•The Doctors Book of•
Home Remedies for
Dogs and Cats

The Doctors Book of Home Remedies for Dogs and Cats

Over 1,000 Solutions to

Your Pet's Problems—

From Top Vets, Trainers,

Breeders and Other

Animal Experts

By the Editors of **PREVENTION** Magazine Health Books
Edited by Matthew Hoffman

Medical Adviser: Amy Marder, V.M.D., animal behavior
consultant to Angell Memorial Animal Hospital in
Boston, clinical assistant professor at Tufts University
School of Veterinary Medicine and pet columnist for
Prevention magazine

Rodale Press, Inc.
Emmaus, Pennsylvania

Copyright © 1996 by Rodale Press, Inc.

Illustrations copyright © 1996 by Dean W. Biechler, Chichaqua Bend Studios

Icon Illustrations copyright © 1996 by Ellen L. Seefelt

Photographs copyright © 1996 by Dennis Mosner

All rights reserved. No part of this publication may be reproduced or transmitted in any form or by any means, electronic or mechanical, including photocopying, recording or any other information storage and retrieval system, without the written permission of the publisher.

Prevention, The Doctors Book and *The Doctors Book of Home Remedies* are registered trademarks of Rodale Press, Inc.

Printed in the United States of America on acid-free (∞), recycled paper ♲

"Vaccination Recommendations for Dogs" and "Vaccination Recommendations for Cats" on page 4 were adapted from *What You Should Know about Vaccination* © 1989 by The American Veterinary Medical Association. Reprinted with permission.

Library of Congress Cataloging-in-Publication Data

The Doctors book of home remedies for dogs and cats: over 1,000 solutions to your pet's problems—from top vets, trainers, breeders and other animal experts / edited by Matthew Hoffman.
     p.   cm.
Includes index.
ISBN 0–87596–294–7 hardcover
ISBN 1–57954–010–4 paperback
   1. Dogs. 2. Cats. 3. Dogs—Health. 4. Cats—Health. 5. Dogs—Diseases. 6. Cats—Diseases. I. Hoffman, Matthew. II. Prevention (Emmaus, Pa.)
SF427.P76 1996
636.7'0896024—dc20   95-46481

Distributed in the book trade by St. Martin's Press

         10   hardcover
2 4 6 8 10 9 7 5 3 1 paperback

OUR PURPOSE

"We inspire and enable people to improve their lives and the world around them."

The Doctors Book of Home Remedies for Dogs and Cats

Editorial Staff

EDITOR: Matthew Hoffman

CONTRIBUTING WRITERS: Laura Catalano, Maryanne Dell, Sally Deneen, Denise Foley, Maria Goodavage, Michael Haederle, Sara J. Henry, Cathy Raymond, Amy D. Shojai, Cheryl S. Smith, Debra Warner, Michelle West, Marielena Zuniga

ASSISTANT RESEARCH MANAGER: Carol Svec

RESEARCH COORDINATOR: Carol J. Gilmore

RESEARCHERS AND FACT-CHECKERS: Derria Monique Byrd, Sandra Salera-Lloyd, Kristina Orchard-Hays

COVER AND BOOK DESIGNER: David Q. Pryor

COVER PHOTOGRAPHER: Dennis Mosner, NYC

PHOTO EDITOR: Susan Pollack

ILLUSTRATOR: Dean W. Biechler

ICON ILLUSTRATOR: Ellen L. Seefelt

ASSOCIATE ART DIRECTOR: Faith Hague

STUDIO MANAGER: Joe Golden

TECHNICAL ARTIST: William L. Allen

SENIOR COPY EDITOR: Jane Sherman

PRODUCTION MANAGER: Helen Clogston

MANUFACTURING COORDINATOR: Patrick T. Smith

OFFICE STAFF: Roberta Mulliner, Julie Kehs, Bernadette Sauerwine, Mary Lou Stephen

Rodale Health and Fitness Books

VICE-PRESIDENT AND EDITORIAL DIRECTOR: Debora T. Yost

ART DIRECTOR: Jane Colby Knutila

RESEARCH MANAGER: Ann Gossy Yermish

COPY MANAGER: Lisa D. Andruscavage

Contents

For an interactive experience, visit our web site
at http://www.petremedies.com

Foreword

The Best Remedies Begin at Home

Throughout my many years in practice as a veterinarian and animal behavior consultant, I have learned that some people don't want to see me. They would rather treat their pets' simple, everyday health problems in the comfort of their homes without going to the veterinarian—and their pets would prefer it also.

Coming to the office requires a stressful trip in the car and sometimes an equally stressful payment for the office visit. Dogs whimper in the waiting room. Cats grip the sides of their carriers to avoid being put on the examining table. And many owners find that just having a sick pet is upsetting enough.

There are times, of course, when your pet must see a veterinarian. A cat that is urinating more often than usual. A dog that's suddenly going bald. A dog or cat that's biting people. For these and many other potentially serious problems, it's essential that your pet receive professional care.

Yet there are many things that you can do at home as well. In *The Doctor's Book of Home Remedies for Dogs and Cats*, you'll learn which conditions need professional attention and which you can tackle on your own. The editors have sought advice from some of the most respected authorities in veterinary medicine. The result is more than 1,000 remedies that are both effective *and* safe.

Many of the chapters include a special feature, "When to See the Vet." Always read this section first. Sometimes a problem that looks simple may be far more serious than you think. If you have questions, don't hesitate to pick up the phone and call the experts. Your veterinarian or an assistant will be more than happy to discuss what's best for your pet.

Enjoy this book. I certainly did. You will learn a lot about a variety of common problems—and what you can do at home to help your pet live a happier, healthier life!

Amy Marder, V.M.D.

Introduction

Pet Care: Staying a Step Ahead

Dogs and cats come from all walks of life. They live in penthouses and farmhouses, studio apartments and mansions. Some chase mice for a living. Others herd sheep. Some even spend their days on soft cushions, contentedly snoozing between nibbles of filet mignon.

Yet all pets, from the daintiest poodle to the toughest alley cat, have one thing in common: They never forget the important thing in life. They don't care if it's raining or the bills are overdue or the bus drivers are out on strike. What they really care about is you. (Although a nice meal and a comfortable place to nap are also nice.)

In return, it's our job to keep our pets happy and fit. It's not always easy. Dogs and cats are intelligent, curious creatures, with a tendency to get themselves—paws, tails, whiskers and all—into trouble. And when pets get hurt or sick, "they can't tell you what the trouble is, so you have to do a little extra work to figure things out," says Albert S. Dorn, D.V.M., professor of surgery at the University of Tennessee College of Veterinary Medicine in Knoxville.

While there's no substitute for regular veterinary care, there's a lot you can do to keep your pets healthy. In fact, some of the best "remedies" begin even before you bring a puppy or kitten home.

Picking the Right Pet

Getting a pet can be the beginning of one of the most rewarding relationships of your life. "Figuring out which pet to get is an extremely important decision," says Barbara Simpson, Ph.D., D.V.M., a certified applied animal behaviorist and adjunct assistant professor at North Carolina State University College of Veterinary Medicine in Raleigh.

Consider your lifestyle. All pets can make good companions, but sometimes their needs and yours come into conflict. If you travel a lot and work long hours, for example, you might want to think twice before getting a dog. "Dogs are very social animals and need lots of inter-action," says Dr. Simpson.

Cats, however, are more independent and can be a good choice for a person on the go—particularly if you get a feline friend to keep them company. "Two cats can keep each other company very nicely for long stretches," says Michael W. Fox, B.V.M., Ph.D., vice-president of bio-ethics and farm animal protection for the Humane Society of the United States in Washington, D.C., and author of *The New Animal Doctor's Answer Book*.

Match your energy levels. While nothing's more adorable than a puppy or kitten, not everyone has the time or patience to perform the house-training and nearly constant surveillance required at this diffi-cult age. For some people, adopting an adult pet makes more sense.

When looking for a "preowned" pet, however, try to learn some-thing of his history first. "You don't want to take on an animal with a lot of problems unless you know what you're doing," says Dr. Dorn.

Shop around. If you have your heart set on owning a particular breed, you may find yourself visiting professional breeders in your area. But if you're not fussy about pedigree, the local animal shelter or hu-mane society is probably overflowing with hopeful dogs and cats eager for a new home.

"Some of the best pets in the world come from shelters," says Carol Moulton, associate director of the American Humane Association's Animal Protection Division in Denver. "It's as if they know you've come to their rescue."

Picking the Right Vet

One of the most important people in your pet's life is the veterinar-ian. Sure, your furry friend probably doesn't realize this. He might even put his paw down when it comes time to get a checkup. (You wouldn't look forward to having your temperature taken that way, either.) But a good vet can play a major role not only in your pet's health but in as-suring your peace of mind as well.

Finding a vet you're comfortable with can be as tricky as finding the right doctor, says Karen Overall, V.M.D., Ph.D., a lecturer specializing in behavioral medicine in the Department of Clinical Studies at the University of Pennsylvania School of Veterinary Medicine in Philadel-phia. "But it's important to choose someone who has the qualities you really want," she says.

In your quest for a vet, here are a few points to consider.

- Does he take time to answer your questions? Is he gentle with your pet? Are you comfortable with his personality?
- Does he see mainly outpatients, or is he also equipped to handle serious medical problems that require overnight hospitalization? If he does take overnight patients, is a friendly assistant on duty around the clock?
- Does he provide emergency care 24 hours a day?
- Are there separate waiting areas for dogs and cats? This comes in handy when you have a cat-chasing dog or a dog-fearing cat.
- Is the staff friendly and helpful? Knowing your pet will get all the attention he needs can be very reassuring.

There's nothing wrong with calling a prospective vet and explaining that you'd like to bring your pet in for a face-to-face meeting, adds Dr. Overall. "It's an excellent way to get a feel for the place that's going to play a big role in your pet's health."

A Pound of Prevention

Vets agree that the best medical care is daily care. A loving home, a good diet, plenty of exercise and regular grooming will go a long way toward keeping your little friend happy and healthy.

"It's so much better and easier on the animal to prevent problems than to cure them," says Harold N. Engel, D.V.M., Ph.D., professor of veterinary anatomy at Oregon State University College of Veterinary Medicine in Corvallis.

To help keep problems from getting serious, you need to catch them early. "People who watch their pets and are familiar with what's normal can sometimes tell, even before obvious signs appear, that there's something wrong," says Dr. Engel.

He recommends giving your pet a nose-to-tail checkup every week. It doesn't take more than a few minutes, and it can help prevent problems—and expenses—down the road.

Start with a body rub. "This relaxes the pet and starts the experience out on the right foot," says Dr. Engel. In addition, your fingers may discover things that the eyes can miss.

- Flaking or scabs. They can be a sign of parasites, allergies or a skin disorder.

A Shot in Time

One of the easiest and most effective ways of preventing your pet from getting sick is by making sure he gets all his vaccinations on a regular basis. This is usually done in the veterinarian's office, although you can buy vaccines (and syringes) from a number of pet supply companies, such as the Omaha Vaccine Com-

Vaccination Recommendations for Dogs

DISEASE	AGE AT FIRST VACCINATION (WEEKS)
Distemper	6–10
Infectious canine hepatitis (CAV-1 or CAV-2)	6–8
Parvovirus infection	6–8
Bordetellosis	6–8
Parainfluenza	6–8
Leptospirosis	10–12
Rabies	12
Coronavirus	6–8

*Check with your veterinarian as to type of vaccine.

Vaccination Recommendations for Cats

DISEASE	AGE AT FIRST VACCINATION (WEEKS)
Panleukopenia	8–10
Viral rhinotracheitis	8–10
Caliciviral disease	8–10
Pneumonitis (chlamydiosis)	8–10
Rabies	12
Feline leukemia	10

*Check with your veterinarian as to type of vaccine.

• Lumps and bumps. These are usually a normal part of aging in pets, but sometimes they can indicate that something is seriously wrong. Catching them early "can help your pet immensely," says Dr. Engel.

• The vertebrae. If you can easily feel all the nooks and crannies in

pany (for a catalog, write to P.O. Box 7228, Omaha, NE 68107, or call 1-800-367-4444). Most vets follow the schedules given below, although there may be some variation from state to state. Some vaccines are given separately, while others may be combined into a single shot, which makes things easier.

Age at Second Vaccination (weeks)	Age at Third Vaccination (weeks)	Revaccination Interval (months)
10–12	14–16	12
10–12	14–16	12
10–12	14–16	12
10–12	14–16	12
10–12	14–16	12
14–16	—	12
64	—	12 or 36*
10–12	12–14	12

Age at Second Vaccination (weeks)	Revaccination Interval (months)
12–16	12
12–16	12
12–16	12
12–16	12
64	12 or 36*
12 and 24*; 13-14*	12

your pet's backbone, perhaps something is causing him to lose weight. If you can't feel the backbone at all, however, he may be too plump.

• Swelling. Depending on where it occurs, this can be a warning sign of parasites, heart trouble or even cancer.

Listen to his breathing. Unless your pet is panting, his breathing should be smooth and quiet. If it's labored, raspy or rattling, he could have a respiratory problem that needs to be checked out.

Check his pulse. The heartbeat should be strong and regular. To check your pet's pulse, place your hand against his chest near his left elbow. Count the number of beats in 15 seconds, then multiply by four.

In cats, the pulse generally runs about 120 beats a minute. For dogs, the rate ranges between 60 and 160 beats. (The heart always beats faster in puppies and kittens.) If your pet's pulse is considerably higher or lower than these rates, call your vet for advice.

Examine the ears. They should be light pink and clean. A foul odor, discharge or redness could be a sign of infection.

Examine the eyes. They should be sparkly and clear. Swelling, squinting, redness or discharge could indicate eye problems such as conjunctivitis or glaucoma.

Look in the mouth. Healthy gums are usually pink, although in some pets they're naturally brownish-black. If you press the gums, they should quickly return to their usual color.

While you're in there, take a look around for lumps or other irregularities. Check to see if the teeth are covered with yellowish tartar. Then take a sniff. "Your pet's breath shouldn't knock your socks off," says Dr. Engel.

In general, keep a sharp eye out for day-to-day changes—in appetite, gait, bowel movements or general behavior, advises Dr. Engel. If you notice something worrisome, call your vet for advice.

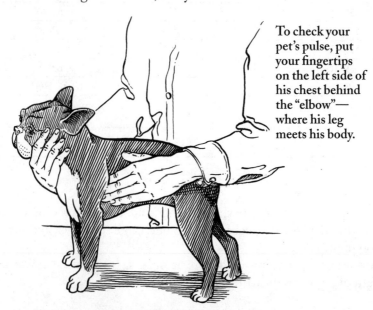

To check your pet's pulse, put your fingertips on the left side of his chest behind the "elbow"— where his leg meets his body.

First-Aid Basics

Accidents can't always be prevented (that's why they're called accidents), but by being prepared you can help keep small problems from turning into big ones.

"Having a first-aid kit at home can be of substantial assistance," says Michael Schaer, D.V.M., professor of medicine and associate chief of staff at the University of Florida College of Veterinary Medicine in Gainesville.

You can buy first-aid kits at pet stores. Or you can stock your own. Here's what it should include.

- Your vet's telephone number, plus the number of an emergency weekend or nighttime vet
- A veterinary first aid manual such as *Emergency Care for Cats and Dogs*
- Gauze rolls or pads
- Adhesive tape
- Absorbent cotton
- Scissors, preferably with rounded tips
- Hydrogen peroxide
- Antibiotic ointment
- Hydrocortisone ointment
- Eyewash
- Tweezers
- Rectal thermometer
- Syringe (without the needle) for giving oral medications
- Antihistamine liquid

Household Protection

Dogs and cats have sharp claws, keen teeth and nearly boundless curiosity. The combination can be a dangerous one, says William B. Buck, D.V.M., professor of toxicology at the University of Illinois College of Veterinary Medicine in Urbana and director of the National Animal Poison Control Center.

To keep your pets safe around the house or in the yard, here's what vets recommend.

Keep medicine cabinets closed. Dogs and cats can't read warning labels. "And just because a container is childproof doesn't mean it's pet-proof," adds Dr. Buck. "He'll chew right through your medicine bottle, childproof or not."

If your pet is one of those intrepid explorers that excel at nosing open closed doors, you might want to consider installing childproof latches, he suggests.

Wash away wastes. Many common household products, like pesticides and antifreeze, are toxic to pets. "A few licks of something like antifreeze is all it takes to be fatal," says Dr. Buck.

Keep your pet at a safe distance whenever you're working with hazardous products, he advises. It's also a good idea to clean up spills immediately, before your friend comes over to investigate.

Beware of bait. Gardeners occasionally set out snail bait, then absentmindedly let the dog or cat out in the yard. "The stuff tastes as good as cookies to them, so they often go right for it. It can be very toxic," Dr. Buck warns.

Keep garbage cans closed. To the average pet, the contents of the trash bin are like a gourmet meal. The smellier it is, the more he likes it. To keep his tummy healthy *and* reduce the mess, make sure the cans are tightly closed and, if possible, out of reach.

Stop him from getting wired. Many dogs and cats like nothing more than chewing on electrical cords, with shocking—and potentially deadly—results.

It's a good idea to unplug appliances when you aren't using them. Try to keep cords out of harm's way by running them behind cabinets or under carpets. For short-term protection from puppies or kittens, you may want to cover exposed cords with a wide strip of electrical tape, which makes them harder to chew. Or you can spray exposed cords with a pet repellent, available in pet stores.

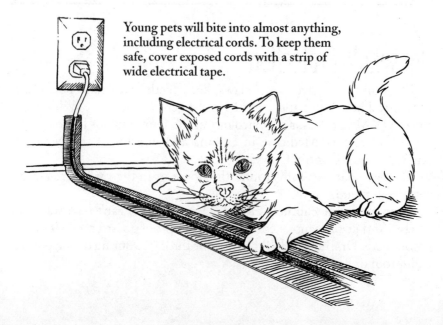

Young pets will bite into almost anything, including electrical cords. To keep them safe, cover exposed cords with a strip of wide electrical tape.

Watch out for water. Although dogs and cats are capable swimmers, if they fall into a swimming pool they may not be able to climb back out. Never let pets, particularly puppies or kittens, play near water except when you're nearby to watch them.

The Medicine Chest

Dogs and cats are a lot like us—at least when it comes to getting sick. They get tummyaches and diarrhea, itchy skin and minor infections. What's more, some of the medications we take for everyday problems will also work for them.

It's best to check with your vet before giving any human medication to pets, says Amy Marder, V.M.D., animal behavior consultant to Angell Memorial Animal Hospital in Boston, clinical assistant professor at Tufts University School of Veterinary Medicine in North Grafton, Massachusetts, and pet columnist for *Prevention* magazine. Here are some general guidelines for treating your pets safely.

- Buffered aspirin. For lowering fever and relieving minor aches and pains in dogs, give one-quarter of a 325-milligram tablet for every ten pounds of pooch once or twice a day. Buffered aspirin is easier on the stomach.

  Aspirin can be extremely dangerous for cats, so never give it without a veterinarian's supervision.
- Acetaminophen and ibuprofen. Both are dangerous for pets, vets say. Don't use them.
- Kaopectate. Helpful for digestive troubles, this soothing over-the-counter medication can be given to dogs and cats every four hours. Give one teaspoon of Kaopectate for each ten pounds of weight. Doses vary widely from pet to pet, however, so be sure to ask your vet for advice.
- Pepto-Bismol. For dogs with tummy trouble, give one teaspoon per 20 pounds of weight every four to six hours. But don't give it to cats, since it contains ingredients they may have trouble metabolizing.
- Dimenhydrinate (Dramamine). For preventing motion sickness, give medium to large dogs 25 to 50 milligrams an hour before traveling. For small dogs and cats, give about 12.5 milligrams. Dramamine comes in 50-milligram tablets that can be split into quarters to provide the right dose.

  While Dramamine is safe for most healthy dogs and cats, it may be dangerous when given to pets with glaucoma or bladder problems. To be safe, check with your vet.

Spaying and Neutering

People have no lack of excuses for not neutering or spaying their pets. Some worry it will make the pets fat or lazy. Others worry that the procedures are dangerous or simply unnatural.

The fears are misguided, Dr. Fox says. Neutering does not cause pets to gain weight or change their personality. No surgical procedure is without risks, but neutering and spaying are both extremely safe. In fact, the procedures can help your pets live longer by reducing the occurrence of certain tumors as well as by making them less likely to roam or fight.

Although most people take excellent care of their dogs and cats, the American Humane Association estimates that about ten million pets are euthanized in animal shelters every year. Reducing the number of *unwanted* pets by having animals spayed or neutered is perhaps the best way to prevent this unhappy fate.

The best time to neuter or spay your pet is between about six and eight months of age. "Even pets that are well along can benefit," adds Dr. Fox.

Basic Training

Every good relationship between people and pets is based on having common goals and clear communication. This is particularly true of dogs, which look to you for leadership and approval, says Dr. Simpson. "Knowing the rules of the road gives them confidence—especially when they're rewarded for good behavior!"

While some canine (and even a few feline) prodigies manage to learn a wide variety of feats, all your dog really needs to know, apart from house-training and basic manners, are five commands: "Sit," "Stay," "Heel," "Down" and "Come." Once he's mastered these skills, he'll be less likely to pounce on guests, dash into traffic or run away in the park. He'll be under your control.

While dogs are excellent candidates for training, most cats are not. Give them a firm talking-to and chances are they'll simply walk away—and avoid you for the rest of the day! But you must hold cats responsible for at least the basics: using the litter box, for example, or staying off the table while you're eating.

While some people successfully train their pets at home, a formal obedience class can be very helpful, says Bob Gutierrez, animal behavior coordinator at the San Francisco Society for the Prevention of Cruelty to Animals. Not only will your pet learn his ABCs, but you'll get some training, too. Plus you'll both get practice in meeting unfamiliar people and pets in a friendly setting.

Pets often start classes after receiving their first vaccinations—usually no earlier than eight weeks of age. "Look for a puppy class that's like a puppy party," suggests Dr. Simpson. "There should be lots of fun interaction between puppies, kids and adults, so the puppy can get used to all kinds of situations."

While it's best to start young, even old dogs can learn new tricks, she adds. "They really respond to positive reinforcement, and it makes them love learning."

Fun and Games

Having a pet in the family can make you feel like a kid again. You get to run around, throw balls, get chased and just plain act ridiculous. And since most pets love taking a good romp—vets recommend getting out for at least 20 minutes twice a day—you both get some vigorous exercise in the bargain.

This is true not only for dogs but in some cases for cats as well, says Dr. Overall. In fact, walking a cat has some advantages over strolling with a canine counterpart. Cats don't lift their legs at every stop, constantly sniff the ground or tug on the leash. "Cats love getting out of the house and going for walks with you, particularly if you get them used to it when they're young," she says.

Cats wriggle out of collars easily, so many vets recommend using a harness instead of the usual choke collar. To get her used to the idea, first put on the harness without the leash. Once she's used to the harness, snap on the leash and take some practice walks around the house. When you both feel comfortable, head outdoors for an enjoyable jaunt.

Don't expect your cat to heel like a dog, however. Basically, she's going to be walking *you*.

You don't always have to leave the yard to have a great time. Pets love to play—some *live* to play—wherever they are. Pet stores stock an enormous variety of toys. But pets aren't picky. A tennis ball sewn in an old sock can provide just as much entertainment as a $20 rubber toy. Every now and then, toss your friend something new—and stick around for the fun.

"Pets can bring so much happiness to your life—and you can bring so much happiness to theirs," says Dr. Overall. "Have a wonderful time!"

Acne

9 Ways to Soothe the Skin

Sure, you won't find your Siamese staring moodily in the mirror, tube of Clearasil in paw. Your Doberman won't have to cancel a prom date or swear off french fries because of skin eruptions. But pets can develop acne that's as uncomfortable and unsightly as any tenth-grader's.

Located on the chin or around the face, acne in pets is typically caused by a bacterial infection inside a blocked oil gland, says Bernadine Cruz, D.V.M., a veterinarian in private practice in Laguna Hills, California. It may occur when normal scratching irritates hair follicles and causes inflammation of the glands. It can also be caused by allergies or hormones that are out of balance. In cats, it can be a result of less-than-thorough grooming.

Acne can occur in cats at any age. Among dogs it's most common in the younger set, says Wayne Rosenkrantz, D.V.M., a veterinary dermatologist in private practice in Garden Grove, California. For some reason it's the big breeds—mastiffs, Great Danes and their jumbo peers—that seem to suffer most, he says.

While acne in pets isn't the social liability it is in humans, it can be uncomfortable, Dr. Cruz says. Here's what experts recommend.

 For Dogs and Cats

Clean it daily. Gently washing your pet's face with soap and a washcloth will remove surface bacteria and help break down material that may be plugging the oil glands, says Dr. Cruz. To be most effective, the washcloth should be "a little warmer than a baby's bath, but not scalding," she says. Scrub gently, then rinse well with warm water to remove the soap.

You can use any mild cleansing soap, or you can buy an antibacterial pet shampoo at a pet store. Don't use human deodorant soaps, which can be irritating, adds Dr. Cruz.

Add some heat. Another way to help open plugged glands is by holding a hot pack to the area, says Dr. Cruz. She recommends wetting a washcloth with hot (not scalding) water. Then wring it out and hold it on the affected area for about five minutes or until the cloth is cool. Do this once a day until the acne goes away, she advises.

Reach for echinacea. Given orally, this infection-battling herb, which is commonly sold in health food stores, may act like a mild antibiotic, stopping acne from the inside out, says Nancy Scanlan, D.V.M., a veterinarian in private practice in Sherman Oaks, California.

Echinacea is usually sold in tablet or liquid form. Dr. Scanlan recommends giving one-half the human dose to a large dog, one-quarter the human dose to a medium-size dog and one-eighth the human dose to a small dog. But don't give echinacea to cats without first checking with your vet, she adds. Some cats may have trouble digesting it.

Put calendula on your calendar. A concentrated tincture made from marigolds, calendula may help quell skin infections and speed healing, says Stephen Blake, D.V.M., a veterinarian in private practice in San Diego. He recommends mixing six drops of the tincture in an ounce of warm water. Using a clean cotton ball, apply the solution to the acne twice a day, he advises.

Raid the planter. Applying a thin layer of gel from an aloe vera plant will help ease discomfort caused by painful acne, says Michael Lemmon, D.V.M., a veterinarian in private practice in Renton, Washington. If you don't have an aloe vera plant, you can buy the gel at most health food stores.

Don't swap medicines. Drugs made for people are unlikely to be helpful when given to pets, says Dr. Rosenkrantz. "Using any acne products formulated for people would probably just worsen the problem," he warns.

Avoid the squeeze. When a serious acne outbreak is making your pet uncomfortable, you may be tempted to squeeze the pimples yourself. Don't do it, advises Dr. Rosenkrantz. Squeezing pimples can be painful and in some cases will cause infected material to spread beneath the skin, causing a deeper infection.

Look at the big picture. While most outbreaks of acne will stick around for a few days and then disappear, sometimes it's a constant problem. It may be that there's something in your pet's environment—a certain type of flea collar, for example, or the presence of household pesticides—that's causing the problem. Try substituting an herbal flea collar for the chemical kind, suggests Dr. Blake.

Go to the source. As in people, acne in pets may be caused by hormonal surges or imbalances. If it's an ongoing problem, you may want to have your pet neutered. "That can do a lot to help," says Dr. Scanlan.

PANEL OF ADVISERS

Stephen Blake, D.V.M., is a veterinarian in private practice in San Diego.

Bernadine Cruz, D.V.M., is a veterinarian in private practice in Laguna Hills, California.

Michael Lemmon, D.V.M., is a veterinarian in private practice in Renton, Washington.

Wayne Rosenkrantz, D.V.M., is a veterinary dermatologist in private practice in Garden Grove, California.

Nancy Scanlan, D.V.M., is a veterinarian in private practice in Sherman Oaks, California.

Aggression

13 Ways to Calm Your Pet

Back in the days when food didn't come in a bag and life was a lot rougher than it is today, dogs and cats needed an aggressive attitude, along with sharp teeth and strong claws, just to survive.

In today's world, however, excessively aggressive behavior, like hissing, growling, showing of teeth or slashing of claws, can be dangerous—not just for people or other pets but for your aggressive friend as well.

There are many reasons dogs and cats are aggressive. Fear of strangers or new situations will cause some pets to show their teeth or claws. A pet that's been abused is more likely to turn his temper—and teeth—on others. In addition, some pets are encouraged by their owners to play rough—and then look surprised when they get a scolding instead of praise.

Don't ever ignore aggressive behavior, says Steve Aiken, owner of Animal Behavior Consultants in Wichita, Kansas. Chances are it won't get better—and it may get worse. Sooner or later, someone—a person or another pet—is going to get hurt, he warns.

To keep your pet calm and under control, here's what experts recommend.

 **For Dogs and Cats**

Remind him who's boss. The next time your pet growls, spits or bites, give him a firm "No!" advises Wayne Hunthausen, D.V.M., an animal behavior consultant in Westwood, Kansas, president of the American Veterinary Society of Animal Behavior and co-author of *Practitioner's Guide to Pet Behavior Problems.* "You want the pet to stop what he's doing immediately and show a submissive lowering of the body," he explains. "You want it to look like, 'Whoa! I don't think I want to do that again.'"

When to See the Vet

A grumpy snarl when a toddler touches her tail. A show of teeth when strangers call. A flash of claws at passing hands. "Living with a truly aggressive animal is like living with a loaded gun," says Andrea Fochios, D.V.M., a veterinarian in private practice in Ferndale, New York.

In some cases aggressive behavior is caused by a painful physical problem—arthritis, for example—that makes a pet cranky. More often, it's a result of behavioral problems that often can be difficult to treat.

If your pet is posing a serious threat, don't try to handle it alone. Call your vet or an animal trainer for advice.

It's important, however, not to scare him or cause serious alarm, he adds. The trick is to be firm but not terrifying. He'll soon get the hint.

Stop him in the act. Dogs and cats, like children, will occasionally act up when you're too busy or embarrassed to scold them—like when the boss is over for dinner.

Take charge anyway. For scolding to be effective, it has to be delivered within a few seconds of the misbehavior, explains Robert K. Anderson, D.V.M., professor and director emeritus of the Animal Behavior Clinic at the University of Minnesota College of Veterinary Medicine in Minneapolis-St. Paul.

Try a time-out. One of the best ways to discipline an aggressive pet is to separate him from what he loves best—you. "Put him in another room by himself for about five minutes," Aiken suggests. "Pets don't like being alone."

Shake him up. Pets hate loud noises, so the next time your pooch gets aggressive, take him down a peg or two by rattling a shake can.

"Take an empty pop can, put some coins in it and tape the top shut," suggests Dr. Hunthausen. When your pet starts misbehaving, tell him "No!" while at the same time giving the can a quick shake. The unpleasant noise will help remind him that he's getting out of line.

Save your hands for loving. It's natural to strike out at a biting dog or hissing cat, but in most cases hitting does more harm than good, says Dr. Hunthausen. In fact, some animals become so afraid of being hit that they automatically bite whenever they feel threatened. "Your hand should be your pet's friend," says Dr. Hunthausen.

 For **Dogs** Only

Introduce him to strangers. Dogs can be very territorial and may get aggressive when strangers—like delivery people and mail carriers—"invade" their turf.

To help your dog make friends of foes, try keeping a stash of treats near the door. When visitors call, hand them a treat and let them offer it to the dog, Aiken suggests. "It's hard for your dog to see a person as a threat when that person's supplying food."

Mail him a bone. Mail carriers often bear the brunt of a dog's unruly behavior. If you have a mail slot leading into the house, you can help your mailman get a first-class reception by taping a treat to the outside of the door, suggests trainer Steve Lindsay, owner of Canine Behavioral Services in Philadelphia. Then the mail carrier can slip in a peace offering along with the mail.

Sign up for class. Perhaps the best way to prevent young dogs from getting uppity later on is to train them well. "Puppy obedience classes provide exposure to other dogs and people and also teach the owner to gain and keep control of the dog," says Margaret English, an obedience instructor in Somers, New York. Most dogs can start classes between 12 and 16 weeks of age.

For **Cats** Only

Give him the silent treatment. The next time your cat gets too rough, lightly flick his nose with your finger. Then ignore him for several minutes, vets advise. He'll soon learn that gentle play has more rewards than being too aggressive.

Have a blast. When your rambunctious cat is making life miserable by leaping at you, claws out, when you're not looking, try discouraging him with a blast from an air canister like those used for cleaning camera lenses, suggests Dr. Hunthausen. Cats hate the hiss and eventually will learn to mind their Ps and Qs.

Give a squirt. Another way to discourage an "attack" cat is to keep a loaded water pistol handy, then squirt him when he gets too tough, Dr. Hunthausen says.

Plan ahead. If you can figure out what's behind your cat's attacks—if he always leaps when you're rustling the newspaper, for example—you can forestall the ambush by tossing him a favorite toy *before* he gets started, says John C. Wright, Ph.D., a certified animal behaviorist, professor of psychology at Mercer University in Macon, Georgia, and a member of the adjunct faculty at the University of Georgia School of Veterinary Medicine in Atlanta.

Keep him busy. Cats have loads of energy, and they'll be less aggressive if you help them burn off steam in more socially acceptable ways. Having vigorous play sessions with exciting toys like table-tennis balls will help keep aggression in check, says Dr. Hunthausen.

PANEL OF ADVISERS

Steve Aiken is owner of Animal Behavior Consultants in Wichita, Kansas.

Robert K. Anderson, D.V.M., is professor and director emeritus of the Animal Behavior Clinic at the University of Minnesota College of Veterinary Medicine in Minneapolis-St. Paul.

Margaret English is an obedience instructor in Somers, New York.

Andrea Fochios, D.V.M., is a veterinarian in private practice in Ferndale, New York.

Wayne Hunthausen, D.V.M., is an animal behavior consultant in Westwood, Kansas, president of the American Veterinary Society of Animal Behavior and co-author of the *Practitioner's Guide to Pet Behavior Problems.*

Steve Lindsay is a trainer and owner of Canine Behavioral Services in Philadelphia.

John C. Wright, Ph.D., is a certified animal behaviorist, professor of psychology at Mercer University in Macon, Georgia, and a member of the adjunct faculty at the University of Georgia School of Veterinary Medicine in Atlanta.

Aging

13 Lifelong Tips

It seems like only yesterday your dog was a little bundle of fur chasing his tail and your cat a playful kitten bouncing after sunbeams.

In fact, relatively speaking, it *was* only a short time ago. Most dogs live no more than 15 or 16 years, and for some larger breeds, 10 years is the usual life span. And although there are plenty of 20-year-old cats basking in their senior years, their two decades of life still put them in the "ancient" category.

Like their owners, many pets live to a healthy old age, while others may experience increasing problems—from mild aches and pains to more serious conditions such as cancer—as the years go by.

While you can't reverse the hands of time, there's a lot you can do to keep an old friend comfortable and by your side for a long time to come.

 **For Dogs and Cats**

Begin with regular checkups. Once your pet enters her middle years, it's a good idea to let your vet have a look at her at least once a year, says Meryl Littman, V.M.D., chief of medicine at the University of Pennsylvania School of Veterinary Medicine in Philadelphia.

For dogs, "middle age" is usually around seven years old—earlier for the largest breeds like Irish wolfhounds or Great Danes. Cats can wait a little longer, usually until they're between eight and ten, says Dr. Littman.

When you take your pet in for her first routine checkup, your vet may recommend that she have a comprehensive examination that tells how she should feel when she's healthy. This will provide a baseline to compare her to as she gets older, Dr. Littman explains.

In addition, ask the vet to check your pet's blood pressure, Dr. Littman adds. High blood pressure can lead to blindness in dogs and is

When to See the Vet

Older pets are prone to a host of minor ailments, as well as a few that aren't so minor. To catch problems early, call your vet if:

- You feel a lump. Any unusual bump on the animal's skin could be a sign of cancer, says Guy L. Pidgeon, D.V.M., a specialist in veterinary internal medicine and director of the Department of Veterinary Affairs for Hill's Pet Nutrition in Topeka, Kansas. Pay special attention to the animal's mouth, because tumors there tend to be the most serious. Other warning signs of cancer include foul odors or unusual discharge or bleeding.
- She seems short of breath. This can be a symptom of heart problems, says Dr. Pidgeon.
- Her appetite changes. This could be a sign of kidney failure or other serious problems.
- She's losing weight. "If an animal is losing weight, you need to get to the bottom of it, and that requires a trip to the vet," says Kathryn Michel, D.V.M., a researcher and nutrition expert in the Department of Clinical Studies at the University of Pennsylvania School of Veterinary Medicine in Philadelphia.
- She is drinking a lot of water and urinating more frequently than usual. This could be a sign of kidney disease or diabetes.

a symptom of high thyroid levels in cats. Untreated, it can also lead to strokes, so it's worth catching early.

Keep those paws moving. Daily exercise will help keep your pet slim and flexible, helping stave off age-related disorders like arthritis or digestive problems, says James B. Dalley, D.V.M., associate professor of small animal clinical sciences at the Michigan State University College of Veterinary Medicine in East Lansing. He recommends walking your pet for at least 20 minutes twice a day. But any amount of exercise is good, he adds.

Watch her weight. "The number one problem in the pet population is obesity," says Guy L. Pidgeon, D.V.M., a specialist in veterinary internal medicine and director of the Department of Veterinary Affairs for Hill's Pet Nutrition in Topeka, Kansas.

In dogs, obesity is a big contributor to age-related problems like arthritis and heart disease. In cats, it can lead to diabetes. In fact, cats that already have diabetes may be able to get it under control just by trimming surplus pounds.

How can you tell what kind of shape your pet is in? Dogs should maintain an "hourglass figure," says Dr. Pidgeon. "As you look down on your dog from above, there should be a decided waist right in front of the rear legs. As you run your hands up and down their chest wall, you should be able to feel their ribs."

The same goes for cats: They should stay fairly sleek throughout their lives. If you can't feel her ribs or see her waist, she's probably overweight.

Give extra fiber. Adding more dietary fiber to your pet's diet is a great way to help her lose weight, says Dr. Dalley. Fiber can also help prevent constipation and improve digestion, making an older pet better able to absorb needed nutrients.

To increase your pet's fiber intake, vets recommend buying foods specially designed for overweight or senior pets. Ask your vet for recommendations.

Meals That Heal

The evidence isn't conclusive, but some researchers suspect that a diet low in protein and phosphorus can help slow the progression of kidney failure, currently the third leading cause of death among elderly pets.

"The restriction of protein is known in some experimental conditions to retard the progression of the disease," says James B. Dalley, D.V.M., associate professor of small animal clinical sciences at the Michigan State University College of Veterinary Medicine in East Lansing.

The kidneys are responsible for metabolizing protein, he explains. Less protein in the body means less work for the kidneys.

Ask your vet if a low-protein diet is a good idea for your pet.

Sharp Relief

The aches of aging hurt twice: once for your pet, and again for you as you stand helplessly by.

While medications can provide some relief from age-related conditions like arthritis, they aren't always safe or effective for long-term use. Some vets are now recommending a more pointed approach. "Acupuncture can be the fountain of youth for older animals," says Deva Khalsa, V.M.D., a veterinarian in private practice in Yardley, Pennsylvania.

A certified acupuncturist, Dr. Khalsa has been practicing this ancient Chinese medical treatment—in which needles are inserted along nerve points just under the skin—on her elderly pet patients for 14 years. The treatments may be helpful for conditions ranging from dysplasia and arthritis to allergies.

Although acupuncture won't cure your pet's aches and pains, it can offer her temporary relief, says Charles Schneck, D.V.M., a veterinarian in private practice in East Brunswick, New Jersey, and past president of the American Holistic Veterinary Medical Society. "It does allow the animal to get around a little better."

Don't get carried away. While a good diet is important for all pets, don't rush to make changes if your pet is already slim and healthy. "Not all older dogs and cats are fat," says Kathryn Michel, D.V.M., a researcher and nutrition expert in the Department of Clinical Studies at the University of Pennsylvania School of Veterinary Medicine in Philadelphia. "A healthy older animal can eat regular food."

Add fresh food to the main course. Holistic veterinarians often recommend that people feed their pets vegetables, fruits and grains instead of commercially prepared pet foods. "If you give animals fresh and healthy foods, it keeps their immune systems up and cuts down on the diseases we see with aging," says Deva Khalsa, V.M.D., a veterinarian in private practice in Yardley, Pennsylvania, and a certified acupuncturist.

Cats are finicky, so they won't always appreciate having fruits or vegetables added to their meals. However, they may eat sprouts. Just mix them well into the regular food, Dr. Khalsa says.

Switch to healthy treats. Giving your pets little snacks "seems to be part of the human/animal bond," says Dr. Michel. But if your pet is elderly or overweight, you could be killing her with kindness.

Dr. Michel recommends substituting healthy snacks—like carrot sticks and fruit—for her regular treats. Of course, you may have a tough time convincing your cat that asparagus is just as tasty as a liver treat!

Slip her a supplement. In lieu of snacks, many vets "reward" their patients with a pet vitamin. "They aren't high in calories, and they have flavoring ingredients pets like," says Dr. Dalley. Pet stores carry a variety of chewable pet vitamins. Ask your vet which is best for your pet.

Slip them some antioxidants. In humans, studies have shown that daily doses of the antioxidant vitamins C and E can help protect against heart disease. Dr. Khalsa recommends giving older dogs at least 400 milligrams a day of vitamin C (larger dogs can take more) and 100 to 400 international units of vitamin E. Cats can take 500 milligrams a day of vitamin C and 50 international units of vitamin E. Check with your vet for precise dosing instructions.

To make things easier, you might want to get a liquid or powdered form of the vitamins and mix them in your pet's food. For cats, try mixing the vitamins with a little canola or olive oil and smearing the mixture on her paw. "She'll just lick it off," Dr. Khalsa says.

Keep the water bowl full. Many pets naturally drink less as they get older, which can cause dehydration. Dr. Pidgeon recommends keeping water bowls in different parts of the house. This is particularly important if your pet doesn't get around as well as she used to.

"Measure the water in the morning and again at night to make sure your pet is drinking," he adds.

Keep her close. As they age, many dogs and cats begin to lose some of their hearing, making them much more vulnerable to accidents. "Keep an old animal confined or on a leash outside," advises Dr. Dalley. "You need to become their ears and take more precautions on their behalf."

Help the kids understand. Like people, many elderly pets get a bit cranky and intolerant of interruption. While your senior cat will probably slink away from any hubbub in the house, you may need to ask the kids to be considerate of an elderly dog. "A lot of times children don't recognize the early signs of grumpiness, and they get bitten," Dr. Dalley warns.

 **For Cats Only**

Change diets carefully. Cats don't like changes in their routine, and changing to a new food can cause them to sulk and leave the table for a few days. More is at stake than just a little hunger, since cats that don't eat can develop a serious, possibly fatal condition called hepatic lipidosis. "You need to change cats' diets very slowly," says Dr. Pidgeon.

If you are changing your cat's diet to help her lose weight, he recommends mixing the new food with the old a little at a time. At first, give her no more than one-quarter of the new food and three-quarters of the old. Every day, add just a little more of the new. "Slowly make the change over a two-week period of time, if not longer," he advises.

PANEL OF ADVISERS

James B. Dalley, D.V.M., is associate professor of small animal clinical sciences at the Michigan State University College of Veterinary Medicine in East Lansing.

Deva Khalsa, V.M.D., is a veterinarian in private practice in Yardley, Pennsylvania, and a certified acupuncturist.

Meryl Littman, V.M.D., is chief of medicine at the University of Pennsylvania School of Veterinary Medicine in Philadelphia.

Kathryn Michel, D.V.M., is a researcher and nutrition expert in the Department of Clinical Studies at the University of Pennsylvania School of Veterinary Medicine in Philadelphia.

Guy L. Pidgeon, D.V.M., is a specialist in veterinary internal medicine and director of the Department of Veterinary Affairs for Hill's Pet Nutrition in Topeka, Kansas.

Charles Schneck, D.V.M., is a veterinarian in private practice in East Brunswick, New Jersey, and past president of the American Holistic Veterinary Medical Society.

Allergies & Hay Fever

9 Tips to Relieve Them

Dogs and cats with hay fever? You bet!

Like their owners, many pets are sensitive to airborne annoyances—not just pollens or molds but also such things as dust, feathers and wool.

But while people with hay fever get red eyes, runny noses and explosive sneezing attacks, pets are more likely to get downright itchy. To soothe their skin and help keep allergies under control, here's what experts recommend.

 ## For Dogs and Cats

Calm it with cool water. Giving your pet a cool-water soak is a quick way to ease itchy skin, says John MacDonald, D.V.M., associate professor of dermatology at the Auburn University College of Veterinary Medicine in Alabama. Bathe your pet for five to ten minutes, he advises. Make sure the water is cool. "Warm water aggravates the itch," Dr. MacDonald says.

Since it's a rare cat that goes willingly to the tub, getting her wet can be a challenge. See "How to Give Your Cat a Bath" on page 186 for tips.

Ease it with oatmeal. To make soaks additionally soothing, vets sometimes recommend adding colloidal oatmeal (like Aveeno) to the bathwater, says Dr. MacDonald. It gives the water a smooth, silky feel that will help calm the crankiest skin.

Alleviate it with antihistamines. "You can often bring allergies under control with antihistamines," says Lowell Ackerman, D.V.M., Ph.D., a veterinary dermatologist in private practice in Scottsdale, Arizona, and author of *Skin and Haircoat Problems in Dogs*.

Your vet may recommend an over-the-counter drug like diphenhydramine (Benadryl). The typical dose is one to three milligrams for every pound of pet, but you should ask your vet for precise dosages.

When to See the Vet

While hay fever and other allergies rarely cause more than a little itching, some pets will scratch themselves into a veritable frenzy, causing hair loss, skin damage or serious infections, says John MacDonald, D.V.M., associate professor of dermatology at the Auburn University College of Veterinary Medicine in Alabama.

For pets that are unusually sensitive, vets sometimes recommend giving a series of allergy shots. Given every few days at first and then about once a week for a period of months or years, the shots can help pets become progressively less sensitive. Eventually they may stop being allergic, at which time they won't need the shots, Dr. MacDonald says.

Not every product is right for every pet, adds Lloyd Reedy, D.V.M., a veterinary dermatologist, clinical associate professor of comparative medicine at the Health Science Center at the University of Texas Southwestern Medical School in Dallas, and author of *Allergic Skin Diseases of Dogs and Cats*. Your vet may recommend several antihistamines before finding the one that works best.

"Probably a four- to six-day trial of each would be indicated before you say it isn't effective," says Dr. Reedy. Once you've found the right medication, don't give it only when symptoms flare, he adds. It's best to give it daily throughout the allergy season.

Subdue it with supplements. To help calm itchy skin, try giving your pet fatty acid supplements, which are also used for relieving mange and other skin disorders, says William H. Miller, Jr., V.M.D., associate professor of medicine at the Cornell University College of Veterinary Medicine in Ithaca, New York. The supplements come in capsules and are available from veterinarians and some pet stores. Ask your vet which dose is right for your pet.

Getting a dog or cat to swallow a capsule can be tricky. An easier way is to take the capsules apart and squeeze the oil into your pet's food. "They're effective in about 20 percent of dogs and perhaps 25 to 30 percent of cats," adds Dr. Ackerman. "They taste fishy, and cats especially really like them."

Keep her indoors. In spring and summer, pollen fills the air—and your furry friend's coat and airways as well. To prevent pollen from pushing your pet around, keep her indoors during peak pollen times—typically early morning and in the evenings.

Smooth the rough edges. Carpeting, heavy drapes and thick upholstery may make you feel warm and snug, but they're veritable magnets for attracting—and holding—dust and pollen particles.

Rather than redecorating your entire house, try keeping your pet in areas that have surfaces that are easy to clean, like bare floors and vinyl blinds.

Clean and clean again. Daily cleaning won't eliminate allergy-causing particles, but it will help keep them at manageable levels. Vets recommend vacuuming and dusting often. It's also a good idea to change furnace or air-conditioner filters monthly.

Plan on washing your pet's bedding at least once a week, vets say. This will help reduce the buildup of dust mites—microscopic critters that thrive on skin flakes and are common causes of allergies in people and pets.

Look to the litter. Many litter-box products contain chemical scents to make your cat's bathroom more appealing—to you if not to her. In some cases, however, both cats and dogs may be sensitive—both to the smell of the litter and to its dust.

Get the Medicine Down

While antihistamines are often effective treatments for hay fever, giving pills to dogs or cats can often be a challenge.

The drugs work best on an empty stomach, so you don't want to hide them in food, vets say. (Clever pets always seem to eat around them anyway.) Here's a better way to get your dog to take her medication. (For tips on how to give pills to cats, see "Help the Medicine Go Down" on page 42.)

Place the palm of your hand over the bridge of your dog's nose. Your thumb and middle finger should circle the muzzle and fit behind each upper canine (long) tooth. Then gently press her lips against her teeth to make her drop her jaw.

With your other hand, quickly poke the pill to the back of her tongue. Then hold her mouth closed and stroke her throat until you see her swallow. When she licks her nose, you'll know she's done.

For Dogs only

Give her a foot soak. Dogs with allergies occasionally suffer from itchy feet, and soaking them in Epsom salts can be a big relief, says Dr. MacDonald.

He recommends filling the tub with just enough cool water to cover your dog's paws. Dissolve several cups of Epsom salts crystals in the water. Stand your dog in the tub for five to ten minutes, then gently dry her feet. Don't let her drink the water, however, since Epsom salts can act as a laxative.

PANEL OF ADVISERS

Lowell Ackerman, D.V.M., Ph.D., is a veterinary dermatologist in private practice in Scottsdale, Arizona, and author of *Skin and Haircoat Problems in Dogs*.

John MacDonald, D.V.M., is associate professor of dermatology at the Auburn University College of Veterinary Medicine in Alabama.

William H. Miller, Jr., V.M.D., is associate professor of medicine at the Cornell University College of Veterinary Medicine in Ithaca, New York.

Lloyd Reedy, D.V.M., is a veterinary dermatologist, clinical associate professor of comparative medicine at the Health Science Center at the University of Texas Southwestern Medical School in Dallas, and author of *Allergic Skin Diseases of Dogs and Cats*.

Anal Sac Problems

2 Steps to Ease Rearward Woes

Maybe you've noticed your pooch scooting on his rear end from one end of the rug to the other. Or perhaps your cat has been tearing around the house, pausing every so often to lick at her backside. While worms often take the bum rap for these awkward ballets, anal sacs are usually to blame, says Douglas J. Heacock, V.M.D., a veterinarian in private practice in Madison, New Jersey.

Your pet has two anal sacs, one on each side of the anus. The sacs contain a strong-smelling liquid that pets use to mark their territory and also to identify each other—which is why they often say hello by sniffing each other's rear end.

The sacs normally release a little fluid through tiny openings whenever your pet has a bowel movement. Sometimes, however, the openings get clogged or the glands produce more fluid than the sacs can comfortably hold. The result can be uncomfortable itching or a feeling of fullness, vets say.

Anal sac problems are most common in miniature dogs, but even large dogs and cats can be affected. To get to the bottom of the problem, here's what experts recommend.

 ## For Dogs and Cats

Scrap the table scraps. Anal sacs typically need pressure from firm stools in order to release fluid properly, says Dr. Heacock. Giving your pet human food can cause the stools to be unusually soft, making it more likely that fluid will build up. To help prevent this, make sure he sticks to an animal-food diet, Dr. Heacock says.

Take the express route. Although it's not an appealing task, emptying (expressing) your pet's anal sacs is perhaps the best way to relieve the problem. "Professionals can often do a more thorough job because they're adept at various techniques," says Howard Hollander, D.V.M., a veterinarian in private practice in Brooklyn. "But there's no reason you can't at least try it at home first." Here's what vets recommend.

1. Tote him to the tub. "That way you can bathe any remaining smell off your pet afterward," says Robert Cross, D.V.M., a veterinarian in private practice in Duncan, Oklahoma, and past president of the Oklahoma Veterinary Medical Association. If your pet won't get in the tub, at least take him to an area without carpeting and protect the floor with a layer of newspapers.
2. Don a pair of latex gloves. It's also a good idea to have a few paper towels or a damp cloth handy to help clean up the mess. "You'll be glad you did," says Dr. Heacock.
3. Get in position. Kneeling at your pet's side (or standing if you put him on a table), lift his tail with one hand and hold a cloth or paper towel in the other to catch the secretions. (Don't stand directly behind him or you could get in the line of fire.)
4. Take aim with your fingers. A dog's anal sacs extend from both sides of the main anal opening to about the five and seven o'clock positions outside the circumference of the anus. For cats, they extend to about four and eight o'clock.

If the sacs are full, you should be able to feel them as two hard bulges, often not much larger than a pea. With the hand that's holding

When to See the Vet

While blocked anal sacs can sometimes be treated at home, there are times you're going to need an expert's care.

For example, if your pet flinches with pain when you touch the anal area, or if you see swelling, sores or growths, he could have abscesses, polyps or an anal sac infection, says Douglas J. Heacock, V.M.D., a veterinarian in private practice in Madison, New Jersey.

See your vet right away if the glands are difficult or impossible to empty or if the expressed fluids contain blood, pus or a pasty black substance. In some cases, your vet may recommend surgery to remove the sacs, particularly if the glands are becoming blocked frequently. "It's not a simple procedure, but in some cases it's necessary for the animal's comfort and health," Dr. Heacock says.

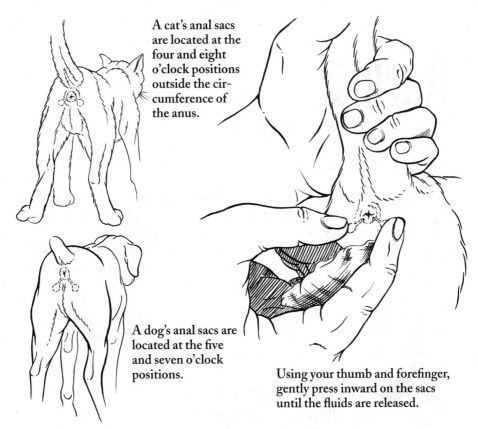

A cat's anal sacs are located at the four and eight o'clock positions outside the circumference of the anus.

A dog's anal sacs are located at the five and seven o'clock positions.

Using your thumb and forefinger, gently press inward on the sacs until the fluids are released.

the towel, place your thumb and forefinger on either side of the anal opening and gently press inward.

Just make sure the anus is covered with the towel, adds Dr. Hollander. "You can actually feel the sacs empty as you squeeze," he says. The fluid that comes out may be thin or thick, with colors ranging from yellow to light gray or brown.

If nothing comes out at first, slightly adjust the position of your fingers and try again. If you still come up dry, take a break and consult your vet. Pushing too hard can be painful for your pet. It can also damage the sacs, Dr. Heacock warns.

PANEL OF ADVISERS

Robert Cross, D.V.M., is a veterinarian in private practice in Duncan, Oklahoma, and past president of the Oklahoma Veterinary Medical Association.

Douglas J. Heacock, V.M.D., is a veterinarian in private practice in Madison, New Jersey.

Howard Hollander, D.V.M., is a veterinarian in private practice in Brooklyn.

Anemia

7 Tips to Iron It Out

Usually your pet has more energy than he knows what to do with, but lately he's been dragging around as if he was up all night watching the late show. He doesn't even rouse himself at suppertime.

Your vet says he has anemia, a condition in which red blood cells aren't carrying enough oxygen to keep him energized. Often a result of blood loss, anemia can be caused by conditions ranging from severe flea or hookworm infestations to ulcers.

Since anemia is a symptom of an underlying problem, a pet with this condition needs to be under a veterinarian's care. In addition, there are things you can do to help get his energy up to par.

 For Dogs and Cats

Get rid of parasites. "Young puppies and kittens can be infested with fleas or born with hookworms, which suck blood, causing anemia," says Carol Macherey, D.V.M., a veterinarian in private practice in Nashville. In severe cases, pets can lose up to one-quarter of their blood to parasites, so getting rid of the pests is a priority.

Some parasites, like fleas, are easy to eliminate, while for others your pet will need a veterinarian's care. Ask your vet for advice.

Ask about medications. There are a number of prescription and over-the-counter drugs, including aspirin and other anti-inflammatory medications, that can cause bleeding in the digestive tract that can lead to anemia. In addition, some drugs may cause the immune system to "attack" otherwise healthy blood cells, reducing the blood's oxygen-carrying capability. If your pet seems under the weather and is also taking medications, ask your vet if there might be a connection.

Beef up the diet. For quick relief from anemia, your pet needs to boost the oxygen-carrying capacity of his blood as quickly as possible. Giving him foods rich in iron and B vitamins, such as cooked liver, will help, says Lee R. Harris, D.V.M., a veterinarian in private practice in Federal Way, Washington.

Vets typically recommend giving a cat one ounce of liver a day for a week or two, or until he's feeling better. A small dog should get two ounces, and a large dog will happily gobble up to four ounces of liver a day.

Reach for the Geritol. Another way to beef up the blood is to give a daily dose of this over-the-counter supplement, which is high in iron and B vitamins, Dr. Harris says. Ask your vet to recommend a safe dose for your pet.

Supplement his diet. "With some kinds of anemia, vitamin supplementation seems to make sense," says Michael Richards, D.V.M., a veterinarian in private practice in Cobbs Creek, Virginia, who answers questions on dog and cat health in the Pet Care Forum on America Online. He recommends giving supplements high in iron and B vitamins; they are available at pet stores and from your vet. Just crush the pills—or if you're using capsules, take them apart—and mix the powder with his food.

Select good chows. While the type of anemia caused by insufficient

When to See the Vet

While the symptoms of anemia can sometimes be relieved temporarily with home treatment, the underlying problem must be treated by a vet.

If you suspect that your pet is anemic, take a look in his mouth—it should be a healthy pink (although some pets' mouths are naturally brown or black). If your pet has anemia, the inside of his mouth may be quite pale, says Carol Macherey, D.V.M., a veterinarian in private practice in Nashville. "If you can't see any pink in the gums, head for the vet," she advises.

Another way to spot anemia is to examine the eyes. "Pull down the lower eyelid and look at the conjunctiva, the membrane that lines the eyelid," suggests Eugene Snyder, D.V.M., a veterinarian in private practice in Kettering, Ohio. While some pets have dark pigment there, usually the conjunctiva is bright pink. If your pet has anemia, however, the conjunctiva will looked washed-out and pale.

iron in the diet usually occurs only in very young pets, it's still a good idea to play it safe by sticking to name-brand dog or cat foods, says Dr. Macherey.

It doesn't matter whether you choose dry, canned or semi-moist foods. However, you should try to stay away from generic or supermarket-brand foods, since the nutrients in these foods may be difficult for dogs or cats to absorb.

Encourage quiet time. Physical activity increases the body's demand for oxygen, which in pets with anemia is already in short supply. "Animals need to stay really quiet if they're anemic," says Dr. Harris.

PANEL OF ADVISERS

Lee R. Harris, D.V.M., is a veterinarian in private practice in Federal Way, Washington.

Carol Macherey, D.V.M., is a veterinarian in private practice in Nashville.

Michael Richards, D.V.M., is a veterinarian in private practice in Cobbs Creek, Virginia, who answers questions on dog and cat health in the Pet Care Forum on America Online.

Eugene Snyder, D.V.M., is a veterinarian in private practice in Kettering, Ohio.

Arthritis

13 Ways to Ease the Aches

When your dog gets out of bed in the morning, does he hobble like a wounded war hero? Is your once-graceful cat shuffling around like Walter Brennan? Arthritis can be a real pain in the neck—not to mention the hip, elbow and back.

While there are many kinds of arthritis, the one most likely to strike your pet is osteoarthritis. Also called degenerative joint disease, it usually comes about after years of wear and tear on hard-working joints.

Large pets are especially vulnerable to osteoarthritis, but even the smallest cat can feel its piercing pangs. "It hurts, and without your help, it's not going to feel better," says Mark M. Smith, D.V.M., associate professor of surgery in the Department of Small Animal Clinical Sciences at Virginia-Maryland Regional College of Veterinary Medicine in Blacksburg, Virginia, and co-author of *Atlas of Approaches for General Surgery of the Dog and Cat.*

Once your pet starts getting arthritis, he's going to need a veterinarian's care. Your vet may advise giving anti-inflammatory drugs, like buffered aspirin or cortisone. Even acupuncture can be a big help. In addition, there are many things you can do at home to help him get around more comfortably.

 For **Dogs** and **Cats**

Lighten his load. Heavy pets are considerably more likely to suffer joint pain than their trimmer counterparts. "Slimming him down is one of the best things you can do for him," says James D. Lincoln, D.V.M., associate professor and chief of small animal surgery at the Washington State University College of Veterinary Medicine in Pullman. "It reduces the stress on the joints and can provide enormous relief."

Helping him shed a few pounds may be as simple as cutting treats and table scraps from his diet. You also may want to switch him to a food that has less fat and more fiber than the one he's been getting. That way he can eat the same amount but consume fewer calories.

Put his best paw forward. Regular exercise is vital to controlling the progression of arthritis, which is why vets often recommend taking pets for a 20-minute walk several times a day.

Many cats adore going for walks, although they often insist on setting the course! Because felines wriggle out of collars so easily, it's usually best to fit them with a harness.

If your cat isn't leash-trained, having a lively play session—with a ball, a pull-toy or some other "active" toy—is a good substitute.

"Good muscle tone and muscle mass will help alleviate undue force on the arthritic joint," Dr. Smith says.

If 20 minutes seems too long, try taking shorter walks up and down small hills. Walking on the beach is also fine, as long as your pet doesn't run or dig too much. "Experiment and see what he likes," says Dr. Smith. "If he's more lame than usual the next day, you know you've done too much. Just use common sense and don't overdo it." It's also a good idea to check with your vet before beginning any new exercise plan.

Try some home improvements. If your pet sleeps outdoors, make sure his usual abode is well-protected. "Cover it with a plastic sheet or insulation so the cold wind doesn't stiffen his joints," says David E. Harling, D.V.M., a veterinarian in private practice in Greensboro, North Carolina, who specializes in orthopedics and ophthalmology.

Let him sleep in. "When it's cold and damp outside, your arthritic pet is going to hurt," says Ralph Womer, D.V.M., a veterinarian in private practice in Auburn, Alabama. "Your pet's joints will thank you if you bring him inside for the night."

Make a cozy bed. "If your pet is sleeping on a hard surface, he'll probably get some relief if you switch to something soft," says Dr. Harling. During the cold months, he'll appreciate curling up on a soft layer of synthetic fleece. You can even invest in a heated pet bed, available in some pet stores and animal supply companies, such as Discount Master Animal Care, a division of Humboldt Industries (for a catalog, write to Humboldt Industrial Park, One Maplewood Drive, Hazleton, PA 18201-9798).

Lay on something warm. A little moist heat, applied directly over painful joints, can be a great comfort to arthritic pets, says Sue Stephens, D.V.M., a veterinarian in private practice in Winston-Salem, North Carolina.

One trick is to use a hot water bottle (filled with warm, not hot, water). Or soak a towel in warm water, wring it out and drape it over the affected area. When the towel cools, replace it with a fresh one.

Apply the heat twice a day, morning and evening, for about 15 minutes each time. "It makes them feel so much better, especially in the morning when they tend to be stiffer," says Dr. Stephens.

But while heat is good, don't take chances with a heating pad, she adds. "They can burn an animal's skin very badly, especially if he has limited mobility and can't easily move away if it gets too hot," she says.

Be the Wizard of Ahs. Have you ever felt really achy, and then some kind soul gave you a soothing massage? "Imagine being able to do that for your pet," says Robert A. Montgomery, D.V.M., a veterinarian in private practice in New Philadelphia, Ohio.

Gently knead the sore area with small, circular motions, Dr. Montgomery says. Gradually extend the massage until you've gone a few inches beyond the painful joint, then gradually work your way back. "Once the animal looks more relaxed than when you started, you've done something right," says Dr. Montgomery.

Raise the dinner table. If your pet has a stiff neck, try putting his food and water bowls up off the floor so he doesn't have to lower his head as much at mealtimes, suggests Dr. Harling. You can put the bowls on a block of wood or a firm box. Or you can buy a pet-bowl stand at pet stores.

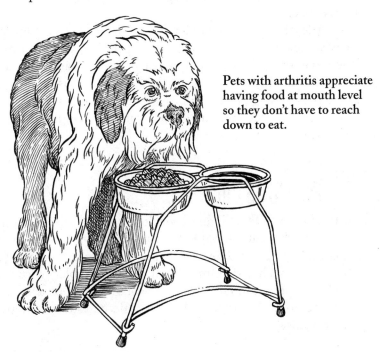

Pets with arthritis appreciate having food at mouth level so they don't have to reach down to eat.

Slinging a towel beneath your pet's belly will help him walk when his joints are acting up.

Help him be a social climber. If your pet is having trouble with stairs, you may want to install a ramp to help him go up and down without assistance.

At the very least, be prepared to lend him a helping hand. "Jumping up or down can really cause pain for arthritic pets," says Dr. Smith.

Try the towel trick. If your pet is having trouble walking, you can help him out by slinging a towel beneath his belly and using it to help him stand upright, suggests Dr. Smith. If he continues to have this much trouble, of course, you should be working paw-in-hand with your veterinarian.

 For Dogs Only

Buffer it with an OTC. Giving your dog buffered aspirin can be a great help for arthritis pain, says Dr. Harling. Experts recommend giving one-quarter of a 325-milligram tablet per 10 pounds of dog twice a day. A 40-pound pooch, for example, will need one tablet twice a day, while a pint-size poodle might need only one-quarter of a tablet or less. To prevent stomach upset, always use buffered aspirin and give it only after mealtimes.

Remember, too, that doses of aspirin that are safe for dogs can be deadly for cats, so never give your cat aspirin without advice from your veterinarian. In addition, don't give dogs or cats other over-the-counter painkillers without first checking with your vet.

Make a splash. Swimming is great exercise because it maintains muscle mass without stressing arthritic joints, says Dr. Smith. "Many arthritic dogs tend to naturally want to swim," he adds.

He recommends taking your pet to a nearby pond, lake, swimming pool or any other body of water where he won't have to fight big waves. For small pets, even a bathtub full of lukewarm water can be a real treat. "Wherever your pet swims, let him swim as long as he wants, as long as he doesn't seem tired," he says.

Of course, some dogs will turn tail at the first sign of water, so don't force the issue if your pet happens to be a landlubber.

Button him up. When the temperature dips, you may want to bundle your pet into a coat or sweater. "Anything you can do to keep him warm could make his arthritis less painful," says Dr. Harling. You can explore the world of *haute couture* at most pet stores.

PANEL OF ADVISERS

David E. Harling, D.V.M., is a veterinarian in private practice in Greensboro, North Carolina, who specializes in orthopedics and ophthalmology.

James D. Lincoln, D.V.M., is associate professor and chief of small animal surgery at the Washington State University College of Veterinary Medicine in Pullman.

Robert A. Montgomery, D.V.M., is a veterinarian in private practice in New Philadelphia, Ohio.

Mark M. Smith, D.V.M., is associate professor of surgery in the Department of Small Animal Clinical Sciences at the Virginia-Maryland Regional College of Veterinary Medicine in Blacksburg, Virginia, and co-author of *Atlas of Approaches for General Surgery of the Dog and Cat.*

Sue Stephens, D.V.M., is a veterinarian in private practice in Winston-Salem, North Carolina.

Ralph Womer, D.V.M., is a veterinarian in private practice in Auburn, Alabama.

Asthma

12 Ways to Ease Breathing

It wasn't so long ago that the only thing in the yard faster than your ferocious feline was the occasional fly lucky enough to get away.

But these days, even short outdoor romps are triggering asthma attacks, causing wheezing, coughing and fatigue. "Coughing and wheezing are common signs of asthma in cats," explains Lisardo J. Martinez, D.V.M., a veterinarian in private practice in Miami.

Typically caused by such things as dust or pollen in the air, asthma in cats occurs when airways in the lungs become inflamed and constricted, making it harder for air to get through. (Dogs are less commonly affected.) While most cats may require medication, there are things you can do at home to keep him breathing easy.

 **For Cats Only**

Shave off a few pounds. While every cat should stay trim, it's particularly important for pets with asthma. "The signs of asthma can be made worse by obesity," says Dr. Martinez. "An overweight cat will have even more problems breathing."

If your cat is roly-poly, gradually decreasing the amount he eats will help him lose those excess pounds. Talk to your vet about beginning a sensible weight-loss plan.

Crank up the humidifier. Breathing dry air irritates the airways, which in turn can trigger asthma attacks. "In many homes the humidity drops as low as 10 percent because of the air-conditioning unit," says Janet R. Childs, D.V.M., a house-call veterinarian in Fairview, Tennessee. In winter, heaters dry out the air as well.

To make the air less irritating, she suggests using a vaporizer or humidifier to boost humidity levels to between 30 and 40 percent. Don't go higher, however, because this can encourage the growth of mold and dust mites, which can also trigger asthma attacks.

Kick the habit. Surely your cat doesn't smoke, but second-hand smoke from you or your friends could make the problem worse. "Pets are a lot more vulnerable to the effects of smoke than people," says Carol Macherey, D.V.M., a veterinarian in private practice in Nashville. "The concentration at floor level is greater than people realize."

If you smoke, you'll being doing your pet (and yourself) a favor by quitting. Or do your puffing outside.

Bring him indoors. If you suspect hay fever is kicking off his asthma attacks, it might help to keep him indoors during the height of the pollen season, says Dr. Macherey. This is particularly true in the early morning and late afternoon, when pollen counts in the air tend to be highest.

Choose the right litter. Most catbox litter puffs up dust whenever your feline friend starts digging. "Look for dust-free litter, or use sand-box sand instead," suggests Dr. Martinez.

Clear the air. Many things you take for granted, like hair spray, perfume or household cleaners, could be irritating your pet's airways and triggering attacks, says Dr. Martinez. "Anything that's irritating to your nasal passages could cause a problem for them," adds Dr. Childs.

When to See the Vet

Although asthma can often be managed at home with a veterinarian's guidance, it's important to remember what's happening inside your cat's airways—inflammation and constriction. If they shut down all the way, your pet could die, explains Carol Macherey, D.V.M., a veterinarian in private practice in Nashville.

If your cat has just started coughing or wheezing, or if she's had asthma before but the symptoms are getting worse, don't take chances. Call your vet right away, advises Dr. Macherey.

In addition, it's a good idea to ask your vet about heartworms. Some cats may react to the worms just as they would to some other allergen, like pollen. "When cats get heartworms, it's sometimes confused with asthma," says Mark Coleman, D.V.M., a veterinarian in private practice in Gainesville, Florida, and president of the American Heartworm Society. Heartworms can be detected with a simple blood test, he adds.

Help the Medicine Go Down

It's not uncommon for cats with serious asthma to require oral medications that help relieve airway inflammation.

To give your cat pills or capsules without getting scratched, first wrap a towel around his chest so his feet are blocked with the towel, suggests Carol Macherey, D.V.M., a veterinarian in private practice in Nashville. Put your hand on the back of his head, with your thumb on one side of his jaw and your fingers on the other. Gently rotate his head until it's tilted back.

The lower jaw will drop by reflex, although you may have to keep it open with your thumb and forefinger, says Dr. Macherey. "Drop the pill in and poke it back with your index finger."

Don't try this technique with your cat's head in a normal position, she adds. Trying to poke pills "uphill" doesn't work.

"If you're giving a liquid dosage, carefully wipe the outside of the dropper so the dropper itself isn't a source of bad flavor," adds Dr. Macherey. She recommends pointing the dropper far back in the cat's mouth so the medicine doesn't hit the taste buds on its way down.

How do you make sure your cantankerous kitty will actually swallow the medication instead of spitting it out in the corner? The best way to get a cat to swallow is to startle it, according to Eugene Snyder, D.V.M., a veterinarian in private practice in Kettering, Ohio. As soon as you have given the medicine and released him, gently blow in his face. "He will reflexively swallow," he says.

Put aside powerful cleaners in favor of milder products like vinegar and baking soda, plus some extra elbow grease, recommends Jeffrey Feinman, V.M.D., a house-call veterinarian in Weston, Connecticut.

When cleaning bathrooms or other areas where mold grows, however, you need to use a mild bleach solution. Be sure to rinse the area well with fresh water, and keep your pet in another room until the room airs out, Dr. Feinman suggests.

Do extra cleaning. Even small amounts of floating dirt and dust can trigger asthma attacks, so it's important to keep your cat's area squeaky clean, says Dr. Feinman.

"You need to dust in corners and move furniture so you can clean under it," he says.

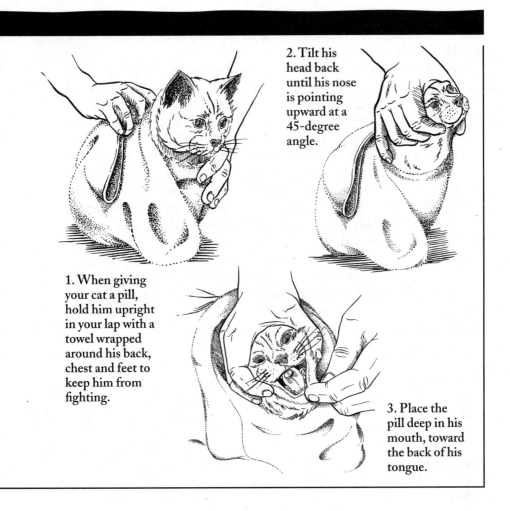

2. Tilt his head back until his nose is pointing upward at a 45-degree angle.

1. When giving your cat a pill, hold him upright in your lap with a towel wrapped around his back, chest and feet to keep him from fighting.

3. Place the pill deep in his mouth, toward the back of his tongue.

While you're cleaning, however, there will be veritable clouds of dust hovering in the air. Keep your pet in a different area until the dust has a chance to settle, he suggests.

Put the muscle on mites. Dust mites are microscopic critters that typically flourish in mattresses and bedding and are common triggers of both allergies and asthma attacks, says Paul Schmitz, D.V.M., a veterinarian in private practice in Joliet, Illinois.

One way to keep mites under control is to enclose mattresses and pillows in vinyl cases. In addition, you should wash all bedding in hot water once a week. This will help keep their numbers down and your pet breathing easy.

Filter out the problem. If your home is heated and cooled with a central system, consider installing an electrostatic filter. While these filters can be expensive, they do seem to filter some types of particles, says Dr. Childs.

Look for culprits. If asthma is a new visitor in your life, it's possible some recent addition—a new carpet or couch, for instance—is behind the problem. In addition, some cats may be sensitive to new detergents or shampoos their owners are using, says Dr. Feinman. Try switching back to your old brands to see if things improve.

Try supplemental protection. Some vets believe that giving pets antioxidant vitamins, which apparently help "neutralize" harmful oxygen molecules in the body, can help relieve a number of health problems, including asthma. Dr. Childs recommends giving your pet an infant's or child's dose of vitamin C or E once a week. Just crumble or sprinkle it on his food, she says.

Calm your kitty's karma. Asthma has long been linked with stress in pets as well as people. When asthma is flaring, it might be a good idea to nix activities that upset your feline—like taking him to the groomer when he doesn't want to go. Dr. Schmitz recommends keeping him indoors and calm until he's feeling better.

PANEL OF ADVISERS

Janet R. Childs, D.V.M., is a house-call veterinarian in Fairview, Tennessee.

Mark Coleman, D.V.M., is a veterinarian in private practice in Gainesville, Florida, and president of the American Heartworm Society.

Jeffrey Feinman, V.M.D., is a house-call veterinarian in Weston, Connecticut.

Carol Macherey, D.V.M., is a veterinarian in private practice in Nashville.

Lisardo J. Martinez, D.V.M., is a veterinarian in private practice in Miami.

Paul Schmitz, D.V.M., is a veterinarian in private practice in Joliet, Illinois.

Eugene Snyder, D.V.M., is a veterinarian in private practice in Kettering, Ohio.

Back & Disk Problems

5 Pointers to Ease the Pain

Our pets don't slump in office chairs or lift heavy bags from the backseat of the car. Most of the time, in fact, their spines are relatively straight, which may be why they get fewer backaches than we do.

But even a posture-perfect pooch may occasionally wrench his back, says Larry Gainsburg, D.V.M., a veterinarian in private practice in Baltimore who specializes in neurology and neurosurgery.

Some back injuries involve nothing worse than sore muscles. Your pet may cry or jerk away when you pet him. Or he may have trouble climbing stairs or getting to his feet in the morning. Pets may also injure their spinal disks, a serious problem that can cause extreme pain, loss of muscle control or severe nerve damage, including paralysis.

Breeds most susceptible to back problems are the long, low dogs like dachshunds or the bigger guys like Great Danes, Dobermans and German shepherds. In addition, dogs that are overweight may be more likely to have back problems than their leaner counterparts.

Cats can also have back problems, but because they're more flexible than dogs, it happens less often, says Dr. Gainsburg.

Here are a few ways to keep back problems under control.

 For Dogs and Cats

Put on some heat. For minor muscle stiffness and back pain, applying a hot pack or warm compress can be very soothing, says Karen Kline, D.V.M., a neurologist and assistant professor at Iowa State University in Ames. Applying heat can also boost circulation to the area, possibly speeding the healing process.

While sitting next to your pet or holding him in your lap, gently place the pack or compress on the sore spot and hold it in place. Providing an ear-rub at the same time will go a long way toward keeping him still.

If he'll hold still for it, apply the hot pack or compress for up to 15 minutes three times a day, Dr. Kline advises.

Checking for Damage

In pets as in humans, not every backache is cause for alarm. "They can get muscle spasms in their backs just as we do," says Lee R. Harris, D.V.M., a veterinarian in private practice in Federal Way, Washington.

So how do you tell the difference between a sore muscle, which isn't a serious problem, and a disk injury, which requires immediate attention?

One way to tell is by checking your pet's "placing response." While he's standing, flip one of his hind feet so the top of the paw is touching the ground. "The dog should pick the foot up and put it right-side up in two seconds or less," says Dr. Harris.

If he doesn't place the foot correctly, he could have an injury that's putting pressure on a spinal nerve. Consider it an emergency and call the vet right away.

Even if your pet passes the test, however, you should call your vet if the pain persists for more than a day or two. Nerve problems don't always show up right away, and he could suffer permanent damage if he doesn't get professional help fairly soon.

While supporting your pet with one hand, flip one of his hind feet so the top of the paw is touching the ground.

He should quickly place the foot right-side up when you let go. If he doesn't, he could have nerve problems and should see a vet right away.

Give his paws pause. To prevent your pet from adding insult to back injury, keep him quiet and close to home until the sore area has a chance to heal. "Make him as immobile as possible for three to four weeks to give the inflammation a chance to subside," says Dr. Gainsburg.

Keeping your dog or cat in a crate is an easy way to help him avoid overdoing it. At the very least, keep him on a leash when you go outside so he doesn't go dashing off and do further damage.

Enforcing some quiet time is particularly important if your pet is taking steroids or other medications that ease pain or swelling, says Dr. Gainsburg. He may be feeling so good he'll forget he's injured—and then hurt himself all over again.

Work out slowly. Once your pet is back on all fours again, don't celebrate right away with a vigorous romp. Begin with light exercise and work up from there.

"Take short leash walks only," says Dr. Kline. "Begin with a couple of hundred yards and increase it weekly. It's a very gradual process."

Ask about aspirin. For fast relief from mild back pain, your vet may recommend giving low doses of buffered aspirin. A safe dose for dogs is one-quarter of a 325-milligram tablet for every ten pounds of dog, given twice a day. Aspirin can be dangerous for cats, however, so don't give it without first checking with your vet.

Also, don't give ibuprofen or acetaminophen, which can be dangerous for pets, says Lee R. Harris, D.V.M., a veterinarian in private practice in Federal Way, Washington.

Watch his weight. Since being overweight can contribute to back problems in pets, keeping your pet trim should be an ongoing process, says E. A. Corley, D.V.M., Ph.D., president and executive director of the Orthopedic Foundation for Animals in Columbia, Missouri.

To check your pet's weight, lightly run your hands over his ribcage. If you can count each rib, he's at a good weight, says Dr. Corley. If all you feel is padding, however, it's time to talk to your vet about a sensible weight-loss plan.

PANEL OF ADVISERS

E. A. Corley, D.V.M., Ph.D., is president and executive director of the Orthopedic Foundation for Animals in Columbia, Missouri.

Larry Gainsburg, D.V.M., is a veterinarian in private practice in Baltimore who specializes in neurology and neurosurgery.

Lee R. Harris, D.V.M., is a veterinarian in private practice in Federal Way, Washington.

Karen Kline, D.V.M., is a neurologist and assistant professor at Iowa State University in Ames.

Bad Breath

15 Tips to Clear the Air

Do friends politely excuse themselves when your dog is panting nearby? Do you suddenly lose your appetite when your cat gives you a kiss? Oooh, that smell. It's enough to make a grown dog wince.

If your pet's breath packs a potent punch, chances are the culprit is plaque, the same bacteria-laden film that develops on your teeth if you don't brush for a while and can lead to a smelly and sometimes dangerous gum infection.

With a little care, however, you can help prevent your pet's breath from turning too pungent.

 ## For Dogs and Cats

Attack the plaque. "Think of how your mouth would smell if you didn't brush your teeth for a few days, much less a few years," says Anthony Shipp, D.V.M., a veterinarian in private practice in Beverly Hills, California, who specializes in dentistry and is co-author of *The Practitioner's Guide to Veterinary Dentistry*. Brushing twice a day would be ideal, says Dr. Shipp, but twice a week is okay.

Start 'em young. Brushing your pet's teeth may sound like a scene in a horror flick, but if you begin when your dog or cat is only a few months old, the experience can quickly become a pleasant one, says Dr. Shipp.

Begin by gently handling and stroking your pet's mouth for a few minutes a day. "Reward with plenty of love or a treat," says Dr. Shipp. After a few days, lift her lip on one side and, with a piece of gauze on your finger, begin brushing in a circular or back-and-forth motion on the outer surface of a few teeth. You should soon be able to graduate to more teeth. Eventually you may be able to use a miniature brush, available in pet stores, that fits over your finger, or even a regular soft-bristled brush designed for pets.

Tickle their taste buds. Some pet toothpastes come in flavors like poultry, beef or malt to make the experience more palatable for your pet. "Meat-flavored pastes may not sound tasty to a human, but mint-flavored toothpaste doesn't sound tasty to most dogs or cats, either," says Albert S. Dorn, D.V.M., professor of surgery at the University of Tennessee College of Veterinary Medicine in Knoxville. Don't use a human toothpaste that foams, warns Dr. Dorn. Pets can't spit, and if they swallow the foam, it can upset their stomachs.

Get in the groove. If your pet doesn't take kindly to having her teeth brushed, some vets recommend going to the pet store and picking up a hard rubber toy that has grooves in it. These toys are specially designed with your pet's teeth in mind. Smear a little meat-flavored toothpaste in the notches, and your pet may end up brushing her own teeth. "Nothing beats a toothbrush, but this is better than nothing," says Dr. Dorn.

Floss with an ox. The next time you make oxtail soup, give your pet the cooked oxtail. Dr. Dorn says the tail's tendons and fibers help massage the teeth and gums and may help clean those hard-to-reach places.

Quell it with carrots. A little bit of raw carrot, given as a midday treat, can act as a mild-mannered tooth scraper, scouring away stink-causing plaque, says Cheryl Schwartz, D.V.M., a veterinarian in private practice in Oakland, California.

Reach for a spray. Many pet stores sell mouth sprays for dogs and cats, which do the same thing as the minty sprays people use. "They're purely cosmetic," says Dr. Shipp. But cosmetic isn't such a bad thing when your pet's breath is petrifying.

Can the canned food. "Switching to dry food may help to improve mouth odor, because it scrapes the surface of the teeth," says Lisa Freeman, D.V.M., clinical instructor and a fellow in clinical nutrition at the Tufts University School of Veterinary Medicine in North Grafton, Massachusetts.

Nix nibbling. If you allow your pet to munch on her food throughout the day, the harmful bacteria in her mouth are always active, says Dr. Dorn. He advises picking up your pet's food bowl if she doesn't finish her meal within 30 minutes to an hour. "If you only feed a dog once or twice a day, you only feed the bacteria once or twice a day," Dr. Dorn says.

Rice to the occasion. Whole grains, like cooked brown rice, can help food move along the digestive tract more readily, says Dr. Schwartz. "Better digestion can play a role in better breath," she says. She recommends replacing a small portion of your pet's regular food with rice at every meal.

Suspicious Odors

Just as the eyes are windows to the soul, the mouth is a window to your pet's health. While a little stinky breath usually isn't cause for alarm, there are a few serious conditions that can cause distinct mouth odors, says Albert S. Dorn, D.V.M., professor of surgery at the University of Tennessee College of Veterinary Medicine in Knoxville. In fact, your vet can often make a preliminary diagnosis based on your pet's breath. Here are some examples.

- A sweet, fruity scent could indicate diabetes, especially if your pet is drinking or urinating more than usual and is losing weight.
- A urinelike smell might mean kidney disease, particularly if it's accompanied by increased thirst and urination and decreased appetite.
- A mouth odor that vets simply describe as foul, when accompanied by vomiting, loss of appetite, swelling of the abdomen or yellowing of the eyes or gums, could indicate a liver disorder.

Scrap the scraps. Breath often reflects the diet, and if you're feeding your dog or cat things like leftover spaghetti flavored with lots of garlic, you may have found the cause of her bad breath.

Go for the green. Chlorophyll tablets, available in pet stores, can aid digestion and sweeten your pet's breath, says Dr. Schwartz.

Or blast it with black. The next time you're choosing biscuits for your pet, opt for the black variety. They may not be as pretty as the pinks or golds, but they usually have one thing the others don't—a dash of charcoal. Charcoal is a binding agent that can absorb bad odors. But don't go overboard, since charcoal can also bind up essential nutrients. Limit treats to one or two a day, vets advise.

 For Dogs Only

Whip it with rawhide. Rawhide bones are good at rasping away plaque buildup, says Dr. Freeman. "The constant scraping action against the teeth may help clean up the mouth," she says.

Toss her a rope. Those soft, bone-shaped rope twists sold in pet stores create a natural flossing action, says Dr. Dorn. "If your dog can get rid of some of the old food and bacteria lodged in the mouth, it could help a bad-breath problem," he says.

PANEL OF ADVISERS

Albert S. Dorn, D.V.M., is professor of surgery at the University of Tennessee College of Veterinary Medicine in Knoxville.

Lisa Freeman, D.V.M., is clinical instructor and a fellow in clinical nutrition at the Tufts University School of Veterinary Medicine in North Grafton, Massachusetts.

Cheryl Schwartz, D.V.M., is a veterinarian in private practice in Oakland, California.

Anthony Shipp, D.V.M., is a veterinarian in private practice in Beverly Hills, California, who specializes in dentistry and is co-author of *The Practitioner's Guide to Veterinary Dentistry.*

Barking

15 Ways to Keep the Peace

Your dog has been barking up the wrong tree lately. In fact, it seems that every time a leaf falls, the mail carrier calls or a car stalls, his outbursts shake the walls.

Barking is normal, and a little is okay. It's just that some dogs have more to say than others. When your pooch doesn't know when to call it quits, try these tips from the experts to help keep the baying at bay.

 For **Dogs** Only

Exercise him often. "A couple of good walks or play sessions a day can help your dog be calm," says Bob Gutierrez, animal behavior coordinator at the San Francisco Society for the Prevention of Cruelty to Animals. "Instead of barking all day, he may sleep all day."

Let him chew it over. Your dog will have a hard time barking if he's busy chewing on bones or doggy toys. "Chewing is a real stress-reducer and occupier of time," says Gutierrez. "If you're going to be gone, give your dog his very favorite chew treat just before you leave."

Give him something to think about. If your dog often gets lonely—and vocal—when you're away, try rubbing your hands all over his chew treat before leaving. "The scent will remind him of you, and he may not miss you as much," Gutierrez says.

Mask outside noises. "If your dog is super-sensitive to noises in the environment, try blocking some of that noise so he's not as inspired to bark," says Gutierrez. White noise machines can do the trick. So can playing your stereo at a normal level.

Catch up on your cleaning. Turning on the vacuum cleaner can also block unwanted noises—the approaching steps of the mail carrier, for example—and prevent your pet from going into a barking frenzy, says Gutierrez.

Thank him for his thoughts. Sometimes just praising your pet will make him hush, says veterinarian Nicholas Dodman, B.V.M.S., professor in the Department of Surgery and director of the Behavior Clinic at the Tufts University School of Veterinary Medicine in North Grafton, Massachusetts. "The dog may be trying to tell you something, and when you acknowledge him, he may realize it's okay to turn off the barking."

Insist on quiet time. Sometimes a dog will keep barking even after you acknowledge his watchdog woofs. "Say 'Quiet!' sharply, but without yelling," advises Dr. Dodman. "If he blinks and stops barking, praise him warmly."

It doesn't hurt to occasionally give your pet a treat after the noise stops. "What you're doing is taking his mind off the barking and making him realize that it's so good when he stops," Dr. Dodman adds.

Leave the party. Some dogs, like people, hate talking without an audience. So if all your praises and commands fail to keep him quiet, leave. "Chances are your dog wants you to hang around, so turning your back and leaving the room can make him see he's doing something wrong," says Dr. Dodman.

To reinforce the lesson, ring a bell (or sound a tuning fork) before leaving. "Let it ring for a couple of seconds, and when you think the dog hears it, leave," Dr. Dodman says. Over time, your dog will learn to associate the ringing with your leaving, and he'll be more likely to keep his thoughts to himself. It also helps to praise your pooch once he stops barking.

Try a homemade shake. A shake can has an effect on dogs that is the canine equivalent of fingernails on a blackboard. Put some coins in an empty soda can and tape the opening shut. When your barking pooch doesn't respond to your command to be quiet, shake the can a couple of times, Gutierrez suggests. "They don't like the sound, so they often stop what they're doing when they hear it," he says.

Dampen his enthusiasm. To remind your dog that you'd appreciate some quiet time, give him a firm "No!" followed by a short blast with a squirt bottle. "If they don't like water, they'll tend to stop," says Gutierrez. It's best to aim for the body and not the face, he adds.

Seek deliverance from the mail carrier. If your dog goes ballistic whenever people come to the door, you may need an accomplice. One possible solution is to have your mail carrier slip a tasty treat through the door slot, suggests Suzanne Hetts, Ph.D., a certified applied animal behavior consultant in Littleton, Colorado. "Your dog may stop seeing these people as threats and might not feel the need to bark," she says.

Bring him inside. If your dog sleeps outside and likes to exercise his vocal cords at night, you may want to bring him indoors. "He'll have less to bark at," says Dr. Hetts.

Try gentle pressure. Many experts recommend trainer collars like the Promise System or the Gentle Leader. Similar to halters worn by horses, the collars come with ten-foot leads. When your dog starts barking, pulling the lead will gently press his mouth closed for the few seconds that you apply pressure.

"The beauty is you never have to scold your dog or even say anything to him," says Robert K. Anderson, D.V.M., professor and director emeritus of the Animal Behavior Clinic at the University of Minnesota College of Veterinary Medicine in Minneapolis-St. Paul. "The collar speaks for itself by stopping the behavior."

The collars are more humane and effective than choke collars, and some dogs will start barking less in as few as one or two training sessions, says Dr. Anderson. The collars are available from veterinarians and animal trainers, who will make sure they fit correctly and will give instructions for their proper use.

Try shock therapy. Your veterinarian may recommend a specialized bark collar, which delivers either a high-frequency sound or a light

Canine 101

Okay, so your dog isn't exactly Lassie. When he barks, you know he's not telling you "Timmy's in the well!" But that doesn't mean you can't learn something by listening carefully to what he says.

"There are many, many different tones of bark," says veterinarian Nicholas Dodman, B.V.M.S., professor in the Department of Surgery and director of the Behavior Clinic at the Tufts University School of Veterinary Medicine in North Grafton, Massachusetts. Dr. Dodman, who was born in England, insists you can learn "bark-speak" just as he learned to recognize a variety of American accents.

If your dog is whining between barks, for example, he may be telling you he's frightened or he doesn't want you to leave the house, says Dr. Dodman. A dog that barks for a long time, with brief pauses between identical-sounding woofs, is probably bored. An exuberant bark, however, means your pooch is probably eager to play. "Eventually, you could get to know what your dog needs just by hearing him," he says.

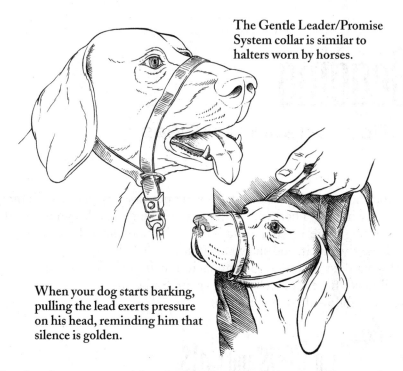

The Gentle Leader/Promise System collar is similar to halters worn by horses.

When your dog starts barking, pulling the lead exerts pressure on his head, reminding him that silence is golden.

shock whenever your dog barks. Some collars go off immediately, while others allow the dog to bark a few times before kicking in. "They can be extremely effective, but you really need to work with someone who can help you get a good collar and training," says Dr. Hetts. See your veterinarian for advice.

Know when to switch strategies. "People often don't know when to call it quits with a particular approach," says Dr. Dodman. "They'll keep doing one thing for months even though it's just not working." If you haven't seen improvement within three to five days of using one anti-bark technique, try another one.

PANEL OF ADVISERS

Robert K. Anderson, D.V.M., is professor and director emeritus of the Animal Behavior Clinic at the University of Minnesota College of Veterinary Medicine in Minneapolis-St. Paul.

Nicholas Dodman, B.V.M.S., is professor in the Department of Surgery and director of the Behavior Clinic at the Tufts University School of Veterinary Medicine in North Grafton, Massachusetts.

Bob Gutierrez is animal behavior coordinator at the San Francisco Society for the Prevention of Cruelty to Animals.

Suzanne Hetts, Ph.D., is a certified applied animal behavior consultant in Littleton, Colorado.

Begging

9 Tips to Table the Pleas

Your heart swells as your loyal, loving pet gazes up at you with those soft brown eyes. Then you notice the whining, the drooling and the unrelenting stare at your fork. This isn't about love. It's about your food—she wants it, and she wants it now.

It's hard to ignore a good mooch, but if you give in, experts say, you'll never have a peaceful meal again. So be strong, hang onto your plate and follow these helpful hints.

 For Dogs and Cats

Feed her first. "If your dog or cat is really full, she just won't be as inspired to ask for more," says Kathryn Segura, who trains animals for television and movies and is co-owner of PHD Animals in Studio City, California.

Don't give in to guilt. No matter how much she manipulates your emotions with those Oliver Twist eyes—"Please, master, may I have some of yours?"—remind yourself that your pet is already well-fed and doesn't need human food, says M. Lynne Kesel, D.V.M., assistant professor of elective surgery in the Department of Clinical Sciences at the Colorado State University College of Veterinary Medicine and Biomedical Sciences in Fort Collins.

Make her leave for leftovers. If you do decide to slip her a snack, don't do it from the table, Dr. Kesel adds. Otherwise your pet will begin confusing your mealtimes with hers. "If I'm eating something healthy and I can't finish it, at the end I'll put a little in their bowls," she says.

Lay down the law. Usually just raising your voice will send your pet scurrying to another room. If that doesn't work, try honking a bike horn or rattling a shake can. "After a few times, they should get the message," says Gary Landsberg, D.V.M., a veterinarian in private prac-

Remove the tab from an empty
can and fill it with coins. Tape
the opening closed.

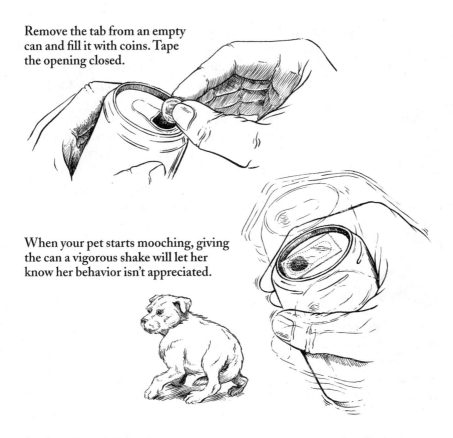

When your pet starts mooching, giving
the can a vigorous shake will let her
know her behavior isn't appreciated.

tice in Thornhill, Ontario, who specializes in animal behavior.

To make a shake can, put some coins inside an empty soda can.
Tape up the hole and you've got a noisemaker extraordinaire.

Say it with spray. Cats can be incorrigible beggars, even jumping on
tables and stealing food when you don't hand over a handout. And
dogs aren't above trying some pretty pushy maneuvers themselves. To
discourage such brazen behavior, surprise your pet with a blast from a
spray bottle. The plastic bottle you use to spray plants will do nicely.
Just aim for whatever part of your pet is handy, says Bob Gutierrez, animal behavior coordinator at the San Francisco Society for the Prevention of Cruelty to Animals.

Isolate the problem. "When your dog or cat is driving you crazy,
tell her 'No!' and calmly put her in another room and shut the door,"
says Dr. Landsberg. You may get complaints in the form of barking or
meowing, but don't let her out until you're done eating. "Eventually
she'll figure out that if she doesn't beg, she doesn't get sent away," says
Dr. Landsberg.

Try a sticky solution. Does your pet's begging repertoire include jumping up on kitchen counters? If so, try putting strips of double-sided tape in strategic spots. Then stand back and watch, says Gutierrez. "They hate the sensation of their paws getting a little stuck," he says. "They're unlikely to return, but just in case, buy an extra-big roll."

Give in—just a little. Some people love feeding their pet at the table and don't want to give it up entirely. As a compromise, try slipping her something healthy, like lettuce, suggests Myrna Milani, D.V.M., a veterinarian in private practice in Charlestown, New Hampshire, and author of *The Body Language and Emotions of Cats* and *The Body Language and Emotions of Dogs*. "If she doesn't like it, you've done your part—and if she does, you're not loading her down with fattening food," she says.

 For Dogs Only

Send her to school. If your pooch's pleas are starting to peeve, why not try obedience school? Once you've both mastered the essential commands like "Stay!" and "Down!" you'll have peace in the family once again. "This way it's not a constant battle at the dinner table," says Dr. Landsberg.

PANEL OF ADVISERS

Bob Gutierrez is animal behavior coordinator at the San Francisco Society for the Prevention of Cruelty to Animals.

M. Lynne Kesel, D.V.M., is assistant professor of elective surgery in the Department of Clinical Sciences at the Colorado State University College of Veterinary Medicine and Biomedical Sciences in Fort Collins.

Gary Landsberg, D.V.M., is a veterinarian in private practice in Thornhill, Ontario, who specializes in animal behavior.

Myrna Milani, D.V.M., is a veterinarian in private practice in Charlestown, New Hampshire, and author of *The Body Language and Emotions of Cats* and *The Body Language and Emotions of Dogs*.

Kathryn Segura trains animals for television and movies and is co-owner of PHD Animals in Studio City, California.

Birthing

9 Ways to Help Her Bear It

She hasn't been eating pickles, knitting pink and blue booties or shopping around for a speedy diaper service, but your pet is obviously quite pregnant. One day soon those kittens or puppies are going to wriggle from her world into yours.

Fear not. While it's a good idea to consult your vet when your pet becomes pregnant, you probably won't need a kitty Lamaze class or a mutt midwife. "Dogs and cats have been doing this for millions of years, and they've usually gotten along perfectly well without our help," says Craig Allan Smith, D.V.M., Ph.D., assistant editor of the *Journal of the American Veterinary Medical Association* in Schaumburg, Illinois.

Still, there are things you can do to ensure that all goes smoothly on the big day. Here's what vets recommend.

 **For Dogs and Cats**

Bring her indoors. Even if your pet normally lives outside, you'll want to keep her inside and safe during the last week or so of her pregnancy. "That way she won't be as likely to have her puppies or kittens outside where they're not as protected," says Vicki N. Meyers-Wallen, V.M.D., Ph.D., associate professor in the Department of Anatomy and a chief of service at the Small Animal Fertility and Infertility Clinic at the Cornell University College of Veterinary Medicine in Ithaca, New York.

Dogs usually give birth 58 to 68 days after conception; for cats it's between 60 and 68 days. You'll know your pet is nearing the end when her appetite markedly increases and her activity levels start to decline.

Make a maternity ward. "Most cats and dogs like to have a place to call their own during whelping and nursing," says Dr. Smith. You can buy a whelping box at pet stores, or you can make your own.

"If you have one of those little kiddie swimming pools around the house, you've got one of my favorite homemade types of whelping boxes," says Dr. Smith.

Another option is to cut down a heavy cardboard box, like those used to ship TVs or dishwashers. Just be sure the box is large enough to allow Mom to stretch out, with adequate room left over for the wee ones. In addition, one side should be low enough so Mom can come and go easily but not so low that the pups or kittens can take to wandering. Also, leave it open at the top so you can keep an eye on things.

Make it comfortable. Whatever type of whelping box you choose, cover the bottom with several layers of newspaper, then add several layers of clean towels. This will help keep the puppies or kittens warm and also absorb moisture and help keep them dry, says Jill Chase, D.V.M., a veterinarian in private practice in San Francisco. Once the little ones are born, change the bedding whenever it gets soiled.

Be quiet. Giving birth is a big experience in your pet's life, and she's going to want privacy. "She's not going to want to be where there's lots of noise or foot traffic," says Victor M. Shille, D.V.M., Ph.D., professor emeritus of theriogenology at the University of Florida College of Vet-

When to See the Vet

The vast majority of births go smoothly and without serious complications. But sometimes you need to call the vet right away. Here are the danger signs.

- Your pet passes a dark green fluid before delivering. This could mean that the placenta—the baby's lifeline—has become separated sooner than it was supposed to.
- She's been straining hard without delivering for more than one hour. This could mean that the puppy or kitten is too large or in the wrong position to come out without assistance.
- She seems weak, nervous or restless more than half an hour after the labor stops. "It could very well mean that someone has been left behind," says Victor M. Shille, D.V.M., Ph.D., professor emeritus of theriogenology at the University of Florida College of Veterinary Medicine in Gainesville and editor of the veterinary journal *Theriogenology*.
- Her muscles start trembling days or weeks after giving birth, or she begins vomiting or having trouble standing up. This could be a sign of eclampsia, a dangerous deficiency of calcium that sometimes occurs after giving birth.

When your pet is approaching her due date, get a large box and pad it well with several layers of newspapers and clean towels. Trim one of the sides so it's convenient for Mom to get in and out but too high for the young ones to escape.

erinary Medicine in Gainesville and editor of the veterinary journal *Theriogenology.* "The kitchen would not be a good idea. A corner of her favorite room, like the bedroom or den, could be just right."

It's also important that the area be free of drafts and comfortably warm and dry. For cats, it should also be fairly dark, experts say.

Help her move in. About one or two weeks before the due date, your pet should start getting used to her box. "Some cats and dogs will be so curious watching you put it together that they'll just hop right in," says Dr. Chase. "Others may need more encouragement."

Putting your pet's favorite blanket or toy inside the box will make it seem more familiar and comfortable, says Dr. Chase. Even so, you may need to lift her in—at least the first time. Don't be surprised if she jumps right out, adds Dr. Chase. When it's actually time to give birth, she'll probably return to the box on her own.

Prepare for the big moment. Anywhere from 6 to 24 hours before giving birth, your pet may begin pacing, panting or shivering. Often she'll walk around nervously, digging at the floor or carpet and looking for a place to nest. "It's hard watching her go through this," says Dr. Smith. "All you can do is stay calm yourself and comfort her if it seems to help."

If you suspect your pet is about to give birth—on your bed or in the closet, for example—encourage her to take refuge in her box. If she insists on staying where she is, try moving the box nearby and helping her in, says Dr. Chase.

Be prepared for a change of plans. Despite your best efforts to
(continued on page 64)

Birthing 101

While dogs and cats are usually well-prepared to give birth on their own, there are times when you'll need to don your midwife's hat and lend a hand.

Sometimes, for example, the puppy or kitten will come only halfway out, despite the mother's persistent straining. When that happens, you may need to assist the birth, says Victor M. Shille, D.V.M., Ph.D., professor emeritus of theriogenology at the University of Florida College of Veterinary Medicine in Gainesville and editor of the veterinary journal *Theriogenology*. While someone holds your pet's head to prevent her from lashing out, gently grasp the young one with a clean towel and pull firmly. If it doesn't slide out quickly and easily, stop pulling and call your veterinarian immediately, Dr. Shille says.

Once a puppy or kitten is born, the mother will usually instinctively tear off the amniotic sac (if it's still covering the body), sever the umbilical cord and roughly lick the baby to stimulate its breathing and circulation. But if she hasn't taken action within about 30 seconds, it's probably time for you to step in.

To remove the amniotic sac, start at the baby's mouth and

1. Grasp the emerging pup or kitten with a terrycloth towel or washcloth and gently pull it free.

2. Starting at the mouth, peel away the amniotic sac.

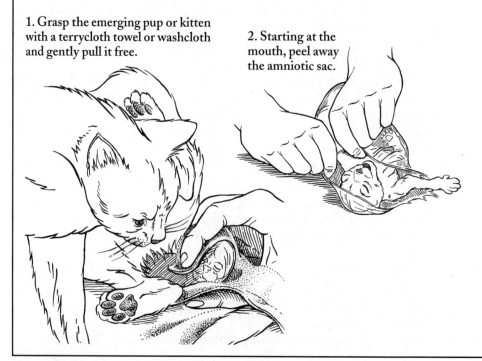

work backward, peeling it off with your fingers. Gently clean the mucus from the mouth with your finger, then rub him vigorously for several seconds with a clean terry towel or washcloth.

At this point you should step back and encourage your pet to lick her baby and sever the umbilical cord. If she doesn't follow through in about a minute, you'll have to cut the cord yourself.

Cut two pieces of sewing thread and wet them in alcohol. Tie them snugly around the cord about 1½ inches from the young one's tummy and 3 or 4 inches from the placenta. Snip the cord between the threads with sharp, sterilized scissors, then dab the end of the cord with iodine to prevent infection.

With the cloth, vigorously rub the puppy or kitten again, holding him head-down to allow secretions in his nose, mouth and ears to run out. Then check his breathing. "If he squeaks, you know he's breathing," says Dr. Shille. "But you can look closely and tell, too," he adds.

Once you're sure the puppy or kitten is in good working order, place him facing his mother's nipples and let her take over.

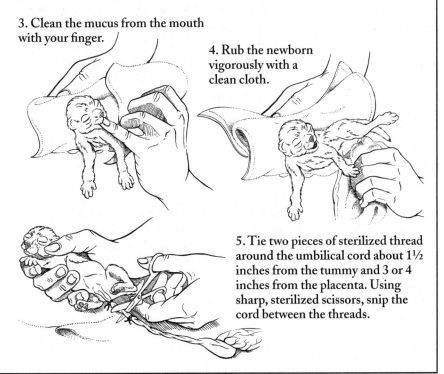

3. Clean the mucus from the mouth with your finger.

4. Rub the newborn vigorously with a clean cloth.

5. Tie two pieces of sterilized thread around the umbilical cord about 1½ inches from the tummy and 3 or 4 inches from the placenta. Using sharp, sterilized scissors, snip the cord between the threads.

make the whelping box comfortable, your pet may refuse to use it. If that happens, just put down some clean towels wherever she happens to be. Then step back and let nature take its course. "The last thing you want to do at this point is move her to a place she doesn't want to be," says Dr. Shille. "It could delay her whelping, which could prove dangerous to the pups or kittens."

Once your pet has given birth, it's okay to move the little ones into the box. In most cases, Mom will soon follow and settle in.

Forget the cameras. "For some reason, some people like to capture these events on film," says Dr. Smith. "Forget it. Bright lights and strange equipment in her face could upset the whole process."

If your pet doesn't mind, however, you can watch her giving birth from a few feet away. It's important to talk quietly, however, and to give her plenty of space. "But if your pet tries to get away from you or you get the sense you're in the way, back off," says Dr. Smith. Just stay close enough so you can be there if she needs help.

Maintain a hands-off policy. While you may want to help your pet by playing midwife, she'll probably do fine without any help from you. In fact, trying to help when it's not needed can result in all sorts of complications, says Dr. Shille.

Just remember: What's unfamiliar and scary to you is perfectly natural for your pet. Some pets, for example—especially first-time mother cats—will issue dramatic yowls during delivery. Some give birth in a squatting position, and many will eat the placenta. "Don't be alarmed," says Dr. Shille. "If you know what's normal and what's not, you'll almost always be able to sit back and let your pet go through this fascinating process on her own."

PANEL OF ADVISERS

Jill Chase, D.V.M., is a veterinarian in private practice in San Francisco.

Vicki N. Meyers-Wallen, V.M.D., Ph.D., is associate professor in the Department of Anatomy and a chief of service at the Small Animal Fertility and Infertility Clinic at the Cornell University College of Veterinary Medicine in Ithaca, New York.

Victor M. Shille, D.V.M., Ph.D., is professor emeritus of theriogenology at the University of Florida College of Veterinary Medicine in Gainesville and editor of the veterinary journal *Theriogenology*.

Craig Allan Smith, D.V.M., Ph.D., is assistant editor of the *Journal of the American Veterinary Medical Association* in Schaumburg, Illinois.

Bites

10 Sharp Tips

They don't call it a dog-eat-dog world for nothing. Big dogs bite little dogs—and vice versa. Dogs chase cats—and cats fight back. Even squirrels, skunks and other critters will occasionally throw their hats into the ring.

Any bite wound is potentially dangerous, says Wayne Wingfield, D.V.M., chief of emergency critical care medicine at the Colorado State University Veterinary Teaching Hospital in Fort Collins. Animal saliva teems with bacteria. In addition, even small bites can seriously damage underlying tissues.

It's a good idea to see a vet any time your pet gets bitten. But here are some things you can do to keep the wounds under control.

 For Dogs and Cats

Start with a muzzle. It's natural for animals in pain to lash out. To protect yourself, wrap your pet's mouth closed before treating the wound, says Susan E. Anderson, D.V.M., clinical instructor of outpatient medicine in the Department of Small Animal Clinical Sciences at the University of Florida College of Veterinary Medicine in Gainesville. "You could get pretty seriously hurt otherwise," she says.

You can improvise a muzzle by wrapping gauze, panty hose or a length of rope or twine several times around your pet's mouth. Then pull the ends back and tie them behind her ears.

Be careful not to cover the nostrils, adds Dr. Anderson. And if your pet starts to get sick or is having difficulty breathing, remove the muzzle immediately.

Or wrap her up. If your dog or cat is too small to wear a muzzle, you can protect yourself by wrapping her head with a towel before starting treatment. Don't leave the towel on too long or wrap it too

When to See the Vet

Animal bites are like icebergs: What looks small on the surface could be large and dangerous underneath, says Wayne Wingfield, D.V.M., chief of emergency critical care medicine at the Colorado State University Veterinary Teaching Hospital in Fort Collins.

Some injuries you can treat yourself, but others always require a veterinarian's care. Danger signs include:

- Severe pain. If touching the area around the wound causes your pet to jerk away, the wound could be infected.
- Severe blood loss. Even if blood isn't visible on the surface, your pet could have internal bleeding. Press a finger against her gums. If they don't turn pink after momentary whiteness, she could have lost large amounts of blood.
- Bites to the abdomen or throat. Injuries in these areas can cause damage to the windpipe or internal bleeding.
- A bite by a wild animal. To be safe, assume the animal was rabid and get your pet to the vet right away.

tightly, however, because it could cut off her air supply.

Take a little off the top. Trimming the hair from around a bite wound makes it easier to clean, says Dr. Wingfield. It will also help the bite heal faster by improving air flow to the area. Clip the hair short with scissors or electric clippers, he suggests. Or use a disposable razor.

But first cover it up. To prevent hair from falling into the wound, some vets recommend smearing on a thin layer of water-soluble jelly such as K-Y Jelly. Cut hairs will be trapped by the jelly, which can then be washed away.

Get it clean. To prevent infection, it's important to clean all bites thoroughly. Flush for at least five minutes with lukewarm running water, says D. J. Krahwinkel, D.V.M., professor and head of the Department of Small Animal Clinical Sciences at the University of Tennessee College of Veterinary Medicine in Knoxville.

If the bite is more than 24 hours old, however, bacteria may already have taken hold. In that case it's best to scrub it well with an antibacterial soap such as Betadine Skin Cleanser and then flush it with running water, Dr. Krahwinkel says.

Add extra protection. After washing and drying the bite, apply an over-the-counter triple antibiotic ointment such as Neosporin, says Dr. Krahwinkel. Then bandage the area with gauze or a clean cloth. You can hold the bandage in place with clear first-aid tape.

Keep it loose. When applying and taping a bandage to a wound, leave enough room to sneak a finger underneath, advises Dr. Krahwinkel. Anything tighter could interfere with your pet's circulation.

Encourage her input. Once the bandage is removed, it's natural for animals to lick their wounds. In most cases this isn't a problem, says Dr. Wingfield. In fact, licking may help speed the healing process by keeping the area clean, he says.

But keep her under control. If your pet is worrying a wound excessively, your vet may recommend fitting her with an Elizabethan collar. These are conical plastic shells that slip over the pet's head and prevent her from reaching the wound, explains William D. Fortney, D.V.M., assistant professor of small animal medicine in the Department of Clinical Sciences at the Kansas State University College of Veterinary Medicine in Manhattan, Kansas.

Elizabethan collars are sold in pet stores, or you can make your own from a plastic bucket by cutting a hole just big enough to go over your

The Snake's Alive!

Dogs and cats have a way of putting their noses right in harm's way—which is why close encounters with the slithering kind typically result in bites to the nose, face or front legs.

Bites from a poisonous snake are scary, but most animals will recover, particularly if they get medical attention right away, says Wayne Wingfield, D.V.M., chief of emergency critical care medicine at the Colorado State University Veterinary Teaching Hospital in Fort Collins.

Symptoms of snake bite include severe swelling and difficulty breathing. Your pet may seem depressed and not be moving very much. In addition, her blink reflex may slow to almost nothing.

If you suspect snake bite, get to the vet right away. Your pet will probably be given steroids to treat shock and antihistamines to counteract chemicals found in the venom. She may also need antibiotics to fight infection, Dr. Wingfield says.

Rabies Alert

Thanks to vaccinations, rabies in this country is rare in dogs and cats. Among wild animals, however, the deadly virus is still very much at large.

The raccoon is perhaps the worst culprit. In one year in New York, for example, raccoons were responsible for approximately 81 percent of all rabies cases. But rabies is also found in skunks, foxes, bats and other carnivores.

Don't make friends with *any* wild animal, vets say. Suspect the worst if a wild critter allows you to get close without running away. This isn't natural behavior and could be a sign that it's infected.

pet's head. Be sure that the collar isn't too tight, however, and that it doesn't prevent your pet from eating normally or getting comfortable.

Keep up with shots. Rabies is a viral disease that, without treatment, is almost always fatal—to pets and to people. In most areas rabies vaccinations are required by law. Be sure to keep your pet's vaccinations current.

PANEL OF ADVISERS

Susan E. Anderson, D.V.M., is clinical instructor of outpatient medicine in the Department of Small Animal Clinical Sciences at the University of Florida College of Veterinary Medicine in Gainesville.

William D. Fortney, D.V.M., is assistant professor of small animal medicine in the Department of Clinical Sciences at the Kansas State University College of Veterinary Medicine in Manhattan, Kansas.

D. J. Krahwinkel, Jr., D.V.M., is professor and head of the Department of Small Animal Clinical Sciences at the University of Tennessee College of Veterinary Medicine in Knoxville.

Wayne Wingfield, D.V.M., is chief of emergency critical care medicine at the Colorado State University Veterinary Teaching Hospital in Fort Collins.

Bladder Control Problems

8 Ways to Keep Things Dry

Few things are less savory than discovering an unpleasant odor emanating from the potted Norfolk pine or—*squish*—a puddle on the living room carpet.

Oh, no—she's done it again.

It's normal for puppies and kittens to make mistakes. But when your formerly fastidious feline or conscientious canine has suddenly stopped making it to the litter box or backyard in time, there could be something physically wrong that needs to be looked into.

Some pets develop nerve, kidney, urinary tract or other internal problems that make accidents hard to prevent. In addition, some older pets gradually lose control. They do their best to wait, but they just can't make it.

Even if your vet can't stop the problem entirely, there are ways to get things dry again.

 **For Dogs and Cats**

Hold the nightcap. To help keep floors dry while you sleep, try putting out only a small amount of water at night, says Wayne Hunthausen, D.V.M., an animal behavior consultant in Westwood, Kansas, president of the American Veterinary Society of Animal Behavior and co-author of *Practitioner's Guide to Pet Behavior Problems*.

Don't stop giving water entirely, however. For some pets, going without water for even short periods can be dangerous. So check with your vet before turning off the taps.

 **For Dogs Only**

Head for the great outdoors. Even if your pooch has the best of intentions, she may need extra opportunities to relieve herself. "Take her out the instant she wakes up, even if she's just been taking a nap," says Karen Overall, V.M.D., Ph.D., a lecturer specializing in behavioral medicine in the Department of Clinical Studies at the University of Pennsylvania School of Veterinary Medicine in Philadelphia. "Reward the dog each time she goes out and does something," she adds.

Drop by the diaper aisle. For dogs with bladder control problems, diapers might be a good idea, says George Lees, D.V.M., a veterinary urologist and assistant head of the Department of Small Animal Medicine and Surgery at the Texas A&M University College of Veterinary Medicine in College Station. Pet diapers are available from vets and at pet stores.

It's important to change diapers frequently, Dr. Lees adds. Otherwise your pet could develop a condition that vets call moist dermatitis, better known as diaper rash.

Watch for warning signs. If your pooch is looking restless, walking in circles or nosing the ground, you can bet she's not looking for a lost ring. Try to get her outside before the accident occurs.

Keep a regular meal schedule. Since some pets need to go outside immediately after eating, controlling their mealtimes will help you keep tabs on their other needs as well. "Make food available one to three times a day, depending on the age of the dog," says Dr. Hunthausen. "Get the dog in gear physiologically to eat and eliminate at predictable times."

Consider a crate. Some dogs get lonely or frightened when they're left alone, with predictable—and damp—results. One solution is to confine your pooch to a crate or cage whenever you leave the house. Most

When to See the Vet

While even the best-behaved pet can have accidents, a sudden change for the worse could mean trouble.

Pets that are urinating frequently or in all the wrong places could have a bladder infection, diabetes, hormone imbalances or even kidney failure, says Meryl Littman, V.M.D., chief of medicine at the University of Pennsylvania School of Veterinary Medicine in Philadelphia. In addition, there are some breeds, like Dobermans, that are prone to congenital bladder problems that may need to be corrected surgically.

Call your vet if any changes in your pet's usual habits persist for more than two days, if the urine is discolored or if it's difficult for her to go.

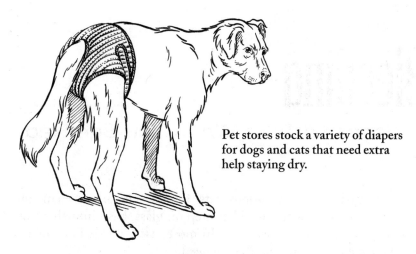

Pet stores stock a variety of diapers for dogs and cats that need extra help staying dry.

pets won't make messes where they sleep, so this will help keep the problem under control. Just be sure to let her out as soon as you get home.

 For Cats Only

Provide extra bathrooms. When your cat has poor control, the last thing she needs is a litter box that's far away. To make sure she can get relief when she needs it, vets recommend having at least one litter box on every floor of the house.

Keep it tidy. Even desperate cats can be finicky, and if the litter isn't kept clean, they may refuse to use it.

"I usually recommend that people have several litter boxes and clean them out often," says Meryl Littman, V.M.D., chief of medicine at the University of Pennsylvania School of Veterinary Medicine. Plan on cleaning the box (or boxes) at least once a day, she advises.

PANEL OF ADVISERS

Wayne Hunthausen, D.V.M., an animal behavior consultant in Westwood, Kansas, president of the American Veterinary Society of Animal Behavior and co-author of *Practitioner's Guide to Pet Behavior Problems.*

George Lees, D.V.M., is a veterinary urologist and assistant head of the Department of Small Animal Medicine and Surgery at the Texas A&M University School of Veterinary Medicine in College Station.

Meryl Littman, V.M.D., is chief of medicine at the University of Pennsylvania School of Veterinary Medicine in Philadelphia.

Karen Overall, V.M.D., Ph.D., is a lecturer specializing in behavioral medicine in the Department of Clinical Studies at the University of Pennsylvania School of Veterinary Medicine in Philadelphia.

Bleeding

11 Steps to Take When You See Red

For dogged dogs and curious cats, minor—and messy—cuts and scrapes are anything but rare. They step on glass, bash into sharp objects or get caught on barbed wire. In most cases, a little first aid, and perhaps some reassurance, is all they need.

To stop the bleeding and keep small wounds from getting serious, here's what vets recommend.

 ## For Dogs and Cats

Press on the wound. With any wound, "the first thing to do is stop the bleeding," says William D. Fortney, D.V.M., assistant professor of small animal medicine in the Department of Clinical Sciences at the Kansas State University College of Veterinary Medicine in Manhattan, Kansas.

Using a handkerchief, a towel or a piece of clean cloth, apply firm pressure directly over the wound. In a pinch, it's okay to press down with your thumb or the palm of your hand, says Dr. Fortney. The bleeding will usually start to slow within a few minutes.

Turn down the pressure. When bleeding is serious, applying pressure directly to the artery (not the wound) can help slow it, says Wayne Wingfield, D.V.M., chief of emergency critical care medicine at the Colorado State University Veterinary Teaching Hospital in Fort Collins.

Dogs and cats have three major pressure points.

- The upper inside of the front legs: Pressing here will help control bleeding from the lower forelegs.
- The upper inside of the rear legs: Pressing here will help control bleeding from the lower hind legs.
- The underside of the tail: Pressing here helps control bleeding from the tail.

Forget the tourniquet. "A lot of limbs have been lost because the blood supply was cut off for too long a period," Dr. Fortney warns.

Give him a trim. Once you have bleeding under control, it's a good idea to trim hair from around the wound, using scissors or electric trimmers, says Dr. Wingfield. This will help keep the wound clean and possibly help speed healing, he says. In addition, some vets recommend applying a thin layer of water-soluble jelly such as K-Y Jelly to keep hair from falling into the wound. Cut hairs will be trapped by the jelly, which can then be washed away.

Protect yourself. An injured animal is a scared animal. If you suspect there's even a chance you might be bitten while giving first aid, "it would be smart to put on a muzzle," says D. J. Krahwinkel, Jr., D.V.M., professor and head of the Department of Small Animal Clinical Sciences at the University of Tennessee College of Veterinary Medicine in Knoxville.

You can improvise a muzzle from a roll of gauze, a length of rope or some panty hose. Wrap it firmly around the animal's mouth, then pull the ends back and tie them behind the ears. If your pet starts to vomit or has trouble breathing, be prepared to remove the muzzle promptly.

Or cover them up. If you have a cat or a dog too small to wear a muzzle, you can protect yourself by wrapping her in a pillowcase, towel

Pets have a number of "pressure points"—areas you can press to stop serious bleeding occurring elsewhere in the body.

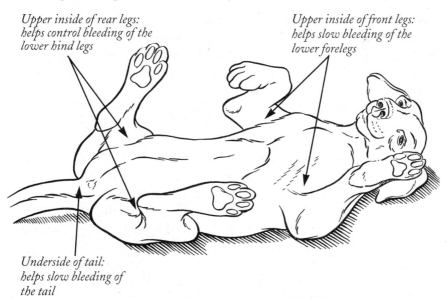

Upper inside of rear legs: helps control bleeding of the lower hind legs

Upper inside of front legs: helps slow bleeding of the lower forelegs

Underside of tail: helps slow bleeding of the tail

When to See the Vet

Most cuts and scrapes can be safely treated at home, but when the wound is deep and there's a lot of blood, you need an expert's care.

Deep wounds, which involve tendons and muscle and not just the upper layers of skin, often cause severe blood loss and increase the risk of infection. Your pet could need a transfusion as well as stitches and anesthesia, says Wayne Wingfield, D.V.M., chief of emergency critical care medicine in the Department of Clinical Sciences at the Colorado State University Veterinary Teaching Hospital in Fort Collins.

And bleeding doesn't always occur where you can see it. Some of the worst injuries are internal. Your pet could be losing pints of blood and you might never know it—until it's too late.

Symptoms of internal bleeding include blood in vomit or urine, pale pink or white gums and listlessness. Don't take chances, Dr. Wingfield advises. If you think an injury is serious, it probably is—and you should see your vet right away.

or blanket before beginning treatment, advises C. B. Chastain, D.V.M., associate dean for academic affairs and professor of veterinary medicine and surgery at the University of Missouri College of Veterinary Medicine in Columbia. Don't wrap her too tightly or for a long time, however, or she may have trouble breathing.

Layer up. If bleeding doesn't stop right away, you may want to tie a bandage loosely around the wound to help slow the flow. If the bandage quickly soaks through, however, just leave it there.

"You don't want to destroy the clot that's trying to form," says Susan E. Anderson, D.V.M., clinical instructor of outpatient medicine in the Department of Small Animal Clinical Sciences at the University of Florida College of Veterinary Medicine in Gainesville. Instead, wrap a second bandage around the first. If the bleeding continues, however, it's a sign that you need to see your vet, she advises.

Clean it well. The danger from most wounds isn't necessarily the bleeding but the infection that may set in later. To prevent this, thoroughly washing the wound is critical, says Dr. Krahwinkel.

If the wound is recent, flush it for at least five minutes with luke-warm running water. For older wounds, it's a good idea to wash the area with an antibacterial soap such as Hibiclens. Or you can apply an over-the-counter antiseptic like Betadine Solution, says Dr. Wingfield. Both of these products are available at drugstores.

Smear on protection. Once the wound is clean, applying an over-the-counter antibiotic ointment like Neosporin will help prevent in-fection by killing bacteria that may be present, Dr. Krahwinkel says.

Wrap it up. To keep the wound clean and protected, it's a good idea to wrap it with gauze. Just make sure the wrapping isn't too tight, which could cut off circulation, says Dr. Krahwinkel.

About once a day, remove the bandage and clean the wound with lukewarm water. Then reapply the antibiotic ointment and wrap it again, Dr. Krahwinkel says.

Pause for paws. While paw injuries are usually not serious, they can bleed a lot, says Dr. Krahwinkel. Slipping a clean white sock over the paw will help keep the wound *and* your floors clean until the bleeding stops.

PANEL OF ADVISERS

Susan E. Anderson, D.V.M., is clinical instructor of outpatient medicine in the De-partment of Small Animal Clinical Sciences at the University of Florida College of Veterinary Medicine in Gainesville.

C. B. Chastain, D.V.M., is associate dean for academic affairs and professor of vet-erinary medicine and surgery at the University of Missouri College of Veterinary Medicine in Columbia.

William D. Fortney, D.V.M., is assistant professor of small animal medicine in the Department of Clinical Sciences at the Kansas State University College of Veteri-nary Medicine in Manhattan, Kansas.

D. J. Krahwinkel, Jr., D.V.M., is professor and head of the Department of Small Animal Clinical Sciences at the University of Tennessee College of Veterinary Medicine in Knoxville.

Wayne Wingfield, D.V.M., is chief of emergency critical care medicine in the De-partment of Clinical Sciences at the Colorado State University Veterinary Teaching Hospital in Fort Collins.

Body Odor

8 Sweetening Strategies

Your pooch is never going to make it big in the perfume business, at least until someone decides to market *eau de dog*. Whew! He smells like old cheese.

While some dogs just naturally smell a little ripe, bad odors often are a sign that they've been rolling in something they shouldn't or that skin oils are turning rancid, says Robert Hilsenroth, D.V.M., executive director of the Morris Animal Foundation in Englewood, Colorado. In other words, dogs are prone to B.O.

Cats, on the other hand, rarely develop strong smells because their daily grooming behavior removes oils and other debris before they get stinky, adds Robert Willyard, D.V.M., a veterinarian in private practice in Las Vegas and president of the Clark County, Nevada, Veterinary Medical Association.

Here's what vets recommend to help you and your pooch through smelly times.

 For **Dogs** Only

Start with a bath. When being around your dog is making your nose wrinkle, what he probably needs is a good washing, says Marilyn Burleson, a groomer and owner of Critter Clipper in Fountain Valley, California.

Get him in the tub and douse him well with lukewarm water. Then work up a good lather with a pet shampoo, she says. Start around the face and nose, then work down the entire body. Rinse him well, then repeat.

Except for a little wet-dog smell when he gets out of the tub, his aroma should be much improved, Burleson says.

Progress to tar. For pets with a particularly oily coat, you may want to skip the mild shampoo and go straight to a tar-based product, says

Dr. Willyard. Shampoos with tar are available at pet stores and will quickly clean the dirtiest coat, he says.

Don't go overboard. While some washing is good, too much can cause the oil glands to boost their output, making the coat even more oily. "The more you wash, the sooner your dog is going to need another bath," warns Dr. Hilsenroth.

In most cases, bathing your pet once a month is plenty, although you can certainly make exceptions if your intrepid canine frequently goes where he shouldn't—like into mud puddles, swamps or other odoriferous wallows.

Brush him often. "Regular brushing helps remove gunk that gets in the fur and causes odors," Burleson says. In addition, brushing helps remove excess oils from the skin and hair before they ripen.

Long-haired pets should be brushed daily, Burleson says, while those with shorter hair can get by with once-a-week sessions.

Keep his ears clean. Ear infections are a common cause of bad odors, says Lisa Degen, D.V.M., a veterinarian in private practice in North Palm Beach, Florida, and president of the Palm Beach Veterinary Society.

While ear infections require a veterinarian's care, you can help prevent them by washing your dog's ears. Pooches prone to problems may need to have their ears scrubbed as often as once a week. Dr. Degen recommends mixing one part white vinegar with two parts water, then gently flushing the ear with a bulb syringe. Rub the ear gently to distribute the liquid, then wipe with a cotton ball.

When to See the Vet

If you've tried brushing, scrubbing and otherwise sanitizing your pet and he still smells like an old shoe, there's a good chance something's wrong. A smelly pet may be a sick pet, says Robert Willyard, D.V.M., a veterinarian in private practice in Las Vegas and president of the Clark County, Nevada, Veterinary Medical Association.

Strong odors can be caused by such things as ear infections, gum or tooth disease, a kidney problem or even skin disease. So don't wait too long if your pet seems unusually stinky. Take him in for a checkup, Dr. Willyard advises.

Do a mouth check. Dogs occasionally get a piece of bone, wood or some other object wedged in the mouth, and it will eventually start smelling like garbage. Take a good look inside your dog's mouth, Dr. Hilsenroth advises. If something's wedged in there and it doesn't come out with gentle pressure, ask your vet for help.

Peek at the teeth. Dogs don't brush their teeth, and when they lick themselves, a lifetime accumulation of morning breath can give them an unpleasant smell.

Dr. Willyard recommends buying a pet toothbrush and giving your dog's choppers a good brushing at least twice a week. Or you can wrap gauze or a washcloth around one finger to clean his teeth.

Just be sure not to use human toothpaste for pets, he adds. Dogs can't spit, and the foam from human pastes, when they swallow it, can upset their stomachs. Always use a pet toothpaste, vets advise.

Try a minty spray. If your dog won't hold still for a good brushing, you can still improve his breath—and his body odor—by spritzing in a little breath freshener. To make your own, dilute a capful of mouthwash in a cup of water and pour it into a spray bottle, Dr. Willyard says. Then give your dog a little spritz the next time his "dog breath" is getting out of control. (For more information on dental care, see the chapters on Bad Breath on page 48 and Dental Problems on page 131.)

PANEL OF ADVISERS

Marilyn Burleson is a groomer and owner of Critter Clipper in Fountain Valley, California.

Lisa Degen, D.V.M., is a veterinarian in private practice in North Palm Beach, Florida, and president of the Palm Beach Veterinary Society.

Robert Hilsenroth, D.V.M., is executive director of the Morris Animal Foundation in Englewood, Colorado.

Robert Willyard, D.V.M., is a veterinarian in private practice in Las Vegas and president of the Clark County, Nevada, Veterinary Medical Association.

Boredom

12 Stimulating Suggestions

By human standards, cats and dogs don't do a whole lot. They sleep, eat, play a bit and then go back to sleep. Give them a little love and attention, and they seem perfectly content to laze the day away.

More often than not, however, your pet may want more excitement in her life than she's been getting—and will tell you in the only way she knows how. "Bored pets are destructive pets," says Liz Palika, a dog obedience instructor in Oceanside, California, columnist for *Dog Fancy* magazine and author of *Fido, Come: Training Your Dog with Love and Understanding* and *Love on a Leash*. "They dig and chew and do other things that make them less frustrated. They're just filling a void."

Giving your pet extra attention is probably the best way to avoid that void. Here are a few easy ways to enliven her day.

 ## For Dogs and Cats

Begin with a romp. "If your cat is destroying your Ming vase collection and your dog is eating your couch, a little exercise might get that energy out of their system," says Stanley Coren, Ph.D., professor of psychology at the University of British Columbia in Vancouver, who teaches at the Vancouver Dog Obedience Training Club and is author of *The Intelligence of Dogs*.

How much exercise depends on what your pet is used to. In most cases, you can begin with a 20-minute walk several times a week and then work up from there. "You don't have to kill them with fatigue, but you want them to feel tired enough to settle down for a while," Dr. Coren says.

Expand the family. Not all pets crave company, but sometimes having a kitty or doggy friend will help chase their blahs away. "You can't expect an animal to sit at home alone waiting for you at least nine hours every day and not get bored," says M. Lynne Kesel, D.V.M., as-

Television can help keep dogs and cats entertained when you're gone all day. You can buy videos made for—and starring—pets.

sistant professor of elective surgery in the Department of Clinical Sciences at the Colorado State University College of Veterinary Medicine and Biomedical Sciences in Fort Collins. "Having another cat, dog or anything that your pet will get along with could do wonders for his spirit and help decrease the bored, destructive behavior."

Turn on the tube. "Television can provide real entertainment and can help alleviate boredom for some dogs and even cats," says Myrna Milani, D.V.M., a veterinarian in private practice in Charlestown, New Hampshire, and author of *The Body Language and Emotions of Cats* and *The Body Language and Emotions of Dogs*. "Leave the television on a channel he might enjoy and see if it helps."

Or play a video. Many pet stores now carry action-packed videos designed especially for dogs and cats. "My cats love them," says Bob Gutierrez, animal behavior coordinator at the San Francisco Society for the Prevention of Cruelty to Animals. "They go insane watching the birds, the cats and the colors."

Make it Montovani. "Filling the room with music can keep things from getting dull," says New York City dog trainer Carol Lea Benjamin, author of *Mother Knows Best: The Natural Way to Train Your Dog* and *Surviving Your Dog's Adolescence*. Some dogs like Beethoven. Your cat might prefer Eric Clapton. "My shepherd likes the corniest Christmas music," Benjamin says. "She could listen to it forever."

Dogs that are vocally inclined will get a special kick out of these music sessions, adds Micky Niego, an animal behavior consultant in Airmont, New York. "I'd put on the opera for my dog, and he'd howl along with great vigor for 45 minutes. He'd be pretty quiet after that," she says.

Phone home. "Some people call from work and leave a message on the answering machine so their pets can hear their voice," Palika says. "That could help, but if your pet is likely to be sleeping, you'd best leave well enough alone."

Watch the birdies. To keep your cat entertained, try setting up a bird feeder outside the window, Palika suggests. Some dogs also enjoy a little bird-watching, she adds.

Or try a few fish. An aquarium full of fish can provide hours of colorful entertainment for you and your pet, says Niego. "My cats absolutely adore it," she says. It's important, however, to use a covered aquarium, which will prevent the evening's entertainment from becoming the main course.

 For **Dogs** Only

Put 'em to work. All dogs were once bred for certain tasks—like retrieving ducks, hunting bear or snagging varmints—and they may feel frustrated when they can't perform their "duties." To keep your dog

---

When Boredom Brings Out the Best

Although a bored pet usually spells trouble, there are times when a little down time gives rise to surprising creativity. "Given the right circumstances, you'll be stunned at what your pet might be capable of doing," says Myrna Milani, D.V.M., a veterinarian in private practice in Charlestown, New Hampshire.

Consider the enterprising Siamese cat that, in her spare time, removed gold chains from her owner's jewelry case and lined them up on the dining room table. Or the frisky feline that pulled dirty socks from the hamper and made a trail down the hall—and then tried to match the socks.

Not all pets are quite so inspired, of course. Dr. Milani admits her corgi is no Edison, but he still finds ways to keep himself—and her—amused. "He takes a humongous bone and throws it up in the air and watches it land," she says. Sometimes genius really is 1 percent inspiration and 99 percent perspiration.

happy, encourage her to do what she does best, Niego suggests.

For a terrier, you might try setting aside a small part of your yard where she can dig. Or give her a big pile of old clothes inside the house that she can burrow into. For a Labrador retriever, nothing beats splashing in cold water, and just about every dog enjoys visiting new territory and getting in a good sniff.

Have a chew-fest. Dogs always like to chew, so make her day with a special treat, suggests Kathy Gaughan, D.V.M., an instructor in the Department of Clinical Sciences at the Kansas State University College of Veterinary Medicine in Manhattan, Kansas. She recommends stuffing a hollow dog toy with peanut butter or your pet's favorite food. "You'll be surprised how long she'll be entertained," she says.

For Cats Only

Help her chase rainbows. Cats are fascinated by almost anything that moves, including light. Crystals hanging in the windows will cast enchanting—and eminently chaseable—patterns on the floors, walls and furniture, keeping many cats occupied for hours at a time, Niego says.

Exercise her mind. When your cat is looking for something to do, give her a mental challenge, advises Dr. Milani. Pet stores sell a variety

A homemade cat puzzler will keep your pet busy and entertained, keeping boredom at bay.

of cat puzzlers, but it's easy to make your own. She recommends cutting holes in the sides of a shirt box or shoebox and putting a table tennis ball inside. "Make the holes big enough for your cat to put her arm through but not so big that the ball can roll right out," she says. "Some cats spend hours trying to get the ball out."

PANEL OF ADVISERS

Carol Lea Benjamin is a dog trainer in New York City and author of *Mother Knows Best: The Natural Way to Train Your Dog* and *Surviving Your Dog's Adolescence*.

Stanley Coren, Ph.D., is professor of psychology at the University of British Columbia in Vancouver, teaches at the Vancouver Dog Obedience Training Club and is author of *The Intelligence of Dogs*.

Kathy Gaughan, D.V.M., is an instructor in the Department of Clinical Sciences at the Kansas State University College of Veterinary Medicine in Manhattan, Kansas.

Bob Gutierrez is animal behavior coordinator at the San Francisco Society for the Prevention of Cruelty to Animals.

M. Lynne Kesel, D.V.M., is assistant professor of elective surgery in the Department of Clinical Sciences at the Colorado State University College of Veterinary Medicine and Biomedical Sciences in Fort Collins.

Myrna Milani, D.V.M., is a veterinarian in private practice in Charlestown, New Hampshire, and author of *The Body Language and Emotions of Cats* and *The Body Language and Emotions of Dogs*.

Micky Niego is an animal behavior consultant in Airmont, New York.

Liz Palika is a dog obedience instructor in Oceanside, California, a columnist for *Dog Fancy* magazine and author of *Fido, Come: Training Your Dog with Love and Understanding* and *Love on a Leash*.

Burrs

8 Solutions to a Prickly Problem

You had a great time hiking through fields and forests, but now it's time to pay the price. It seems your companion brought home a coat filled with bristly souvenirs—and you're in charge of Operation Unstick.

Burrs are the rough, prickly seedcases of certain plants, and they seem to leap out whenever your pet passes by. Depending on where they lodge, burrs can cause matting, skin irritation or infection. What's more, they can be as hard to remove as chewing gum.

To get around this thorny problem, try these tips from the experts.

 For **Dogs** and **Cats**

Look for hideaways. Burrs can stick in the darnedest places, so you'll want to inspect your pet closely for these hidden prickly pains, says Hazel Christiansen, owner of Blue Ribbon Pet Grooming in Lewiston, Idaho, and president of the American Grooming Shop Association. "Check between all the toes, on top of the feet, around the testicles and in the armpits—just about anyplace there's a little crevice," she says.

Take the dry road. Once burrs get snarled into your pet's coat, be sure to remove them before he manages to get himself wet. "The tangled hair around the burr will shrink like a wool sweater after it gets wet, and you'll have an extra-hard time trying to get the burr out," says Linda A. Law, a certified master groomer and director of the Canine Clippers School of Pet Grooming in Dumfries, Virginia.

Put your fingers to work. "It's really important to remove burrs as soon as you can so they don't dig in and create mats and irritations," says Law.

If the burr has only recently lodged, you may be able to remove it with just your fingers or a pair of tweezers. If it's been there longer, however, it may be tangled inside a hair mat. To undo the mat, pull it apart with your fingers little by little, working from the end of the hairs

Outfoxing Foxtails

Unlike burrs, which stop at the hair, foxtails can puncture skin in a matter of hours. In some cases they travel all the way through a pet's body, tearing tissue as they go, says David T. Roen, D.V.M., a veterinarian in private practice in Clarkston, Washington.

In extreme cases, foxtails have been known to puncture organs, including the brain. More commonly, they stick between the toes or lodge in the ears or nose, where they can cause a painful abscess, says Stephen A. Gardner, D.V.M., a veterinarian in private practice in Albany, California.

"The best policy with foxtails is to avoid them completely," says Dr. Gardner. "If you can't do that, check your pet thoroughly and keep his coat short during foxtail season."

He recommends carefully inspecting your pet's entire coat, including between the toes and around body openings, after outdoor jaunts. If you find even the smallest sliver, be sure to get it out or it may migrate inward, he warns.

If your pet has been romping in a foxtail-infested area and begins sneezing, pawing at his eyes or shaking or tilting his head, he could have a foxtail embedded in a dangerous place. You'll want to call your vet right away.

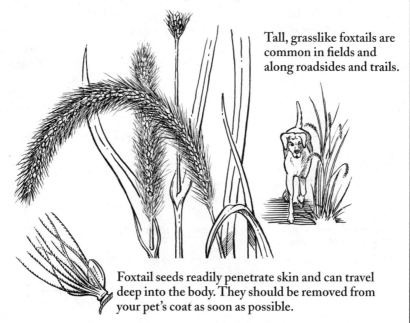

Tall, grasslike foxtails are common in fields and along roadsides and trails.

Foxtail seeds readily penetrate skin and can travel deep into the body. They should be removed from your pet's coat as soon as possible.

down toward the roots. After you get the burr out, run a comb or brush through the hair to really smooth things out, advises Law.

Loosen 'em with a lube job. When a burr is really tangled, applying a little vegetable oil will help get it loose, says Shirlee Kalstone, a New York City groomer and author of *The Complete Poodle Clipping and Grooming Book.* A spritz of detangling spray, available at pet stores, can also help. If you're buying a detangling spray for your cat, however, read the label to make sure it's feline-friendly, Kalstone adds.

Try the kindest cut. If you're having trouble removing burrs with your fingers, try cutting them out, says Kathe Barsotti, a certified master groomer and owner of Featherle Pet Care in Herndon and Sterling, Virginia. She recommends using blunt-tipped scissors to avoid accidentally gouging your pet. It's best to cut perpendicular to the mat, not parallel to it. "Just make sure you're cutting hair and not skin," she says.

Take your time. Removing burrs can be a time-consuming and sometimes painful process. "Take frequent breaks when you're dealing with a dog or cat with lots of burrs," says Law. "You don't want it to be a terrible experience for them."

She recommends removing burrs for no more than ten minutes at a time. Then praise your pet and reward him with a toy or treat before going back to work.

Keep it short. Keeping your pet's coat neatly trimmed won't prevent burrs from sticking, but it will make them easier to remove. "Then at least the burrs won't stick so badly," Barsotti says.

Pass up prickly places. In the future, the one sure way to avoid burrs is to stay away from infested areas. "If you've had a problem with one trail or field, walk your animal somewhere else next time," says Kalstone.

PANEL OF ADVISERS

Kathe Barsotti is a certified master groomer and owner of Featherle Pet Care in Herndon and Sterling, Virginia.

Hazel Christiansen is owner of Blue Ribbon Pet Grooming in Lewiston, Idaho, and president of the American Grooming Shop Association.

Stephen A. Gardner, D.V.M., is a veterinarian in private practice in Albany, California.

Shirlee Kalstone is a New York City groomer and author of *The Complete Poodle Clipping and Grooming Book.*

Linda A. Law is a certified master groomer and director of the Canine Clippers School of Pet Grooming in Dumfries, Virginia.

David T. Roen, D.V.M., is a veterinarian in private practice in Clarkston, Washington.

Car Chasing

7 Ways to Apply the Brakes

Some dogs like to chase sticks. Others prefer tennis balls. Unfortunately, plenty of pooches have a penchant for pounding the pavement in pursuit of Porsches and Pontiacs.

"It's a very natural instinct for a dog to chase prey, to herd or to run after something invading its territory. These things are at the core of car chasing," says Al Stinson, D.V.M., professor emeritus of animal behavior at the Michigan State University College of Veterinary Medicine in East Lansing. "Sadly, with car chasing, the thrill of the chase often ends in injury or worse."

If your dog tends to take to the road, these tips will help break his hazardous habits.

 For **Dogs** Only

Tie one on. To help your pooch learn his limits, attach a 10- or 20-foot lead to his choke collar. (To prevent him from getting hurt, be sure the collar is positioned so the leash attaches on top of his neck for quick release.) Then have a friend—someone the dog isn't familiar with—drive by. When the dog takes chase, let him run several feet, then quickly tighten and release pressure on his collar while giving him a sharp "No!"

"This will stop him, surprise him and start getting him conditioned to the idea that this isn't a good thing to do," Dr. Stinson says.

He recommends working with your dog for 30 minutes once a day until he learns to abandon the chase. When he's able to just watch a car go by, praise him profusely, adds Dr. Stinson.

Say it with balloons. According to Gary Landsberg, D.V.M., a veterinarian in private practice in Thornhill, Ontario, who specializes in animal behavior, the following technique is an effective, albeit wet, way to teach your dog not to chase.

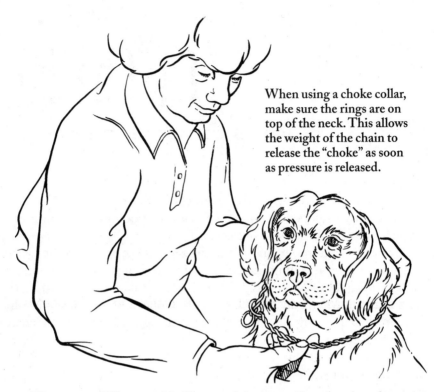

When using a choke collar, make sure the rings are on top of the neck. This allows the weight of the chain to release the "choke" as soon as pressure is released.

- The setup: Fill several balloons with water, then hunker down in the backseat of a friend's car. (It should be a car your dog won't recognize.) In the meantime, have another friend stand outside, holding your dog on a long lead.
- The sting: Slowly cruise by the house until your pooch starts chasing. When he gets within a few feet of the car, have your friend stop. "That's when you start throwing balloons toward the dog," says Dr. Landsberg. "Your dog will probably be very surprised and might think twice about car chasing again," he says.

Repeat the trick once a day for a few days. It doesn't always work, but some dogs may give up their chasing for good. Just be sure to reward your dog with a treat if he restrains himself and just watches the car go by.

Trumpet the message. Like balloons, loud noises can be a deterrent, says Dr. Landsberg. Using the same drive-by strategy, arm yourself with a noisemaker such as an air horn. When your dog starts to chase, sound the horn.

"They don't like those loud noises, and the dog could come to learn that chasing cars is an unpleasant experience," Dr. Landsberg says. You can buy air horns at boating supply stores.

Keep his feet off the street. The only sure way to curb a dog's lust for the chase is to keep him off the road in the first place. "Keep him in a fenced yard, or go for walks and watch him all the time," says Dr. Stinson.

Have a ball together. If you give your dog plenty of exercise, he may lose his desire to chase cars, says Patricia O'Handley, V.M.D., associate professor of small animal medicine at the Michigan State University College of Veterinary Medicine. "Dogs can get so bored and restless that they end up chasing cars just to do something," she says.

Dr. O'Handley recommends taking your pooch for two walks a day—anything from a 20-minute shuffle to a two-hour hike. It's also important to include some kind of chasing exercise in his daily routine. "Throw a ball or a stick for him until he's tired," she says. "Just take care of that chase instinct."

Solve it with schooling. Dog school might be just what the professor ordered for your car-chasing dog. "A good obedience program will put you back in control of your dog," says Dr. Stinson. What you want is a class that will teach your dog to stop in his tracks when you say "Down!" or "Stay!" "It takes some work, but it can be a lifesaver," he says.

Teach him boundaries. If you don't have a fenced yard, find an obedience instructor who can help you train your dog to recognize where he's allowed to go and where he's not. While the training can involve a lot of work, once a dog knows his boundaries he'll usually stick with them, says Dr. O'Handley.

PANEL OF ADVISERS

Gary Landsberg, D.V.M., is a veterinarian in private practice in Thornhill, Ontario, who specializes in animal behavior.

Patricia O'Handley, V.M.D., is associate professor of small animal medicine at the Michigan State University College of Veterinary Medicine in East Lansing.

Al Stinson, D.V.M., is professor emeritus of animal behavior at the Michigan State University College of Veterinary Medicine in East Lansing.

Car Sickness

10 Hints to Help Your Pet Stomach It

You're enjoying a leisurely Sunday drive, but your dog obviously would rather be on terra firma. His stomach's rumbling, he's starting to drool, and beneath his fur (you suspect) he's probably a queasy shade of green. It's enough to make *you* sick.

Car sickness is quite common, especially in young animals, says Lynda Bond, D.V.M., a veterinarian in private practice in Cape Elizabeth, Maine, who hosts a weekly pet segment for a Portland television station. Until they outgrow it, the messy consequences can make even short trips seem way too long.

But you don't have to leave your friend at home. Here are a few ways to keep his stomach settled and the upholstery clean.

 For **Dogs** and **Cats**

Travel on empty. It's a good idea not to feed your pet six to eight hours before embarking on a road trip, advises Clayton MacKay, D.V.M., director of the veterinary teaching hospital at Ontario Veterinary College at the University of Guelph in Canada and president of the American Animal Hospital Association. Having an empty stomach will make him less likely to throw up. "And if he does get sick, there's no food in the vomit, so at least it's easier to clean up," he says. Giving your pet water, however, won't upset his stomach and may make him more comfortable.

Or put in a quarter-tank. While some pets travel best on an empty stomach, others will feel more comfortable after eating a small meal. "They just need a little food in their stomach to help keep them from getting sick," says Dr. MacKay.

Take frequent rest breaks. While some pets can travel for hours without having problems, others start getting queasy after a few miles. "Get to know your pet's pattern," says Dr. MacKay. He recommends stopping at least every hour or two and taking a quick walk to help your pet get his land-legs back. It's also a good idea to pour him a little water, since he may not feel like drinking when he's in the car.

Cruise carefully. "Be considerate of your carsick pet, just as you would if you had a carsick child," says Gary Beard, D.V.M., assistant dean at the Auburn University College of Veterinary Medicine in Alabama. "Don't fly around curves, and take it slower than you normally would."

Be up-front with him. "There's not as much movement in the front of the car as in the back, so it might help your pet if you let him ride in the front seat," says William G. Brewer, D.V.M., assistant professor of small animal internal medicine in the Department of Small Animal Surgery and Medicine at the Auburn University College of Veterinary Medicine. To keep your friend safe, you may want to invest in a doggy seatbelt. Or you can buy a small kennel that buckles into the seat. Both items are available at pet stores.

Expand his horizons. Pets, like people, are less likely to get carsick when they can watch the passing scenery. "Allow your pet to look out the window, and he'll probably fare much better than if he has nothing to set his sights on," says Bernhard P. Pukay, D.V.M., a veterinarian in private practice in Ottawa, Canada, and host of the Discovery Channel's *Pet Connection*.

Crank down the windows. "Fresh air is good for anyone who's feeling a little carsick, including your dog or cat," says Dr. Pukay. "But don't open the window enough so he can escape or get his head way out," he adds.

Try a motion potion. Dimenhydrinate (Dramamine)—the same drug people take to ward off car sickness—also works for pets, says James B. Dalley, D.V.M., associate professor of small animal clinical sciences at the Michigan State University College of Veterinary Medicine in East Lansing. Medium to large dogs should be given 25 to 50 milligrams of Dramamine at least an hour before traveling, says Dr. Dalley. Cats and small dogs should get about 12.5 milligrams.

Dramamine is available in 50-milligram tablets that can be split into quarters to provide the right dose for your pet. Vets say it's safe for most healthy dogs and cats, although pets with glaucoma or bladder problems shouldn't take it without a veterinarian's approval.

Don't drive him to despair. For many pets, it's not motion that causes car sickness but fear. "Don't make going to the vet the only time your pet rides in the car, or you're asking for an anxious and possibly sick pet," says David Hammond, D.V.M., a veterinarian in private practice in Pleasant Hill, Oregon, and veterinary affairs manager for Hill's Pet Nutrition. Allowing him to accompany you occasionally on more pleasant jaunts will help keep his tummy calm at all times.

Allay his anxiety. Some pets become almost panicky about being in a moving vehicle, says Dr. MacKay. To help him overcome his fear—as well as the resulting nausea—try making the car a pleasant place to be. "Take your pet to the car and just sit there without the engine on," suggests Dr. MacKay. "Give him a treat if you like. Do this for seven to ten days. Then one day, start the car. Praise him, talk to him, possibly give him a treat. Do this for several minutes a day for the next few days."

Once your pet is used to just sitting in the car, try taking short trips, suggests Dr. MacKay. Begin by driving around the block, then gradually work up to longer distances. His car sickness should eventually start to improve. "It takes time," says Dr. MacKay, "but it's worth the work."

PANEL OF ADVISERS

Gary Beard, D.V.M., is assistant dean at the Auburn University College of Veterinary Medicine in Alabama.

Lynda Bond, D.V.M., is a veterinarian in private practice in Cape Elizabeth, Maine, who hosts a weekly pet segment for a Portland television station.

William G. Brewer, D.V.M., is assistant professor of small animal internal medicine in the Department of Small Animal Surgery and Medicine at the Auburn University College of Veterinary Medicine in Alabama.

James B. Dalley, D.V.M., is associate professor of small animal clinical sciences at the Michigan State University College of Veterinary Medicine in East Lansing.

David Hammond, D.V.M., is a veterinarian in private practice in Pleasant Hill, Oregon, and veterinary affairs manager for Hill's Pet Nutrition.

Clayton MacKay, D.V.M., is director of the veterinary teaching hospital at the Ontario Veterinary College at the University of Guelph in Canada and president of the American Animal Hospital Association.

Bernhard P. Pukay, D.V.M., is a veterinarian in private practice in Ottawa and host of the Discovery Channel's *Pet Connection.*

Cataracts

4 Clear Tips for Cloudy Eyes

You don't call your pooch Hawkeye or ask him to read an eye chart, but lately you've noticed his eyes seem to be getting a little cloudy. Should you be worried about his sight?

Probably not. Cataracts in people often cause problems, but in pets they usually aren't serious enough to raise an eyebrow over. After all, a dog's normal vision isn't much better than Mr. Magoo's. The difference in sight caused by cataracts is usually minimal, says Waldo Keller, D.V.M., a veterinary ophthalmologist and dean of the Michigan State University College of Veterinary Medicine in East Lansing.

Dogs usually get cataracts when they're young, often between one and three years old. (Cats, however, rarely get cataracts.) In most cases, a dog's other senses are so keen that even if his vision starts to go, you may not notice there's a problem, says Dr. Keller.

If he does need help getting around—or if you're concerned about preventing cataracts in the future—here are some tips from vets.

 For **Dogs** Only

Be consistent. There's no place like home—until one day you put the couch where the TV used to be. Then your dog's usual territory can suddenly seem like a new and possibly bumpy place. "They can really have a problem if you rearrange the furniture," says William Crane, V.M.D., a veterinarian in private practice in Colmar, Pennsylvania.

Give him a tour. If you do move things around or if your pet has just recently begun having vision problems, gently lead him around the house so he'll learn where everything is, says Dr. Crane.

Keep him in reach. Don't take chances if your pet seems to be having serious vision problems. Unless the yard is securely fenced, keep him on a leash whenever you go outside.

Keep up with checkups. After heredity, the leading cause of cataracts in dogs is diabetes. (Golden retrievers, Labradors and poodles are particularly susceptible.) When this condition is caught early, however, cataracts may be delayed or even prevented altogether, says Guy L. Pidgeon, D.V.M., a specialist in veterinary internal medicine and director of the Department of Veterinary Affairs for Hill's Pet Nutrition in Topeka, Kansas.

While pets with diabetes need a veterinarian's care, there is some evidence that dietary fiber can help control blood sugar levels and perhaps lower the risk of developing cataracts, says Kathryn Michel, D.V.M., a researcher and nutrition expert in the Department of Clinical Studies at the University of Pennsylvania School of Veterinary Medicine in Philadelphia.

She recommends buying a "special" dog food that's designed for overweight pets. (If your pet is already thin, however, check with your vet before switching foods.)

Whether your pooch is fat or thin, however, he will probably appreciate getting carrot sticks or apple slices as snacks. Most dogs like them, and they're a great way to up his fiber intake, says Dr. Michel.

When to See the Vet

Your vet said not to worry about the cataracts, but he didn't say anything about your pet getting squinty, bloodshot eyes. These days your pooch looks like a gangster (without the cigar). What's going on?

Dogs with cataracts will occasionally develop a condition called phacolytic uveitis, which occurs when lens material from the cataract leaks out, causing a painful inflammation of the iris and the part of the eye behind it.

If your dog already has cataracts, it's important to see your vet as soon as you notice squinting or other symptoms. "If untreated, it can become glaucoma, which is more serious than the cataract," says Kerry Ketring, D.V.M., a veterinary ophthalmologist with practices in Ohio, Michigan and Kentucky.

Caught early and treated with topical anti-inflammatory drugs, however, the condition usually will clear right up. Sometimes the cataract will shrink as well.

Shades of Blue

Maybe you've watched *Cool Hand Luke* too many times, but suddenly it seems as though your retriever's brown eyes are as blue as Paul Newman's.

No, you're not dreaming of blue eyes. As the eyes get older, fibers in the lens get denser and reflect light differently, sometimes making brown eyes appear a hazy blue. Vets call this condition lenticular sclerosis, and it's one of many normal changes that can occur with aging.

Although you'll want to see your vet just to be sure, this condition doesn't affect your pet's vision, and it doesn't require treatment, says Waldo Keller, D.V.M., a veterinary ophthalmologist and dean of the Michigan State University College of Veterinary Medicine in East Lansing.

PANEL OF ADVISERS

William Crane, V.M.D., is a veterinarian in private practice in Colmar, Pennsylvania.

Waldo Keller, D.V.M., is a veterinary ophthalmologist and dean of the Michigan State University College of Veterinary Medicine in East Lansing.

Kerry Ketring, D.V.M., is a veterinary ophthalmologist with practices in Ohio, Michigan and Kentucky.

Kathryn Michel, D.V.M., is a researcher and nutrition expert in the Department of Clinical Studies at the University of Pennsylvania School of Veterinary Medicine in Philadelphia.

Guy L. Pidgeon, D.V.M., is a specialist in veterinary internal medicine and director of the Department of Veterinary Affairs for Hill's Pet Nutrition in Topeka, Kansas.

Cat Flu

9 Soothing Hints

You won't find your cat perusing drugstore shelves or see her propped up in bed with a thermometer in her mouth, but even hardy felines can come down with upper respiratory infections, better known as flu.

Cat flu, like the common cold in humans, is a viral illness that results in weepy eyes, a runny nose and perhaps sudden sneezing attacks. (Dogs aren't susceptible to these viruses.) In adult cats this highly contagious condition will usually clear up on its own in a week to ten days. Here are a few ways to keep your cat comfortable in the meantime.

 **For Cats Only**

Fight it with food. While a sick cat is rarely a hungry cat, it's important to encourage her to eat, says Susan M. Cotter, D.V.M., professor of medicine and head of the Section of Small Animal Medicine at the Tufts University School of Veterinary Medicine in North Grafton, Massachusetts. A good diet will help keep her immune system strong, making her better able to fight off infection, Dr. Cotter says.

To stimulate her appetite, try giving her a warm meal, she suggests. Add warm water to her kibble to make a gravy or just pop her food in the microwave until it's warm.

Order something odoriferous. Since your cat probably has a stuffed-up nose, you can tempt her taste buds by giving her something with big flavor—and smell. Canned tuna is always a good choice, says Dr. Cotter. You can put some alone on a plate or mix it with her regular food.

Cats also like high-protein foods like cottage cheese, scrambled eggs and chicken, says H. Ellen Whiteley, D.V.M., a veterinary consultant in private practice in Guadalupita, New Mexico, and author of *Understanding and Training Your Cat or Kitten.*

"Pop a skinless, boneless chicken breast in the microwave and then cut it up real fine," she suggests. "Most cats will eat something like that."

It's not a good idea to give human food to cats for more than a few days, however. Once she starts to feel better, switch her back to her regular chow, Dr. Cotter advises.

Lend a hand. If your finicky feline just sniffs your special offerings and walks away, try dabbing a little food on her nose or paw for her to clean off, says Dr. Whiteley.

Give it a whirl. If your cat won't eat no matter what you give her, try running her food through the blender or food processor to make it liquid, Dr. Whiteley suggests. Even pets that don't feel like eating are often willing to lap a tasty and nutritious gravy.

Give her a hankie. Cats with flu often get an uncomfortable buildup of mucus around the eyes and nose. To help your pet breathe easy and feel more comfortable, "keeping the eyes and nose clean is important," says Dr. Cotter.

Dampen a soft washcloth or cotton ball with warm water and gently swab away the secretions, she suggests. Or you can use premoistened baby towelettes, which contain soothing ingredients like lanolin and aloe vera, says Jim Humphries, D.V.M., a veterinary consultant in private practice in Dallas and author of *Dr. Jim's Animal Clinic for Cats* and *Dr. Jim's Animal Clinic for Dogs*.

Soothe with saline. If your cat is having difficulty breathing, giving her saline nose drops will thin sticky mucus and help clear her nose, Dr. Whiteley says.

When to See the Vet

Cat flu is generally no more serious among the feline crowd than the common cold is for us. Sometimes, however, the germs stick around longer than they should. "Some cases can get really serious," says H. Ellen Whiteley, D.V.M., a veterinary consultant in private practice in Guadalupita, New Mexico.

In severe cases, cat flu can lead to problems like pneumonia, anemia or dehydration. And in kittens, it can be extremely dangerous. So if your pet seems unusually sick or if secretions from her nose or eyes are thick and discolored, call your vet right away.

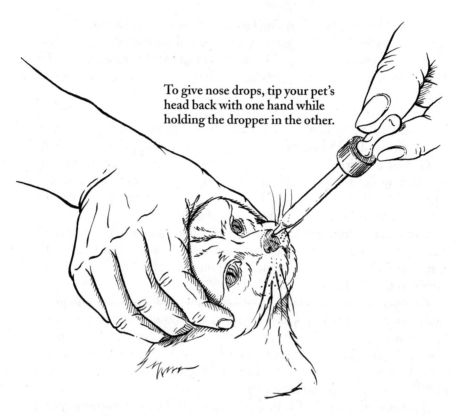

To give nose drops, tip your pet's head back with one hand while holding the dropper in the other.

With the dropper in one hand, tip her head back with the other. Place one or two drops in each nostril, then keep her head elevated for a minute to give them time to work, she says. You can repeat this twice a day, or more often if it seems to help.

Give eye relief. You can also use saline drops to help relieve sore, weepy eyes. (If you use the same dropper, however, be sure to rinse it thoroughly between uses.) Just put a drop or two in each eye; repeat three to five times a day, says Dr. Whiteley. Or you can use over-the-counter eyedrops containing boric acid, she adds.

Help with humidity. Putting extra moisture into the air with a humidifier will help ease congestion and improve breathing, says Dr. Cotter.

Another alternative is to take your pet into the bathroom when you bathe or shower, suggests James Richards, D.V.M., assistant director of the Feline Health Center at the Cornell University College of Veterinary Medicine in Ithaca, New York.

Take protective measures. Veterinarians often recommend a vaccine that's very effective at preventing cat flu. While it doesn't work

100 percent of the time, it will dramatically improve your cat's chances for staying healthy. Even if she does get sick, the symptoms will be less serious, Dr. Richards says.

PANEL OF ADVISERS

Susan M. Cotter, D.V.M., is professor of medicine and head of the Section of Small Animal Medicine at the Tufts University School of Veterinary Medicine in North Grafton, Massachusetts.

Jim Humphries, D.V.M., is a veterinary consultant in private practice in Dallas and author of *Dr. Jim's Animal Clinic for Cats* and *Dr. Jim's Animal Clinic for Dogs*.

James Richards, D.V.M., is assistant director of the Feline Health Center at the Cornell University College of Veterinary Medicine in Ithaca, New York.

H. Ellen Whiteley, D.V.M., is a veterinary consultant in private practice in Guadalupita, New Mexico, and author of *Understanding and Training Your Cat or Kitten.*

Chewing

7 Tips to Grind Out the Urge

Dogs are born chewers, and when the urge to be oral strikes, almost any object will do. Even cats, which tend to use their nails to carve paths of destruction, will sometimes set their teeth around such delectable items as carpets and computer cords.

"Chewing knows few bounds. It's a popular pastime among all kinds of animals," says Bob Gutierrez, animal behavior coordinator at the San Francisco Society for the Prevention of Cruelty to Animals.

But while unauthorized munching may be a source of great amusement for your dog or cat, it can wreak havoc around the house. So if your pet's chewing is gnawing at your patience, don't stand around biting your nails. Try these suggestions.

 ## For Dogs and Cats

Just say no. Letting your pet get away with chewing even once can set the stage for a lifetime of bad habits, says Liz Palika, a dog obedience instructor in Oceanside, California, columnist for *Dog Fancy* magazine and author of *Fido, Come: Training Your Dog with Love and Understanding* and *Love on a Leash.* When you catch your pet chewing something he shouldn't, say "No!" Then replace the object with an appropriate chew toy and praise him when he takes interest in it, Palika says. "They learn pretty fast this way."

Rotate his toys. Instead of lavishing your pet with a dozen of his favorite chew toys all at once, give him one or two at a time. Then change them every couple of days, says Palika. "This makes life more interesting," she says. "There's always something new to do."

Make the good better. Particularly when they're young, pets can't always figure out why it's okay to chew rawhide but wrong to feast on the Corinthian leather couch. To help him figure it out, it helps to make his toys really appealing, Gutierrez says.

He recommends dragging a chew toy on a string until your pet gets interested. Or try coating the toy with peanut butter, soaking it in chicken or beef broth or even rubbing it between your hands to get your scent all over it. "When he starts chewing, get all excited and tell him 'Good, chew! Chew, chew, chew!' After a while, you'll just have to say 'Chew!' and your pet will know what to do," says Gutierrez.

Make the bad bitter. If your dog or cat persists in noshing things he should leave alone, try using pet repellent, suggests Kathryn Segura, who trains animals for television and movies and is co-owner of PHD Animals in Studio City, California. Pet stores sell a variety of repellents with names like Get Off My Garden and Habit Breaker. Segura's favorite is bitter apple repellent. "Just wipe it on furniture or spray a little on objects you want them to stay away from," she says. "They hate the bitter taste, and they learn quickly."

Spice up his life. Putting a dash of hot pepper sauce on whatever your pet is chewing will quickly quell his desire to come back for more, says Gutierrez, who sometimes uses Tabasco sauce. "It wipes off furniture, walls and lots of other chewables almost as easily as it wipes on—and it works," he says. But he adds a caution: Try a test spot first to make sure it won't permanently stain your belongings orange.

Have bad scents. Most pets dislike the smell of perfumes and colognes, so Gutierrez recommends mixing one part perfume with ten parts water and spraying the solution on whatever your pet shouldn't be chewing. "The cheaper the perfume, the better—they won't even come near it," he says. "Then again, it may not exactly be a sensory joyride for you, either," he adds.

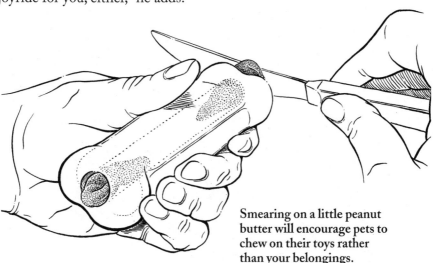

Smearing on a little peanut butter will encourage pets to chew on their toys rather than your belongings.

Hide the shoes. People often wonder why pets always seem to go for their favorite belongings. The reason, says Palika, is that these objects smell like you. "Your pet thrives on your scent, especially when you're gone." Shoes are a real favorite, she adds. Not only are they overflowing with your scent, but the leather is fun to chew. "If you have a pair of $500 Gucci shoes and a dog that still doesn't know what to chew, simply put the shoes out of his reach," she says.

PANEL OF ADVISERS

Bob Gutierrez is animal behavior coordinator at the San Francisco Society for the Prevention of Cruelty to Animals.

Liz Palika is a dog obedience instructor in Oceanside, California, a columnist for *Dog Fancy* magazine and author of *Fido, Come: Training Your Dog with Love and Understanding* and *Love on a Leash*.

Kathryn Segura trains animals for television and movies and is co-owner of PHD Animals in Studio City, California.

Claw Problems

11 Tips for Toe Woes

Click, click, click—is that the sound of your pooch walking across the kitchen floor? Rip, rip, rip—is that what you hear as your fractious feline shreds the lace curtains?

"Owners often don't realize how long their dog's or cat's nails are," says Joanne Stefanatos, D.V.M., a veterinarian in private practice in Las Vegas. "If the claws are actually snagging in the carpet, you know they're much too long."

In the old days dogs and cats wore their nails down naturally as they ran, dug and scratched their way through the great outdoors. Today, however, their claws typically get less of a workout and are more likely to get torn or ripped or even grow into the pad like an ingrown nail.

Add to this such things as infections and bad manicures, and even the most mild-mannered pet can suffer a case of the terrible toes.

To keep your pet up and running, here's what vets recommend.

 For **Dogs** and **Cats**

Trim them often. To prevent claws from getting too long and causing problems, they should be trimmed every six to eight weeks, says M. Lynne Kesel, D.V.M., assistant professor of elective surgery in the Department of Clinical Sciences at the Colorado State University College of Veterinary Medicine and Biomedical Sciences in Fort Collins.

If your pet doesn't often get outside (and on hard ground), however, more frequent clippings may be necessary. Some experts recommend clipping every two to four weeks for less active dogs and every month for indoor cats.

Start 'em young. "You should teach a kitten or puppy early on that he is to sit still to have his nails trimmed," Dr. Kesel says.

Don't lunge at him all at once, however. To help your pet get used to the idea of pedicures, spend some time touching his feet before you

When to See the Vet

While most claw problems are minor and can be treated at home, sometimes the problem runs deep—like into the foot pad itself or even deep inside the bone.

Like people, pets will occasionally develop ingrown nails, in which the sharp little spike penetrates deeply into the pad, says Scott Weldy, D.V.M., a veterinarian in private practice in El Toro, California. Or sometimes a long nail gets snagged on carpet or underbrush and tears loose. Either way, your pet is probably going to need surgery to correct the problem.

In addition, if bleeding doesn't stop in ten minutes, wrap the area with a gauze bandage and call your vet. Some pets have difficulty forming blood clots and can bleed heavily if they don't receive professional assistance.

Not all nail problems are caused by accidents. Occasionally a bacterial infection or internal illness may cause nails to grow twisted and deformed, says Jan A. Hall, D.V.M., a veterinary dermatologist and referral specialist in Ville St. Laurent in Montreal.

If the claw looks normal but the area where the claw and skin meet looks puffy, your pet could have a serious infection, says Dr. Weldy. See your vet right away.

---

actually start clipping, advises Anitra Frazier of New York City, author of *The New Natural Cat*. Once he's used to having his feet handled, he'll be less likely to rebel when you bring out the clippers.

Cut carefully. To make sure you don't cut too far and into the quick—the pink part of the nail that contains nerves and blood vessels—"don't think of shortening the claw," Frazier says. "Think of blunting the tip."

For cats, this means cutting no farther down than is needed to remove the sharp tip. A lot of dogs, however, have dark nails, which makes it difficult to distinguish the dead, trimmable part of the nail from the quick. To be safe, trim just to the point where the nail starts to curve downward, says Dr. Kesel.

Treat them like jewels. If your pet won't sit still for clippers, maybe he'll do better if you use a jeweler's file, says Hazel Christiansen, owner of Blue Ribbon Pet Grooming in Lewiston, Idaho, and president of the American Grooming Shop Association. "Just file and take off a short bit at a time," she says. Jeweler's files can be purchased at hardware stores.

Work in shifts. "When a pet is nervous, I suggest clipping one claw a day," says Frazier. "People think they've got to do everything at once, but there is nothing wrong with stealth, cunning and patience."

Reach for the shaving kit. Many nail injuries occur when owners accidentally trim too close to the quick, says Mollyann Holland, D.V.M., a resident veterinarian in small animal medicine in the Department of Veterinary Medicine and Surgery at the University of Missouri College of Veterinary Medicine in Columbia. To staunch the bleeding, rub the cut place with a styptic pencil or coagulant powder, she advises. The chemicals used to stop bleeding may sting for a moment, so hold your pet snugly when applying them.

Turn to flour power. Another way to stop nail bleeding is to dip the toe in flour and pat the powder in, says Scott Weldy, D.V.M., a veterinarian in private practice in El Toro, California.

Protect with a cleaning. If your pet has recently torn or cracked a nail and is bleeding or in pain, you'll want to clean the nail well to pre-

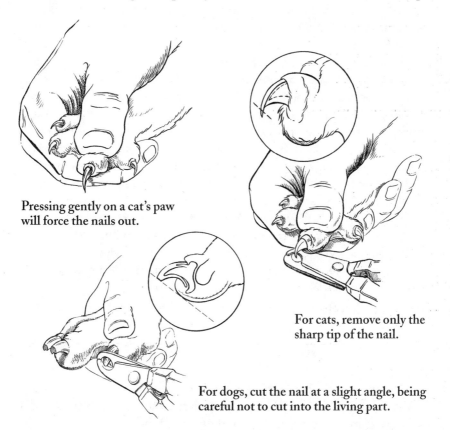

Pressing gently on a cat's paw will force the nails out.

For cats, remove only the sharp tip of the nail.

For dogs, cut the nail at a slight angle, being careful not to cut into the living part.

Scotch the Scratching

First he disemboweled the leather couch. Now he is scratching a hieroglyphic masterpiece into the cherrywood chest. Your cat is sweet and charming, but he's clawing his way out of your heart.

To prevent household cat-astrophes, many owners turn to declawing, and that's a shame, says veterinarian Nicholas Dodman, B.V.M.S., professor in the Department of Surgery and director of the Behavior Clinic at the Tufts University School of Veterinary Medicine in North Grafton, Massachusetts.

Rather than having your pet undergo painful surgery, Dr. Dodman says, why not try retraining him? Here's what he recommends.

Put out a scratching post. Cats can't resist sinking their claws into a rough, sisal surface—which is why a scratching post could be the salvation of your household goods. Whichever post you choose, however, don't get rid of it when it starts looking tatty. "If it looks tatty, that's because he's using it and it has his scent," Dr. Dodman says.

Be sure the post is tall enough for the cat to reach up as he scratches. "It's got to be absolutely stable. If it rocks, he'll lose his confidence and not use it," Dr. Dodman adds.

Finally, put the post in the middle of the action—right by the sofa, for example, or wherever your cat's been doing his scratching, says Dr. Dodman. Once he starts using it, then you can move it, a few inches at a time, to a more remote location.

Remove the odor. One of the purposes of scratching is to deposit a familiar scent; it's your cat's way of marking his territory. Removing his scent with an odor neutralizer, sold in pet stores, may help prevent him from scratching there in the future.

In addition, you can actively repel cats by applying citrus, an odor they hate, Dr. Dodman adds. Try hiding dried orange or lemon peels under cushions. Rub wood furniture with lemon-scented oil or put a lemon-scented air freshener nearby and replace it every few months.

vent infection from setting in, says Dr. Weldy.

Wash the area well with soap and water, then gently towel it dry and apply a small dab of antibacterial ointment, he advises.

Pad the paw. To keep the injured area protected, wrap a thin gauze bandage lightly around the paw. Change the bandage every day until the nail is healed, vets advise.

To keep the bandage clean and in place, cover it with a lightweight cotton sock. For small pets, use a child's sock.

 ## For Dogs Only

Do the dew. Since the dewclaws, located on the inside of either the front or hind legs (or both), get zero wear, they can easily get too long and snag on something, causing serious injury, says Dr. Holland. "They bleed terribly when they get pulled," she says.

You must remember to trim the dewclaws at the same time you do your pet's other claws, says Dr. Weldy. Or if your pooch is still a pup, your vet may recommend having the dewclaws surgically removed. If done within a few days of birth, the procedure typically doesn't require anesthetic, says Dr. Weldy.

 ## For Cats Only

Give paws a squeeze. Unlike a dog's nails, a cat's are slightly recessed. To get them out for trimming, gently squeeze the toe from top to bottom, says Dr. Kesel. This forces the nail out so you can blunt the tip.

PANEL OF ADVISERS

Hazel Christiansen is owner of Blue Ribbon Pet Grooming in Lewiston, Idaho, and president of the American Grooming Shop Association.

Nicholas Dodman, B.V.M.S., is professor in the Department of Surgery and director of the Behavior Clinic at the Tufts University School of Veterinary Medicine in North Grafton, Massachusetts.

Anitra Frazier lives in New York City and is author of *The New Natural Cat.*

Jan A. Hall, D.V.M., is a veterinary dermatologist and referral specialist in Ville St. Laurent in Montreal.

Mollyann Holland, D.V.M., is a resident veterinarian in small animal medicine in the Department of Veterinary Medicine and Surgery at the University of Missouri College of Veterinary Medicine in Columbia.

M. Lynne Kesel, D.V.M., is assistant professor of elective surgery in the Department of Clinical Sciences at the Colorado State University College of Veterinary Medicine and Biomedical Sciences in Fort Collins.

Joanne Stefanatos, D.V.M., is a veterinarian in private practice in Las Vegas.

Scott Weldy, D.V.M., is a veterinarian in private practice in El Toro, California.

Cold-Weather Concerns

15 Warming Tips

You know it's getting cold when your furry Persian won't leave her perch beside the stove and your woolly sheepdog looks like he'd appreciate an extra coat.

While dogs and cats are never really underdressed—they wear their favorite furs year-round—Jack Frost's nip can still give a painful bite.

Without protection from the elements, dogs and cats can develop frostbite or hypothermia—a potentially deadly condition that may occur if their temperature drops even a few degrees. At the very least they can be cold and miserable—or even have ice balls form between their toes.

With a few simple precautions you can keep your pets cozy no matter what winter throws your way—and even save their lives should they accidentally spend too much time in the bitter cold.

 For **Dogs** and **Cats**

Consider his background. Not all pets are equally at home in the cold. While a Labrador or sheepdog might be comfortable outside on all but the coldest days, a miniature poodle or short-haired cat might get chilly even when it's balmy, says Tom Bradley, owner of Luftnase Kennel in Watertown, New York.

Check with your vet if you're not sure if your pet is bred for chilly climes. If he's not, you'll want to keep him where it's warm—in the house, garage or a comfortable outbuilding.

Check his wardrobe. While most cats are comfortable in the cold, "only dogs that grow thick coats can really stay outdoors," Bradley says. "My Labradors, it doesn't matter what the weather is. They go out and play in the snow. My German short-haired pointers, on the other hand, go out, do what they have to do and then come in and get underneath the woodstove."

Keep his hair combed. "If your animal grows a thick hair coat for the winter, you want to make sure it doesn't get matted," says Kenneth Sperling, D.V.M., a veterinarian in private practice in Anchorage, Alaska. "Wet, matted hair can lead to diseases of the skin because the dead hair traps dirt and debris."

Lend him something warm. On particularly cold days, your pet may appreciate being bundled up before he goes outdoors. This is especially true of breeds such as toy poodles, which typically have thin coats and aren't well-suited for the cold. "Dog sweaters are perfectly fine," says Dr. Sperling. Check out the canine couture at pet stores.

But forget the foot-warmers. Although pet stores sell booties to keep your pets' feet warm, most animals aren't comfortable wearing them and will quickly pull them off. In most cases, they're more trouble than they're worth, vets say.

When to See the Vet

If your pet has been outside too long and you suspect he has frostbite—symptoms commonly include flushing, swelling and itching of the affected part—rub him gently with a blanket or your hands to gradually raise the temperature of the frozen parts. "Don't do a lot of rubbing or you'll cause more damage," says Kenneth Sperling, D.V.M., a veterinarian in private practice in Anchorage, Alaska.

Frostbite is serious, so you'll want to get your pet to the vet as soon as possible, he adds.

The same advice applies if you suspect your pet has developed hypothermia, or low body temperature, which can cause shallow breathing, a weak pulse or shivering muscles. (If he's not shivering, however, it could mean that your pet has suffered severe exposure to cold and that his metabolism isn't capable of spontaneously increasing body temperature.) "You need to bring him into a warm environment and slowly allow him to rewarm," advises Robert J. Murtaugh, D.V.M., associate professor in the Department of Medicine at the Tufts University School of Veterinary Medicine in North Grafton, Massachusetts.

But avoid using the heat from lamps, heating pads or open ovens, because your pet could be burned. Instead, wrap him in a warm blanket and hold him close so your body temperature will help raise his. Then get him to the vet as soon as you can.

Build a Better Doghouse

All outdoor dogs need shelter from the cold, rain and snow—even though some, like Snoopy, spend more time outside the house than in. To keep your pooch cozy, here's what vets recommend.

Size it right. "If the doghouse is too big, the dog's body temperature isn't going to keep him warmed up," says Kenneth Sperling, D.V.M., a veterinarian in private practice in Anchorage, Alaska. "It should be just big enough for the dog to get in there, turn around and lie down comfortably."

Build it tight. To keep your pooch cozy, the house should be well-built and waterproof. "Line it with some kind of easily cleaned, warmth-retaining lining like straw or wood shavings to keep down heat loss through the floor and also to give him something he can burrow down into to build up warmth," says Mark Raffe, D.V.M., professor of anesthesia and critical care at the University of Minnesota College of Veterinary Medicine in St. Paul.

Raise it high. The doorway should be high enough off the ground to prevent water from flowing in. It should also be fairly small to minimize heat loss. To make it even more secure, hang a plastic flap to keep the wind from whipping through.

In addition, Dr. Sperling recommends putting a roof over the "porch" to provide some protection for pets that don't know enough to come in from the cold.

The most expensive doghouse in the world won't do any good if your pet refuses to use it. It should be warm and cozy—large enough for him to turn around in yet small enough to make him feel snug.

Give him time to adjust. After spending a nice sunny season warming himself in the yard, your pet may not be prepared for winter's chill. It usually takes between three and six weeks after the temperature drops before your pet's winter coat gets thick enough to stave off winter's chill, says Mark Raffe, D.V.M., professor of anesthesiology and critical care at the University of Minnesota College of Veterinary Medicine in St. Paul.

"Allow the pet to slowly adapt to the environment," he says. "Give him progressive periods outside, starting with 15 minutes a day."

Do your share of skin care. Winter air can be extremely drying, and even pets that never set a paw outdoors can get dry, itchy skin, says Dr. Sperling. To prevent this, he recommends giving all pets a B-complex vitamin that contains fatty acids, which will help keep their skin from drying out. The vitamins are available at pet stores.

Give him shelter. "If it's going to be minus 20 degrees for the next week, even if you have an outdoor pet, make arrangements to bring him into the garage or some other warmer place for a few days," advises Robert J. Murtaugh, D.V.M., associate professor in the Department of Medicine at the Tufts University School of Veterinary Medicine in North Grafton, Massachusetts.

In fact, even hardy pets pet should have shelter once the temperature dips into the teens or single digits. For dogs, a comfortable, weatherproof, well-padded doghouse will help keep the chill out. Cats will be comfortable in a barn or other outbuilding. Just make sure there's a way for them to get in and out, says Dr. Raffe.

Watch the windchill. Even if the thermometer reads a relatively comfy 25°, a breeze can make it feel a heck of a lot colder. "With the windchill factor it could feel like 25 below," says Dr. Sperling, so be prepared to bring your pet in when it's blowing.

Listen to his appetite. If your pet lives outdoors, he'll burn up a lot more calories in the winter just trying to stay warm.

If your dog spends a lot of time outdoors, "you may need to increase his calorie intake by 25 to 50 percent," says Dr. Raffe. "They need those extra calories not only for energy demands but also to get a thicker coat."

Keep the water bowl full—and fluid. When the temperature drops, water freezes. "An animal can go for only 20 hours without water before becoming dehydrated," warns Dr. Sperling.

He recommends providing fresh water frequently throughout the day to keep the water bowl full. Or you can buy an electric warming device that will keep the water liquid on even the coldest days. "Just be careful not to run an electrical cord where the animal can chew it," he adds.

Safer Car Care

For pets, one of the most lethal winter hazards is parked right in your driveway—and it kills without moving an inch.

Every year pets die as a result of lapping up ethylene glycol—the active ingredient in antifreeze that's extremely toxic to pets, even in amounts as small as one to two ounces. Even more diabolical, it has a sweet taste that pets enjoy, vets warn.

Obviously, the best precaution is to never leave antifreeze lying around, either in an open container or in puddles under the car.

You should switch to an antifreeze that's safer for pets, says Robert J. Murtaugh, D.V.M., associate professor in the Department of Medicine at the Tufts University School of Veterinary Medicine in North Grafton, Massachusetts. One product, Sierra, contains an ingredient called propylene glycol. While it may upset your pet's stomach or cause mild nervous system reactions, it's unlikely to cause lethal problems such as kidney failure, he says.

Regardless of what kind of antifreeze your pet laps up, however, you'll still want to see the vet right away, Dr. Murtaugh adds.

Trim around the toes. While many dogs and cats love romping through the snow, they'll occasionally develop small ice balls between their toes that can lead to frostbitten feet. "You should regularly trim out the long hair between the foot pads so it doesn't become the focus for ice-ball formation," says Dr. Raffe.

Turn on the heat. If your pet already has ice balls between his toes, you can melt them quickly with a hair dryer, says Ronald Stone, D.V.M., clinical assistant professor of surgery at the University of Miami School of Veterinary Medicine and national executive secretary of the American Association of Pet Industry Veterinarians.

Hold the dryer about six inches away and keep it moving until all the ice is melted. "Just keep it on a low setting so you don't burn them," he warns.

Look for damage. While you're doing the *pet*-icure, check to see if ice has scraped or cut the pads. If it has, apply a little first aid ointment containing an antiseptic to help prevent infection. Then rub on a little hand lotion or aloe vera to keep the pads soft, he says.

 For Cats only

Do an engine check. During the cold months many outdoor cats will creep into the engine compartment of cars to take advantage of the "central heating"—and then get hurt when someone turns the key. Before starting the car in the morning, you may want to check under the hood for visitors, vets advise. It takes only a minute and could save your pet's life.

PANEL OF ADVISERS

Tom Bradley is owner of Luftnase Kennel in Watertown, New York.

Robert J. Murtaugh, D.V.M., is associate professor in the Department of Medicine at the Tufts University School of Veterinary Medicine in North Grafton, Massachusetts.

Mark Raffe, D.V.M., is professor of anesthesiology and critical care at the University of Minnesota College of Veterinary Medicine in St. Paul.

Kenneth Sperling, D.V.M., is a veterinarian in private practice in Anchorage, Alaska.

Ronald Stone, D.V.M., is clinical assistant professor of surgery at the University of Miami School of Veterinary Medicine and national executive secretary of the American Association of Pet Industry Veterinarians.

Constipation

11 Ways to Keep Things Moving

Your cat's litter box hasn't been disturbed all day. Your dog's pooper scooper is beginning to collect dust. You always knew your pets were a little unusual, but could they also be irregular?

"Dogs and cats tend not to get constipated, but it happens, and it's not much fun for them," says Clayton MacKay, D.V.M., director of the veterinary teaching hospital at Ontario Veterinary College at the University of Guelph in Canada and president of the American Animal Hospital Association.

If your pet is straining with little or no success for a whole day (or more), you'll want to see the vet to make sure nothing serious is wrong. Meanwhile, try these remedies to help get her moving again.

 For **Dogs** and **Cats**

Give her high-fiber fare. "A high-fiber diet isn't just good for humans. It can be just what a constipated dog or cat needs," says David Hammond, D.V.M., a veterinarian in private practice in Pleasant Hill, Oregon, and veterinary affairs manager for Hill's Pet Nutrition. He recommends buying a pet food that contains 7 to 13 percent fiber. You'll find the fiber percentage on the label. By regularly eating a high-fiber diet, "your pet may never be constipated again," he says.

Mobilize with Metamucil. This over-the-counter laxative contains psyllium seed husks, which pull water into the stool and help move it along, says Dr. Hammond. He recommends giving about ½ teaspoon twice a day to small pets and about 2 teaspoons twice a day to large dogs.

To make Metamucil more palatable, try mixing it with a small portion of canned food. Or if you're adding it to dry kibble, mix in some warm broth or water. Just be sure to give your pet plenty of water so the Metamucil doesn't congeal in her stomach, adds Dr. Hammond.

Bring on the bran. A sprinkle of oat bran every day can help keep constipation away, says Laura Downey, D.V.M., clinical instructor at the Small Animal Hospital at the Purdue University School of Veterinary Medicine in West Lafayette, Indiana. Depending on the size of your pet, she advises adding from 1/2 teaspoon to 2 tablespoons of oat bran to her food daily. Adding warm broth to the food will help make the bran easier to get down.

Or try getting flaky. A good source of dietary fiber is Grape-Nuts Flakes, says Charles W. Hickey, D.V.M., a veterinarian in private practice in Richmond, Virginia. He recommends doling out one to three teaspoonfuls several times a day until the constipation clears. "But if your pet happens to have a hankering for Grape-Nuts, she can eat them forever without a problem," says Dr. Hickey.

Pass it with pumpkin. "Canned pumpkin is an excellent source of fiber that can make your pet regular again. The bonus is that dogs and cats seem to enjoy it," says Dr. Hammond. He advises mixing a tablespoon or two with your pet's food for several days or until she's more regular again.

Send in the cows. "We're always advising people not to give much milk to their cats or dogs because it can cause diarrhea. But when you have a constipated pet, milk could be just what she needs," says Veronika Kiklevich, D.V.M., instructor and head of the community practice division of the Washington State University College of Veterinary Medicine in Pullman. She recommends giving small pets 1/8 cup twice a day and large dogs about 1/2 cup. When your pet is regular again, wean her off the milk over a period to three to four days, she says.

Water her well. "Water is essential to keeping your pet's digestive system healthy. Always have plenty available," says William G. Brewer, D.V.M., assistant professor of small animal internal medicine in the Department of Small Animal Surgery and Medicine at the Auburn University College of Veterinary Medicine in Alabama. If your pet would rather be lazy than walk across the house for a good swig of water, try placing water dishes in several rooms to make it easy, he recommends. Adding water to dry food is yet another way to increase her fluid intake.

Put on your walking shoes. Taking your pet out for a 20-minute romp several times a day is an excellent way to get things moving in the right direction, says Dr. MacKay.

Listen for nature's call. Some pets get constipated simply because

False Alarms

Just because your pet is straining to move her bowels does not mean she's constipated. Appearances to the contrary, vets say, the problem is far more likely to be something else.

"Ninety-nine percent of straining dogs actually have diarrhea, which is very common," says Clayton MacKay, D.V.M., director of the veterinary teaching hospital at Ontario Veterinary College at the University of Guelph in Canada and president of the American Animal Hospital Association. "The dog probably already emptied its bowel and still feels the urge to go, even though it's not producing anything."

Cats can also fool you. Unlike dogs, however, their straining may be caused by a blocked urethra, the tube that carries urine from the bladder, says Veronika Kiklevich, D.V.M., instructor and head of the community practice division of the Washington State University College of Veterinary Medicine in Pullman. "The owners see the cat straining to urinate, but they interpret it as constipation."

A blocked urethra can be serious, so you'll want to inspect the litter box to see if your cat's been urinating, says David Hammond, D.V.M., a veterinarian in private practice in Pleasant Hill, Oregon, and veterinary affairs manager for Hill's Pet Nutrition. If she continues to strain and the litter box stays dry, take her to the vet right away.

---

they haven't had the time or opportunity to go. "The longer your pet keeps it in, the harder and drier the stool gets," says Dr. MacKay. "That can lead to problems fairly quickly."

It's important, he says, to give your pets plenty of potty time. For cats, make sure the litter box is always available and not behind a closed door. Try to let your dog out several times a day. Or install a doggy door so he can come and go when he pleases.

Say no to bones. Eating ribs or other crunchable bones can cause things to get blocked up inside. "Only give your pets bones they can chew on, not eat," says Dr. Hickey.

Take a little off the back. For pets of the long-haired persuasion, tangled hair on the rear end will sometimes prevent them from having a bowel movement. Vets call this mechanical constipation. "They strain and strain and nothing comes out," says Dr. MacKay. "It can lead to true constipation, because the longer the animal doesn't go, the drier things get inside."

The solution? Get out the blunt scissors and carefully give her a trim. "If mechanical constipation is the problem, you'll know right away," says Dr. MacKay.

PANEL OF ADVISERS

William G. Brewer, D.V.M., is assistant professor of small animal internal medicine in the Department of Small Animal Surgery and Medicine at the Auburn University College of Veterinary Medicine in Alabama.

Laura Downey, D.V.M., is clinical instructor at the Small Animal Hospital at the Purdue University School of Veterinary Medicine in West Lafayette, Indiana.

David Hammond, D.V.M., is a veterinarian in private practice in Pleasant Hill, Oregon, and veterinary affairs manager for Hill's Pet Nutrition.

Charles W. Hickey, D.V.M., is a veterinarian in private practice in Richmond, Virginia.

Veronika Kiklevich, D.V.M., is instructor and head of the community practice division of the Washington State University College of Veterinary Medicine in Pullman.

Clayton MacKay, D.V.M., is director of the veterinary teaching hospital at Ontario Veterinary College at the University of Guelph in Canada and president of the American Animal Hospital Association.

Coughing
9 Strategies to Stop the Hacking

In people, coughing is nature's way of saying good-bye—to dust, bacteria, tickly hairs and all the other itchy, twitchy things that sail into our throats and windpipes every day.

In pets, however, coughing is unusual. While the occasional *harumph*—from a hairball, for example—isn't anything to worry about, coughing that goes on for more than a day could be a sign that something serious is wrong. In the short run, however, there are ways to calm the coughs. Here's what vets recommend.

 ## For Dogs and Cats

Protect him from the elements. Like people, pets will occasionally cough in response to pollen, dust or even fumes from household cleaners, says Lee R. Harris, D.V.M., a veterinarian in private practice in Federal Way, Washington. Try keeping your pet in another room when you're vacuuming or dusting, he suggests. Open windows if you're using heavy-duty cleaners. And in the warm months, keeping him indoors in the early morning and late afternoon will help reduce his exposure to pollen.

Put out the smokes. You already know that smoking isn't good for you. It can be even worse for your pet, since the heavier elements in smoke can drift down to his level.

"One dog that I saw developed very severe emphysema" from its owners' smoking, says Walter Weirich, D.V.M., Ph.D., professor of surgery and cardiology at the Purdue University School of Veterinary Medicine in West Lafayette, Indiana.

Up the humidity. When air is dry, mucus in the throat and airways gets thick and sticky, signaling the body to cough. "It does help to humidify the air," says Dr. Harris. "Take the pet in the bathroom when you shower and let him breathe the moist air." Using a humidifier or vaporizer can also help reduce the dryness of the air, he says.

Choose a harness. While pets that are leash-trained can manage a traditional choke collar, more eager pets will often lunge against the lead, putting irritating pressure on the larynx (voicebox) or windpipe. "I usually recommend walking them in a harness instead of a collar," says Eugene Snyder, D.V.M., a veterinarian in private practice in Kettering, Ohio.

Stop it at the source. "If your pet is coughing more than once an hour, he can probably benefit from a cough suppressant," says Dr. Harris. He recommends using a product containing the active ingredient dextromethorphan, such as Robitussin Maximum Strength Cough Syrup. Ask your vet which dose is right for your pet.

Be sure, however, to pick a product that contains *only* the active ingredient you want. Some cough medications also contain drugs like aspirin or acetaminophen, which can be dangerous for pets.

Slip it down. If the cough suppressant comes in liquid form, "tip the animal's head up, pull the loose skin up from around the mouth and make a funnel," says Dr. Harris. Then spoon in the appropriate amount.

Try another OTC. When coughing is caused by hay fever, giving

When to See the Vet

When pets start coughing, it's sometimes a warning sign that something serious—like pneumonia, asthma, bronchitis, a collapsed windpipe or even a heart attack—is going on. How can you tell when to be concerned?

"In a dog, if he's been coughing more than 24 hours, something is wrong and the animal should be checked out," says Carol Macherey, D.V.M., a veterinarian in private practice in Nashville. Coughing is rare in cats, with the exception of expelling hair balls, and should always be seen by a vet.

"Coughing is the most frequent sign of heart disease," adds James Buchanan, D.V.M., professor of cardiology at the University of Pennsylvania School of Veterinary Medicine in Philadelphia. If your dog is coughing and is breathing rapidly or seems short of breath, or if he has a swollen abdomen, get to the vet immediately.

an over-the-counter antihistamine like diphenhydramine (Benadryl) can help reduce irritation, says Paul Schmitz, D.V.M., a veterinarian in private practice in Joliet, Illinois.

Dosing amounts vary, but plan on giving about one to three milligrams of medication for every pound of pet. Ask your vet for exact amounts.

Keep him trim. "Weight is often a significant factor in older dogs that have chronic coughs," says Dr. Harris. "If we can get a few pounds off them, a lot of the coughing will disappear."

Keep him calm. Stressful situations can trigger cough attacks, says Carol Macherey, D.V.M., a veterinarian in private practice in Nashville. So when your dog's symptoms flare, give him extra love until things calm down, she suggests.

PANEL OF ADVISERS

James Buchanan, D.V.M., is professor of cardiology at the University of Pennsylvania School of Veterinary Medicine in Philadelphia.

Lee R. Harris, D.V.M., is a veterinarian in private practice in Federal Way, Washington.

Carol Macherey, D.V.M., is a veterinarian in private practice in Nashville.

Paul Schmitz, D.V.M., is a veterinarian in private practice in Joliet, Illinois.

Eugene Snyder, D.V.M., is a veterinarian in private practice in Kettering, Ohio.

Walter Weirich, D.V.M., Ph.D., is professor of surgery and cardiology at the Purdue University School of Veterinary Medicine in West Lafayette, Indiana.

Dandruff

8 Hints to Keep His Coat Clean

You knew he might shed, scratch the floors or dig holes by the begonias. But the last thing you expected from your furry friend was a blizzard of flaky skin. Doggy dandruff on the divan? Crusty kitty cascade on the carpet? Oh, great!

"Pet dandruff looks like a really bad case of people dandruff—you can easily see it with most animals," says Nancy Scanlan, D.V.M., a veterinarian in private practice in Sherman Oaks, California.

While occasionally dandruff can indicate a serious health problem, like allergies, parasites or skin infections, more often it occurs when skin cells naturally proliferate—form, die and flake off—at an accelerated rate.

To forgo the flakes, here's what experts suggest.

 **For Dogs and Cats**

Take the plunge. Since dandruff is a sign of flaky skin, giving your pet regular baths will help wash the flakes away before they accumulate, says Scott Weldy, D.V.M., a veterinarian in private practice in El Toro, California. Bathing your pet once a month in winter and twice a month in summer may clear up the problem for good, he says.

To bathe your pet, use warm, not hot, water. Use a mild shampoo like baby shampoo and massage it well into your pet's skin. Then rinse thoroughly and dry him well, says Dr. Scanlan.

For cats, the big struggle isn't getting rid of the dandruff, it's getting them into the bath in the first place. For tips, see "How to Give Your Cat a Bath" on page 186.

Go for more power. If baby shampoo doesn't seem to help, try using a pet dandruff shampoo that contains sulfur or salicylic acid. Leave the lather in place for about five minutes to give the active ingredients time to work, advises Dr. Weldy.

You can buy medicated shampoos in pet stores. Don't use med-

When to See the Vet

If you've tried shampoos, regular brushing and new foods and it still looks like winter on your pet's coat, you're probably going to need professional help, says Jan A. Hall, D.V.M., a veterinary dermatologist and referral specialist in Ville St. Laurent in Montreal.

While dandruff is usually nothing more than flaky skin, in some cases it can indicate serious problems like allergies, parasites or skin infections. Warning signs to watch for, besides the flakes, include scabs, crusting or itching, says Dr. Hall.

"Problems with the skin can be an indication of internal disease," she says. "After a month or so, if there is no improvement, you should take your pet to the vet." See a vet right away if the symptoms suddenly get worse, she adds.

icated shampoos made for humans, because they can be harmful for pets, adds Wayne Rosenkrantz, D.V.M., a veterinary dermatologist in private practice in Garden Grove, California. It's also a good idea, when buying shampoo for your cat, to check the label carefully. Products that are safe for dogs may be harmful for cats.

And to prevent making dandruff worse, avoid using shampoos that also include an insecticide, says Bernadine Cruz, D.V.M., a veterinarian in private practice in Laguna Hills, California. "Most of the flea shampoos are very drying, even those with added moisturizers," she says.

Add oatmeal to the bath. The same colloidal oatmeal (Aveeno) that people use for dry skin can also help relieve flaking in pets, says Dr. Cruz. "Aveeno is marvelous for pets with dandruff because it moisturizes dry skin," she says. It does take a little extra elbow grease to work it into a lather, though.

Give him a spritz. If you live in a dry climate, spraying your pet's coat with an oil rinse, available at pet stores, will help lubricate the skin and lock in moisture, says Dr. Rosenkrantz.

Rub in a moisturizer. To get moisture down really deep, you can rub your pet's coat with the same moisturizing lotion or cream you use on your hands, says M. Lynne Kesel, D.V.M., assistant professor of elective surgery in the Department of Clinical Sciences at the Colorado State University College of Veterinary Medicine and Biomedical Sciences in Fort Collins.

Give him the brush-off. Grooming your pet regularly helps distribute natural oils evenly over dry skin, which will help keep dandruff down, says Dr. Kesel. "Lots of cases will be resolved after the owner brushes the pet several times," she says.

Choose a brush that's not too harsh. "You can tell by rubbing the brush on the back of your hand if it's going to hurt," Dr. Kesel says. "Something you could use on your own head is going to be pleasant for the animal."

Check the oil. "Sometimes we'll see dandruff when animals aren't getting enough fat in their diets," says Mollyann Holland, D.V.M., a resident veterinarian in small animal medicine in the Department of Veterinary Medicine and Surgery at the University of Missouri College of Veterinary Medicine in Columbia.

Giving your pet fish-oil supplements will help improve the metabolism of fats in skin tissue, Dr. Weldy explains. Try mixing ½ to 1 teaspoon of fish oil into your pet's food every day. Using the same amount of safflower or corn oil can also help, says Jan A. Hall, D.V.M., a veterinary dermatologist and referral specialist in Ville St. Laurent in Montreal.

Upgrade his diet. Some generic pet foods do not provide the full range of vitamins and minerals your pet needs to maintain healthy skin. "I have seen dogs taken off generic dog food and put on a quality, name-brand pet food, and the owners have gotten rid of the dandruff," says Dr. Scanlan.

PANEL OF ADVISERS

Bernadine Cruz, D.V.M., is a veterinarian in private practice in Laguna Hills, California.

Jan A. Hall, D.V.M., is a veterinary dermatologist and referral specialist in Ville St. Laurent in Montreal.

Mollyann Holland, D.V.M., is a resident veterinarian in small animal medicine in the Department of Veterinary Medicine and Surgery at the University of Missouri College of Veterinary Medicine in Columbia.

M. Lynne Kesel, D.V.M., is assistant professor of elective surgery in the Department of Clinical Sciences at the Colorado State University College of Veterinary Medicine and Biomedical Sciences in Fort Collins.

Wayne Rosenkrantz, D.V.M., is a veterinary dermatologist in private practice in Garden Grove, California.

Nancy Scanlan, D.V.M., is a veterinarian in private practice in Sherman Oaks, California.

Scott Weldy, D.V.M., is a veterinarian in private practice in El Toro, California.

Deafness

11 Sound Coping Tips

Your dog doesn't raise an ear when the doorbell rings or you call her name. Your cat seems oblivious to most noises—even the whir of the electric can opener. Now the vet has confirmed your fears: Your pet isn't stubborn or sick. She's deaf.

Some dogs and cats are born deaf. Others lose their hearing with age or because of injuries or chronic ear infections. Fortunately, with a little extra care, many pets that are partially or even totally deaf will do just fine. "They're remarkably adaptive," says Michael Moore, D.V.M., chief of small animal medicine at the Washington State University College of Veterinary Medicine in Pullman.

To help your pet deal with deafness, listen to the advice of these experts.

 For **Dogs** and **Cats**

Give her a leash on life. A leash can literally be your deaf pet's lifeline, says Janis H. Audin, D.V.M., editor-in-chief of the *Journal of the American Veterinary Medical Association* in Schaumburg, Illinois. "Never let a deaf pet roam around outside. Always take her on a leash," she says. "They can't hear traffic or predators, and they can end up in real trouble."

Practice patience. Living with a deaf pet can be a challenge. They're often harder to train than other pets and may not play with you as much as you'd like. "You really need to be kind and patient," says Dr. Moore. "It will pay off. Realize that your deaf pet wants to make things normal as much as you do, so be willing to work gently to help her out."

Try a new language. Your pet can't hear your commands, but it's possible for her to *see* them. "Hand signals are very effective ways of communicating with a deaf dog," says Dr. Moore. Even cats that are deaf can benefit from a little signal training, vets say.

One important command that's easy to teach is "come." With your pet watching, beckon her to come to you by using several quick, big movements of your hand, the same way you'd signal a friend, suggests Howard Hollander, D.V.M., a veterinarian in private practice in Brooklyn. At the same time, crouch down or hold a treat in your free hand—whatever you think will entice your pet to come to you. Then reward her with lots of love and sometimes a treat, says Dr. Hollander. Again, patience is required. A few pets may respond in a day, but others will take weeks or even months to learn what the signals mean. To learn more about communicating with hand signals, talk to your vet or obedience trainer.

Lead her by the nose. Dogs and cats have powerful senses of smell. In many cases you can summon them by creating olfactory "waves"— waving fishy pet nibbles or a piece of dried liver through the air. Once your pet gets a whiff, she'll be at your side in a hurry, experts say.

Be on tap. To get your pet's attention when she's sleeping or not looking in your direction, walk in front of her and tap her gently, suggests Dr. Moore. "A deaf animal can't hear the normal cues that someone is approaching. You don't want to suddenly burst in with no warning and scare the animal," he says.

Bring out the bells and whistles. While your pet may have trouble hearing your voice, sharp sounds that are easily distinguishable from

When to See the Vet

Ear infections are fairly common and simple to treat. If they're ignored, however, the middle ear and eardrum may be damaged, leading to deafness, says Robert Cross, D.V.M., a veterinarian in private practice in Duncan, Oklahoma, and past president of the Oklahoma Veterinary Medical Association.

"Keeping your pet's ears clean and healthy is about the only way an owner can actually help prevent deafness," he says.

If you notice a foul odor coming from your pet's ears or she is often busy scratching and rubbing them, take her in for a checkup. In some cases your vet may recommend that you clean her ears daily or weekly to keep infections at bay, says Dr. Cross. "That's a small price to pay for keeping her hearing," he adds.

When cleaning your pet's ears, use only products recommended by your vet. Ear-care products that are safe for humans may be toxic to pets.

Sign Up for Sign Language

Juliette, a Dalmatian from Spokane, Washington, isn't your ordinary deaf dog: This pooch knows more than 20 words in American Sign Language, the language typically used by the human hearing-impaired.

"She picked it up so fast!" says Juliette's owner, Jody Eisenman, a homemaker who, along with the rest of her family, is conversant in American Sign Language.

Juliette's vocabulary now includes "I love you," "go car ride," "no," "sit," "play ball," "food" and "beautiful girl." "You can really communicate with her," marvels Eisenman. "She thrives on this. It's not as limited as ordinary hand signals."

What the Eisenmans did for Juliette, you might be able to do for your deaf pet. To try your hand at sign language, Eisenman suggests taking a class or referring to a sign language book to learn the words you'd like to communicate, or sign.

Juliette, for instance, knows it's chow time when a member of her family points at her, then cups a hand toward their body and moves it downward. Translation: "You hungry?"

"Teach only one sign at a time and teach it with love and patience," advises Eisenman. "If it eventually works, that's great. If not, you're no worse off than when you started," she says.

For pets that are hard of hearing, sign language helps them understand what's going on. A pet's favorite sign: "Food."

background noise may come in loud and clear, says Douglas J. Heacock, V.M.D., a veterinarian in private practice in Madison, New Jersey. He recommends whistling or ringing a bell to get her attention.

It's important, however, to start fairly quietly so your pet isn't startled by that initial explosion of sound. If she doesn't hear the noise at first, gradually make it louder. If she still doesn't flick an ear, quit trying and just give her a little nudge, says Dr. Heacock.

Give her a hand. "Quite a few partially deaf animals can still hear a good clap," says Dr. Heacock. Clap quietly at first so you don't startle her. If there's no response, clap more loudly. If your pet still doesn't respond, don't burst into applause to get her attention. "You'll know within a very few claps if you're being heard," says Dr. Heacock.

Give her good vibrations. If you're on one end of a room and your pet is on the other, stomp your foot. "The vibration through the floor can often make her look right in your direction," says Dr. Hollander.

Show her the lights. At night, flashing the lights can help get your pet's attention, says Dr. Moore. As soon as she looks up, give her the hand signal that tells her what you'd like her to do. Or walk over and gently lead her where you want her to go. Then reward her with love or a treat. "Eventually your dog may come to realize that when you flash the porch lights, it's time to come in," he says.

Get her a companion. Even if your deaf pet can't hear a stranger at the door, she can still get clues from watching a companion. "If the other dog runs to the door and starts barking, the deaf dog may well follow and do the same thing," says Dr. Heacock. "A deaf cat may watch her companion to see when it's time to eat or if someone is coming. These relationships can be invaluable."

Keep her informed. When leaving the house or going into another room, give your pet a little tap so she knows you're going, says Dr. Moore. "Otherwise when she wakes up or turns around and finds you're not there when she thought you were, it can be confusing. She can get quite anxious."

PANEL OF ADVISERS

Janis H. Audin, D.V.M., is editor-in-chief of the *Journal of the American Veterinary Medical Association* in Schaumburg, Illinois.

Robert Cross, D.V.M., is a veterinarian in private practice in Duncan, Oklahoma, and past president of the Oklahoma Veterinary Medical Association.

Jody Eisenman lives in Spokane, Washington, and owns Juliette, a deaf Dalmatian that has learned American Sign Language.

Douglas J. Heacock, V.M.D., is a veterinarian in private practice in Madison, New Jersey.

Howard Hollander, D.V.M., is a veterinarian in private practice in Brooklyn.

Michael Moore, D.V.M., is chief of small animal medicine at the Washington State University College of Veterinary Medicine in Pullman.

Dehydration

7 Ways to Wet Her Whistle

You wouldn't know it to look at her, but your pet is a veritable ocean of water. She needs all that fluid to keep her tissues moist and to transport ions, proteins and essential nutrients throughout her body.

In pets (and people), maintaining constant fluid levels is essential. That's why dehydration—in which fluids are depleted due to vomiting, diarrhea, overheating or not receiving enough to drink—is so dangerous, says Harold N. Engel, D.V.M., Ph.D., professor of veterinary anatomy at the Oregon State University College of Veterinary Medicine in Corvallis. Cats are less likely than dogs to get overheated and dehydrated, but their fluid levels can also fall too low, especially when they get sick.

Symptoms of dehydration include a dry mouth, sunken eyes, loss of elasticity in the skin and extreme exhaustion, says Dr. Engel. This condition always requires a veterinarian's care. (For more on dehydration and overheating, see Hot-Weather Concerns on page 215.) In addition, here are some valuable tips to help you prevent dehydration and keep your pet healthy and in the swim.

 For **Dogs** and **Cats**

Moisten her muzzle. While dogs and cats don't sweat much—they have only a few sweat glands between their toes—they can lose a lot of fluid through panting, says Dr. Engel. To make sure your pet always has enough to drink, it's a good idea to keep two water bowls filled at all times. That way she'll have water even if she kicks one of the bowls over.

But don't let her guzzle. If your pet has gone a long time without drinking, letting her gulp down an entire bowl of water all at once may result in vomiting—which can result in *less* fluids getting in, says Albert S. Dorn, D.V.M., professor of surgery at the University of Tennessee College of Veterinary Medicine in Knoxville.

Take the bowl away after she's had a few laps, he suggests. Wait a minute or two, then let her drink some more.

Electrolyte up her life. Dehydration can cause your pet to lose electrolytes, minerals like potassium and sodium that transmit electrical impulses throughout the body.

While giving plain water will replace most electrolytes, you can help your pet recover from lack of water even more quickly by giving her an electrolyte-enriched drink such as Pedialyte, says Raymond Deiter, V.M.D., a veterinarian in private practice in Sausalito, California, who specializes in acupuncture. You can buy electrolyte solutions at grocery stores and pharmacies.

Pour a sports drink. If your hot dog (or cat) seems reluctant to drink, try tempting her with an electrolyte-containing sports drink such as Gatorade, advises Ralph Womer, D.V.M., a veterinarian in private practice in Auburn, Alabama. "Some pets have a thing for sweet, fruity flavors, and they enjoy Gatorade," he says.

Let her lick ice. Pets that have gone a long time without water may have trouble keeping fluids down. A helpful alternative is to give her an ice cube, suggests David Hammond, D.V.M., a veterinarian in private practice in Pleasant Hill, Oregon, and veterinary affairs manager for Hill's Pet Nutrition. "As she licks it, she'll slowly hydrate her system," he says.

Check her mouth. Occasionally dogs or cats will stop drinking if

When to See the Vet

Hot dogs and thirsty cats generally don't need anything more than a little rest and a long drink of cool water to prevent dehydration. But when dehydration has already occurred, the body's systems may start to fail, says Harold N. Engel, D.V.M., Ph.D., professor of veterinary anatomy at the Oregon State University College of Veterinary Medicine in Corvallis.

Here's a test vets use for diagnosing dehydration: Gently lift the skin along your pet's back. Normally it will snap back into place when you let go. In dehydrated pets, however, the skin loses elasticity, causing it to stay up in a ridge.

If this occurs, it's an emergency. Get your pet to a vet right away, says Dr. Engel.

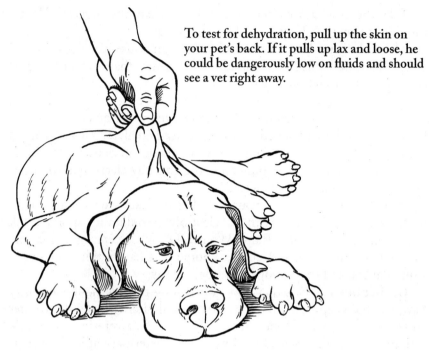

To test for dehydration, pull up the skin on your pet's back. If it pulls up lax and loose, he could be dangerously low on fluids and should see a vet right away.

they get something lodged inside the mouth, like a burr, says Dr. Dorn. If your pet isn't drinking, he recommends taking a careful look around. If you spy something in the mouth that shouldn't be there, try to get it out yourself or call your vet for advice.

Get water to go. To prevent dehydration from occurring, it's important to provide your pet with water even when you're out of the house, says Dr. Deiter. When he travels with his pets, for instance, he keeps a no-spill water bowl in the car. Pet stores also sell collapsible pet bowls that fit into a pants pocket as well as a variety of spillproof containers.

PANEL OF ADVISERS

Raymond Deiter, V.M.D., is a veterinarian in private practice in Sausalito, California, who specializes in acupuncture.

Albert S. Dorn, D.V.M., is professor of surgery at the University of Tennessee College of Veterinary Medicine in Knoxville.

Harold N. Engel, D.V.M., Ph.D., is professor of veterinary anatomy at the Oregon State University College of Veterinary Medicine in Corvallis.

David Hammond, D.V.M., is a veterinarian in private practice in Pleasant Hill, Oregon, and veterinary affairs manager for Hill's Pet Nutrition.

Ralph Womer, D.V.M., is a veterinarian in private practice in Auburn, Alabama.

Dental Problems

17 Ways to Lick Them

Your cat doesn't have to flash his pearly whites for family portraits. Your pooch doesn't do smoochy love scenes for romantic movies or get up close and personal with execs at business luncheons.

So why worry about his teeth?

"If you ignore your pet's teeth, they may go away, or worse," says Peter Emily, D.D.S., director of animal dentistry at the Colorado State University College of Veterinary Medicine and Biomedical Sciences in Fort Collins, president of the American Veterinary Dental Society and co-author of *The Manual of Veterinary Dentistry*. "You should care every bit as much about your pet's teeth as you do about your children's or your own. They're just as vulnerable," he adds.

Although dogs and cats rarely get cavities, more than 80 percent of pets three years and older have some degree of periodontal disease, Dr. Emily explains. Periodontal disease is an infection caused by plaque, a thin, bacteria-laden film that can form on teeth. Over time, periodontal disease can lead to erosion of gum tissue and bones supporting the teeth, causing teeth to loosen and fall out. In rare cases, bacteria can spread from the mouth throughout the body, possibly causing infection in major organs such as the kidneys or heart.

Once your pet has periodontal disease or other dental problems, he'll need to see a vet for treatment and possibly a thorough tooth cleaning. But with regular care, you can prevent problems from getting started. Here's what tooth experts recommend to help keep your pet smiling.

 For **Dogs** and **Cats**

Use mainly dry food. Feeding your pet dry kibble rather than canned food can help reduce plaque on teeth because it's slightly abrasive, says Steven Holmstrom, D.V.M., a veterinarian in private practice in Belmont, California, president of the American Veterinary Dental

When to See the Vet

While a toothbrush used regularly can help prevent many dental disorders, it's not a magic wand, says Peter Emily, D.D.S., director of animal dentistry at the Colorado State University College of Veterinary Medicine and Biomedical Sciences in Fort Collins and president of the American Veterinary Dental Society. While brushing your pet's teeth you should also watch out for problems that may need a veterinarian's care.

Red gums, for example, could indicate your pet has periodontal disease. Lumps or bumps could indicate an abscessed tooth or even a tumor. Other danger signs include inflamed or bleeding gums, foreign bodies you can't remove easily, tartar stains, damaged teeth, pimples around the mouth or a sudden onset of drooling or bad breath.

In addition, if your pet doesn't seem to be eating or is favoring one side of his mouth when he chews, it could be because he has a painful dental disorder.

Keep in mind that while virtually every vet can handle simple dental problems, you may need a specialist for more serious disorders. Some vets devote their careers to pet dentistry and can do everything from root canals to orthodontics.

College and author of *Veterinary Dental Techniques*.

Dogs are luckier than cats on this front because a food designed expressly to deal with doggy dental hygiene is now available by prescription. Called Hill's Prescription Diet Canine T/D, it is oversize kibble that doesn't crumble at the first bite. Instead it holds together until the teeth penetrate almost all the way through. This helps wipe the teeth clean as your dog is eating, says Dr. Holmstrom.

Bone up on biscuits. "If you're going to give your pet a treat, a good choice for his teeth is a crunchy pet biscuit," says Dr. Emily. The abrasive action of the biscuits will help keep his teeth well-scrubbed and clean.

But beware of bones. Your pet may adore gnawing on big bones from your favorite cut of meat, but they can be mighty tough on teeth, says Dr. Holmstrom. "If you don't want your pet's teeth to fracture, avoid really hard things like bones," he advises. And of course you'll want to stay away from bones that splinter, such as chicken bones.

Whip it with a windpipe. While cow or pig tracheas aren't likely to be on display in your supermarket (you can find them in some specialty shops), they make great dental aids, says Dr. Emily. While your pet chews, the tough fibers and cartilage massage his teeth and gums and help clean plaque from hard-to-reach places.

Dr. Emily recommends cutting the trachea into three-inch segments and boiling it. It should be cooked "as you'd cook a bone—maybe 5 to 15 minutes, depending on the size," he says. Then give it to your dog or cat as a treat. "They really enjoy it," says Dr. Emily.

Or use a tail to tame it. Oxtails are much easier to find at your grocer's than tracheas, and they provide the same plaque-busting, tooth-cleaning benefits, says Dr. Emily. Boil an oxtail for about five to ten minutes, let it cool and pass it on to your pet.

Reach for the rubber. Giving your pet a hard rubber toy with grooves is a great way to help keep his teeth white and clean, says Dr. Emily. As he chews, the rubber scrapes under the gum tissue, helping dislodge material that could lead to infection. To encourage him to chew, try filling the grooves with his favorite pet toothpaste, says Dr. Emily.

Pet stores stock a variety of rubber toys. Vets often recommend Kong brand, which are expressly designed for your pet's chewing satisfaction, says Dr. Emily.

Launch a plaque attack. The idea of brushing your pet's teeth daily can be a bit daunting at first, but it's the best thing you can do to help keep gum disease from getting started. Even if you decide to do it only two days a week, it can make a big difference.

Start off easy. Rather than lunging at your pet with toothbrush in hand, give him time to get used to the idea, suggests Anthony Shipp, D.V.M., a veterinarian in private practice in Beverly Hills, California, who specializes in dentistry and is co-author of *The Practitioner's Guide to Veterinary Dentistry*. Start off by handling his mouth for about a minute a day for a few days, he says. Talk gently to him while you stroke around his mouth. Then reward him with plenty of love or a treat. "Getting your dog or cat comfortable with having his mouth handled is half the battle," Dr. Shipp says.

Graduate to gauze. Once your pet is comfortable with having his mouth touched, it's time to move on to his teeth. But rather than beginning with a brush, it's easier to go in with gauze, says Dr. Shipp. (If you don't have gauze, a bit of nylon stocking will also work.)

Lift your pet's lip on one side and, with a little gauze wrapped around your finger, rub the outer surfaces of the upper and lower teeth.

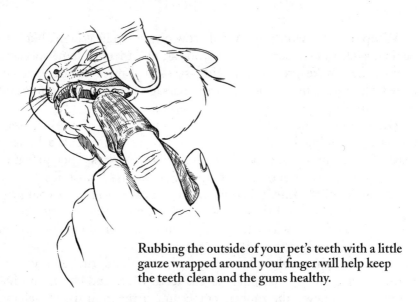

Rubbing the outside of your pet's teeth with a little gauze wrapped around your finger will help keep the teeth clean and the gums healthy.

Then switch to the other side. Try to keep the whole operation under a minute so your pet doesn't get antsy—and don't forget the reward. Doing this once a day for about a week will help your pet get used to having your fingers inside his mouth and will make it easier for you to move on to the next step: a toothbrush.

Bring out the brush. "A good brushing is vital to keeping plaque at bay," says Dr. Holmstrom. He recommends using a soft, child-size toothbrush or one designed specifically for dogs or cats. You can also buy brushes that fit over your index finger.

Hold the brush at a 45-degree angle to the teeth and with a gentle, circular motion, brush the outer surfaces of the teeth. Be sure to cover the entire tooth, especially the area where the base of the tooth meets the gum, says Dr. Holmstrom.

Use paste with taste. These days, pet toothpaste comes in so many lip-smacking flavors that few dogs and cats will turn up their noses at it. "Use whatever flavor you think your pet will like, based on what he likes to eat," says Wendy Beers, D.V.M., a veterinarian in private practice in Albany, California, who specializes in dentistry. Many pets like beef- and poultry-flavored pastes. Others prefer malt. For extra protection, however, your vet may recommend that you use a prescription, plaque-retardant paste instead.

But don't use toothpastes made for humans, since these usually contain detergents, she warns. Since dogs and cats are more likely to swallow than spit and rinse, human toothpaste can cause stomach upset.

Go for the garlic. If your pet doesn't seem to like any of the toothpaste flavors, try adding a bit of garlic powder to lukewarm water and use that to moisten the brush. "I think all dogs and cats must be part Italian, because they all seem to love garlic," says Dr. Emily.

Bring on the bouillon. If garlic water doesn't tickle his taste buds—or if you can't stand having a pet with garlic breath—try dipping the brush in chicken or beef broth. "Nothing beats the effectiveness of a good toothpaste, but at least these may help your pet accept a brushing," Dr. Emily says.

Do something fishy. Another favorite alternative to using toothpaste, especially among cats, is to moisten the toothbrush with water from a can of water-packed tuna, says Dr. Emily. Just beware: Your pet's mouth may not smell exactly minty-fresh afterward.

Make brushing a spectator sport. Your pet will be more likely to relax when you brush his teeth if he sees you brushing your own, says Dr. Beers. So leave the bathroom door open the next time you brush. Or, if you don't mind taking your brush to another room, sit in front of your pet's bed and brush your teeth there. "He may realize it's nothing that's going to hurt him if he watches you doing it to yourself," she says.

Plug in, plaque out. Fearless dogs and cats can benefit from the use of an electric toothbrush, says Dr. Emily. "The same ones that are good for people can be good for pets. Just remember, the quieter the better," he says.

Go to a pro. To keep your pet's teeth in tip-top shape, most vets recommend having them examined about once a year by your vet. "It's important to catch problems before they become serious," says Gary Beard, D.V.M., assistant dean at the Auburn University College of Veterinary Medicine in Alabama. Your vet may recommend that your pet have periodic professional cleanings as well.

PANEL OF ADVISERS

Gary Beard, D.V.M., is assistant dean at the Auburn University College of Veterinary Medicine in Alabama.

Wendy Beers, D.V.M., is a veterinarian in private practice in Albany, California, who specializes in dentistry.

Peter Emily, D.D.S., is director of animal dentistry at the Colorado State University College of Veterinary Medicine and Biomedical Sciences in Fort Collins, president of the American Veterinary Dental Society and co-author of *The Manual of Veterinary Dentistry.*

Steven Holmstrom, D.V.M., is a veterinarian in private practice in Belmont, California, president of the American Veterinary Dental College and author of *Veterinary Dental Techniques.*

Anthony Shipp, D.V.M., is a veterinarian in private practice in Beverly Hills, California, who specializes in dentistry and is co-author of *The Practitioner's Guide to Veterinary Dentistry.*

Depression

20 Blues Busters

No one greets you at the door. The rattle of the leash goes unnoticed. Even a steak bone fails to generate much excitement. If your pouty pet doesn't start showing some enthusiasm soon, you're going to change her name to Gloom and Doom.

It's not uncommon for pets to come down with the blues. Caused by such things as illness, loneliness, lack of exercise or even winter darkness, depression can make pets lethargic, mopey and sad, says Steve Lindsay, a trainer and owner of Canine Behavioral Services in Philadelphia.

Sudden changes in lifestyle can also cause emotional upheavals in pets, says Ian Dunbar, D.V.M., a veterinarian, trainer and animal behaviorist at the Center for Applied Animal Behavior in Berkeley, California. Dogs and cats may get depressed following the death of one of their friends, for example, or after moving to a new house. Cats can get depressed just from having the furniture rearranged.

To raise your pet's spirits, here's what experts recommend.

 For **Dogs** and **Cats**

Make every day play day. Throwing yourself into some wholehearted play with your pet is perhaps the best way to take her mind off her troubles. "Get on the floor and tickle her tummy and be silly," says Vicki L. White, an assistant trainer and behavior consultant at the Marin Humane Society in Novato, California. "Let your pet know it's okay to play."

Reflect some fun. Putting up a mirror where your pet can see her own reflection will give her a sense that she's not alone and help keep her from feeling lonely, Lindsay says.

Walk away her problems. Taking your pet for a vigorous romp does more than get her out of the house. Exercise also stimulates the release of endorphins, chemicals in the body that heighten good feelings.

Don't reward the moping. About the worst thing you can do when your pet is depressed is stroke, pamper or otherwise "reward" her for feeling bad, says Wayne Hunthausen, D.V.M., an animal behavior consultant in Westwood, Kansas, president of the American Veterinary Society of Animal Behavior and co-author of *Practitioner's Guide to Pet Behavior Problems*. "You'll probably make things worse," he says.

It's good to give her attention, but only if you stay upbeat and cheerful. If you're enthusiastic, there's a good chance your pet will be, too.

Make your friends exciting. It's common for pets to feel left out when someone new—like a boyfriend or another pet—enters the owner's life, says Elizabeth Marshall Thomas, an anthropologist in Peterborough, New Hampshire, and author of *The Hidden Life of Dogs* and *The Tribe of Tiger*. "We are our pets' loved ones, and they don't want to share our love with other pets or other people," she says.

To help your pet get used to new friends, Dr. Dunbar suggests this strategy: Ignore your pet, just a little bit, when the two of you are alone. Then turn on the attention when the new person (or pet) is around. Go for a walk. Have a play session on the floor. Or just give her an extra treat. Pretty soon your pet will associate the new person with good times and will be less likely to mope, Dr. Dunbar explains.

Prepare her for baby. Having a new baby in the family will often make pets jealous and depressed. To lighten the blow, "don't drop a bomb on them suddenly," says Pam Johnson, a feline behaviorist in

When to See the Vet

While depression in pets is usually nothing more than a short-term bout with the blues, it can also be a warning sign that something serious is wrong.

A dog or cat that's lethargic, not eating and generally moping about could have a physical problem, like thyroid disease, pancreatitis or even heartworms, says Andrea Fochios, D.V.M., a veterinarian in private practice in Ferndale, New York.

Even if the problem turns out to be behavioral or emotional, the symptoms of depression, such as not eating, can make your pet sick. Don't take chances. For dogs, call your vet if he's mopey and hasn't eaten in 48 hours. For cats, 36 hours is the maximum, Dr. Fochios says.

Nashville and author of *Twisted Whiskers: Solving Your Cat's Behavior Problems.*

"If you're pregnant, start wearing baby powder and baby lotion so the pet gets used to the smells," she suggests. "You can also play a tape of a baby crying so your pet gets used to the 'strange' sound."

Include her in the fun. "If you separate the new baby from the pet and don't pay any attention to your pet anymore, you'll probably end up with problems," says Petra Mertens, D.V.M., a veterinarian who practices at the Institute for Ethology and Animal Welfare in Munich, Germany.

Dog trainer Bardi McLennan, of Weston, Connecticut, author of *Dogs and Kids: Parenting Tips*, recommends putting a lattice-type gate across the door to the nursery. This will keep your pet outside while still allowing her to keep tabs on what's going on.

Take a little piece of home. Moving to a new house or apartment can be a depressing experience for dogs and cats. To make the transition less trying, prepare a special box or pet carrier. Line it with your pet's usual bedding and put in some of her favorite toys, Johnson suggests. With a "safe" place to retire to, she'll feel more secure and confident in her new abode, she explains.

Plant surprises. For pets, home is where the good smells (and treats) are. Some vets recommend "salting" the new place with exciting toys or tasty treats, which she'll discover on her own. Instead of being depressing, moving day will become an adventure day.

Don't forget to call home. Dogs and cats may feel lonely when you're gone all day. To perk up your pet, periodically call home and leave a message on the answering machine (with the volume turned up so she'll hear your voice).

Another way to give your pet company when you're gone is to tape-record your voice and let it play during the day. "Hearing your voice may do wonders," Johnson says.

Cheer her up with music. Dogs and cats often enjoy music and are less likely to feel depressed when something pleasant is playing. "Classical music—particularly gentle flutes and string instruments—could have a relaxing effect," says Michael W. Fox, B.V.M., Ph.D., vice-president of bioethics and farm animal protection for the Humane Society of the United States in Washington, D.C., and author of *The New Animal Doctor's Answer Book.*

Play it their way. Rather than playing human music for your pets, why not play some of their own? The record *Jingle Cats Meowy Christ-*

mas, which features cat sounds made into holiday carols, is a popular choice, says Kate Gamble, a feline behaviorist in private practice in San Francisco and consultant to the San Francisco Society for the Prevention of Cruelty to Animals.

Go to the movies. Another way to keep your pets perky is to play an animal video. A series of short videos includes a number of adventure "tails," featuring the likes of Betty Bird, Larry Lizard, Freddy Fish and Krazy Kats.

You can turn on the video when you leave the house in the morning or set a timer so it comes on later in the day.

Give time to mourn. It's not uncommon when a pet dies or runs away for her friends to suffer deep depression. "Pets demonstrate a deep love for each other, just as people do," says Dr. Fox. There's no instant cure for grief, but giving your pet plenty of love will help him get through the difficult time, he says.

Give her a new friend. While it's not always possible to "replace" a pet, many cats and dogs will feel better when they have another furry companion to play with, says Andrea Fochios, D.V.M., a veterinarian in private practice in Ferndale, New York.

 For **Dogs** Only

Try a new setting. Rather than taking the same old walk on the same old street or in the same old park, try taking your mopey pet someplace new, suggests John C. Wright, Ph.D., a certified animal behaviorist, professor of psychology at Mercer University in Macon, Georgia, and a member of the adjunct faculty at the University of Georgia School of Veterinary Medicine in Atlanta. The new smells, sights and sounds will go a long way toward raising his spirits, he says.

Consider drop-in care. Dogs are extremely social animals, and being home alone all day can make them sad and lonely. Try having a neighbor or professional pet sitter come in once a day. "They can make a dog's day," Lindsay says.

Throw a party. Dogs love excitement as much as people do, and it's hard for them to stay depressed when all their friends show up. Warren Eckstein, in his book *How to Get Your Dog to Do What You Want*, recommends filling the house with his four-legged friends. He suggests throwing several parties for your dog and inviting some of his canine comrades over.

 For Cats Only

Give a room with a view. Without a lot of stimulation, many cats get bored and depressed. To help keep your feline friend entertained, make sure she has a windowsill or cat perch. Watching birds, butterflies or even people going by will often help keep her spirits high.

Attract a show. To get even more entertainment value from your windows, install a birdhouse or feeder outside. Many cats will watch the ongoing "show" for hours at time.

Destructive Behavior

17 House-Saving Strategies

They knock things over, tear things up and go where they're not supposed to go. And no matter how many toys you scatter around the house, they always seem to sink teeth or claws into your favorite furniture instead.

If you've ever had a puppy or kitten, you already know how destructive young animals can be. But sometimes even grown pets start misbehaving, at least on occasion. What gets into them?

"The vast majority of behavior problems that you have with dogs and cats are normal behavior patterns, but inappropriate for the setting in which they're occurring," says Daniel Q. Estep, Ph.D., a certified applied animal behaviorist in private practice in Littleton, Colorado.

In other words, it's normal for a cat to scratch and a dog to chew— but inappropriate when the object of their affection happens to be your new $1,000 sofa.

But most pets are quick learners, and with common sense and a few simple training tips, you can help channel their energies in less destructive directions.

 For **Dogs** and **Cats**

Give them plenty of toys. While puppies literally need things to chew on to help ease the pain of teething, older pets can use some amusement, too—particularly when you're not around to play. Dogs are fond of chew toys, while cats are partial to catnip mice and other things they can bat around. Just don't forget to praise them when they do take an interest in "approved" toys.

But don't give them *your* toys. "If you teach your dog to play tug with a tennis shoe, how is he going to distinguish that from all other tennis shoes?" says Karen Overall, V.M.D., Ph.D., a lecturer specializing in behavioral medicine in the Department of Clinical Studies at the University of Pennsylvania School of Veterinary Medicine in Philadelphia.

Stop them fast. Letting your pet wreak havoc on your possessions even once can result in a lifetime of problems, vets say. So the first time you catch your pet chewing something he shouldn't, say "No!" Then replace the object with an appropriate toy.

Move it or lose it. Like kids, even the best-behaved pets will occasionally get into mischief—not to mention the trash, houseplants or your best shoes.

"The easiest way to prevent this behavior is to remove the object so they don't get into it," says Bonnie V. Beaver, D.V.M., professor and chief of medicine in the Department of Small Animal Medicine at the Texas A&M University School of Veterinary Medicine in College Station and author of *Feline Behavior: A Guide for Veterinarians.* "You may want to leave the wastepaper basket out in the bathroom, but you can't reason with these guys, so you simply have to move it."

Raise the alarm. If your pets sneak onto the furniture the minute you're gone, maybe it's time to give them the "off" signal—in the form of a motion-sensing alarm. "Many dogs are sensitive to noise and will run away," says Debra Horwitz, D.V.M., a veterinarian and animal behavior consultant in private practice in St. Louis.

Motion-sensing alarms are often effective for cats, although some felines won't realize *they're* the ones causing the ruckus. They'll simply look around and wonder what's up, Dr. Horwitz says.

Motion-detecting alarms are available from hardware or building supply stores.

Give him a charge. As an alternative to noise alarms, your vet may recommend that you try a device that delivers a slight electrical jolt when your pet goes where he shouldn't. While the devices can be effective, be sure to choose one that's designed specifically for a pet the size of yours, Dr. Horwitz says. The alarms are available at some pet stores and from pet supply companies, such as Doctors Foster and Smith (for a catalog, write to 2253 Air Park Road, P.O. Box 100, Hollander, WI 54501, or call 1-800-562-7169).

Give him a room of his own. Keeping your pet confined—either by shutting him in a certain room or by putting him in a cage or crate—is an easy way to curb his destructive instincts when you're gone. "Pets can injure themselves by chewing on cords or getting into household poisons," says Dr. Horwitz. "Crates protect property and protect the pet. They can also help with house-training," she adds.

Punish him promptly—or not at all. "Unless you reward or punish in a very short amount of time—and we're talking seconds here—an animal is not going to associate the reward or punishment with what they're doing," Dr. Horwitz points out. If you do catch him wreaking havoc, give him a firm "No!" Eventually he'll take the hint.

 For **Dogs** Only

Add a little flavor. You want to make sure your pooch likes his chew toys better than, say, your new Italian loafers. "The way to do that is to enhance them," says Dr. Horwitz. "Dogs like the taste of oil, garlic salt, meat and cheese."

She recommends spraying cloth toys with cooking oil and maybe sprinkling on a little garlic salt as well. "There are also some types of chew toys that are hollow," she adds. "You can put a little peanut butter or cheese spread inside to entice the dog."

Leave him good memories. Since your dog probably does his most dastardly deeds when he's alone (and lonely), try to get him calmed down before you even leave the house. Rub his belly for a while. Or make him sit or lie down and then reward him with a treat, suggests Dr. Overall.

"Once your dog is giving you that happy RCA Victor look, you can bring your briefcase in," she suggests. If he starts looking nervous, take a few minutes to get him calmed down again. Then leave the house. Hopefully he'll be feeling secure and calm enough that he won't work out his frustrations on your furnishings.

"All of this requires some forethought and may require you to get up a half-hour earlier, but it will sometimes work," she says.

Have Rover come over. If your dog is often destructive when you're away, maybe he'd like some company. You don't necessarily have to get another dog, says Dr. Estep. An easier solution might be to find a neighbor who also leaves her pet alone during the day and then get the two together.

"Have Rover come over and stay with your dog some days, and have your dog stay with Rover some days," Dr. Estep suggests.

If this isn't practical, look in the phone book for a pet-sitting service or day care center or check with your veterinarian or pet store for referrals. Another alternative is to pay a small fee to a responsible neighborhood child who will walk and play with your dog after school.

For Cats Only

Get a post to please them. It's a common misunderstanding that cats scratch furniture to sharpen their claws. They're really doing it to mark their territory. (They have scent glands in their paws that leave a distinctive "mark.")

"They want to shred and tear," says Dr. Horwitz. "They want something like sisal or burlap that is going to rip and tear."

To make the post particularly appealing, try putting catnip or oil from canned tuna on it, Dr. Horwitz adds, or hang a little toy from the top.

Put it in the right place. Since cats scratch to mark their territory, you have to put the post in a place that's important to them.

"If you bring the marking post and put it in the living room near the object the cat has been scratching, you'll be more successful in getting him to use it," says Dr. Horwitz. "Once he starts using it, you may be able to gradually move it to a less conspicuous place."

Put out the "Not Welcome" mat. "While you're training your cats to use the scratching post, cover up the area where he's been scratching with another surface that doesn't feel as good," like plastic or aluminum foil, suggests Dr. Estep.

"You can also use duct tape," adds Dr. Horwitz. "Fold it into a circle

Don't throw away a scratching post when it starts getting tatty. It's obviously being well-used—and appreciated.

and put it on the spot where he scratches. Usually it doesn't harm the furniture, and the cat is not going to want to get all sticky."

Begin a bonus plan. "If your cats look at the scratching post, give them a small reward like a food treat," suggests Wayne Hunthausen, D.V.M., a behavior consultant in Westwood, Kansas, president of the American Veterinary Society of Animal Behavior and co-author of *Practitioner's Guide to Pet Behavior Problems.* "If they touch it, give them a bigger reward. And if they use it, give them a huge reward, something they really love."

Lay on the tough love. If your cat persists in exercising his feet on the furniture, try giving him a blast with a squirt bottle or water pistol, suggests Dr. Hunthausen. Or shake a can filled with coins—the noise may drive him off.

Put on protection. If nothing else works, your vet may recommend you try a product called Soft Paws—rubber or plastic caps that you glue on your cat's sharp little claws. "They last eight weeks before they have to be replaced," says Dr. Estep. While they don't stop your cat from scratching, they do help eliminate the damage.

PANEL OF ADVISERS

Bonnie V. Beaver, D.V.M., is professor and chief of medicine in the Department of Small Animal Medicine and Surgery at the Texas A&M University School of Veterinary Medicine in College Station and author of *Feline Behavior: A Guide for Veterinarians.*

Daniel Q. Estep, Ph.D., is a certified applied animal behaviorist in private practice in Littleton, Colorado.

Debra Horwitz, D.V.M., is a veterinarian and animal behavior consultant in private practice in St. Louis.

Wayne Hunthausen, D.V.M., is an animal behavior consultant in Westwood, Kansas, president of the American Veterinary Society of Animal Behavior and co-author of *Practitioner's Guide to Pet Behavior Problems.*

Karen Overall, V.M.D., Ph.D., is a lecturer specializing in behavioral medicine in the Department of Clinical Studies at the University of Pennsylvania School of Veterinary Medicine in Philadelphia.

Diabetes

7 Helpful Hints

Like people, pets produce a hormone called insulin that enables the cells to take up the blood sugar (glucose) they use for fuel. Animals with diabetes, however, either don't produce enough insulin, or the insulin they do make doesn't work efficiently. In either case they don't get all the fuel they need to run at full steam.

In dogs, diabetes may be caused by diseases that affect the pancreas; they usually need injections of synthetic insulin to correct the condition. In cats, however, diabetes is often caused by being overweight. They can often beat the disease by making "lifestyle" changes, like dropping a few pounds, says endocrinologist Deborah S. Greco, D.V.M., Ph.D., assistant professor of small animal medicine in the Department of Clinical Sciences at the Colorado State University College of Veterinary Medicine and Biomedical Sciences in Fort Collins.

While diabetes always requires a veterinarian's care, there are things you can do at home to help keep it under control.

 For **Dogs** and **Cats**

Keep her trim. Being overweight can make diabetes much more difficult to control, says Lee R. Harris, D.V.M., a veterinarian in private practice in Federal Way, Washington. "We see these 16-pound cats that are producing insulin, but not enough."

To keep your pet at a healthy weight, he recommends measuring her food to make sure you're not giving too much. You should also hold back the table scraps, which can pile on the pounds.

Switch to a high-fiber diet. Giving your pet high-fiber foods can help stabilize the rate at which fuels enter the cells, keeping blood sugar levels more constant.

"You can buy a brand such as Hill's Prescription Diet W/D or Fit and Trim from Purina," says Lisardo J. Martinez, D.V.M., a veterinarian in private practice in Miami. "It helps the carbohydrates in food be absorbed more slowly."

Feed her smaller meals. Rather than giving your pet one big meal a day, you may want to feed her several smaller ones to even out the rate at which sugars enter the bloodstream. Give dogs two meals a day and cats four small meals, suggests Dr. Martinez. "The important thing is to have a feeding routine that you stick to," he adds.

Keep those paws moving. "Exercise is important because it helps control weight," says Dr. Martinez. In addition, the more your pet exercises, the less insulin her body requires, explains Dr. Greco.

Ask your vet how much exercise your pet should be getting every day, then try to stick with it. "Don't jog a mile one day and not do it the next, because every change in exercise will affect the insulin requirement," says Dr. Martinez.

Give medications regularly. Perhaps the most important aspect of treating diabetes is to prevent blood sugar levels from swinging wildly from high to low. That's why vets recommend giving medications at the same times every day.

"Most dogs are on twice-daily insulin injections," says Dr. Greco. "Once a day is not ideal for managing blood sugar." Cats should also

When to See the Vet

Diabetes can be hard to spot. The disease comes on so gradually that it may be months before you notice symptoms—like weight loss or weakness—and by then it could be well advanced.

Diabetes is often accompanied by three classic signs: drinking a lot, eating a lot and urinating a lot. In addition, some pets with diabetes will develop sweet breath—a sign that blood sugar levels have risen too high, says endocrinologist Deborah S. Greco, D.V.M., Ph.D., assistant professor of small animal medicine in the Department of Clinical Sciences at the Colorado State University College of Veterinary Medicine and Biomedical Sciences in Fort Collins.

If you notice any of these symptoms—or if your pet is shaking, seems weak or tired or is steadily losing weight—get her to a vet right away.

be given their medications at the same times twice a day. Don't make any changes in your pet's medication without first checking with your veterinarian.

Reward her for good behavior. No one enjoys getting shots, your pets included. To make the experience as comfortable as possible, be extremely patient and gentle. Then reward her with plenty of love and perhaps a small treat when you're done.

"Some animals actually come and nudge their owners when it's time for their shot," Dr. Martinez says.

Keep a sweet handy. Giving a pet insulin will sometimes cause her blood sugar to plunge too low, a condition vets call hypoglycemia. "Always be sure, if you have a diabetic pet, that you have a source of sugar readily available," says Dr. Martinez.

He recommends always keeping a small container of honey or Karo syrup on hand. "Take some Karo syrup or honey and rub it on the gums until the animal stops shaking," says Dr. Martinez.

Then head for the vet. Hypoglycemia is an emergency, and your pet may need intravenous glucose to make a sure recovery.

PANEL OF ADVISERS

Deborah S. Greco, D.V.M., Ph.D., is an endocrinologist and assistant professor of small animal medicine in the Department of Clinical Sciences at the Colorado State University College of Veterinary Medicine and Biomedical Sciences in Fort Collins.

Lee R. Harris, D.V.M., is a veterinarian in private practice in Federal Way, Washington.

Lisardo J. Martinez, D.V.M., is a veterinarian in private practice in Miami.

Diarrhea

9 Tips to Slow the Flow

Does diarrhea have your doggy down in the dumps? Is your feline dashing to the litter box—and not always making it in time? Your poor pet may not bellyache about it, but having the runs can be a real pain in the gut.

Diarrhea in pets often occurs because they've gobbled something rank, like garbage or rotten things outside. An intestinal virus or sudden change in their usual diet can also lead to watery woes. But while diarrhea isn't much fun, "it's actually a wonderful defense mechanism," says James H. Sokolowski, D.V.M., veterinary communications manager for Waltham USA in Vernon, California. "It helps speed bad things out of the system."

What's good for your pet, however, isn't necessarily good for the carpets. So here are a few easy ways to help speed her recovery.

 **For Dogs and Cats**

Don't let her eat and run. "Quit putting stuff in your pet, and stuff will stop coming out," says Clayton MacKay, D.V.M., director of the veterinary teaching hospital at Ontario Veterinary College at the University of Guelph in Canada and president of the American Animal Hospital Association.

He recommends not feeding your pet for 24 hours after the onset of diarrhea. If she still isn't better even after a day of no food, there could be something seriously wrong, and you should call your vet, he advises.

Try your hand at bland. When your pet is ready to eat again, keep her digestive system calm by giving her cooked white rice mixed with boiled hamburger or skinless white meat chicken. Vets recommend mixing two parts rice to one part meat and feeding your pet small amounts every four hours for two days.

When to See the Vet

Although diarrhea is usually nothing worse than a bad restaurant review—proof that your ravenous beast made a three-course meal of something she shouldn't have—it can also indicate more serious problems like diabetes, distemper or pancreatitis, says Fred Oehme, D.V.M., Ph.D., professor of toxicology, medicine and physiology at the Kansas State University College of Veterinary Medicine in Manhattan, Kansas.

So if your furry friend has severe diarrhea for more than 24 hours, or if the diarrhea is accompanied by fever, vomiting, abdominal pain or excessive thirst, take her to the vet right away.

"Even with these symptoms, the diarrhea could be something minor, but on the chance that it's a sign of a bigger problem, it's important to know right away," says Dr. Oehme.

If your cat doesn't care for rice (and many don't), you can try substituting pasta or mashed potatoes, says Gale Bowman, D.V.M., a veterinarian in private practice in Raleigh, North Carolina.

Then blend the bland. After two days you can begin switching your pet back to her regular diet. Rather than changing foods all at once, which could thrust her insides back into overdrive, try substituting the bland diet for about a fourth of her regular food once a day for four days.

Firm it with fiber. If your pet's stools are still a little soft—either after or during the bland diet phase—try adding a little Metamucil to her food, suggests Martin J. Fettman, D.V.M., Ph.D., professor of pathology and clinical nutrition at the Colorado State University College of Veterinary Medicine and Biomedical Sciences in Fort Collins. Fiber helps draw water out of the stool, and its fermenting action in the colon will help bring things back to normal, he explains.

Depending on your pet's size, he recommends giving between $1\frac{1}{4}$ teaspoon and 1 tablespoon of Metamucil a day for one or two days. Just mix it with water and pour it on her food. "I know it sounds strange to fight diarrhea with fiber, but sometimes it works very well," he says.

Keep her liquid levels high. Since diarrhea can rapidly deplete the body of essential fluids, be sure to keep her water bowl full. It's also a good idea to fill a separate bowl with Gatorade, suggests Ralph Womer, D.V.M., a veterinarian in private practice in Auburn, Alabama. Like other sports drinks, Gatorade will help replenish minerals the body needs, like potassium and sodium. "The original flavor was good, but dogs and cats seem to like the fruit punch flavor better," he says.

Cut out the dairy. Most adult dogs and cats have difficulty digesting milk because they lack the enzyme (lactase) needed to digest a sugar (lactose) in milk, says Kathryn Michel, D.V.M., a researcher and nutrition expert in the Department of Clinical Studies at the University of Pennsylvania School of Veterinary Medicine in Philadelphia. "If you're giving your pet milk and she has diarrhea, cut the milk and you should see some real improvement in a few days," she says.

Outwalk the runs. Taking a 15-minute walk twice a day will help stimulate a part of the nervous system that is responsible for keeping the gut calm, says Dr. Bowman. "It can have a very good effect on diarrhea," he says. It's important, however, to walk your pet only if she seems to have the energy for it. "If she lags or is shaky or doesn't even want to get up, let her be," Dr. Bowman advises.

Suppress the stress. Visiting the vet, moving or having a new pet at home are just a few of the things that can upset your pet. To prevent emotional upheavals from getting the upper hand, "Talk to her gently, reassure her and spend extra time with her," says Dr. Bowman.

Say no to drugs. While there are a number of over-the-counter medications that can help ease the runs, many vets feel it's best to let the illness run its course. "There's a reason your pet has diarrhea," says Dr. Bowman. "Forget about rushing for anything that will keep the stool in unless your vet thinks it's a good idea," she says.

PANEL OF ADVISERS

Gale Bowman, D.V.M., is a veterinarian in private practice in Raleigh, North Carolina.

Martin J. Fettman, D.V.M., Ph.D., is professor of pathology and clinical nutrition at the Colorado State University College of Veterinary Medicine and Biomedical Sciences in Fort Collins.

Clayton MacKay, D.V.M., is director of the veterinary teaching hospital at Ontario Veterinary College at the University of Guelph in Canada and president of the American Animal Hospital Association.

Kathryn Michel, D.V.M., is a researcher and nutrition expert in the Department of Clinical Studies at the University of Pennsylvania School of Veterinary Medicine in Philadelphia.

Fred Oehme, D.V.M., Ph.D., is professor of toxicology, medicine and physiology at the Kansas State University College of Veterinary Medicine in Manhattan, Kansas.

James H. Sokolowski, D.V.M., is veterinary communications manager for Waltham USA in Vernon, California.

Ralph Womer, D.V.M., is a veterinarian in private practice in Auburn, Alabama.

Digging

13 Ways to End Excavations

Your dog digs ditches—but you want him to ditch digging. You dig your cat—but she digs your houseplants.

If life with your pets seems like a regular hole-y war sometimes, you're not alone. Cats will often dig in off-limits places when the litter box just won't do. For dogs, "it's a very natural, highly enjoyable behavior," says Debra L. Forthman, Ph.D., a certified applied animal behaviorist at Zoo Atlanta in Georgia.

If you think your pet's digging is the pits, try these tips.

 For **Dogs** Only

Make his paws pooped. "A well-exercised dog is much less likely to dig because he's already used up all that energy," says Dr. Forthman. She recommends taking your pooch for at least one good half-hour walk every day. "Do whatever exercise he enjoys doing," she adds. "You could see a marked difference in the digging."

Play it cool. If your dog digs overtime during the warm months, he might be looking for a cool place to rest, says Patricia McConnell, Ph.D., a certified applied animal behaviorist and adjunct assistant professor in the Department of Zoology at the University of Wisconsin in Madison. "The earth is a great insulator," she says. "Many dogs seem to know this instinctively, and they'll dig a nice cool hole to lie in."

As soon as the hole warms up, of course, your dog will often get the urge to dig deeper—or to start another hole. "It can become a real mess," says Dr. McConnell.

To keep your yard from looking like a minefield, make sure your hot-diggety dog has plenty of water and can cool off inside when it's hot out. When he's outside, let him have access to a spot that's cool, shaded and damp, such as beneath the porch or under a large, leafy tree.

Try a warmer approach. Just as your dog digs to keep cool in summer, he may use the same strategy to stay warm in winter. "The insulative qualities of the earth work both ways," says Dr. McConnell. Make sure your dog can come inside when it's cold. If he's not allowed in the house, provide him with a sheltered place outside where he can be warm and cozy.

Garden alone. When your dog sees you digging away in the garden, he may say to himself, "What fun!" and return later to try it on his own, says Dr. McConnell. "Some dogs do copy when their owners dig," she says. So you may want to leave your pet inside when you're doing your own digging outside.

Stop the offense with a fence. "We tend to forget the obvious, but a fence can do a fine job of keeping your dog from sensitive areas in your garden or yard," says Chip Golden, owner of Golden Canine dog training in Columbus, Ohio. Just make sure the fence is tall enough so your dog can't easily scale it in pursuit of a good dig. Chicken wire on strong support posts is relatively inexpensive and can be quite effective.

If your dog is digging in order to get out of his yard or pen, you may need an escape-proof fence, says Dr. Forthman. Some experts recommend erecting a fence that extends several feet into the ground. Ask your vet which options might work best for you.

Diminish his drive. Your dog may not feel the urge to tunnel out if he doesn't feel the urge to mate, says Suzanne Hetts, Ph.D., a certified applied animal behavior consultant in Littleton, Colorado. "Neutering or spaying your dog may be all you need to prevent escape digging," she says.

Stage a coverup. Spreading canvas or another kind of heavy cloth and weighing it down with bricks is an easy way to stop your dog from digging where he shouldn't, says Dr. Hetts. Or you can lay chain-link fencing flat on top of his digging ground. "What you want to do is interfere with the habit," says Dr. Hetts. Once your dog has forgotten the joys of digging, you may be able to safely remove the coverings.

Create a work stoppage. The next time you spot your four-legged backhoe excavating the backyard, tell him "No!" in a loud, sharp voice. "If that doesn't stop him, clap your hands loudly, blow an air horn or make some noise to startle him," says Dr. Hetts. Giving a headstrong pooch a spritz from a spray bottle can work, too.

Give him a distraction. Once your dog obeys your command to stop digging, praise him immediately. Then get him involved with another activity, like fetching a ball or chewing a favorite toy, says Dr. Hetts. "This will teach him that there's something that's interesting to do other than digging," she says.

Giving your dog his own "dig zone" will
help keep the rest of the yard intact.

Give him a hole to call his own. Experts admit there are some dogs
that love digging so much they just won't quit. "In these cases it's best
to provide an outlet for the digging or it will be a constant battle," says
Dr. McConnell.

She recommends giving the dig-meister his own digging pit—a
comfortable, shaded area about three feet wide, six feet long and two
feet deep. While your pooch is watching, loosen up the soil—you can
even add sand if the dirt is excessively hard—and bury a few of his toys
an inch or two down. Then encourage him to dig.

"You may have to get down on your hands and knees and paw at the
dirt yourself; your neighbors may think you're crazy, but that's okay,"
says Dr. McConnell. Once your dog joins you, tell him "Dig, dig, dig,
dig!" Then bury his toys a little deeper and encourage him to dig some
more. Eventually, all you'll have to say is "Dig!" and he'll run to his pit
for a happy dirt-fest.

 For Cats Only

Tidy his toilet. If you haven't cleaned the litter box lately, your cat
may dig up a few plants while looking for a cleaner place to go, says Dr.

Forthman. Experts recommend cleaning the litter box once a day and changing the litter at least once a week. In addition, adding a little baking soda to the litter will help absorb odors your cat may find offensive.

Provide plenty of rest stops. "When a cat is desperate and its litter box isn't near, a nearby plant will often do—the cat will dig it to pieces," says Dr. Forthman. Vets recommend putting at least one litter box on each floor of the house; plan on having at least one litter box per cat. "That way it's easy for the cat to find a box whenever he needs to go," Dr. Forthman says.

Switch litters. If your cat's kitty litter resembles potting soil, confusion—and unwanted digging—may result. Dr. Forthman recommends choosing a litter that's easily distinguished from plant soil.

PANEL OF ADVISERS

Debra L. Forthman, Ph.D., is a certified applied animal behaviorist at Zoo Atlanta in Georgia.

Chip Golden is owner of Golden Canine dog training in Columbus, Ohio.

Suzanne Hetts, Ph.D., is a certified applied animal behavior consultant in Littleton, Colorado.

Patricia McConnell, Ph.D., is a certified applied animal behaviorist and adjunct assistant professor in the Department of Zoology at the University of Wisconsin in Madison.

Drooling

6 Ways to Deal with the Deluge

Pavlov's dog had nothing on your pet. In fact, had the famous Russian physiologist—who learned to make dogs slobber at the ring of a bell—seen the way your pet salivates, he probably would have hired him on the spot.

While breeds like basset hounds and Saint Bernards are notorious droolers—largely because of the excessive skin around their mouths—many dogs simply drool as part of their repertoire. "Some are so bad you want to fit them with a spit cup," says Gary Beard, D.V.M., assistant dean at the College of Veterinary Medicine at Auburn University in Alabama. "They can probably drool a cup or more an hour when they're worked up." Nausea is another common cause of drooling, vets say.

Cats, on the other hand, rarely drool, and even most breeds of dogs drool only sparingly. But sometimes the mouths of even the most refined pets wax a wee bit on the wet side. Try these tips from the experts to help slow the flow.

 For Dogs and Cats

Do a mouth check. If your pet is suddenly drooling more than usual, it could be because he has a foreign object lodged in his mouth. Slivers of plastic or wood are frequent causes of drippy mouths, says Dr. Beard. "Foreign material stimulates the salivary glands and can make a dog or cat quite drippy," he says. "You may be surprised at what you find."

If you do find an object in the mouth and can't readily remove it yourself, take your pet to the vet, he adds.

Table the scraps. Those rich leftovers may suit your palate, but they can have messy and uncomfortable effects on your pet. "Drooling is one of the first signs of dietary distress," warns Dr. Beard. "Watch what you feed your pet if you don't want a drooling or sick animal."

Travel in comfort. Even pets that are normally dry about the mouth can get somewhat drippy and queasy when riding in a car or boat. To prevent this, vets recommend feeding your pet nothing or very little for a few hours before traveling. (Giving them water is okay.) Once you're under way, opening a window or letting your pet ride up front can help, says Dr. Beard. Taking frequent rest stops will also help keep his tummy calm.

 For **Dogs** Only

Practice damage control. If your dog is a natural drooler whose fur frequently gets a little damp, tying a bandanna around his neck will help protect him, says Steven Holmstrom, D.V.M., a veterinarian in private practice in Belmont, California, president of the American Veterinary Dental College and author of *Veterinary Dental Techniques*.

To make a bandanna bib, fold a bandanna in half and tie it so the triangular side covers your dog's chest. "Bandannas are like fashionable

When to See the Vet

Your pooch has always been a dry pet, but lately he's been dribbling so much that if the NBA doesn't draft him, the drought-busters will.

Since the causes of sudden drooling can range from a chipped tooth to poisoning, it's a good idea to call your vet right away, says Peter Emily, D.D.S., director of animal dentistry at the Colorado State University College of Veterinary Medicine and Biomedical Sciences in Fort Collins and president of the American Veterinary Dental Society.

Dental problems are the most common cause of drooling in pets that don't normally salivate heavily, adds Gary Beard, D.V.M., assistant dean at the Auburn University College of Veterinary Medicine in Alabama. "The cause could be a gum infection, a loose tooth or anything that causes pain in the mouth," he says.

More serious is the risk of poisoning—from household chemicals, for example—of which drooling may be the first symptom. Drooling also may be caused by rabies or other diseases. So if your pet is suddenly drooling and not acting like his usual self, call your vet immediately, Dr. Beard advises.

Tying a bandanna around your dog's neck will help keep his coat—and his immediate surroundings—somewhat drier.

bibs," he says. "A lot of show dogs wear them before they show."

Wipe his jowl with a towel. Even dogs that usually drool just a little can get uncommonly wet when they're in high spirits and running around. To keep your pet (and those he comes in contact with) slobber-free, use a paper or terrycloth towel to wipe his mouth .

In addition, if your pooch has been excitedly slobbering over another dog's head, good doggy etiquette demands that you wipe off *both* dogs, says Charles A. Williams, D.V.M., a veterinarian in private practice in Vienna, Virginia, who specializes in dentistry. "Friends will appreciate it if you take a towel along when you go to the park," he says.

Put placemats in his place. The mere idea of food can make even the driest dog a veritable Niagara of enthusiastic anticipation. To keep your floors dry, Dr. Beard recommends rolling out the placemats when mealtime rolls around. "A large placemat under your dog's bowl can help keep the place dry," he says.

PANEL OF ADVISERS

Gary Beard, D.V.M., is assistant dean at the Auburn University College of Veterinary Medicine in Alabama.

Peter Emily, D.D.S., is director of animal dentistry at the Colorado State University College of Veterinary Medicine and Biomedical Sciences in Fort Collins, president of the American Veterinary Dental Society and co-author of *The Manual of Veterinary Dentistry.*

Steven Holmstrom, D.V.M., is a veterinarian in private practice in Belmont, California, president of the American Veterinary Dental College and author of *Veterinary Dental Techniques.*

Charles A. Williams, D.V.M., is a veterinarian in private practice in Vienna, Virginia, who specializes in dentistry.

Dung Eating

13 Appetite Suppressants

You always knew your pooch was voracious, but how did he sink so low? Breakfast from the cat box? Oh, no!

No one's sure why, but many dogs develop a habit so distasteful that vets politely refer to it by its Greek name, *coprophagia*. In English it means "dung eating," and once a dog gets started, it can be difficult to make him stop.

Vets speculate that some dogs start eating wastes—either their own or those of other animals—out of boredom, or because they're seeking nutrients not found in their diets. Others may simply like the taste, says Katherine Houpt, V.M.D., Ph.D., professor of physiology and director of the Animal Behavior Clinic at the Cornell University College of Veterinary Medicine in Ithaca, New York.

Cats don't indulge, presumably because they're more refined than their canine counterparts.

"Most dogs do it occasionally," adds Carol McConnell, D.V.M., a veterinarian in private practice in Wilmington, Delaware. "It's very common."

While eating dung rarely causes health problems, it doesn't exactly make your pooch a joy to be around. Here's what vets recommend to change his tastes.

 For Dogs Only

Supplement his diet. Some vets speculate that dung eating may occur when dogs are lacking certain vitamins or minerals in their diets. Adding a multivitamin to his food will help ensure that he's getting all the necessary nutrients, says Dr. Houpt.

Remove temptation. When your pooch is looking for a ready snack, the cat's litter box on the floor might as well have a big sign saying "*Bon appetit.*" Try putting the box in a location that's easy for the cat to get to but out of your dog's reach, such as behind a cabinet, advises Dr. Houpt.

When to See the Vet

While dung eating is usually more of an unpleasant habit than a genuine health threat, sometimes it's a sign of trouble.

In cats, for example, eating dung is extremely rare. When it occurs it could be a sign of parasites, pancreatitis or even feline leukemia, says Bonnie V. Beaver, D.V.M., professor and chief of medicine in the Department of Small Animal Medicine and Surgery at the Texas A&M University School of Veterinary Medicine in College Station. So if your kitty starts eating what she shouldn't, call your vet right away.

Among the canine crew, trouble can·arise if dogs accidentally swallow large amounts of kitty litter, which can cause intestinal obstructions, says Katherine Houpt, V.M.D., Ph.D., professor of physiology and director of the Animal Behavior Clinic at the Cornell University College of Veterinary Medicine in Ithaca, New York.

In addition, your pooch may pick up parasites from the waste, which can eventually result in nutritional deficiencies or blood loss, says Dr. Houpt. So if your dog has been eating waste and also seems to be tired or losing weight, call your vet right away.

Install a private entrance. Another way to keep the litter box off the menu is to put it in a room or closet equipped with a cat door, says Dr. Houpt. Make sure the door is small enough that unauthorized guests can't squeeze through when you're not looking.

Bar the door. To keep the pooch out of the cat's powder room, try attaching a hook-and-eye fastener to the door. Adjust the hook so the door opens just enough for the cat to slide in but not wide enough to admit the dog, suggests David Spiegel, V.M.D., a veterinarian and animal behavior expert in private practice in Wilmington, Delaware.

Cover it up. If you don't want to move the litter box, try replacing it with a covered, walk-in-style box, suggests Dr. Houpt. Covered boxes have cat-size entrances that will keep dogs out, plus they usually contain a charcoal air filter that reduces odors.

Add some spice. Dogs dislike fiery spices, so sprinkling cayenne pepper on wastes—either in the litter box or in the yard—will help take the fun out of foraging.

"Some dogs learn to associate the smell of the pepper with the spicy taste and avoid anything that's been baited," says Dr. Houpt. In fact, if you repeat the spicing on a regular basis, your pooch may eventually learn it's safest to limit his eating expeditions to proper meals.

Change the taste. Some dogs will develop a taste for their own waste. To stop the cycle, experts sometimes recommend a product called ForBid. ForBid, a powder that gives the waste a taste dogs hate, is available from vets and some pet supply companies, including the Omaha Vaccine Company (for a catalog, write to P.O. Box 7228, Omaha, NE 68107, or call 1-800-367-4444).

If you're lucky, the dog will learn to associate his grazing with the unpleasant taste and give it up for good, says Dr. Spiegel. If he returns to his old ways, try giving him another dose, he advises. Many dogs will eventually take the hint.

Patrol with a scoop. If your dog persists in his habits, your best bet may be to clean up after him (or other pets) before temptation strikes, advises Charles Abbate, D.V.M., a veterinarian in private practice in Warwick, Rhode Island.

Send a signal. If your dog is a long-term offender, your vet may recommend fitting him with a remote-control collar, which will get his attention by activating a high-pitched tone, says Dr. Spiegel.

When he starts grazing, activating the tone may encourage him to change his mind. After four or five "reminders," some dogs will give up their bad habits for good. Just be sure to reinforce the lesson by giving your dog a treat and plenty of love when he turns away from forbidden "foods," says Dr. Spiegel.

Give him lead time. To help your beast learn right from wrong, keep him on a leash even when you're walking inside the yard. If he starts to take a bite, pull sharply on the leash and give a firm "No!" says Dr. Spiegel.

"Because of your reprimand, he'll associate anxiety with the behavior. This will help inhibit him from doing it in the future," says Dr. Spiegel.

Keep him busy. Many dogs seem to develop bad habits when they have too much time on their paws. Scheduling ample playtime into the day will help keep his mind off less wholesome activities, says Dr. Spiegel.

"It's best to devote two big chunks of time a day, maybe a half-hour or 45 minutes, to play," he says. "A lot of owners give their dogs just a few minutes of attention, not enough to really satisfy them."

Increase the toy inventory. Giving your dog a variety of exciting toys to play with will help keep him out of harm's way, says Dr. Houpt. For example, you might bring out a tennis ball on Monday, a rawhide bone on Tuesday, a rope pull toy on Wednesday and so on. The busier he is, the less time he'll have to get into trouble.

Limit crate time. While many vets recommend using crates to house-train young dogs, it's important to let your pets out often—and also to keep the crate clean. Otherwise your dog may try to keep it clean the only way he knows how, says Dr. Houpt.

PANEL OF ADVISERS

Charles Abbate, D.V.M., is a veterinarian in private practice in Warwick, Rhode Island.

Bonnie V. Beaver, D.V.M., is professor and chief of medicine in the Department of Small Animal Medicine and Surgery at the Texas A&M University School of Veterinary Medicine in College Station and author of *Feline Behavior: A Guide for Veterinarians.*

Katherine Houpt, V.M.D., Ph.D., is professor of physiology and director of the Animal Behavior Clinic at the Cornell University College of Veterinary Medicine in Ithaca, New York.

Carol McConnell, D.V.M., is a veterinarian in private practice in Wilmington, Delaware.

David Spiegel, V.M.D., is a veterinarian and animal behavior expert in private practice in Wilmington, Delaware.

Ear Mites

8 Tips to Get Up to Scratch

A pat behind the ears no longer brings a grin to your furry friend's face. Instead it fires up a scratching frenzy that sends her back leg whirling like an eggbeater.

Itchy ears are sometimes a symptom of ear mites—tiny, eight-legged pests that can take up residence by the thousands in the ear canals. When they get stirred up—as a result of a vigorous head-scratching, for example—your pet may feel as though she has an earful of jumping beans. Without treatment, dogs and cats have been known to scratch themselves raw, sometimes causing skin infections.

Ear mites are readily passed from animal to animal, so unless your pet spends most of her time alone, they can be difficult to prevent. But with patience and persistence (and advice from your vet), you can successfully fight mites. Here's what vets recommend.

 **For Dogs and Cats**

Clear the debris. When treating your pet for ear mites, it's important to clear away the crust inside the ear before using medications, says Susan E. Anderson, D.V.M., clinical instructor of outpatient medicine in the Department of Small Animal Clinical Sciences at the University of Florida College of Veterinary Medicine in Gainesville. Otherwise the mites will take cover underneath the crust, where the medication won't reach.

Using a small dropper, deposit several drops of mineral oil inside the ear canal and wait several hours for the crust to soften. Then fill a rubber ear-cleaning syringe with equal portions of lukewarm white vinegar and distilled water and gently flush debris from the ear canal.

"Don't use too much pressure," warns Dr. Anderson. "What I do is squeeze and release, squeeze and release—you don't want a constant stream," she says.

When you're finished rinsing, gently press cotton inside the ear and

When to See the Vet

When ear mites don't go away within a month of home treatment or if your pet develops an ear rash or painful irritation, put away the over-the-counter medications and see your vet. He may prescribe a stronger solution that contains an antibiotic to prevent infection and a topical steroid to ease inflammation and pain.

move it around to clean up the gunk. Repeat the process as often as necessary until the entire ear is clean, Dr. Anderson advises.

Get a drop on them. Once your pet's ears are clean, vets usually recommend putting in a few drops of an over-the-counter medication containing pyrethrins—an insecticide made from chrysanthemums. "That should work," says Linda Frank, D.V.M., assistant professor of dermatology in the Department of Small Animal Clinical Sciences at the University of Tennessee School of Veterinary Medicine in Knoxville.

Medicated ear drops are available in pet stores. Directions will vary according to the product, but the procedure is simple: Place the drops in the ear canal, then gently massage the base of the ear for three to five minutes to allow the drops to penetrate. Then step back and let your pet shake her head, which will remove some of the liquid inside. Wipe up the remainder with cotton or a soft tissue.

Dr. Anderson recommends repeating this treatment every day for ten days, then skipping ten days and treating again for another ten. "You should start seeing real improvement over a week or ten days," she adds.

Try an oil treatment. Instead of using medications, you may want to try putting in a drop or two of mineral oil or baby oil once every day or so. This will smother some of the mites and help soothe your pet's sore, itchy ears, says Donald J. Klingborg, D.V.M., assistant dean at the University of California, Davis, School of Veterinary Medicine.

Heat the oil until it's just warm to the touch. Fill a small dropper and put in just enough oil to coat the ear canal. Don't flood it, adds Dr. Klingborg. Although the oil won't eradicate all the mites, it will reduce their numbers and help keep your pet comfortable for a day or two, he says.

"The important thing is to continue doing it for up to a month," adds Anne Lampru, D.V.M., a veterinarian in private practice in

Tampa, Florida. "That causes the mites that are popping out of the eggs to die before they're old enough to produce more eggs."

Go Italian. Garlic and olive oil aren't just for pizza—they can soothe the itch of ear mites as well, says Michele Yasson, D.V.M., a veterinarian in private practice in Rosendale, New York.

She recommends crushing four cloves of garlic and letting them steep overnight in one cup of olive oil. Then discard the garlic, heat the oil until it's warm to the touch and put several drops into your pet's ears.

You can repeat the treatment as often as every other day or as seldom as once a week, depending on the severity of the condition. "Any kind of oil will smother the mites, and this solution is soothing," she says.

Go after pioneers. While ear mites rarely leave their secure little homes, a few adventurers may roam outside—and then return days or weeks later to set up another infestation. "You may have to treat the entire animal," Dr. Anderson says.

She recommends using flea sprays or powders twice weekly or flea dips once a week for four weeks to kill mites that may have wandered.

Mites It Might Not Be

There are a number of conditions other than ear mites that can set up an itchy—and sometimes dangerous—ear infection. Some warning signs include:

- Dark, creamy wax that resembles peanut butter and smells like yeast. Your pet could have a yeast infection, particularly if she's been in the water recently. "They get swimmer's ear," says Linda Frank, D.V.M., assistant professor of dermatology in the Department of Small Animal Clinical Sciences at the University of Tennessee School of Veterinary Medicine in Knoxville.
- The ear canal is red and there's a moist yellow paste with a fruity or strong smell. This could indicate a bacterial infection, which may require oral or topical antibiotics.
- She's tilting her head continually. This could signal problems with the inner ear, such as a punctured eardrum. "In chronic inflammation of the ear canal, the eardrum is perforated (torn) in half the cases," says C. B. Chastain, D.V.M., associate dean for academic affairs and professor of veterinary medicine and surgery at the University of Missouri School of Veterinary Medicine in Columbia.

Spotting the Mite Blight

If you suspect your pet has ear mites but you aren't entirely sure, start with the ear test. Gently pull her ear flap down and rub it over the opening. If her hind leg swings into action, it may be mites—an uninfected pet won't scratch, says C. B. Chastain, D.V.M., associate dean for academic affairs and professor of veterinary medicine and surgery at the University of Missouri College of Veterinary Medicine in Columbia.

Another way to diagnose ear mites is to gently swab the ear canal with a cotton swab, then rub the swab on a dark piece of paper. Shine a bright light on the paper and look for wiggly white specks.

Mites are comfortable where it's dark, and the light will send them into a frenzy of activity, says Allan Paul, D.V.M., a small animal extension veterinarian at the University of Illinois College of Veterinary Medicine at Urbana-Champaign.

Another way to spot mites is to look in the ear. Mites typically leave behind a dry, crumbly, reddish-black crust that looks like coffee grounds, Dr. Paul says.

One way to tell if your pet has ear mites is to gently pull the ear flap down and rub it over the opening. If there are mites inside, the rubbing can stir them up, causing your pet's hind leg to swing into motion.

While you're at it, it's a good idea to spray your home and yard, since mites can survive for months without a furry host.

Since medications that are safe for dogs may be harmful for cats, be sure to read the label carefully before using any powder or spray, she adds.

Stop the cycle. Ear mites sometimes travel from pet to pet, so if one of your pets has been infected, chances are good that others will be joining her soon. "All the animals in the household have to be treated at the same time," says Dr. Lampru.

Be persistent. It takes about three weeks for a mite to undergo the transition from egg to a major pain in the ear. So regardless of the treatment you choose, it's important to continue treating your pet through the entire growth cycle in order to eradicate present and future generations.

Stick it out for a month, advises Dr. Lampru. "Ear mites are easily treated, but most people stop too soon."

Start a clean routine. Keeping your pets' ears clean can help ward off future infestations by removing ear mites before they have a chance to colonize, says Allan Paul, D.V.M., a small animal extension veterinarian at the University of Illinois College of Veterinary Medicine at Urbana-Champaign.

Use a cotton swab—dry or dipped in hydrogen peroxide—to gently clean out the canal. Don't go in too deep, adds C. B. Chastain, D.V.M., associate dean for academic affairs and professor of veterinary medicine and surgery at the University of Missouri College of Veterinary Medicine in Columbia. (If you can't see the cotton tip, you're in too far.) Plan on cleaning the ears about once a month. After bathing is often a convenient time, says Dr. Paul.

"A lot of dogs kind of like it," he adds. "You'll see them turn their heads like they're in doggy heaven."

PANEL OF ADVISERS

Susan E. Anderson, D.V.M., is clinical instructor of outpatient medicine in the Department of Small Animal Clinical Sciences at the University of Florida College of Veterinary Medicine in Gainesville.

C. B. Chastain, D.V.M., is associate dean for academic affairs and professor of veterinary medicine and surgery at the University of Missouri College of Veterinary Medicine in Columbia.

Linda Frank, D.V.M., is assistant professor of dermatology in the Department of Small Animal Clinical Sciences at the University of Tennessee School of Veterinary Medicine in Knoxville.

Donald J. Klingborg, D.V.M., is assistant dean at the University of California, Davis, School of Veterinary Medicine.

Anne Lampru, D.V.M., is a veterinarian in private practice in Tampa, Florida.

Allan Paul, D.V.M., is a small animal extension veterinarian at the University of Illinois College of Veterinary Medicine at Urbana-Champaign.

Michele Yasson, D.V.M., is a veterinarian in private practice in Rosendale, New York.

Eye Irritation

6 Solutions to a Sticky Problem

Your dog's eyes are so weepy you suspect he's been watching *Old Yeller* on TV again. Your cat is spending more time pawing at her crusty eyes than playing with her catnip toy.

One of the most common eye problems for dogs and cats is conjunctivitis. Also known as pinkeye, conjunctivitis is an inflammation of the membrane covering the inside of the eyelids and the front of the eye. Caused by such things as allergies, infections or even distemper, it can make your pet's eyes crusty, itchy and red, with an ugly abundance of pus or tears.

To ease the discomfort, here's what vets recommend.

 ## For Dogs and Cats

Wipe it out. To speed healing and make your pet more comfortable, you'll want to clean the discharge from her eyelids, says Gary M. Bryan, D.V.M., professor of ophthalmology at the Washington State University College of Veterinary Medicine in Pullman.

Wet a soft, clean cloth or cotton ball with lukewarm water, squeeze it out and gently wipe away the goop from around your pet's eyes, he says. Repeat twice a day or as often as needed.

Or try a scrub. Instead of using water, you may want to try an over-the-counter eye scrub. Eye scrubs are pH-balanced and may cause less stinging than water.

You can buy eye scrubs at pet stores, but scrubs formulated for humans are just as effective, says Mary B. Glaze, D.V.M., professor of ophthalmology at the Louisiana State University School of Veterinary Medicine in Baton Rouge and co-author of *The Atlas of Feline Ophthalmology.* "Just follow the directions as if your pet were human," she says.

Help her shed some tears. While eye scrubs can help keep the lids clean, you'll also want to wash the surface of the eye. A good way to do this is with artificial tears, which can help wash away particles that may be causing the problem, says David C. Smith, D.V.M., a veterinarian and expert in eye care in private practice in Tulsa.

Coddle her with a compress. Covering your pet's eyes with a damp, warm compress can be very soothing, says Art J. Quinn, D.V.M., professor of ophthalmology at the Oklahoma State University College of Veterinary Medicine in Stillwater. Wet a soft, clean cloth in lukewarm water, wring it out, and gently hold it across her eyes for five minutes. "This can make your pet's eyes feel much better, and it goes a long way toward keeping her eyes clean," he says.

If your pet balks at having both eyes covered, apply the compress to one eye for about five minutes. Then rinse the cloth and place it on the other eye. Of course, you can skip this step if only one eye is affected.

Take her to the barber. Regular grooming can help prevent eye irritations before they get started. "Hair in your pet's eyes can cause irritation that can lead to conjunctivitis if it's matted up around the corners," says Dr. Smith. "Brushing the hair back away from the eyes or getting a groomer to cut excess hair can help prevent conjunctivitis."

Keep the windows at half-mast. When traveling in the car, don't

When to See the Vet

While conjunctivitis isn't difficult to treat, any eye infection can result in permanent damage, so you'll want to see your vet at the first sign of problems.

In some cases your pet may need antibiotics to clear up an infection, says Art J. Quinn, D.V.M., professor of ophthalmology at the Oklahoma State University College of Veterinary Medicine in Stillwater.

In addition, some dogs that appear to have conjunctivitis actually have a condition known as dry eye, or *keratoconjunctivitis sicca* (cats are rarely affected). It occurs when there aren't enough tears to keep the eyes properly lubricated, Dr. Quinn explains.

Your vet can test your dog's tears to see if she has dry eye. If she does, treating the problem with artificial tears may be all that's needed, although some pets will need antibiotics or steroids as well.

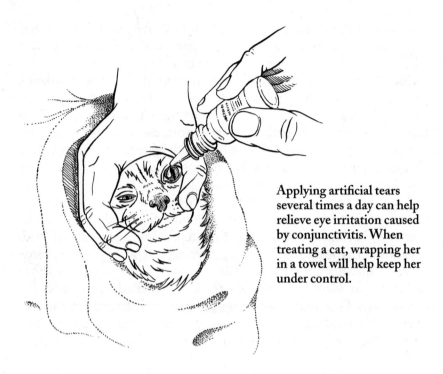

Applying artificial tears several times a day can help relieve eye irritation caused by conjunctivitis. When treating a cat, wrapping her in a towel will help keep her under control.

let your pet cruise with her head out the window, advises Janis H. Audin, D.V.M., editor-in-chief of the *Journal of the American Veterinary Medical Association* in Schaumburg, Illinois. "Debris can get in the eye, and the eye becomes more prone to infection," she says.

PANEL OF ADVISERS

Janis H. Audin, D.V.M., is editor-in-chief of the *Journal of the American Veterinary Medical Association* in Schaumburg, Illinois.

Gary M. Bryan, D.V.M., is professor of ophthalmology at the Washington State University College of Veterinary Medicine in Pullman.

Mary B. Glaze, D.V.M., is professor of ophthalmology at the Louisiana State University School of Veterinary Medicine in Baton Rouge and co-author of *The Atlas of Feline Ophthalmology.*

Art J. Quinn, D.V.M., is professor of ophthalmology at the Oklahoma State University College of Veterinary Medicine in Stillwater.

David C. Smith, D.V.M., is a veterinarian and expert in eye care in private practice in Tulsa.

Fears

8 Reassuring Strategies

A thunderstorm turns your golden retriever into a quivering mass. A car ride to the vet's office sets your cat howling like a banshee. You count yourself lucky if you don't sustain serious injuries just getting them to the groomer to have their nails trimmed. On top of all this, you have to fork over the extra charge for "difficult" clients.

Like people, some pets become phobic—irrationally frightened of the simplest things, such as unfamiliar people, places or animals. Other common scaremongers are loud noises, like fireworks or gunfire.

To keep your pet calm and the fears in check, here's what vets recommend.

 ## For Dogs and Cats

Start safely. While your instincts may tell you to throw your arms around a panicking pet, it's usually better to take a step back. A fearful animal often lashes out aggressively, even at his beloved owner.

"Don't try to interact with a pet that's so panicky he tries to remove body parts," says Karen Overall, V.M.D., Ph.D., a lecturer specializing in behavioral medicine in the Department of Clinical Studies at the University of Pennsylvania School of Veterinary Medicine in Philadelphia. Wait until your pet has calmed down before you approach him.

Help him relax. Your pet can't do yoga or deep-breathing exercises, but there are other relaxing things you can help him do, says Dr. Overall.

She recommends putting your pet through some of the same paces he learned in school, like sitting or lying down. Doing something familiar will help him relax. Plus, seeing you calm and collected will help him calm down, too.

Don't reward the fear. If you have a dog that's afraid of thunder, and you pamper and cuddle him when it thunders, you're rewarding him for being fearful—and increasing the likelihood that he will make a big

When to See the Vet

While every pet owner occasionally has to reassure a frightened friend, sometimes the fears can't be calmed. Phobic pets may urinate, claw or bite. Others may run and hide.

Any animal that is regularly experiencing high anxiety is dangerous—both to himself and to you. You're going to need to consult an expert, says Daniel Q. Estep, Ph.D., a certified applied animal behaviorist in private practice in Littleton, Colorado.

In most cases, the treatment of choice is desensitization therapy, in which the pet is gradually exposed to what scares him—until it no longer does. Your vet may teach you to do this on your own, or he may recommend you call an animal behavior consultant. With time and patience, this type of therapy can be very effective, Dr. Estep says, but he adds that some pets may also need anti-anxiety medication.

production out of being scared, says Debra Horwitz, D.V.M., a veterinarian and animal behavior consultant in private practice in St. Louis.

There's nothing wrong with giving a nervous pet a few kind words and a gentle touch, she adds. Just don't cater to him. When he sees you're not making a big deal out of whatever's bothering him, he'll eventually learn to deal with it on his own.

Get a leash on fears. At some point you or your vet may want to begin working with your pet to help him overcome the underlying cause of his anxiety.

The way to do this is to expose him, a little at a time, to whatever it is he's afraid of, says Wayne Hunthausen, D.V.M., an animal behavior consultant in Westwood, Kansas, president of the American Veterinary Society of Animal Behavior and co-author of *Practitioner's Guide to Pet Behavior Problems*.

Suppose, for example, your cat is afraid of strangers. "It may be that your cat can see a man at 30 feet and feel safe, but when the man comes within 10 feet, he gets scared," says Dr. Hunthausen. To help him get over this, have a friend stand 30 feet away, then slowly come a little closer—say, to 20 or 25 feet. Then give your pet a little treat. You can repeat this process, a little bit at a time, over days, weeks or months.

"You keep doing this, moving the man closer and closer until he actually feeds the cat," Dr. Hunthausen says.

Record his fears. If your dog is afraid of thunderstorms, try playing an audiotape of a storm, suggests Daniel Q. Estep, Ph.D., a certified applied animal behaviorist in private practice in Littleton, Colorado. Play it at very low volume to start, and reward your dog with a treat if he manages to stay calm. Then gradually increase the volume. Eventually he may start feeling safer during real storms as well.

Go for a "park." Many pets associate getting in the car with going to the vet. You might want to demonstrate that going for rides can have more pleasant outcomes as well.

For starters, encourage your pet to jump in the car when you aren't going anywhere. Just sit in the car with him and give him little strokes and maybe a treat, says Dr. Estep. When he starts getting comfortable, start the car. Then give him time to get used to that. Eventually work up to backing out of the driveway and pulling back in.

When you finally do go for a real drive, *don't* go to the vet! Take him to the park instead.

Speak highly. Some pets get fearful when they hear a man's voice. "Men have deeper voices, which tend to be like the growling vocalization dogs use with each other," says Dr. Estep. "I find if I use a high, happy voice, they tend to do a little better."

Stop fears from starting. People who train show dogs gently introduce their pets to just about every stressful experience they're ever likely to encounter, from being handled by strangers to hearing loud applause, says Dr. Hunthausen.

"Start handling the pet right away," he suggests. "Every chance you get, start brushing him. Look in his ears and mouth. Examine his paw. Put him on a tabletop. Then reward good behavior. If he associates these experiences with something good, he's going to look forward to getting on the vet's or groomer's table."

PANEL OF ADVISERS

Daniel Q. Estep, Ph.D., is a certified applied animal behaviorist in private practice in Littleton, Colorado.

Debra Horwitz, D.V.M., is a veterinarian and animal behavior consultant in private practice in St. Louis.

Wayne Hunthausen, D.V.M., is an animal behavior consultant in Westwood, Kansas, president of the American Veterinary Society of Animal Behavior and co-author of *Practitioner's Guide to Pet Behavior Problems.*

Karen Overall, V.M.D., Ph.D., is a lecturer specializing in behavioral medicine in the Department of Clinical Studies at the University of Pennsylvania School of Veterinary Medicine in Philadelphia.

Fever

5 Cooling Solutions

You always knew your pet was hot stuff, but today he really does seem to be overheating. Worse, he's moping about and doesn't even want to eat. What's turning up the heat?

It's probably just a virus. Normal temperature for dogs and cats is between 100.5° and 102.5°F. Once the thermometer registers over 103°, you can bet they're getting sick, and you may want to call the vet, says Lisardo Martinez, D.V.M., a veterinarian in private practice in Miami.

Fevers are rarely dangerous, and in most cases a fever will go away as soon as the illness does. But to make your pet feel more comfortable and help bring the temperature down, here's what vets recommend.

 **For Dogs and Cats**

Press away the heat. One soothing way to lower your pet's temperature is with cool-water compresses, suggests Jeffrey Feinman, V.M.D., a house-call veterinarian in Weston, Connecticut. Soak a washcloth in cold water, wring it out and gently pat it on your pet's belly, he suggests.

You can also pat his belly with a washcloth moistened with isopropyl alcohol, he adds. The alcohol evaporates quickly from the skin, helping to bring the temperature down.

Run a cool bath. If your pet will hold still for it, putting him in a cool (not cold) bath for five or ten minutes will help bring the fever down, says Dr. Martinez.

Give him the wrap-around. To lower a fever in a cat or small dog, "just place a towel soaked in cool water around him," says Paul Schmitz, D.V.M., a veterinarian in private practice in Joliet, Illinois. Most pets will enjoy the coolness, particularly if you periodically wet the towel with fresh water to keep it cool and comfortable.

Keep the water bowl full. A pet with fever runs the risk of dehydration, so it's important to keep his water bowl full. If he doesn't seem to want to drink, try giving him ice cubes instead. Many pets enjoy the crunch, and they'll get extra fluid.

Ask about aspirin. While vets are cautious when it comes to giving human medication to pets, aspirin can sometimes be used to help bring a fever down, says Dr. Schmitz. For dogs, a safe dose would be about one-quarter of a 325-milligram tablet of buffered aspirin for

When to See the Vet

While most fevers are caused by minor viral infections, they can also be a sign of something more serious, such as hepatitis, pneumonia or Lyme disease, says Lisardo Martinez, D.V.M., a veterinarian in private practice in Miami.

To check your pet's temperature, lightly coat a rectal thermometer with petroleum jelly. (A human thermometer is fine, although you should have an extra one just for your pet.) Holding the thermometer in one hand and your pet's tail out of the way with the other, gently slide the thermometer two-thirds of its length into the rectum. Hold it in for two or three minutes. If it reads over 103°F, play it safe and call your vet right away.

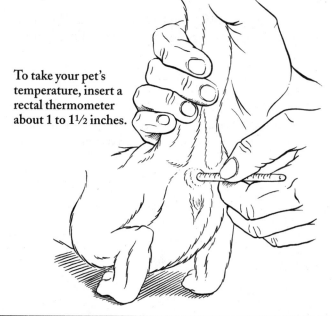

To take your pet's temperature, insert a rectal thermometer about 1 to 1½ inches.

Does the Nose Know?

Just as we check a child's temperature by feeling his forehead, we automatically reach for our pets' noses when they're feeling ill.

While dogs and cats certainly appreciate the attention, the nose is not an accurate gauge of temperature, says Paul Schmitz, D.V.M., a veterinarian in private practice in Joliet, Illinois.

Pets have mucus glands in the lining of the nose that naturally keep it moist. A pet with a fever *could* have a warm, dry nose. It's just as likely, however, that his nose could be cool and moist, says Dr. Schmitz.

Don't trust your hands to take an accurate temperature, he adds. Use a thermometer instead.

every ten pounds of weight. Aspirin can be dangerous for cats, however, so don't give it without checking with your veterinarian. Also, don't give your pet ibuprofen or acetaminophen instead of aspirin. These and other aspirin "substitutes" can be dangerous when given to dogs or cats.

Of course, you should always get your vet's okay before giving aspirin or any other human medication to your pet, Dr. Schmitz adds.

PANEL OF ADVISERS

Jeffrey Feinman, V.M.D., is a house-call veterinarian in Weston, Connecticut.

Lisardo J. Martinez, D.V.M., is a veterinarian in private practice in Miami.

Paul Schmitz, D.V.M., is a veterinarian in private practice in Joliet, Illinois.

Fighting

16 Tips to Halt the Brawling

Every night your cat goes out looking for trouble—and comes back looking like he tangled with a Waring blender. Your pooch is calm and dignified—until he catches sight of another canine. Then he's instantly transformed into Cujo from the Stephen King novel.

While fighting is scary to watch and dangerous for the combatants, it's extremely common, says Wayne Hunthausen, D.V.M., an animal behavior consultant in Westwood, Kansas, president of the American Veterinary Society of Animal Behavior and co-author of *Practitioner's Guide to Pet Behavior Problems*.

But there are ways to stop battles before casualties occur. Here's what vets recommend.

 ## For Dogs and Cats

Don't get in the middle. Dogs and cats in the heat of battle aren't discriminating about what (or whom) they bite. Many owners have been mauled while trying to break up a fight, so, keep your hands clear, says Steve Aiken, owner of Animal Behavior Consultants in Wichita, Kansas.

If you absolutely have to reach into a fight—to prevent your pet from being seriously injured, for example—throw a heavy blanket over the combatants. This will help protect your hands when you go for the grab.

Go deep and loud. When you see a fight brewing, interrupt the aggression with the loudest, deepest "No!" you can muster, says Vicki L. White, an assistant trainer and behavior consultant at the Marin Humane Society in Novato, California.

Pets associate a low-pitched voice with a threatening growl and take it more seriously than they would a high-pitched command, she explains.

Give them a blast. If the squabble occurs in the vicinity of a garden hose, giving the combatants a shot of water will help quench their gladiatorial ardor. Cooling them off with a pitcher of water will serve the same purpose, White says. Some hot-tempered pets are hard to convince, so be prepared to use a *lot* of water.

Sit out minor brawls. When dogs or cats meet, you can expect a certain amount of posturing, hissing, growling or tussling. In most cases it's just their way of getting acquainted, Aiken says. Even if they start squabbling, chances are the ruckus will calm down in a minute or two.

Organize get-togethers. To help your pets understand that a strange pet isn't always hostile, it helps to let them be around their peers as often as possible. "I'm a big believer in early training and socialization," says Dr. Hunthausen.

Vets recommend introducing pets to others of their kind—either in a formal setting like a class or just by walking in the park—as soon as they've had their first set of vaccinations, usually at about 12 weeks of age.

Plan meetings ahead of time. When introducing two (or more) four-legged strangers, try to do it at a time of day when they're naturally feeling peaceful. "It's best to meet after a big meal when the animals are sleepy or after a long walk or play period," says Aiken.

Introduce them on neutral ground. Rather than bringing animals together at home, where territorial feelings often run high, let them meet in a neutral place such as the park, advises Anita Fahrenwald, co-owner of the Good Neighbor Dog Training School in Hansen, Idaho.

Neuter them young. Fighting is greatly reduced in males that have been neutered, Aiken says. Even in females, spaying can reduce some of the aggressive tendencies that lead to fighting. "If you do it before six months, many problems never develop in the first place," he says.

 For Dogs Only

Keep him under control. Always have your dog on a leash when you're out in public, advises Marti Kincaid, co-owner of the Good Neighbor Dog Training School. If a fight seems to be brewing, you can quickly pull him out of danger.

When dogs meet, "let them sniff the shoulder and the back end," she advises. "Then count to five and say, 'Good dog!' and pull your dog away."

Keep the leash low. Although it's natural to pull on the leash when

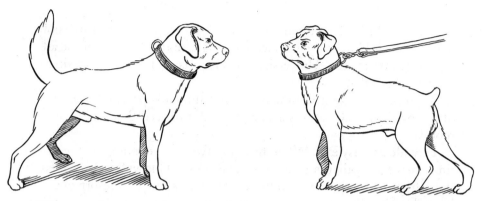

When two dogs meet, it's natural to hold the leash high and tight. Unfortunately, this pulls the dog's head up, making him look aggressive and ready to fight.

Keeping the leash low and loose allows pets to say "Hi" to each other without accidentally giving the wrong impression.

another dog approaches, "this pulls your dog's head into fighting posture," Kincaid says. This unintentional body language may cause the other dog to attack. "Keep the leash low and loose," she advises.

Respect the hierarchy. Dogs are pack animals with rigid rules of social behavior. To prevent fights in the family, older dogs generally should be given more respect and attention than the young upstarts.

"The dog that has been around longer must be allowed a lot of privileges," says Kincaid. "The older dog gets greeted first, gets groomed first and gets his treat first."

 For Cats Only

Give them separate quarters. Bringing a new cat into the family can raise tensions for both the newcomer and the old hand, says John

C. Wright, Ph.D., a certified animal behaviorist, professor of psychology at Mercer University in Macon, Georgia, and a member of the adjunct faculty at the University of Georgia School of Veterinary Medicine in Atlanta.

To keep fights to a minimum, he recommends providing separate litter boxes for each cat. It's also a good idea to feed them in separate rooms.

Provide an easy exit. When bringing two cats together for the first time, make sure there's an easy escape route. This will help prevent them from feeling trapped and make them less likely to resort to violence, Dr. Wright advises.

Waft an introductory smell. Rather than putting two cats together all at once, you can smooth the process by first "introducing" them to each other's scent, Aiken suggests. Put a blanket or toy from one cat into an area where the other one will find it. When they finally do meet, it will almost seem like old times.

Get them in twos. "If you want to have two cats, get them at the same time, as kittens," advises Andrea Fochios, D.V.M., a veterinarian in private practice in Ferndale, New York. Cats that grow up together are less likely to tussle than those that meet later on.

Keep them indoors. "If you really love your cat, you'll want to keep him indoors," says Aiken. "The average life span for an outdoor cat is 1 to 2 years; for an indoor cat it's 12 to 14 years."

PANEL OF ADVISERS

Steve Aiken is owner of Animal Behavior Consultants in Wichita, Kansas.

Anita Fahrenwald is co-owner of Good Neighbor Dog Training School in Hansen, Idaho.

Andrea Fochios, D.V.M., is a veterinarian in private practice in Ferndale, New York.

Wayne Hunthausen, D.V.M., is an animal behavior consultant in Westwood, Kansas, president of the American Veterinary Society of Animal Behavior and co-author of *Practitioner's Guide to Pet Behavior Problems.*

Marti Kincaid is co-owner of Good Neighbor Dog Training School in Hansen, Idaho.

Vicki L. White is an assistant trainer and behavior consultant at the Marin Humane Society in Novato, California.

John C. Wright, Ph.D., is a certified animal behaviorist, professor of psychology at Mercer University in Macon, Georgia, and a member of the adjunct faculty at the University of Georgia School of Veterinary Medicine in Atlanta.

Flatulence

13 Ways to Fight the Fumes

It's no secret when Rex passes gas. But he can't help being a four-pawed faux pas. After all, intestinal gas is a natural part of digestion. "It's just that some animals produce more than others," says William D. Fortney, D.V.M., assistant professor of small animal medicine in the Department of Clinical Sciences at the Kansas State University College of Veterinary Medicine in Manhattan, Kansas.

Cats are also prone to flatulence, although their diets and eating habits tend to make them less gassy than dogs. "Besides, there's a big difference between a flatulent little cat and a flatulent 80-pound dog," says Dr. Fortney.

No matter the perpetrator, flatulence is an ill wind that blows no good. So if you find yourself crying foul when your pet's around, try these tips.

 **For Dogs and Cats**

Work it out with a walk. Exercise helps move gas out of the intestine, and if your pet happens to relieve himself on his walk, even more gas will be released. "Just make sure to stay upwind," Dr. Fortney advises.

Oy! Soy! If your pet is frequently gassy, the culprit could be soybeans. Packed with protein, soybeans comprise up to 25 percent of some pet foods. While that's not a problem for most dogs and cats, some may find soy hard to digest, says Kathryn Michel, D.V.M., a researcher and nutrition expert in the Department of Clinical Studies at the University of Pennsylvania School of Veterinary Medicine in Philadelphia. "Changing to a food with less soy or no soy could make a big difference," she says.

To determine how much soy a product contains, look at the label. Ingredients positioned near the top of the list comprise the bulk of a product, while those farther down are included in smaller amounts.

Switch brands slowly. If you notice a sudden change for the worse in air quality after changing foods, you might have gone too quickly. "It takes a while for the bacteria in the colon to adjust to a new diet," says Richard Hill, B.V.M., Ph.D., assistant professor of clinical nutrition and a specialist in internal medicine in the Department of Small Animal Sciences at the University of Florida College of Veterinary Medicine in Gainesville. He suggests switching over a period of three days, substituting one-third of the new food for one-third of the old each day.

Stash the trash. "If your dog or cat gets into the garbage, the digestive system is bound to run amok for a while. The results can be rank," says Lawrence McGill, D.V.M., Ph.D., a veterinary pathologist in Salt Lake City.

Go on pig-out patrol. Does your beast like to feast? Then it's time to face facts: Gluttons can get gas, says M. Lynne Kesel, D.V.M., assistant professor of elective surgery in the Department of Clinical Sciences at the College of Veterinary Medicine and Biomedical Sciences at Colorado State University in Fort Collins. "Overeating can overload the gut, so things end up fermenting that normally wouldn't," she says.

Steer clear of supplements. While many people like to give their pets extra vitamins and minerals, the use of supplements can stimulate bacterial action in the gut that can lead to gas, says Mark L. Morris, Jr., D.V.M., Ph.D., a nutrition consultant in Topeka, Kansas, creator of Science Diet pet foods and co-author of *Small Animal Clinical Nutrition.* "Unless there's a medical reason to be taking supplements, your pet may be better off without them," he says.

Lay off the dairy. Most adult dogs and cats can digest only tiny amounts of milk, says Dr. Michel. That's because they don't produce enough of an enzyme called lactase, which is needed to digest the lactose found in milk. "If your flatulent pet is getting milk, take it away for a few days and see if things improve," she advises. You can also try switching to lactose-reduced milk, she adds.

Try a little culture. Many yogurts contain digestion-friendly bacteria that can help decrease flatulence, says Ann-si Li, D.V.M., an expert in Oriental veterinary medicine in Oakland, California. She recommends giving ¼ teaspoon of plain yogurt to cats and small dogs, 1 teaspoon to dogs 15 to 20 pounds and 1 tablespoon to large dogs. Most pets like the taste, so you won't need to hide it in their food. She notes that even pets that can't handle lactose can usually enjoy yogurt without any problems.

Check it with charcoal. "Activated charcoal is messy, but it can absorb the smell pretty effectively," says Dr. Kesel. For small pets, she recommends adding ⅛ to ¼ teaspoon to their food daily. For larger pets, ½ teaspoon is about right, she says.

Keep in mind, however, that activated charcoal—which is available over the counter in most pharmacies—can absorb nutrients as well as gas from the digestive tract. It shouldn't be used for more than a few days at a time, experts say.

Calm it with CurTail. Sold by veterinarians, this anti-gas product contains an enzyme that helps break down foods so they can be digested more efficiently—and with less combustion. "The stuff really works," says Katherine Brown, D.V.M., a veterinarian in private practice in Salt Lake City.

Reduce mealtime competition. When you feed two or more pets at the same time, one may be wolfing his meal to prevent another pet from nabbing it. The result is swallowed air, which comes out as belches, flatulence or—lucky you—both. Feeding pets separately will allow them to eat more slowly and with fewer unpleasant consequences, says Dr. Michel.

Extend the dinner hour. Another tactic to reduce air-swallowing is to put a fairly large object—a large ball, for example—into your pet's food bowl. "He'll have to nose around and work harder to get the food, so he'll be forced to slow down," says Dr. Michel. Just be sure the object is large enough so that your pet doesn't accidentally wolf it down along with his food. "I've seen dogs come in with objects you could never dream of in their stomachs, so be careful what you use," she says.

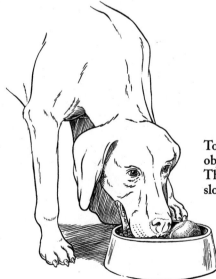

To reduce flatulence, put a large object in your pet's food bowl. This will cause him to eat more slowly and swallow less air.

End the bends. Yet another way to keep air out of your pet's system is to raise the food dish off the floor, says Dr. Fortney. "If he's not bending his neck so far down, he'll swallow less air," he says. He suggests placing the food bowl securely on a box. Or you can invest in a specially designed stand that holds the food and water bowls at mouth level.

PANEL OF ADVISERS

Katherine Brown, D.V.M., is a veterinarian in private practice in Salt Lake City.

William D. Fortney, D.V.M., is assistant professor of small animal medicine in the Department of Clinical Sciences at the Kansas State University College of Veterinary Medicine in Manhattan, Kansas.

Richard Hill, B.V.M., Ph.D., is assistant professor of clinical nutrition and a specialist in internal medicine in the Department of Small Animal Sciences at the University of Florida College of Veterinary Medicine in Gainesville.

M. Lynne Kesel, D.V.M., is assistant professor of elective surgery in the Department of Clinical Sciences at the Colorado State University College of Veterinary Medicine and Biomedical Sciences in Fort Collins.

Ann-si Li, D.V.M., is an expert in Oriental veterinary medicine in Oakland, California.

Lawrence McGill, D.V.M., Ph.D., is a veterinary pathologist in Salt Lake City.

Kathryn Michel, D.V.M., is a researcher and nutrition expert in the Department of Clinical Studies at the University of Pennsylvania School of Veterinary Medicine in Philadelphia.

Mark L. Morris Jr., D.V.M., Ph.D., is a nutrition consultant in Topeka, Kansas, creator of Science Diet pet foods and co-author of *Small Animal Clinical Nutrition*.

Fleas

19 Ways to Foil Them

See that itsy flea on your itchy pet? Well, you ain't seen nothing yet. Within the next month, that flea (with a little help from her girlfriends) could fill your house with up to 250,000 descendants.

What's more, for every flea you see on your pet, you can bet there are up to 100 more, in one form or another, that are not on your pet—they're in the yard, on the floors and in the linen, says Michael Dryden, D.V.M., Ph.D., associate professor of veterinary parasitology at the Kansas State University College of Veterinary Medicine in Manhattan, Kansas. "It can be quite daunting."

The little pests can be incredibly difficult to get rid of. In fact, you may never be able to eradicate them 100 percent from your house or yard. But you can still prevent your pet from going buggy from fleas. "You have to realize it's a never-ending battle, but if you're diligent, you can win," says Philip Kass, D.V.M., Ph.D., associate professor of epidemiology at the University of California, Davis, School of Veterinary Medicine. Here's what you need to do.

 **For Dogs and Cats**

Begin with a bath. If your pet is willing to climb into the bathtub, washing his coat with a gentle, nonmedicated pet shampoo will send many fleas right down the drain, says Pete Schaubhut, D.V.M., a veterinarian in private practice in New York City. If he's still scratching after his first bath, try again, this time using a flea shampoo.

When washing cats—assuming yours is one of those rare felines that will actually let you do it—use only shampoos designed especially for them. A product that's safe for dogs could be dangerous when used on cats, warns Dr. Kass. Check the label first. (For tips on bathing cats, see "How to Give Your Cat a Bath" on page 186.)

How to Give Your Cat a Bath

Trying to get a cat to take a bath—for flea control or anything else—is about as easy as wrestling with barbed wire.

"If your cat hates it, she will climb right out and over you," says Dawn Logas, D.V.M., assistant professor of dermatology at the University of Florida College of Veterinary Medicine in Gainesville.

To clean your kitty without getting killed, here's what vets recommend.

Plan ahead. Cats hate the sound of running water, so fill the tub first, then bring kitty in.

Keep her face dry. Getting wet above the neck will give almost any cat conniptions. To prevent this, gently lower her into the tub, being careful to keep splashing to a minimum.

Bring an anchor. To keep your ferocious feline under control, you may want to invest in a kitty harness that's attached to a leash, with a suction cup on one end. The suction cup sticks to the tub or shower wall and will help keep your cat in the tub while leaving your hands free to do the washing, says Carol Emsley, a groomer at Blue Ribbon Groomer in Livonia, Michigan, and a member of the board of directors of the American Grooming Shop Association.

Help her get a grip. Putting a plastic milk crate, rubber mat or some other object in the tub will give your clutching kitty something to grab. That way she's less likely to sink her claws into you, Emsley says.

Or keep him high and dry. As an alternative to bathing, try using a "dry" shampoo, one that foams without water. "It's better if your pet will tolerate a real shampoo, but this is certainly better than not bathing him at all," says Dr. Kass.

Again, when treating cats, be sure to check the label to make sure the shampoo is feline-friendly.

Use herbs to perturb. Mixing a few drops of pennyroyal or eucalyptus oil into your pet's usual shampoo will help repel fleas, says Richard H. Pitcairn, D.V.M., Ph.D., a veterinarian in private practice in Eugene, Oregon, and author of *Dr. Pitcairn's Complete Guide to Natural Health for Dogs and Cats*. Undiluted pennyroyal oil can be toxic,

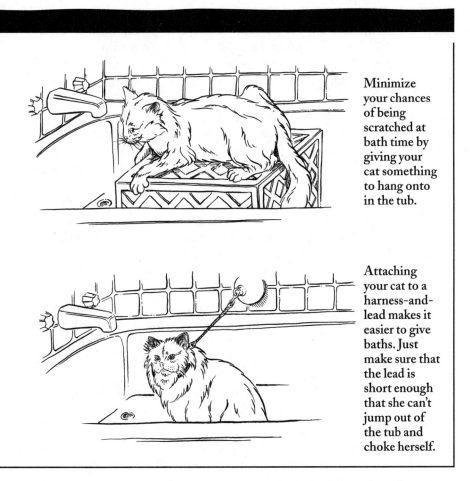

Minimize your chances of being scratched at bath time by giving your cat something to hang onto in the tub.

Attaching your cat to a harness-and-lead makes it easier to give baths. Just make sure that the lead is short enough that she can't jump out of the tub and choke herself.

though, so it should never be used full-strength.

Give him a good grooming. Pulling a flea comb through your pet's coat once a day will help keep the critters away, says Dr. Kass. Between strokes, dip the comb in a bowl of soapy water to drown any fleas that may be hanging on.

Give your pet bad taste. "Blecch!" is what you want fleas to think when they bite into your pet. One way to taint their taste buds is to mix a little garlic and brewer's yeast into your pet's breakfast. Many pets like the taste, so you won't have to disguise it. "It may very well make the animal unappetizing," says Dr. Schaubhut.

Choose collars carefully. Traditional flea collars impregnated with insecticides can't always handle heavy infestations. In addition, they can be irritating to your pet's skin, says Dr. Dryden. A better bet might be to buy a collar that contains a synthetic flea-controlling hormone like methoprene. "They're virtually nontoxic to mammals, and they sterilize flea eggs before they can roll off and continue the life cycle," Dr. Dryden says.

In the warm months when fleas thrive, you may be tempted to buy an electronic, ultrasonic flea collar with all the bells and whistles. "Don't waste your money," advises Dr. Dryden. Not only are the collars not effective, they emit sounds that may be within the hearing range of cats and dogs and could be annoying.

Use sprays to keep them at bay. Treating your pet's coat with flea spray will quickly wipe out any visitors that may be dining in. There's a variety of products to choose from. Those containing the insecticides D-limonene or pyrethrins (made from chrysanthemums) are effective and less toxic than some other sprays, says Dr. Kass. You can also buy sprays containing methoprene.

When spraying your pet, be sure to keep insecticide out of his eyes, ears, nose and mouth. You can do this by spritzing a square of gauze and using it to apply the insecticide to his face. Since many cats will run from the hissing sound of spray bottles, you may have to treat them entirely with moistened gauze.

When buying any insecticide, make sure the label specifies that it's safe for your pet, warns Dr. Kass. Sprays that are safe for dogs can be extremely dangerous for cats.

Powder him from head to toes. Flea powders aren't usually as effective as sprays, but they still can play an important role in flea control. Powder your pet from his neck to his feet, and don't forget the tail. Then work the powder down close to the skin with a comb or brush.

When powdering his face, put tiny amounts of powder on your fingertips and gently work it in, avoiding the area around the eyes and nose, says Dr. Kass.

Go for a dip. More potent than sprays or powders, flea dip—an insecticide solution in which you immerse your pet—can provide long-lasting protection. "In bad infestations they may be necessary, but use them with caution," warns Dr. Kass. "And read the labels carefully. Dips that are okay for dogs can be deadly for cats."

Bring out the artillery. When fleas are showing up in record numbers, you may need to treat the entire house with a house fogger, says Dr. Dryden. He recommends using products containing methoprene or fenoxycarb, another flea-controlling hormone. Insecticides contain-

Critter Control

Planned parenthood for fleas is no longer a leap away. The Food and Drug Administration has approved a medication called Program that could change the way Americans fight the war against fleas.

Unlike flea sprays and powders, the drug contains no insecticides, says Michael Dryden, D.V.M., Ph.D., associate professor of veterinary parasitology at the Kansas State University College of Veterinary Medicine in Manhattan, Kansas. Instead it contains a compound called lufenuron that prevents flea eggs from maturing.

When a female flea feeds on a treated pet, she essentially becomes sterile, explains Dr. Dryden. "It won't eliminate the need for other forms of flea control, but it should definitely make the problem easier to manage," he says.

ing pyrethrins are also safe and effective, says Dr. Kass.

Do 'em in with diatoms. Also known as diatomaceous earth or chinchilla dust, these microscopic algae are safe alternatives to insecticides. They absorb a flea's waxy coating, causing it to dry up and die, says Tanya Drlik, pest management specialist at Bio-Integral Resource Center, a nonprofit group that researches pesticide alternatives, in Berkeley, California.

Sprinkle the diatomaceous earth on carpeting and upholstered furniture. You can also sweep it into cracks and crevices around baseboards by using a small hand duster. Wear a dust mask and goggles so the tiny particles don't drift into your lungs or eyes. Work them in with a broom, then vacuum them up a few days later, Drlik says.

Diatoms, which are sold in pet stores, are inactivated by water, so they can be used only indoors, she says. Be sure to use amorphous diatomaceous earth, Drlik adds. The glassified diatomaceous earth used for swimming pool filters isn't effective against fleas and can be harmful if inhaled.

Suck 'em up. "Vacuuming at least once a week is an extremely effective, nontoxic way to keep the flea population down," says Drlik.

Concentrate on areas where your pet spends lots of time, like around his bedding. Be sure to vacuum cracks, crevices and baseboards, and spend plenty of time on rugs, says Drlik.

Hit them when they're down. To prevent voracious fleas from emerging from your Hoover, remove the bag, seal it securely in plastic and place it in the freezer or in direct sunlight. The extreme temperature—either cold or heat—will help kill the fleas, Drlik says.

Take away their hiding places. "The more clutter in your home, the more places there are for fleas to escape your attempts to get rid of them," says Robert Hilsenroth, D.V.M., executive director of the Morris Animal Foundation in Englewood, Colorado. "Keep floors as clear of things like boxes, toys and books as possible."

Lay a trap. Wherever fleas are a problem, plug in a night light and put a wide pan partially filled with water underneath. (A lasagna pan will do nicely.) Since fleas are attracted to warmth, some will leap toward the light—and make a splashdown in the water, where they'll drown, says Mary L. Brennan, D.V.M., a veterinarian in private practice in Atlanta and co-author of *The Natural Dog: A Complete Guide for Caring Owners*. This won't solve your problem, but in the war against fleas, every body counts.

Limit the rooms where your pet roams. "The fewer rooms your pet has access to, the fewer rooms you'll have to worry about," says Drlik. "Shutting a few doors probably isn't going to upset your pet too much, and it could save you lots of work."

Make it laundry day. Washing your pet's bedding at least once a week will help keep fleas at bay, says Dr. Pitcairn.

If your pet sleeps on a pad or thick bed that's tough to wash, get in the habit of protecting it with a small sheet or a large towel that you can wash once a week. When you remove the towel, however, be sure to roll it up carefully in order to trap fleas and their eggs. "Otherwise they can fall off and scatter everywhere," says Dr. Pitcairn.

Practice car care. If you take your pet on trips, cover the area where he sits with a sheet that can be washed regularly, says George G. Doering, D.V.M., a veterinarian in private practice in Walnut Creek, California, who specializes in dermatology. "There's nothing like a car full of fleas," he says.

It's a good idea to vacuum the car frequently, and you may also have to bomb it periodically with a household flea spray.

Use worms to make 'em squirm. To control yard infestations, many experts recommend using nematodes—microscopic worms that prey on the larvae and pupae of many insects, including fleas, says Dr. Dryden.

Nematodes are available at pet and garden stores (a 300-gram canister contains about 100 *million* little worms). Following the directions on the label, just put them in a hose sprayer and blast away, taking particular aim at damp, shaded areas where fleas thrive, says Dr. Dryden. When the fleas disappear, so will the nematodes.

PANEL OF ADVISERS

Mary L. Brennan, D.V.M., is a veterinarian in private practice in Atlanta and co-author of *The Natural Dog: A Complete Guide for Caring Owners.*

George G. Doering, D.V.M., is a veterinary dermatologist in private practice in Walnut Creek, California.

Tanya Drlik is a pest management specialist at Bio-Integral Resource Center, a nonprofit group that researches pesticide alternatives, in Berkeley, California.

Michael Dryden, D.V.M., Ph.D., is associate professor of veterinary parasitology at the Kansas State University College of Veterinary Medicine in Manhattan, Kansas.

Carol Emsley is a pet groomer at Blue Ribbon Groomer in Livonia, Michigan, and a member of the board of directors of the American Grooming Shop Association.

Robert Hilsenroth, D.V.M., is executive director of the Morris Animal Foundation in Englewood, Colorado.

Philip Kass, D.V.M., Ph.D., is associate professor of epidemiology at the University of California, Davis, School of Veterinary Medicine.

Dawn Logas, D.V.M., is assistant professor of dermatology at the University of Florida College of Veterinary Medicine in Gainesville.

Richard H. Pitcairn, D.V.M., Ph.D., is a veterinarian in private practice in Eugene, Oregon, and author of *Dr. Pitcairn's Complete Guide to Natural Health for Dogs and Cats.*

Pete Schaubhut, D.V.M., is a veterinarian in private practice in New York City.

Food Allergy & Sensitivity

9 Steps to Stop Food from Eating Her

Does your pet eat her kibble and then lose her lunch? Is her hind leg perpetually stuck in scratching gear?

For dogs and cats with food allergies and sensitivities, eating the wrong chow can unleash a torrent of uncomfortable symptoms, ranging from vomiting or diarrhea to never-ending itchiness.

In most cases, however, "food problems are easy to treat," says Alexander Werner, V.M.D., a veterinarian in private practice in Studio City, California, who specializes in dermatology. "Stop feeding the same old diet and find a new one your pet can tolerate."

To make mealtimes fun times again, here's what experts recommend.

 For **Dogs** and **Cats**

Don't share from your plate. There are a number of human foods that can cause problems in pets. Slipping your pet such goodies as fermented cheese, beef sausage, canned tuna, egg whites or even tomatoes could cause allergy symptoms to flare, says Dan Carey, D.V.M., a veterinarian and director of technical communications for the IAMS Company in Dayton, Ohio.

Forget the dairy. Some pets have difficulty digesting milk or cheese because they lack the enzyme (lactase) needed to digest a sugar (lactose) found in dairy products. "Milk often gives pets diarrhea when they can't digest the lactose," Dr. Carey adds.

Try an elimination diet. The only way to know for sure what food or ingredient is causing your friend's culinary distress is to eliminate it from her diet for up to 12 weeks and see if she improves, says Richard W. Markham, D.V.M., veterinary consultation service manager for Hill's Pet Nutrition in Topeka, Kansas.

Since you won't know at first what the culprit is, your vet may recommend putting your pet on an elimination diet. This means feeding her a totally new food until her symptoms go away. Then you gradually reintroduce her old foods, one at a time, until her symptoms flare again. Then you'll know what's been causing the problem.

Choose a "safe" food. For an elimination diet to be effective, you have to feed your pet an entirely new food—one with ingredients she's never been exposed to. It's not enough just to change brands, since many commercial foods contain the same ingredients. "The ideal diet has a unique protein source the pet has not been exposed to before," says James Jeffers, V.M.D., a veterinary dermatologist in private practice in Gaithersburg, Maryland.

Read the label on her old food. The ingredients probably include such things as beef, fish, chicken, egg, milk, wheat, soy or corn. Now you know what your pet has already been exposed to. The next step is to find a food *without* any of these ingredients.

Prepare a home-cooked meal. One way to control what your pet eats during the elimination diet is to make "hypoallergenic" foods at home, says Lowell Ackerman, D.V.M., Ph.D., a veterinary dermatologist in private practice in Scottsdale, Arizona, and author of *Skin and Haircoat Problems in Dogs.*

For dogs, a combination of rice flavored with baby food containing lamb is often a good choice (assuming, of course, her usual food doesn't already contain lamb). Cats don't like rice, so try giving them only the baby food instead.

Try a commercial brand. If you don't feel like preparing your pet's meals yourself, your vet can recommend a commercially prepared diet. There are a number of foods made from "unusual" protein sources— like rabbit or venison—that can be used to help nail down food allergies, says Dr. Werner.

Nix the nibbles. Being on an elimination diet also means forgoing special treats such as pet snacks, rawhide chews or even flavored vitamins. Until you know for sure what's causing your pet's problems, "nothing should pass her lips except for the diet and preferably distilled water," says Dr. Werner.

Challenge the chow. Once your pet's symptoms have cleared up, it's time to start reintroducing new foods *one at a time* to see which one makes her react. Feed her each new food for about five days.

To check for a soy allergy, for example, give your pet a little tofu. Other allergies to test for include beef, chicken, wheat, corn and eggs. "Most dogs and cats react to only one or two ingredients," says Dr. Werner.

Suspicious Links

Food allergies can be tough to pin down. Dogs and cats may be allergic to a variety of proteins. In addition, they may be sensitive to other things, like fleas or pollen, as well, says John MacDonald, D.V.M., associate professor of dermatology at the Auburn University College of Veterinary Medicine in Alabama. In some cases, the only time a pet has symptoms is when he's been exposed to all of the different factors at the same time.

While this type of *multiple sensitivity* can be difficult to diagnose, it isn't necessarily hard to treat. Getting rid of even one of the allergens—the fleas, for example—may relieve the food sensitivity as well.

"You should be able to turn a food reaction on and off like a light switch," he adds. "If the signs come back, you've got a cause and effect."

Find a diet to depend on. Once you know what your pet has to avoid, "you can walk into a store and probably find 20 to 30 different foods that will work for her," says Dr. Werner.

PANEL OF ADVISERS

Lowell Ackerman, D.V.M., Ph.D., is a veterinary dermatologist in private practice in Scottsdale, Arizona, and author of *Skin and Haircoat Problems in Dogs*.

Dan Carey, D.V.M., is a veterinarian and director of technical communications for the IAMS Company in Dayton, Ohio.

James Jeffers, V.M.D., is a veterinary dermatologist in private practice in Gaithersburg, Maryland.

John MacDonald, D.V.M., is associate professor of dermatology at the Auburn University College of Veterinary Medicine in Alabama.

Richard W. Markham, D.V.M., is veterinary consultation service manager for Hill's Pet Nutrition in Topeka, Kansas.

Alexander Werner, V.M.D., is a veterinarian in Studio City, California, who specializes in dermatology.

Fussy Eating

6 Appetizing Solutions

You probably remember Morris, the finicky feline whose fussy eating catapulted him to commercial fame. But if you're living with your own fussy eater, Morris probably seems like a dream cat. At least he liked *some* foods, while your pet turns up his whiskers at just about everything.

Don't fret, experts say. Dogs and cats can skip an occasional meal without suffering anything worse than hunger pangs, says nutrition expert Tony Buffington, D.V.M., Ph.D., associate professor in the Department of Veterinary Clinical Sciences at the Ohio State University College of Veterinary Medicine in Columbus. In addition, there are a number of ways to make meals more palatable. Here's what experts recommend.

 For **Dogs** and **Cats**

Never beg. "If I were a dog or cat and my owner got on his hands and knees and begged me to eat, I would realize the great entertainment value of the scene," says Dr. Buffington. "Why would I risk it by eating immediately?" So instead of pleading, put down the food and walk away, he suggests. Your pet will eventually learn to eat his dinner without the show.

Set a time limit. If your pet isn't finished eating in an hour, pick up his food and put it away, advises Dr. Buffington. Later, bring it back out—but again, give him only one hour to eat. "We've found that the most finicky pets usually have food available all the time," he says. "When they learn it's either eat or go hungry for a while, they tend to eat."

Table the scraps. While your pet undoubtedly appreciates leftovers and mealtime handouts, those rich goodies may be spoiling his appetite, raising his expectations and contributing to a variety of poten-

When to See the Vet

You know there's a problem when you whip up your pet's favorite tuna-and-chicken casserole and he doesn't even lick his chops. Obviously, fussy eating isn't the problem. What is?

Most of the time, it's nothing you need to worry about, experts say. It's common for even the heartiest eaters to skip a meal or two—because of an upset tummy, for example, or because they're bothered by a recent commotion such as moving to a new house or having strangers in the house.

Generally, a healthy dog can go three to four days without eating before you need to worry. With cats, however, liver function can be impaired after even short periods without food. So if your cat hasn't eaten for a day or more, call your vet right away. "You just don't fool around if your cat's not eating anything," says nutrition expert William Burkholder, D.V.M., Ph.D., clinical assistant professor in the Department of Small Animal Nutrition at the Texas A&M University College of Veterinary Medicine in College Station.

tially serious diseases. "Would you want to eat dog food if you knew you could get steak every night?" says Lisa Freeman, D.V.M., clinical instructor and a fellow in clinical nutrition at the Tufts University School of Veterinary Medicine in North Grafton, Massachusetts.

Some like it hot. If your pet normally walks away from dry kibble, try adding a little warm water. This will soften the food and make it as appetizing as homemade stew. "Who doesn't enjoy a warm meal once in a while?" says Dr. Buffington.

If your pet normally eats canned food, scoop some into a bowl and heat it in the microwave until it's just warm, adds Dr. Freeman.

Tantalize his taste buds. "A sprinkle of something out of the ordinary could be all it takes for your pet to take an interest in food again," says Kathy Gaughan, D.V.M., an instructor in the Department of Clinical Sciences at the Kansas State University College of Veterinary Medicine in Manhattan, Kansas. Just don't overdo the succulent add-ons—scraps from last night's pot roast, for example—or you could end up with another problem: an unusually plump pet.

Create a stink. When you shop for pet foods, look for one that really smells. "The smellier it is, the tastier dogs and cats—particularly cats—will find it," says Dr. Freeman. Cats often favor fish-flavored vittles, while dogs tend to prefer liver and beef.

PANEL OF ADVISERS

Tony Buffington, D.V.M., Ph.D., is a nutrition expert and associate professor in the Department of Veterinary Clinical Sciences at the Ohio State University College of Veterinary Medicine in Columbus.

William Burkholder, D.V.M., Ph.D., is a nutrition expert and clinical assistant professor in the Department of Small Animal Nutrition at the Texas A&M University College of Veterinary Medicine in College Station.

Lisa Freeman, D.V.M., is clinical instructor and a fellow in clinical nutrition at the Tufts University School of Veterinary Medicine in North Grafton, Massachusetts.

Kathy Gaughan, D.V.M., is instructor in the Department of Clinical Sciences at the Kansas State University College of Veterinary Medicine in Manhattan, Kansas.

Hair Balls

8 Ways to Lick the Problem

Few creatures are as fastidious as felines. They can spend hours licking their coats, and when they've covered every inch, they'll happily start again. They don't seem to mind swallowing a little hair—it's all part of good grooming.

Sometimes, however, fur that should pass right through the digestive system gets trapped in the stomach. As more and more hair arrives, it begins forming an uncomfortable wad. That's when your pet starts gagging, hacking and trying to vomit it up.

While his retching may look wretched, hair balls are rarely a serious problem. "Most cats get hair balls at some point in their lives, and everything usually comes out fine," says Charles W. Hickey, D.V.M., a veterinarian in private practice in Richmond, Virginia. Try these tips to help make the process a little easier.

 **For Cats Only**

Pass it with petroleum. When your pet first starts hacking, try giving him ¼ teaspoon of petroleum jelly. This will help ease the hair ball through his digestive tract rather than upward onto the carpet, says Lynda Bond, D.V.M., a veterinarian in private practice in Cape Elizabeth, Maine, who hosts a weekly pet segment for a Portland television station. If your cat doesn't like the taste of petroleum jelly, you can take advantage of his fastidious nature and put it on a front paw or under his nose. "Being a cat, he's inclined to clean it off, and in cleaning it off he eats it up," says Dr. Bond. Do this once a day for about four days, she advises.

Try a tasty alternative. Some hair-ball lubricants are downright delicious to cats. Pet stores sell several delectable kinds, like Laxatone and Petromalt. "I had a cat that loved his hair-ball remedy so much that he was always looking around the house for it," says Dr. Hickey.

Butter him up. One of the most effective hair-ball remedies is butter, and cats lap it up, says James B. Dalley, D.V.M., associate professor of small animal clinical sciences at the Michigan State University College of Veterinary Medicine in East Lansing. "Besides being a natural lubricant, butter makes the gallbladder contract and empty bile, a mild laxative, into the digestive tract," he says. This helps speed hair balls out of a cat's system before they cause trouble. He advises giving $\frac{1}{2}$ to 1 teaspoon of butter once a day for up to a week. You don't want to use butter too often, though, he adds, because your cat could go from having hair balls to being a butterball.

Fix it with fiber. "Sometimes a higher-fiber pet food is all it takes to accelerate the passage of a hair ball," says Martin J. Fettman, D.V.M., Ph.D., professor of pathology and clinical nutrition at the Colorado State University College of Veterinary Medicine and Biomedical Sciences in Fort Collins. When shopping for a high-fiber food, look for one containing 3.5 to 10 percent fiber. The fiber percentage is listed on the label.

Foil his fleas. If your cat is infested, he could be grooming himself more than usual and consequently swallowing more hair, says Dr. Hickey. "If you have a tried-and-true flea-busting method, use it, and your cat's hair-ball problems should improve," he says.

Coif your kitty. Combing and brushing your cat's fur every day can do wonders for hair-ball prevention, says Gary Beard, D.V.M., assis-

When to See the Vet

Although most hair balls are, well, hair today and gone tomorrow, some are longer-lasting—and much more dangerous.

"I once saw a hair ball, if you could call it that, that had gathered so much hair that it was 12 inches long. It went from halfway down the cat's esophagus all the way deep into the intestinal tract," says Charles W. Hickey, D.V.M., a veterinarian in private practice in Richmond, Virginia.

Sometimes even normal-size hair balls can cause intestinal blockage or choking, he adds. That's why experts advise a trip to the vet if the retching continues for more than three days or if your cat is constipated or refuses food for more than a day. "A hair ball that blocks the digestive tract can be deadly, so catching it early is important," says Dr. Hickey.

tant dean at the Auburn University College of Veterinary Medicine in Alabama. "Cats can shed hundreds of hairs a day, especially in spring and summer. If you brush these hairs away, your cat's not going to be swallowing so many," he says.

Then wipe him down. After grooming your cat, use a moist washcloth to remove loose hairs your comb or brush might have missed, advises Dr. Dalley.

Take his mind off his fur. "Some cats have personalities that make them compulsive lickers—they can't get enough of grooming themselves," says Dr. Fettman. Overgrooming can also be a response to stress. To give your cat a much-needed distraction, he recommends playing with him more often. "If you give him something else to put his energy into, his grooming may become more normal and his hair balls may diminish," he says.

PANEL OF ADVISERS

Gary Beard, D.V.M., is assistant dean at the Auburn University College of Veterinary Medicine in Alabama.

Lynda Bond, D.V.M., is a veterinarian in private practice in Cape Elizabeth, Maine, who hosts a weekly pet segment for a Portland television station.

James B. Dalley, D.V.M., is associate professor of small animal clinical sciences at the Michigan State University College of Veterinary Medicine in East Lansing.

Martin J. Fettman, D.V.M., Ph.D., is professor of pathology and clinical nutrition at the Colorado State University College of Veterinary Medicine and Biomedical Sciences in Fort Collins.

Charles W. Hickey, D.V.M., is a veterinarian in private practice in Richmond, Virginia.

Heart Problems

7 Healthy Hints

No matter how many rich foods or succulent snacks your pets devour each day, they don't get clogged arteries the way people do.

But their hearts, like any pump, can still have problems, such as heart murmurs, that keep them from working at peak efficiency. While any kind of heart disease requires a veterinarian's care, there are things you can do to help them keep the beat.

 ## For Dogs and Cats

Make eating easier. Eating one big meal a day puts more stress on the body than eating several smaller meals, says Janet R. Childs, D.V.M., a house-call veterinarian in Fairview, Tennessee. Feeding your pet smaller meals two or three times a day will keep her stomach satisfied and could help keep her heart working more smoothly, she says.

Ask about fish oils. Studies suggest that feeding pets omega-3 fatty acids may lower blood pressure and reduce the occurrence of blood clots, which can cause heart attacks, says Walter Weirich, D.V.M., Ph.D., professor of surgery and cardiology at the School of Veterinary Medicine at Purdue University in West Lafayette, Indiana.

It's expensive, but feeding your pet fresh or canned fish—like herring, mackerel, salmon or tuna—several times a week will provide plenty of omega-3's. An easier way is to give her fatty acid supplements. The supplements come as capsules and are available at health food stores and some pet stores. Ask your vet which supplements (and doses) are best.

Watch the scales. Being overweight can put a substantial load on the heart. "The heart does function better if it does not have to pump against all that resistance," says Dr. Weirich. Extra weight also stresses bones and joints, he adds.

Your pet should be lean enough that you can feel all of her ribs when you run your hands over her sides. If you can't feel anything but flab, talk to your vet about putting your pet on a sensible weight-loss plan.

Cut back on salt. While most dogs and cats can get normal amounts of salt in their diets without having difficulty, those with heart problems need to be particularly careful, says Lee R. Harris, D.V.M., a veterinarian in private practice in Federal Way, Washington.

While most commercial pet foods are acceptably low in salt, pets with heart problems may need to go even lower. Try a special low-salt food such as Hill's Prescription Diet, says Dr. Harris.

Keep her moving. Regular exercise is one of the best ways to keep the heart and lungs working at peak capacity. Try to take your pet out twice a day for a least 15 to 20 minutes. Unless your pet is already in good shape, however, don't overdo it, adds Michael Richards, D.V.M., a veterinarian in private practice in Cobbs Creek, Virginia, who also answers questions about dog and cat health in the Pet Care Forum on America Online. "Build up to a moderate exercise level gradually," he advises. And if your pet already has a history of heart problems, be sure to check with your vet before beginning any new exercise program.

Ask about aspirin. Giving pets low doses of aspirin on a regular basis "thins" the blood, helping to reduce the possibility of dangerous blood clots, says Dr. Weirich. This treatment isn't recommended for

When to See the Vet

While pets are less likely than people to have heart attacks, any problem with the heart requires fast treatment.

Signs of heart problems include gasping for breath, coughing, swelling of the abdomen or a blue tint on the insides of the lips—a sign of oxygen deprivation, says James Buchanan, D.V.M., professor of cardiology at the University of Pennsylvania School of Veterinary Medicine in Philadelphia.

The speed at which your pet's heart beats is another indicator of how well—or poorly—the heart is performing. To check her pulse, place your hand against her chest near her left elbow. Count the number of beats in 15 seconds, then multiply by four.

A cat's heart normally beats about 120 times a minute, while a dog's normal range (depending on the breed) can be anywhere from 60 to 160. A fast, slow or erratic beat could mean something serious is wrong, says Dr. Buchanan. If you're worried, call your vet right away.

Brush Away Heart Disease

It's been said that the nearest way to your pet's heart is through her stomach. When it comes to heart disease, however, it's possible that her teeth could provide a dangerous shortcut.

"When we lift the lip and see bad teeth, we know the animal could have a heart problem," says Lee R. Harris, D.V.M., a veterinarian in private practice in Federal Way, Washington.

"When a pet has bad teeth, bacteria can get into the circulation around the gums," he explains. "The bacteria float around the bloodstream and tend to settle on the heart valve. After five or six years of this, it can scar the valve."

He recommends keeping your pet's teeth clean and white with regular mouth care. This means brushing or scrubbing the teeth daily. In addition, giving your pet raw carrots or hard rubber toys to chew will help keep her teeth clean. (For more on mouth care, see Dental Problems on page 131.)

all pets, however, so ask your veterinarian first.

In addition, never replace aspirin with an aspirin substitute without checking with your vet. Some over-the-counter painkillers can be dangerous when given to pets, Dr. Weirich warns.

Reach for the vitamins. Research suggests that giving your pet daily doses of vitamin C, E or beta-carotene—the antioxidant vitamins—can help neutralize harmful oxygen molecules in the cells that can lead to heart damage. "Antioxidants can help slow the progression of heart disease," says Dr. Childs. Ask your vet to recommend a dose that's safe for your pet.

PANEL OF ADVISERS

James Buchanan, D.V.M., is professor of cardiology at the University of Pennsylvania School of Veterinary Medicine in Philadelphia.

Janet R. Childs., D.V.M., is a house-call veterinarian in Fairview, Tennessee.

Lee R. Harris, D.V.M., is a veterinarian in private practice in Federal Way, Washington.

Michael Richards, D.V.M., is a veterinarian in private practice in Cobbs Creek, Virginia, who also answers questions on dog and cat health in the Pet Care Forum on America Online.

Walter Weirich, D.V.M., Ph.D., is professor of surgery and cardiology at the Purdue University School of Veterinary Medicine in West Lafayette, Indiana.

Heartworms

8 Smart Safeguards

It's bad enough when you get bitten by a hungry mosquito—and spend the rest of the day scratching the results.

For dogs and cats, however, mosquitoes are more than just an itchy annoyance. In most parts of the country, particularly on the Gulf and Atlantic coasts, they can carry heartworms. Unless your pet is taking preventive medication, a bite from an infected mosquito could pass this dangerous parasite on to him.

As the name suggests, heartworms literally take up residence in the heart, often causing coughing, rapid breathing, weight loss and sometimes death. Most heartworm cases occur in dogs, although cats can be infected, too.

Since there's no certain way to keep your pet from being bitten by a mosquito, taking preventive measures is essential, says Walter Weirich, D.V.M, Ph.D., professor of surgery and cardiology at the Purdue University School of Veterinary Medicine in West Lafayette, Indiana.

 For **Dogs** and **Cats**

Stop them at the gates. Vets recommend that all dogs (and some cats) be given preventive medication. That way, even if your pet is bitten by an infected mosquito, the medication in his bloodstream will destroy the heartworms before they mature and cause problems.

The medication is available in two types: One pill is formulated to be given daily, the other to be given monthly. If you live in an area with cold winters—and hence no mosquitoes during those months—your vet may recommend that your pet take the pills only during mosquito season. But many vets opt to play it safe and prescribe the pills all year, says Paul Schmitz, D.V.M., a veterinarian in private practice in Joliet, Illinois.

Don't be overconfident. Even if your pet never ventures outside, it's always possible that a mosquito may slip in. Both indoor and outdoor pets should be taking heartworm medication, says Carol Macherey, D.V.M., a veterinarian in private practice in Nashville.

Don't neglect the test. It may be dangerous to give heartworm preventive to a dog or cat that's already infected, which is why vets usually perform a blood test before prescribing the pills. Once you know your pet isn't infected, he can begin taking the medication, says Dr. Schmitz.

Review the records. Some of the older tests for heartworm weren't entirely accurate, Dr. Schmitz adds. It's always a good idea to have your vet take a look at your pet's records to see if he needs to have a newer, more accurate test.

Don't swap pills. Heartworm medication comes in a variety of different strengths. The dose that's right for one pet could be ineffective when given to another. In addition, doses that are safe for dogs could be dangerous for cats. So don't mix and match. Have each of your pets tested individually, then give them their own pills, vets advise.

Invest in snug screens. While you can't entirely exclude mosquitoes from your life (or the house), putting up tight-fitting window and door screens will help keep their numbers down, says Dr. Schmitz. Patch or replace damaged screens as soon as possible, he adds.

Invite some friends for dinner. Putting a purple martin birdhouse in your yard will attract these voracious birds, which can eat thousands of insects a day. This will help keep the mosquito population down—and with it the risk of infection, says Dr. Schmitz. It's also a good idea to eliminate pools of standing water where mosquitoes breed, he adds.

When to See the Vet

Once your pet gets heartworms, it's a difficult condition to treat. The drugs used to eradicate the worms contain arsenic, which can be more dangerous than the disease, says Mark Coleman, D.V.M., a veterinarian in private practice in Gainesville, Florida, and president of the American Heartworm Association.

When heartworms are caught early, however, they are far easier to treat than at later stages, he says. That's why it's critical to see your vet at the first sign of symptoms, which include coughing, rapid breathing and fatigue.

Putting a purple martin birdhouse in your yard will attract these hungry birds, which can eat thousands of mosquitoes a day. This will help reduce the mosquito population—and with it the risk that your pet will get heartworms.

 **For Cats Only**

Avoid high-risk jaunts. Heartworms occur less often in cats than in dogs, which is why cats usually aren't given the preventive medicine.

But cats can get infected, so try to keep your pet out of harm's way, says Mark Coleman, D.V.M., a veterinarian in private practice in Gainesville, Florida, and president of the American Heartworm Association.

"Keep him indoors, especially during the hours of the day when mosquitoes are more prevalent, such as late afternoon and evening," he advises.

PANEL OF ADVISERS

Mark Coleman, D.V.M., is a veterinarian in private practice in Gainesville, Florida, and president of the American Heartworm Society.

Carol Macherey, D.V.M., is a veterinarian in private practice in Nashville.

Paul Schmitz, D.V.M., is a veterinarian in private practice in Joliet, Illinois.

Walter Weirich, D.V.M., Ph.D., is professor of surgery and cardiology at the Purdue University School of Veterinary Medicine in West Lafayette, Indiana.

Hip Dysplasia
10 Soothing Suggestions

Your pooch used to run around like wildfire, but lately his hind legs are so sore and stiff he can barely get out of bed in the morning.

Chances are, he's suffering from hip dysplasia. Rare in cats but common in larger dogs, this is an inherited condition in which the hip joint doesn't fit together as tightly as it should. Over time this can cause painful wear and tear and sometimes lead to arthritis as well.

A diagnosis of hip dysplasia isn't always a dire decree. "Many dogs with hip dysplasia adjust to the problem and live out perfectly healthy, normal lives—with a little assistance from their owners," says E. A. Corley, D.V.M., Ph.D., president and executive director of the Orthopedic Foundation for Animals in Columbia, Missouri.

Here are some tips from the experts on how you can help.

 For **Dogs** Only

Keep him light on his paws. "It's terrible seeing a fat dog with hip dysplasia," says Dr. Corley. "The last thing he needs is to add even more stress to the hip joint." If your pooch is a little plump, trim his tummy by cutting back on snacks and table scraps and switching him to a food that's high in fiber and low in fat.

Keep those paws moving. Regular exercise will help strengthen the muscles that support your pet's hips, says James D. Lincoln, D.V.M., associate professor and chief of small animal surgery at the Washington State University College of Veterinary Medicine in Pullman.

He recommends taking a 20-minute walk twice a day, although longer walks are fine if your pet seems to be enjoying them. It's important, however, to let your pet set the pace. "Don't overdo it with exercise, because you can make things even worse," Dr. Lincoln says. "Consistency and moderation are the keys."

Take the plunge. "Swimming is the greatest exercise there is for

It's Hip to Be Lean

Few things are cuter than a plump puppy. But if your corpulent little canine belongs to one of the breeds that are prone to hip dysplasia—those most at risk include German shepherds, golden retrievers and other large dogs—the extra pudge could mean trouble.

Experts suspect that when a puppy is going through his most rapid growth phase—usually between four and nine months—being overweight could put damaging stress on growing bones. "A fat puppy's hips may start developing incorrectly," says E. A. Corley, D.V.M., Ph.D., president and executive director of the Orthopedic Foundation for Animals in Columbia, Missouri.

This doesn't mean that lean pups will never get hip dysplasia, he adds, but it will at least help keep them healthy longer.

He recommends giving your pet high-quality puppy chow, but only about three-quarters of the amount recommended on the label. "Look at his eyes, his coat and his energy level," says Dr. Corley. "If everything is fine, and it probably will be, this should be a good diet for him."

dysplastic dogs," says Dr. Corley. "It keeps the muscles around the joints toned, and there's not lots of wear and tear. Besides that, some dogs live to swim."

Dr. Corley recommends letting your pet swim for as long as he likes. "Just be sure not to let him get tired out," he adds.

Keep him warm. Sore hips do best when it's warm and dry. "Don't make him sleep outside," says Dr. Corley. "His pain can increase terribly with chilly, damp weather."

Choose the right bed. Better yet, let him choose. "He knows what feels best, so listen to him," says Dr. Lincoln. "If he just likes a blanket, that's fine. If he likes thick foam pads or your old pillow, that's not going to hurt him either."

Some like it hot. Applying a hot water bottle to the hips for 10 to 15 minutes twice a day will go a long way toward easing the ache, says David E. Harling, D.V.M., a veterinarian in private practice in Greensboro, North Carolina, who specializes in orthopedics and ophthalmology.

Rub him the right way. Massaging the muscles around the hip joint will help relax spasms and ease the pain, says Dr. Corley. He advises massaging in a circular motion over the hip joint, using gentle pressure with your fingertips or your palm. "If the dog shows any signs of discomfort, use less pressure or stop massaging," he says. "Otherwise, you can massage each side for a good ten minutes or more, whatever you and the dog feel like," he says.

Help him be upwardly mobile. Climbing stairs or hopping into a car, truck or van can be difficult—and painful—for dogs with hip dysplasia. Using a ramp will make life easier for both of you, says Mark M. Smith, V.M.D., associate professor of surgery in the Department of Small Animal Clinical Sciences at the Virginia-Maryland Regional College of Veterinary Medicine in Blacksburg, Virginia, and co-author of *Atlas of Approaches for General Surgery of the Dog and Cat.* If you use a ramp, "you don't have to pick him up all the time, which can be tough for both you and the dog."

A hint from the pros: Carpeting the ramp will help keep your dog from sliding downhill.

Lay down some traction. "Slippery floors aren't much fun for dogs with hip dysplasia," says Peter Theran, V.M.D., vice-president of the hospital division at the Massachusetts Society for the Prevention of Cruelty to Animals/American Humane Education Society in Boston. He recommends putting down throw rugs to help your pet walk without worry.

Try an OTC. Aspirin is one of the best remedies for easing dysplasia pain, says Dr. Corley. Vets recommend giving about one-quarter of a 325-milligram tablet per ten pounds of dog twice a day. It's best to give buffered aspirin, which is less likely than regular aspirin to upset their tummies.

PANEL OF ADVISERS

E. A. Corley, D.V.M., Ph.D., is president and executive director of the Orthopedic Foundation for Animals in Columbia, Missouri.

David E. Harling, D.V.M., is a veterinarian in private practice in Greensboro, North Carolina, who specializes in orthopedics and ophthalmology.

James D. Lincoln, D.V.M., is associate professor and chief of small animal surgery at the College of Veterinary Medicine at Washington State University in Pullman.

Mark M. Smith, V.M.D., is associate professor of surgery in the Department of Small Animal Clinical Sciences at the Virginia-Maryland Regional College of Veterinary Medicine in Blacksburg, Virginia, and co-author of *Atlas of Approaches for General Surgery of the Dog and Cat.*

Peter Theran, V.M.D., is vice-president of the hospital division of the Massachusetts Society for the Prevention of Cruelty to Animals/American Humane Education Society in Boston.

Hives

5 Ways to Stop the Scratching

When your pet's hind leg starts whirling like a propeller and you hear that "thump, thump, thump" on the floor, you know there's something itchy going on.

While fleas are one common cause of itching, your pet could have hives—red, raised welts on the skin that are the body's response to allergens like insect stings or pollen. Or he could be sensitive to something in his food.

While hives aren't particularly common, when they do occur they can make your pet terribly itchy for a day or two. In most cases the hives will disappear on their own within 24 hours, although in animals with allergies they may recur often, says Richard Anderson, D.V.M., a veterinary dermatologist in private practice in Boston.

Hives that don't go away fairly quickly or that keep coming back should be seen by a vet. In the meantime, here's what experts recommend.

 For Dogs and Cats

Try an antihistamine. Over-the-counter medications like diphenhydramine (Benadryl) block the effects of histamine, a body chemical that causes itching, says William Crane, V.M.D., a veterinarian in private practice in Colmar, Pennsylvania.

The dose you give depends on your pet's weight. A rule of thumb is to give one to three milligrams per pound, but you should call your veterinarian for dosage advice.

Scratch the ointments. While topical medications like calamine or hydrocortisone cream can help relieve itching in people, they aren't as effective in pets because the animals usually lick them off, says Dr. Crane.

Hands off. Rare is the cat or dog that won't appreciate your giving him an assertive scratch. In the case of hives, however, scratching only makes the itching worse. So keep your fingers to yourself, vets advise.

Consider his history. Since hives are often caused by allergies, you may have to do some detective work to figure out what's going on, says Dr. Anderson. Write down when the hives began, when they worsened (or got better), and what your pet was eating or was exposed to. You'll also want to note whether other animals in the family were also affected.

Pinpointing the culprit can take time, says Dr. Crane. But what you eventually learn may be surprising. In one case, for example, a dog's owners kept track of everything he was exposed to, no matter how ridiculous it seemed. "They did this for a very long time," says Dr. Crane. The cause of the problem: a deodorant worn by one of the family members.

Try an elimination diet. Some animals develop hives because they are allergic to a protein found in their diets, says Dr. Anderson. Your vet may recommend that you temporarily switch to a commercially prepared food that contains proteins your pet has never been exposed to and that he won't react to.

Dogs may be put on a special food made from fish and potato, says Kathryn Michel, D.V.M., a researcher and nutrition expert in the Department of Clinical Studies at the University of Pennsylvania School of Veterinary Medicine in Philadelphia. For cats, rabbit and rice is often good.

If your pet's hives go away after a few days or weeks on the new diet, then the culprit probably was something in his supper bowl. You're going to have to switch foods. Your vet can recommend a variety of commercially prepared foods for allergic pets, or he may supply you with recipes for making your own.

PANEL OF ADVISERS

Richard Anderson, D.V.M., is a veterinary dermatologist in private practice in Boston.

William Crane, V.M.D., is a veterinarian in private practice in Colmar, Pennsylvania.

Kathryn Michel, D.V.M., is a researcher and nutrition expert in the Department of Clinical Studies at the University of Pennsylvania School of Veterinary Medicine in Philadelphia.

Hot Spots

11 Soothing Solutions

In the morning you noticed a bare spot about the size of a dime right above her tail. By noon it was as big as a quarter, and that evening it was silver dollar–size. You're beginning to suspect that spot won't stop. What's going on?

She may have a hot spot—a painful circle of inflammation that occurs when pets rub, scratch, lick or bite their way into baldness. Vets call this condition pyotraumatic dermatitis, and it usually occurs when something irritating, like fleas, starts bothering the skin.

The more it itches, the more she scratches—and the larger the hot spot grows, says Jan A. Hall, D.V.M., a veterinary dermatologist and referral specialist in Ville St. Laurent in Montreal.

Here are a few ways to soothe sore skin.

 For **Dogs** and **Cats**

Start with a trim. Since hot spots need regular cleaning, it's helpful to trim the hair around the entire area, says James Jeffers, V.M.D., a veterinary dermatologist in private practice in Gaithersburg, Maryland.

In some cases, however, even a quick haircut can be excruciatingly painful. If your pet won't hold still, put off the trim for another day.

Clean the area well. "If the hot spot is only moderately tender, wash it with a nice cleansing solution," says William H. Miller, Jr., V.M.D., associate professor of medicine at the Cornell University College of Veterinary Medicine in Ithaca, New York. Use an antibacterial soap like pHisoDerm or any mild, nonperfumed soap you happen to have around.

Another way to get the area clean and bacteria-free is to dab it with cotton soaked in an antiseptic solution such as Betadine Solution, adds Dr. Hall. Repeat the procedure two or three times a day, she advises.

Compress with care. To ease discomfort and help with cleaning, apply a soothing compress to the hot spot several times a day. "The advantage of a compress is to soften up any crust so you can gently wipe it away and then better clean the area," Dr. Hall says.

Wet a soft, clean cloth in cool water. Wring it well, then apply it to the area for 10 to 15 minutes, reapplying as needed.

Try a stronger brew. To help speed healing, some vets recommend washing hot spots with strong black or green brewed tea. Tea contains tannic acid, which will help dry the area and help the sore heal. Don't apply hot tea, however; make sure it's cool to the touch.

Dry it with Burow's. Another way to dry hot spots is by applying diluted Burow's solution (aluminum acetate) three times a day. "This agent will keep the area dry and help promote healing," Dr. Jeffers says.

Burow's solution is available in pharmacies. It can be applied as a compress or by pouring it into a bottle and then applying it as a spray.

Ease the inflammation. To reduce swelling and discomfort, try applying a thin layer of hydrocortisone cream, says Kim Herrman, V.M.D., a veterinarian in private practice in Newark, Delaware.

Hydrocortisone cream is available over the counter. Look for the 1 percent concentration and apply it twice a day.

Although the medication penetrates the skin quickly, you may have to distract your pet to prevent her from licking it off before it has time to work. (If she licks it off later, don't worry: In small amounts the medication is safe for pets, inside and out.)

When to See the Vet

The scary thing about hot spots isn't only how ugly they look or how much pain they can cause but also how fast they can spread. It's not uncommon for these warm, swollen patches, exuding pus and giving off a foul odor, to become several inches in size in just a few hours.

While some hot spots will disappear on their own, others may result in dangerous bacterial infections, says Jan A. Hall, D.V.M., a veterinary dermatologist and referral specialist in Ville St. Laurent in Montreal.

It's best to call a vet if the hot spot hasn't improved within 24 hours, says Dr. Hall. Your pet may need topical or oral antibiotics to help calm her angry skin.

Soothe it with vitamin E. Sold in health food stores, pharmacies and grocery stores, vitamin E is a great way to soothe irritated skin. Just open the capsule and apply the gel to the hot spot once or twice a day, says Dr. Jeffers.

Put on plant protection. Applying the gel from an aloe vera plant will quickly help ease the pain of hot spots and also speed healing, some vets say.

Try gentle restraint. When your pet won't leave the painful area alone, you may need to restrain her with an Elizabethan collar—a plastic ring that slips around her head. "It won't allow the pet to get to the hot spot," Dr. Jeffers explains.

Say farewell to fleas. Since many hot spots are initially caused by flea bites, you may want to spray or powder your pet with a product containing D-limonene or pyrethrins—chemicals that are safe and effective for eliminating fleas. Or try a spray containing methoprene, a hormone that prevents flea eggs from maturing.

Ask about allergies. Hot spots are occasionally caused by food allergies or hay fever, which sometimes result in itchy, irritated skin.

"In the rare cases when hot spots are caused by food allergies, it will take about a month on a new diet to see if the pet is getting better," says Jean Greek, D.V.M., a veterinarian in private practice in Oberlin Park, Kansas, who specializes in dermatology.

PANEL OF ADVISERS

Jean Greek, D.V.M., is a veterinarian in private practice in Oberlin Park, Kansas, who specializes in dermatology.

Jan A. Hall, D.V.M., is a veterinary dermatologist and referral specialist in Ville St. Laurent in Montreal.

Kim Herrman, V.M.D., is a veterinarian in private practice in Newark, Delaware.

James Jeffers, V.M.D., is a veterinary dermatologist in private practice in Gaithersburg, Maryland.

William H. Miller, Jr., V.M.D., is associate professor of medicine at the Cornell University College of Veterinary Medicine in Ithaca, New York.

Hot-Weather Concerns

12 Cool Concepts

Whether they're lying under chairs, lapping up water or sleeping from dawn to dusk, dogs and cats are champs at beating summer's heat.

They have to be. Unlike people, whose perspiration keeps them cool, pets have hardly any sweat glands at all. "They do sweat between their toes, but it's not enough to carry heat away," says Robert Hilsenroth, D.V.M., executive director of the Morris Animal Foundation in Englewood, Colorado.

What they do instead is pant. (Cats are less likely than dogs to overheat, which is why they pant less often.) Panting helps dispel some heat, but it really isn't very efficient, says Kim Michels, D.V.M., a veterinarian in private practice in Kenner, Louisiana, and public relations chairperson for the Louisiana Veterinary Medical Association. Which is why hot weather, for both dogs and cats, is uncomfortable weather.

To help your pets beat the heat, here's what experts recommend.

 ## For Dogs and Cats

Double the water. Even if your pet has a water bowl the size of a birdbath, chances are he occasionally kicks it over—and perhaps goes without water the rest of the day. To prevent him from going thirsty, provide two bowls of water and always keep them filled, says Dr. Hilsenroth.

Let 'em drip. One way to make sure outdoor pets always have a fresh supply of cool water is to place their bowl under a faucet that's allowed to drip, says Robert Willyard, D.V.M., a veterinarian in private practice in Las Vegas and president of the Clark County, Nevada, Veterinary Medical Association.

Give them shelter. Direct sunshine raises body temperature fast,

When to See the Vet

In most cases, a little rest and a cool drink of water is all your hot, panting pet needs to recover from the heat. But if he gets too hot, he could develop heatstroke, which means he needs a vet fast.

Heatstroke may occur whenever a dog or cat's temperature rises above 104°. But you don't have to take your pet's temperature to recognize the warning signs. Visible symptoms of heatstroke include exhaustion, heavy panting and a lurching gait, says Robert Hilsenroth, D.V.M., executive director of the Morris Animal Foundation in Englewood, Colorado. Some pets may get so weak they can't even raise their heads.

Pets with heatstroke can suffer brain damage or worse, so don't take chances if you suspect there's a problem. Get him to a vet right away. In the meantime, you can lower his temperature fast by dousing him with a hose and then wrapping him in a cool, damp blanket while you wait for assistance.

You should encourage him to drink, but don't force him, adds Dr. Hilsenroth. Pets with heatstroke may not swallow properly, and forcing him to drink could make him drown.

which is why dogs and cats need cool places where they can go to escape the sun. You don't need anything fancy, says Dr. Michels. As long as their territory includes a porch, an umbrella or even a leafy tree, they'll find ways to stay cool.

Do a home check. While doghouses, garages or other outbuildings often stay comfortably cool, in some cases the temperature rises fast. So don't automatically assume your pet has a pleasant place to escape the heat.

Wait until the hottest part of the day, then check the temperature of his hideaway yourself, says Dr. Willyard. If it feels uncomfortable to you, it's probably too hot for him. You'll need to arrange for other, more comfortable accommodations, he advises.

Smear on sun protection. Although dogs and cats don't take off their clothes in summer (they never even remove their coats), they can still get sunburn, particularly on their noses, ears and other pink spots, says Dr. Willyard.

If your pet spends time outside, it's a good idea to smear exposed skin with sunscreen, preferably one with an SPF (sun protection factor) of 15 or higher, at least once a day. You'll probably want to apply it more often, since many pets like the taste and will lick it off.

Most sunscreens aren't toxic when taken internally. You should avoid those containing zinc, however, which can be dangerous when licked, warns Paul Brandt, D.V.M., a veterinarian in private practice and president of the Capital Area Veterinary Medical Association in Austin, Texas.

Beat the heat. Rather than taking your pet outside during the hottest times of day, try scheduling your romps in the morning or evening, when temperatures are cooler, says Lisa Degen, D.V.M., a veterinarian in private practice in North Palm Beach, Florida, and president of the Palm Beach Veterinary Society.

Keep the cruising cool. Even when you have the windows open, it's often hotter inside the car than it is outside. To keep your pet comfortable, give him a window seat where he can catch the breeze, vets say. (Make sure the windows are closed far enough to prevent a daredevil jump.) Or let him lie on the floor near an air conditioner vent.

On long trips, it's also a good idea to take water and an extra bowl so he can have a drink when he needs one, says Dr. Degen.

Park carefully. The temperatures inside a parked car can get almost oven-hot in just a few minutes. You should never leave your pet inside a parked car, vets say. If you must leave him in the car during a trip—while you pick up groceries, for example—always park in a cool, shady spot. Leave two or more windows open to allow air to circulate (but not so wide that he can jump out). And don't ever leave him there for more than a minute or two.

Don't push too hard. Dogs and cats that play all day during the cool months may find themselves slowing down when it's hot outside. Don't push them too hard, particularly when they start panting. "Pets don't always know their limits. We have to put the brakes on for them," Dr. Degen says.

Forget the haircut. It seems logical, when temperatures rise, to take your pet to the groomer for a summer 'do. But while a long coat may look hot, in many cases it helps insulate your pet and keeps him cooler, says Dr. Brandt.

It's okay to give him a trim, he adds. Just don't give him a buzz cut unless that's his usual style.

Don't fret about feed. Most dogs and cats naturally eat less during the summer months, so don't be alarmed if your pet's appetite falls off a little bit, says Dr. Hilsenroth. "He's not expending as much energy keeping his body warm, so he needs less food," he explains.

 For Dogs Only

Put in a pool. Dogs often enjoy taking a cool dip on a hot day. Fill a small wading pool with an inch or two of cool water to give them a pleasant place to cool off, Dr. Willyard says.

PANEL OF ADVISERS

Paul Brandt, D.V.M., is a veterinarian in private practice and president of the Capital Area Veterinary Medical Association in Austin, Texas.

Lisa Degen, D.V.M., is a veterinarian in private practice in North Palm Beach, Florida, and president of the Palm Beach Veterinary Society.

Robert Hilsenroth, D.V.M., is executive director of the Morris Animal Foundation in Englewood, Colorado.

Kim Michels, D.V.M., is a veterinarian in private practice in Kenner, Louisiana, and public relations chairperson for the Louisiana Veterinary Medical Association.

Robert Willyard, D.V.M., is a veterinarian in private practice in Las Vegas and president of the Clark County, Nevada, Veterinary Medical Association.

House-Training

18 No-Miss Methods

You've just gotten an adorable new puppy, but you're beginning to suspect she's a leaky model. The way things are going, you'll have only two choices for her name: Spot or Puddles.

"House-training isn't necessarily one of the biggest joys of owning a pet, but it's the most vital training you can give them," says Cara Paasch, D.V.M., a veterinarian in private practice in San Francisco.

To get your pet moving in the right direction—preferably outside or toward the litter box—here's what vets recommend.

 ## For Dogs and Cats

Be kind about accidents. Virtually all pets have occasional mishaps, and it doesn't help to yell or rub their nose in it. "The puppy or kitten doesn't know the rules yet and will be scared and confused," says Liz Palika, a dog obedience instructor in Oceanside, California, a columnist for *Dog Fancy* magazine and author of *Fido, Come: Training Your Dog with Love and Understanding* and *Love on a Leash.*

Show her the bathroom. If you catch your pet going in the wrong place, simply say "No!" and immediately pick her up and take her where she's supposed to go. Then wait for her to finish, and praise her plenty when she does, advises Palika.

Hide the scent. Some vets suspect that when dogs or cats can smell where they've gone before, they're more likely to return to the same spot. You'll have to clean the area thoroughly, says Dr. Paasch.

Dr. Paasch recommends mixing ¼ cup of white vinegar and a squirt of liquid detergent in a quart of warm water. Scrub the area thoroughly with the solution, then apply an odor-masking spray or liquid, such as Urine Kleen or Odormute. Both are available in pet stores.

When to See the Vet

Until recently, your pet has had a spotless record, but now she seems to have misplaced her toilet skills. She may just have an upset tummy, but a sudden and recurring loss of control can also be a sign of trouble, says Cara Paasch, D.V.M., a veterinarian in private practice in San Francisco.

There are a number of serious illnesses that can make accidents all but unavoidable, says Dr. Paasch. Some of the usual suspects include colitis, an intestinal or urinary tract infection or possibly a tumor. So if your pet has been making messes and she's also lethargic, feverish, passing blood in her stool or straining to go, you'll want to see a vet right away.

 For **Dogs** Only

There are two basic styles for house-training a puppy: crate training and paper training. Many experts believe crate training is more effective at helping your puppy learn control, although it's also more labor-intensive—you have to be nearby whenever she has to go. Here's how each technique works.

Begin with a crate. When you first bring your puppy home, set her up in her own indoor kennel, or crate. Put her favorite blanket and toy inside to make it comfy—an inviting place where she'll sleep, nap and hang out when you're not actually watching her, says Katherine Brown, D.V.M., a veterinarian in private practice in Salt Lake City.

Before putting her inside, be sure to remove her collar and tags so they don't get caught on the sides of the crate.

Stay nearby. "The idea is to take her out frequently so she never has an accident in her crate," says Dr. Brown. "Since most animals don't like to soil the area where they sleep, this method really works."

Young puppies will usually have to go out about every two hours during the day when they're active and every four hours at night. After about five months, most dogs will be able to go all night without accidents.

Pick up the papers. As an alternative or supplement to crate-training, you may want to use newspapers. This method is particularly good when you can't be home to let your pup outside. What you do is confine her to a small room in which the floor is covered with newspapers. The idea is to let her out as soon as you can and praise her when she goes outside. And if she happens to make a mess, well, that's what the papers are for.

Give her a smaller target. As your pup gains more control, gradually decrease the area covered by newspapers until she's using only a small corner of the room. By this time she'll have more control and probably won't need the papers much longer.

Anticipate her needs. Whether you're training your pup with papers or a crate, the goal is always to get her outside before it's too late. Signals that spell "bathroom" include crouching, pawing the ground or walking in circles while sniffing the ground. Gently whisk her outside as soon as you suspect trouble.

Have a word with her. Once you've taken your puppy outside, give her a pep talk. Say a key word or two, such as "business," "hurry up" or "go pee," suggests Dr. Paasch. "Puppies are so eager to please. Once it clicks that you're asking them to go to the bathroom, they'll do their best."

Be a cheerleader. "You can't give her too much praise for going where she's supposed to," says Palika. "Hug her, love her, make her know she did a good thing so she'll do it again next time."

Set the alarm. During the first few weeks of house-training, plan on getting up halfway through the night to take your pup outside, says Palika. "Even though she may be trying hard, she's just not going to be able to hold it," she says.

Keep a regular schedule. Even house-trained dogs will need to go outside at least every ten hours or so. Twelve hours is pushing it for

A crate provides a cozy retreat while at the same time preventing your pup from wandering—and making messes—where she shouldn't.

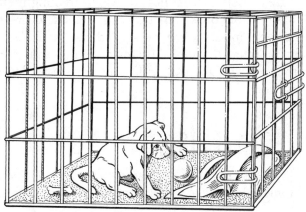

When Your Cat Goes Bad

There's nothing quite like collapsing on the couch at the end of the day only to discover that your furry friend has been there first—and left you a little reminder of her visit.

But while illness can make your cat accident-prone, a more likely scenario is that something around the house isn't to her liking—and she's telling you about it in the only way she knows how.

A dirty litter box may cause your cat to go elsewhere. So can placing the box near her food or in a busy place, such as a hallway, says Myrna Milani, D.V.M., a veterinarian in private practice in Charlestown, New Hampshire. Even changing litter brands can send her in search of another bathroom.

"If she goes at the front door all the time, there could be a new cat in the neighborhood and she's being a sentry," says Bob Gutierrez, animal behavior coordinator at the San Francisco Society for the Prevention of Cruelty to Animals. "Just about any kind of change can bring about house-soiling in certain cats."

Noticing where the "accidents" occur can provide important clues, adds Gutierrez. He tells of one cat that kept spraying by her owner's bureau. "We finally realized the problem: The cat didn't like her new perfume," Gutierrez remembers. "She got rid of the perfume and everything was fine."

---

most dogs. "Don't go for drinks after work unless you have someone to walk your dog or you have a doggy door," says Carol Lea Benjamin, a dog trainer in New York City and author of *Mother Knows Best: The Natural Way to Train Your Dog* and *Surviving Your Dog's Adolescence*.

Be realistic. Regardless of which training method you use, young dogs (and old ones, too) are going to make mistakes. Some pups learn the ropes in just a few weeks. Others, particularly smaller dogs, take six months or more. "If you're doing things right, they'll come around," says Dr. Paasch. "I've never found a dog that can't be house-trained."

 For Cats Only

Kittens get an "A" for house-training. After spending eight weeks at Mom's side, they're usually first in the class at litter-box basics. But if

If your cat suddenly becomes accident-prone, there's probably something going on—like an unwanted "visitor" in the yard—that isn't to her liking. Putting up some frosted "privacy" paper may help: Out of sight is out of mind!

your kitty hasn't quite gotten the concept, try these tips.

Begin with basic training. "Pick her up and take her over to the litter box," says Dr. Brown. "Sometimes all she needs to do is see where it is and she automatically knows what it's for."

Make it easy for her. Just to ensure that your kitten doesn't mistake the antique bedspread for her box, confine her to the bathroom—along with the litter box—soon after eating. When she uses the box, praise her and let her out.

"Cats are naturally fastidious and pick up on this training quickly," says Micky Niego, an animal behavior consultant in Airmont, New York. To prevent misunderstandings, however, you may want to remove the bath mats before shutting kitty in.

Some cats, incidentally, seem to prefer the bathtub to their litter box. Filling the tub with a fraction of an inch of water should stop her cold, experts say.

Make it convenient. Providing your cat with more than one litter box can help prevent her from leaving little surprises around the house, says Dr. Brown. "When kittens have to go, they have to go, and they're not always going to make it across the house or down the stairs. The more litter boxes, the better."

She recommends having at least one litter box on every floor. As a general rule, you'll want a box for each cat, plus an extra box just to be sure.

Low sides are best. For kittens particularly, a high-sided litter box is like putting up a "Do Not Enter" sign. "It's harder for them to get into some of the normal adult-size boxes, and that can slow their house-training progress," says Myrna Milani, D.V.M., a veterinarian in private practice in Charlestown, New Hampshire, and author of *The Body Language and Emotions of Cats* and *The Body Language and Emotions of Dogs*.

"Plastic sweater boxes with fairly low sides are excellent for this purpose, and they're reasonably priced," she adds.

Be a neatnik. Some pets are fussier than others, and keeping the litter box clean will make everyone comfortable. Palika recommends cleaning the box at least once a day and changing the litter as often as three times a week. (Adding a little baking soda will help absorb odors.) "They're not going to be happy with a soiled box and may well refuse to go in it," she says.

PANEL OF ADVISERS

Carol Lea Benjamin is a dog trainer in New York City and author of *Mother Knows Best: The Natural Way to Train Your Dog* and *Surviving Your Dog's Adolescence*.

Katherine Brown, D.V.M., is a veterinarian in private practice in Salt Lake City.

Bob Gutierrez is animal behavior coordinator at the San Francisco Society for the Prevention of Cruelty to Animals.

Myrna Milani, D.V.M., is a veterinarian in private practice in Charlestown, New Hampshire, and author of *The Body Language and Emotions of Dogs* and *The Body Language and Emotions of Cats*.

Micky Niego is an animal behavior consultant in Airmont, New York.

Cara Paasch, D.V.M., is a veterinarian in private practice in San Francisco.

Liz Palika is a dog obedience instructor in Oceanside, California, a columnist for *Dog Fancy* magazine and author of *Fido, Come: Training Your Dog with Love and Understanding* and *Love on a Leash*.

In Heat

12 Tips to Keep Her Calm

When your pet is in heat, she'll do everything but pick the lock with her rabies tag and shimmy out the window in search of romance.

The love bug bites female dogs about every six months, while female felines become seductive once every three weeks from February to October. Each of the heats typically lasts from about six to ten days.

Cats in heat will yowl and howl, while affectionately rubbing against everything in sight. Female dogs get restless and disturbed. Even prospective boyfriends become increasingly obnoxious, particularly when a furry femme fatale encourages their advances. "When the hormones are raging, Romeo needs to be with Juliet," says Mary Jo Mersol-Barg, a cat breeder in Michigan.

Spaying your pet is the only way to put a permanent stop to the shenanigans. Many vets say this is the best strategy, not only for preventing unwanted pregnancies but also for preventing the discomfort that accompanies the cycles. If you plan on breeding your pet, however, but would still like a little peace in the meantime, here are a few ways to cool the heat.

 For **Dogs** and **Cats**

Lay on the love. Your pet's amorous actions and not-so-lovely serenades are really demands for attention. Giving her some extra strokes and perhaps a treat will help take her mind off her problems. "I always try to give them a little extra love to help calm them down," says cat breeder Elaine Wenner Gilbertson of Vista, California, author of *A Feline Affair: Guide to Raising and Breeding Purebred Cats.*

Offer diversions. Although your pet may seem to have a one-track mind, she'll still appreciate getting other forms of attention. "Try playing a game with a favorite toy," Gilbertson suggests. Or simply get down on the floor and give her a belly rub. A vigorous play session will help take her mind off her desires.

Play something soothing. Pets in heat will sometimes settle down when you turn on soothing music. "Pets respond to classical music, especially Mozart," says Pam Johnson, a Nashville, Tennessee, feline behaviorist and author of *Twisted Whiskers: Solving Your Cat's Behavior Problems.*

But beware of strident music with a driving beat that may resemble the sounds of other animals. "Certain tonal qualities actually evoke sexual arousal," says Michael W. Fox, B.V.M., Ph.D., vice-president of bioethics and farm animal protection for the Humane Society of the United States in Washington, D.C., and author of *The New Animal Doctor's Answer Book.*

Keep the windows closed. Male dogs and cats can find females in heat just by sniffing the breeze. In fact, a cat can smell romance a mile away, while a dog's range is about three miles.

"When the girls are in heat, keep your windows closed so you don't have unwelcome males on the doorstep," says Gilbertson.

Nix it with Vicks. The strong smell of this over-the-counter ointment may help keep roaming Romeos away, says Chris Walkowicz, who breeds bearded collies in Sherrard, Illinois, and is co-author of *The Atlas of Dog Breeds of the World* and *Successful Dog Breeding.*

"Put a little on the fur near the girl's tail," she suggests. "If you have a male, put some on his nose."

Try a little chlorophyll. Giving your pet chlorophyll tablets, which are available in health food stores, may help mask the odor of the heat, says H. Ellen Whiteley, D.V.M., a veterinary consultant in private practice in Guadalupita, New Mexico, and author of *Understanding and Training Your Cat or Kitten.*

Limit their territory. Dogs in heat have a bloody discharge that can stain furniture and carpets. Cats don't have the discharge, but they may spray urine about the house to announce their availability to potential partners.

"Try to keep the pet isolated as much as possible in a bathroom or a crate that's easily cleaned," suggests Mersol-Barg.

Keep her under lock and key. Dogs and cats in heat will try almost anything to get outside. Be particularly careful that she doesn't slip by when you're going outside—to get the paper, for example, or when leaving for work in the morning.

If she's an outdoor pet, "confine her in a kennel or a fenced yard where a male can't reach her," says Marion Hunt, who breeds cocker spaniels in Howe, Texas.

"Beware of males jumping the fence," adds Dr. Whiteley. While you're at it, watch out for the guy next door. It's not unheard of for pets to breed right *through* a chain-link fence. "Pets get very creative," she says.

 ## For Dogs Only

Keep her clean. Regularly cleaning away the discharge that occurs during heat can help reduce the odor that attracts male dogs, says Walkowicz. "Particularly during the middle week of season, bathe her rear quarters and legs once or twice a day," she suggests.

Mask the smell. A product called Lust Buster, when sprayed on a female's rear and leg areas, makes her smell as though she's already been bred. This in turn causes marauding males to lose interest. The spray is available in pet stores.

Put on protection. To prevent your dog's discharge from making a mess in the house, put her in diapers, suggests Walkowicz. Pet diapers are available from vets and in pet stores. They come in a variety of sizes, from petite Chihuahua and kitty sizes to Saint Bernard–size jumbo pants. The diapers are fitted with disposable absorbent pads and sport an opening in the rear to accommodate the tail.

Stimulate her appetite. It's not uncommon for a pet's appetite to flag during heat. "After all, she has other things on her mind," Gilbertson says. To encourage your pet to eat and keep up her strength, try offering some special treats, like baby food or a little cooked liver.

PANEL OF ADVISERS

Michael W. Fox, B.V.M., Ph.D., is vice-president of bioethics and farm animal protection for the Humane Society of the United States in Washington, D.C., and author of *The New Animal Doctor's Answer Book.*

Elaine Wenner Gilbertson is a cat breeder in Vista, California, and author of *A Feline Affair: Guide to Raising and Breeding Purebred Cats.*

Marion Hunt breeds cocker spaniels in Howe, Texas.

Pam Johnson is a feline behaviorist in Nashville and author of *Twisted Whiskers: Solving Your Cat's Behavior Problems.*

Mary Jo Mersol-Barg is a cat breeder in Michigan.

Chris Walkowicz breeds bearded collies in Sherrard, Illinois, and is co-author of *The Atlas of Dog Breeds of the World* and *Successful Dog Breeding.*

H. Ellen Whiteley, D.V.M., is a veterinary consultant in private practice in Guadalupita, New Mexico, and author of *Understanding and Training Your Cat or Kitten.*

Insect Bites & Stings

10 Ways to Bite Back

To mosquitoes and other biting members of the insect world, your pets are a four-legged free lunch. Bees, hornets and wasps, however, may be too irritated to lunch. They just sting.

While close encounters of the buggy kind are rarely dangerous, they can be painful. Here are some tips for relieving your friend's stung feelings.

 For **Dogs** and **Cats**

Get the point. If your pet has been targeted by a bee, somewhere in his coat a stinger has probably been left behind. To get it out, carefully part his hair to get a good view. Then remove it with your fingers or a tweezers, says Tam Garland, D.V.M., Ph.D., veterinary toxicologist at the Texas A&M University College of Veterinary Medicine in College Station.

Better yet, if the stinger is in an area that's easy to get to, try scraping it out with your fingernail or the corner of a credit card. That way you're less likely to squeeze additional venom into the wound.

Soothe it with soda. Applying a paste of baking soda and water to the bite or sting several times a day can help ease discomfort, says Larry Thompson, D.V.M., clinical veterinary toxicologist at the Diagnostic Laboratory at the Cornell University College of Veterinary Medicine in Ithaca, New York. "The alkalinity helps relieve the itch," he explains. A dab of calamine can also help, he adds.

Try milk of magnesia. This over-the-counter medication contains magnesium hydroxide, which will also help reduce the itch and irritation, says Dr. Thompson. As with baking soda, you can apply a soothing coat of milk of magnesia several times a day.

Get help from the kitchen. Meat tenderizers contain enzymes that help break down the poison in insect stings, reducing the irritation, says Dr. Thompson.

Make a paste by adding water to the tenderizer. Then apply it directly to the sting, he advises. Repeat as often as needed.

Dab on some ammonia. Experts aren't sure why it works, but ammonia helps cut the pain of bug bites and stings, says E. Murl Bailey, Jr., D.V.M., Ph.D., professor of toxicology in the Department of Veterinary Physiology and Pharmacology at the Texas A&M University College of Veterinary Medicine. "Dab it on the spots with cotton," he says.

Get help from the windowsill. Applying a thin layer of gel from an aloe vera plant will help ease discomfort and possibly speed healing. "Aloe vera is very good for skin irritations," says Dr. Thompson.

If you don't have an aloe vera plant, you can buy the gel in health food stores.

Try an OTC. For areas that are sore and irritated, try applying a thin layer of hydrocortisone cream. "Use Cortaid or another cream with 0.5 percent hydrocortisone," suggests Lowell Ackerman, D.V.M., Ph.D., a veterinary dermatologist in private practice in Scottsdale, Arizona, and author of *Skin and Haircoat Problems in Dogs*.

Chill it down. Applying a cold compress to stings helps take the swelling down and dulls the pain, Dr. Garland says. Wrap a handful of

When to See the Vet

While most bites and stings do nothing more than make your pet a little itchy, sometimes the results can be deadly.

Dogs and cats typically approach the world nose first. As a result they often get stung on the face or in the nose or mouth. "If they swell up in the nose or throat region, they may not be able to breathe," says Tam Garland, D.V.M., Ph.D., veterinary toxicologist at the Texas A&M University College of Veterinary Medicine in College Station.

Watch carefully to see if the swelling is minor or if that fat lip could potentially balloon to dangerous proportions. "If they're stung at 2:00, and at 2:30 there's mild swelling and irritation, that's not going to be a really critical problem," says Larry Thompson, D.V.M., clinical veterinary toxicologist at the Diagnostic Laboratory at the Cornell University College of Veterinary Medicine in Ithaca, New York. "But if they're stung at 2:00 and at 2:05 the swelling is big, they're having a very sensitive reaction and need immediate veterinary care."

ice cubes in a washcloth or small towel and hold it on the area for at least five minutes—longer if your pet will hold still. "It might help calm the animal, too," adds Dr. Garland.

Take to the tub. If your pet is very uncomfortable, a cool soak in colloidal oatmeal (like Aveeno) can help, says Dr. Ackerman.

If you don't have colloidal oatmeal, you can substitute regular oatmeal, adds Dr. Garland. Put the oatmeal in an old sock, attach the sock to the tub faucet and run water through it, she says.

Repel the problem. Dousing your pet with Avon Skin-So-Soft will not only make him smell good, it may also help repel fleas, flies, mosquitoes and other biting things, says Dr. Garland. She recommends mixing about ¼ capful in a quart of water. Put it in a spray bottle and give him a spritz every week or so. "If you use more than that, you're going to get an oily pet," Dr. Garland adds.

PANEL OF ADVISERS

Lowell Ackerman, D.V.M., Ph.D., is a veterinary dermatologist in private practice in Scottsdale, Arizona, and author of *Skin and Haircoat Problems in Dogs*.

E. Murl Bailey, Jr., D.V.M., Ph.D., is professor of toxicology in the Department of Veterinary Physiology and Pharmacology at the Texas A&M University College of Veterinary Medicine in College Station.

Tam Garland, D.V.M., Ph.D., is a veterinary toxicologist at the Texas A&M University College of Veterinary Medicine in College Station.

Larry Thompson, D.V.M., is a clinical veterinary toxicologist at the Diagnostic Laboratory at the Cornell University College of Veterinary Medicine in Ithaca, New York.

Itching

7 Skin Savers

Has the upholstery worn thin where your cat rubs her hide? Does your dog's thumping foot keep you awake at night? Please, would someone stop that itch!

Constant itchiness in pets is usually caused by such things as fleas, hay fever or other allergies. Or it can be caused by nothing more serious than dry skin. By itself, itching isn't a problem. The constant *scratching*, however, can lead to hair loss, skin damage and serious infections.

To curb the itch and scotch the scratch, here's what vets recommend.

 ## For Dogs and Cats

Soothe with a dip. "The easiest way to soothe an itchy pet fast is to give him a cool bath," says Lowell Ackerman, D.V.M., Ph.D., a veterinary dermatologist in private practice in Scottsdale, Arizona, and author of *Skin and Haircoat Problems in Dogs.* The temporary relief from a cool dip can last from several hours to as long as several days, he says. Try to keep your pet in the water for about ten minutes, he advises, but if he won't stay still that long, even a few minutes in the tub will probably help.

Not surprisingly, many cats would rather fight than bathe. For tips on easier bathing, see "How to Give Your Cat a Bath" on page 186.

Soothe it with cereal. "Oatmeal baths can be helpful to animals just as they're helpful to people," says Tam Garland, D.V.M., Ph.D., a veterinary toxicologist at the Texas A&M University College of Veterinary Medicine in College Station. She recommends washing your pet with an oatmeal shampoo or putting colloidal oatmeal (like Aveeno) in the bath water.

If you don't have colloidal oatmeal, you can substitute regular oatmeal from the kitchen, she adds. Take an old sock and fill it with oat-

Name That Itch

Does your dog flail with a hind leg or nibble between his toes? Does your cat rub her face or chew her tail?

Where your pet itches can tell a lot about what's causing the problem, says Steven A. Melman, V.M.D., a veterinarian with practices in Palm Springs, California, and Potomac, Maryland.

Pets with fleas, for example, usually scratch the rear half of their bodies, especially above the tail and down the back of the legs. "The pattern is like a Christmas tree pattern along their back," says Dr. Melman.

If your dog has hay fever, however, it is usually the front half that itches, says Alexander Werner, V.M.D., a veterinarian in private practice in Studio City, California, who specializes in dermatology. "Front-half itching causes face-rubbing, foot-licking, armpit-scratching and neck- and chest-scratching," he explains.

Unlike dogs, cats with hay fever often itch all over. In addition, they may develop little scabby bumps underneath their fur, Dr. Melman says.

If your dog is itching all over, he could have a food allergy. Cats with food allergies, however, are more likely to itch around the face and neck, Dr. Melman says.

Some pets that itch all over also have flaky skin or greasy coats—a condition vets call seborrhea. But if those flakes of skin start to move, watch out: Your pet may have a case of "walking dandruff," which is really a skin parasite called Cheyletiella.

meal. "Tie the sock over your bathtub spout so the water comes through the oatmeal," she suggests.

Try a foot soak. If your pet has been biting or licking his paws, he could have itchy feet. John MacDonald, D.V.M., associate professor of dermatology at the Auburn University College of Veterinary Medicine in Alabama, recommends soothing those paws with an Epsom salts soak.

Run several inches of cool water into the tub. Add two cups of Epsom salts and lift him in for a five- to ten-minute furry-foot soak, he suggests.

Oil the itch. Since itchy skin is often dry skin, using a moisturizer can help relieve the problem. "Avon Skin-So-Soft or Alpha-Keri Oil is good for the itchy pet with dry skin," says Dr. Garland. Dilute one tablespoon per gallon of water and use it as an after-bath rinse. Or spritz your pet's coat once a week or so, she suggests.

Fight fleas. "A lot of itching in pets is due to a flea allergy," says Dan Carey, D.V.M., a veterinarian and director of technical communications for the IAMS Company in Dayton, Ohio. And there doesn't have to be a ferocious horde. "One bite could make your pet itch for days," Dr. Carey says.

Washing your pet with a flea shampoo will get rid of pests that often cause itching, says Philip Kass, D.V.M., Ph.D., associate professor of epidemiology at the University of California, Davis, School of Veterinary Medicine.

It's also a good idea to spray or powder your pet with insecticides containing D-limonene or pyrethrins. Outdoors, keeping the grass mowed, the yard raked and brush cleared will also help keep fleas away, says Michael Dryden, D.V.M., associate professor of parasitology at the Kansas State University College of Veterinary Medicine in Manhattan, Kansas. You also may want to consider using outdoor flea sprays, he adds.

Try supplemental protection. Giving your pet supplements containing essential fatty acids may help calm itchy skin while adding sheen to his coat, says Steven A. Melman, V.M.D., a veterinarian with practices in Palm Springs, California, and Potomac, Maryland, and author of *Skin Diseases of Dogs and Cats.*

He recommends combination supplements containing linoleic acid, gamma-linoleic acid, eicosapentaenoic acid and docosahexaenoic acid, which are available in pet stores. Fatty acids don't work quickly, but you should see results within two months, says Dr. Ackerman.

Try an OTC. Since itching is often caused by hay fever, giving an antihistamine like diphenhydramine (Benadryl) can help, says Lloyd Reedy, D.V.M., a veterinary dermatologist, clinical associate professor of comparative medicine at the Health Science Center of the University of Texas Southwestern Medical School in Dallas and author of *Allergic Skin Diseases of Dogs and Cats.*

Many vets recommend giving one to three milligrams for every pound of pet; ask your vet for precise dosing instructions. For best results, don't give the medication only when itching flares. "It should be given throughout allergy season," Dr. Reedy says.

Jealousy

18 Ways to Work It Out

Life with your pet used to be rosy. But these days the emotional hue is more jealous-green because someone new—a beau, a baby or even another pet—has entered your life.

While pets don't feel jealousy in exactly the same way people do, that's not to say your little darlin' isn't without selfish motives. "There definitely can be some aspect of competition, because you're the best bone in the world, and your pet may not want to share," says Patricia McConnell, Ph.D., a certified applied animal behaviorist and adjunct assistant professor in the Department of Zoology at the University of Wisconsin in Madison.

Pets have ways of showing their displeasure. Maybe your cat is hiding, urinating in odd places or scratching furniture to smithereens. Your dog may be aggressive, overly exuberant or mopey. Or he could be chewing the house apart or forgetting his house-training.

Pets need to feel loved. So when jealousy rears its head, try these tips from the experts to keep your pet feeling wanted.

 ## For Dogs and Cats

Don't demote him. No one enjoys being bottom dog, so try to make your pet feel just as loved as he did before the source of his stress arrived. "Spending quality time playing together and doing the things you used to do is really important in alleviating the problem," says Dr. McConnell.

Stick with the same routine. Even though there's someone new in your life, try to stick as closely as possible to your old schedule, says Patricia O'Handley, V.M.D., associate professor of small animal medicine at the Michigan State University College of Veterinary Medicine in East Lansing.

"Feed your pet at the same time, walk him at the same time and give him a belly-scratch session at the same time every day if that's what he's used to," Dr. O'Handley says. "Routines are very important,

When to See the Vet

Your pet has always been no-miss when it comes to getting to the bathroom on time. Lately, however, he just can't seem to get it right. You're pretty sure the problem is linked to that new person in your life, so you bide your time, figuring things will get better soon enough.

You could be making a mistake. While jealousy and stress can cause pets to forget their manners, there could also be a medical problem—a urinary tract infection, for example, or even a urinary blockage.

"Get to the vet and don't take chances," advises Barbara Simpson, Ph.D., D.V.M., a certified veterinary behaviorist and adjunct assistant professor at the North Carolina State University College of Veterinary Medicine in Raleigh.

Sudden aggression toward a person or another pet in the family also warrants a trip to the vet, she adds. "You don't just wait around, hoping the aggression will go away by itself. A professional can help save the day."

and if they're disrupted, your pet can get very stressed."

Feed him first. If a new pet is causing your pet to see green, be sure to give your "original" pet priority, advises Sandy Sawchuk, D.V.M., clinical instructor of small animal medicine at the University of Wisconsin School of Veterinary Medicine in Madison. "No matter how irresistible a new pet may be, try to feed your old pet first," she says. "Do the same when giving out attention and petting."

But don't let him pig out. Pets that are jealous or stressed tend to overeat, says Michael W. Fox, B.V.M., Ph.D., vice-president of bioethics and farm animal protection for the Humane Society of the United States in Washington, D.C., and author of *The New Animal Doctor's Answer Book*. Control his food intake by putting out only as much food as he should eat, suggests Dr. Fox. And keep your eyes peeled to make sure he's not sneaking grub from other pets.

Tread gently. You might think that the new person in your life is making your furry friend jealous, but it's possible the emotion the newcomer is really inspiring is fear, says Dr. O'Handley.

Her advice: Have your new friend speak gently whenever he or she is near the pet. With cats, be patient and let them make the first move. "The person shouldn't approach the cat and insist on being friends. That never works," she says.

Let the good times roll. "The new person should become your pet's window to fun," says Al Stinson, D.V.M., professor emeritus of animal behavior at the Michigan State University College of Veterinary Medicine in East Lansing. "When your pet sees him or her, he should think, 'Oh, boy, here come good times.'"

He recommends letting the new person frequently walk, feed and play with your pet. "They should soon become fast friends. No more jealousy." But don't try to force things, he adds. "Give it time and it usually works out fine."

Prepare for baby. Pets need time to get used to the sight, smell and sound of strollers, cribs, swings and all the other equipment that goes along with babies. "It's better not to wait until the last minute when the pet has the additional stress of the baby," says Barbara Simpson, Ph.D., D.V.M., a certified applied animal behaviorist and adjunct assistant professor at the North Carolina State University College of Veterinary Medicine in Raleigh. Instead, bring in some of the equipment beforehand. "The earlier you prepare the house for the arrival of a new baby, the better."

Make room in the bed. If your pet currently sleeps with you but you're planning on moving him out when the baby comes, start getting him used to it a few weeks ahead of time. "That way the pet won't feel replaced and rejected because of the infant," says Dr. McConnell.

Recruit a warm-up act. "A baby's cry can be very distressing to a pet who's never heard it before," says Dr. Simpson. She recommends having friends visit with their babies so your pet can get used to the new sounds. "This will help your pet adjust more readily to the situation when you bring home your own baby," she says.

Or play a tape. If you don't know anyone with a baby, get a sound-effects tape that includes baby cries. Play the recording at a normal volume, suggests Dr. Simpson. If your pet gets nervous, turn down the volume until he's calmer, but keep it loud enough so he still can hear the crying. "That way he'll learn to relax even while the baby is crying," she says.

Send home a scent. Before you bring your baby home from the hospital, have a friend bring home some clothes your baby has worn, says Dr. Simpson. "This helps habituate the pet to the new odors that will be everywhere," she says. "Anything you can do like this to make the animal more at ease with the transition will help eliminate problems later."

Have a ball together. "A common mistake people make is that they lavish attention on their pet only when the baby is asleep. They tell the pet to go away when they're handling the baby," says Dr. Sawchuck. "That just makes the pet see the baby as competition for you."

A better way is to give your pet extra attention when you're holding the baby. "When you're nursing the baby, give your pet some treats," she says. "Play with your pet when your baby is right there in his little automatic swing. Make it so the pet equates the baby with fun."

Don't leave your pet and infant alone together, however. "It's too easy for an accident to happen," she warns.

Get yourself a helper. As long as your pet is gentle, allow your child to be the bearer of treats, says Dr. Sawchuk. "The pet will look at the child as a wonderful creature, a sweet dispenser of food," she says. "This helps forge a great relationship between the pet and child."

Dr. Sawchuk says her daughter started giving her dogs treats at the ripe old age of eight months. "They loved her for it," she says.

Provide an escape hatch. It's not easy being a dog or cat with young human siblings. They wail, pull tails and disrupt the peace without fail. "Set aside a closet or a corner of a quiet room and let that be your pet's time-out place," Dr. O'Handley says. "This is a place the children must never go, a place your pet knows he can go to sleep and relax any time he feels a need to escape."

 ## For Dogs Only

Make him a social butterfly. "If you expose your dog to lots of different people and dogs from an early age, he's less likely to be jealous about newcomers," says Dr. O'Handley. You can take your pooch to obedience classes so he can meet other dogs in a controlled setting. Another great place for your dog to make friends is at a park where dogs and people hang out, she says.

Let them meet on neutral turf. When it's time to introduce your pet to a new adult in your life, try to do it away from home, suggests Dr. Stinson. "Dogs have a very special, protective relationship to their territory. Have everyone meet at a park so they can have fun and bond and not feel defensive," he says.

For Cats Only

Put him on a pedestal. "It's important to realize that cats feel more secure when they have a high vantage point," says Jeanne Saddler, owner of Myriad Dog Training in Manhattan, Kansas. "So make sure your cat has a place to climb to where he can inspect new situations and people."

If your cat doesn't have easy access to high places, Saddler recommends getting a cat tree, a carpet-covered pole that goes from floor to

A cat tree puts your feline at a comfortable distance from the goings-on down below.

ceiling and has several carpeted platforms. "They climb up, perch and relax," she says. Cat trees are available at pet stores.

Make introductions slowly. If you've just gotten a new pet, don't give him the run of the house right away. "This will just make the first cat go nuts," says Dr. Sawchuk. Keep the cats in separate areas for a day or two. Then trade their areas so they can get used to each other's scent. If the cats seem okay after a couple of days, let them meet. If their fur goes up and they start hissing, however, keep them separated for a while longer.

PANEL OF ADVISERS

Michael W. Fox, B.V.M., Ph.D., is vice-president of bioethics and farm animal protection for the Humane Society of the United States in Washington, D.C. He is author of *The New Animal Doctor's Answer Book.*

Patricia McConnell, Ph.D., is a certified applied animal behaviorist and adjunct assistant professor in the Department of Zoology at the University of Wisconsin in Madison.

Patricia O'Handley, V.M.D., is associate professor of small animal medicine at the Michigan State University College of Veterinary Medicine in East Lansing.

Jeanne Saddler is owner of Myriad Dog Training in Manhattan, Kansas.

Sandy Sawchuk, D.V.M., is clinical instructor of small animal medicine at the University of Wisconsin School of Veterinary Medicine in Madison.

Barbara Simpson, D.V.M., Ph.D., is a certified applied animal behaviorist and adjunct assistant professor at the North Carolina State University College of Veterinary Medicine in Raleigh.

Al Stinson, D.V.M., is professor emeritus of animal behavior at the Michigan State University College of Veterinary Medicine in East Lansing.

Jumping Up

11 Ways to Bring 'Em Down

You might say your dog is upwardly mobile. He jumps up to greet you in the morning. He jumps up when you come home from the store. He even jumps up on kids and elderly people in the park. When he was a puppy, you thought it was kind of cute, but now you realize it's kind of dangerous.

"Jumping up is one of the most common complaints of dog owners," says Barbara Simpson, D.V.M., Ph.D., a certified applied animal behaviorist and adjunct assistant professor at the North Carolina State University College of Veterinary Medicine in Raleigh.

In the dog-meet-dog world, they jump up to show dominance or just to say hello, Dr. Simpson explains. "But it doesn't fit in with human relationships, and it can be annoying or dangerous." Cats also may be jumpy, but they leap onto laps and countertops more than on upright humans. As a result, this feline behavior usually isn't as great a problem.

Try these tips from the experts to keep your dog's four paws planted firmly on the ground.

 For **Dogs** Only

Don't get him started. "The easiest way to avoid the problem of jumping up is to never, ever encourage it, even when your dog is a cute little puppy," says Al Stinson, D.V.M., professor emeritus of animal behavior at the Michigan State University College of Veterinary Medicine in East Lansing.

"He'll start thinking it's good to jump, and it's very hard to untrain this," he says. When your puppy first starts jumping on you, push him off gently and firmly tell him "Off!"

Give him his just rewards. It's important to not only criticize bad behavior but also reward the good. Any time your dog would normally jump but doesn't, give him plenty of love and praise, says Gary Landsberg, D.V.M., a veterinarian in private practice in Thornhill, Ontario, who specializes in animal behavior.

"If he sits there when you walk in or he walks up to you but stays down, reward him with food treats, love, whatever he likes," says Dr. Landsberg. "Positive reinforcement of the desired behavior is the best thing you can do for a dog."

Make homecomings mellow. Your dog is apt to be much calmer if you don't make a big deal out of coming home at the end of the day, says Jeanne Saddler, owner of Myriad Dog Training in Manhattan, Kansas. "If you greet your dog with a big, excited 'Hi, boy!' after he's been alone all day, he's much more likely to jump up on you as his way of greeting," she says.

In the future when you come home, just walk in the door. If your dog doesn't jump on you, give him some loving pats. When you (and he) are all settled, then you can lavish him with attention, she says.

Come face-to-face. Rather than towering over your dog when you come home, try getting down to his level before he has a chance to jump up, suggests Dr. Stinson. "Your dog wants to smell your face, to relate with your eyes," he says. "So before he jumps you can bend or kneel down or even sit and exchange all the joy you want."

Clear the decks. It's difficult even for well-trained dogs not to get excited when company calls. One way to keep your pooch in line is simply to keep him away from the door, suggests Dr. Simpson.

"It's a simple approach, but if you don't want your dog jumping all over your company, keep him in another room until everyone's had a chance to settle in. Then bring him out to meet guests," she says.

Step to the back. The next time your dog is getting ready to jump up, take a couple of quick steps back—just enough so your dog misses you entirely on his way up—and firmly tell him "Off!"

"He lands back on the ground kind of confused, his purpose thwarted," says Dr. Stinson. "After a few associations of jumping up, hitting the ground instead of you and hearing 'Off!' he can probably figure out that jumping is not the action of choice."

Or forge ahead. Another way to keep him grounded is to wait until he's about three feet away and ready to jump. Then take one or two big steps forward, telling him "Off!" advises Dennis Fetko, Ph.D., an applied animal behaviorist who hosts a pet segment for a San Diego radio station. "Dogs don't like you rushing them when they're jumping," he explains.

If you happen to be standing on a hard surface, you can emphasize

Taking a quick step back when your dog jumps up will cause him to rethink his style of greeting.

When your dog jumps up, quickly push your hand up to—but not touching—his face. Dogs dislike hands coming at them and will quickly learn to back off.

Raise your knee so it's at the level of his chest. With his jump thwarted, he'll learn calmer ways of saying "Hello."

your footwork by stomping loudly when your foot hits the floor. "He'll look at your foot and think 'hmmm,'" says Dr. Fetko. "While he's being quiet for that moment, give him lots of love. This can work pretty quickly."

Give him a hand. The next time your dog comes charging for a jump, spread the fingers of your hand wide and move your palm quickly toward him, accompanied by a firm "Off!" Saddler suggests.

Your hand should come almost up to his face but shouldn't touch it. "Dogs don't like hands coming at their face like that, and they learn to back off," she says.

Sound the alarm. Responding to a pending jump with a loud blast from a personal alarm will deter all but the most enthusiastic dogs. Available at electronics stores and small enough to fit in your purse or jacket pocket, the alarms emit a high-decibel whistle or beep. Dogs dislike the noise and quickly come to realize that their jumping up is what's causing it, says Dr. Simpson. "It's not an elegant solution, but it's a good one," she says.

Do the bump. "A nudge from your knee may convince your dog that jumping isn't appreciated," says Dennis O'Brien, D.V.M., Ph.D., associate professor of neurology at the University of Missouri College of Veterinary Medicine in Columbia.

As your dog runs at you, lift your knee so it's at the level of his chest when he jumps up. Don't do it forcefully, just enough so the knee gets in the way of the jump, he says. After the dog-to-knee encounter, get your dog to sit, if possible, and reward him for sitting quietly, says Dr. O'Brien.

Vets advise using this technique only as a last resort, since it could hurt the dog or make him afraid of you in the future.

Sign up for school. Teaching your dog to sit and stay is one of the best ways to help control jumping up, says Dr. Simpson. Once he knows the commands, he should be able to wait calmly until you tell him it's okay to move. "It's a great aid in parks and other places where your dog might jump to greet a stranger," adds Dr. Simpson.

You can learn the basic commands at any obedience school. Check the phone book or ask your vet for recommendations.

PANEL OF ADVISERS

Dennis Fetko, Ph.D., is an applied animal behaviorist who hosts a pet segment for a San Diego radio station.

Gary Landsberg, D.V.M., is a veterinarian in private practice in Thornhill, Ontario, who specializes in animal behavior.

Dennis O'Brien, D.V.M., Ph.D., is associate professor of neurology at the University of Missouri College of Veterinary Medicine in Columbia.

Jeanne Saddler is owner of Myriad Dog Training in Manhattan, Kansas.

Barbara Simpson, D.V.M., Ph.D., is a certified applied animal behaviorist and adjunct assistant professor at the North Carolina State University College of Veterinary Medicine in Raleigh.

Al Stinson, D.V.M., is professor emeritus of animal behavior at the Michigan State University College of Veterinary Medicine in East Lansing.

Kennel Cough

6 Strategies to Beat Infection

You thought you were leaving your pooch in good hands when you dropped him off with friends for the weekend, but now you suspect he was hanging out with the wrong crowd. He's letting loose with a dry, raspy noise that sounds like he has smoker's cough.

What he probably has, however, is kennel cough—a type of bronchitis caused by a highly contagious virus that's readily passed from dog to dog. (Cats don't get this condition.)

Kennel cough gets its name from the fact that—at least in the past—dogs staying in kennels were often exposed to germs from other dogs that had the disease. Today most kennels require dogs to be immunized against the disease before checking in for the night. But in the outside world, kennel cough can occur whenever two or more dogs get together and swap germs.

While kennel cough may be prevented with vaccinations, there are ways to keep your pet comfortable should she come down with it. Here's what vets recommend.

 For **Dogs** Only

Clear the air. For a pet with irritated airways, clean air is important, says Lee R. Harris, D.V.M., a veterinarian in private practice in Federal Way, Washington. This means protecting your pet from fireplace smoke or smoke from cigarettes, as well as from such things as household chemical fumes.

Put moisture in the air. Keeping humidity high will help tame the cough by soothing your dog's throat and airways, says Carol Macherey, D.V.M., a veterinarian in private practice in Nashville. She recommends running a humidifier or vaporizer during the course of the illness. For temporary relief, you can also take your dog into the bathroom when you shower or bathe.

Reach for the cough medicine. If your poor pooch is coughing more than once an hour, you may want to give her a cough suppressant, says Michael Richards, D.V.M., a veterinarian in private practice in Cobbs Creek, Virginia, who also answers questions on dog and cat health in the Pet Care Forum on America Online.

He recommends using a product formulated for humans that contains dextromethorphan, such as Vicks 44D or Robitussin Maximum Strength Cough Suppressant. (Make sure the product does *not* contain acetaminophen, which can be dangerous to dogs.) He recommends giving 2 teaspoons to a dog 40 pounds and over, 1 teaspoon to a 20-pound dog and ½ teaspoon or less to a smaller dog. Check with your vet to make sure these doses are right for your pet.

Move her gently. When your dog is coughing and congested, taking a slow, gentle walk can help her airways drain, says Dr. Harris. But avoid letting her get tired or overheated, which can set off further bouts of coughing. It's also a good idea to avoid choke chains and tight collars, which can bring on a coughing spell.

Keep her alone. Since kennel cough is contagious, you'll want to keep the "patient" away from other dogs until she has recovered, says Dr. Macherey.

Plan ahead. To prevent your dog from getting kennel cough in the

When to See the Vet

While kennel cough often goes away on its own within seven to ten days, it can also get worse. In some cases it leads to pneumonia, which may be accompanied by spitting up white foam.

"Some pets will require a cough suppressant plus antibiotics and an anti-inflammatory drug," says Carol Macherey, D.V.M., a veterinarian in private practice in Nashville.

One way to tell if your dog needs a vet is to take his temperature. Coat a rectal thermometer with petroleum jelly, insert it gently into his rectum and hold it there for two to three minutes. A dog's normal temperature is 100.5° to 102.5°. Anything higher could mean the illness is serious and requires veterinary care, says Jeffrey Feinman, V.M.D., a house-call veterinarian in Weston, Connecticut.

In addition, if your pet's coughing is accompanied by a loss of appetite, you should probably call your vet right away.

Making the Diagnosis

Like people, dogs may simply cough now and then—if for no other reason than because they have a tickle in the throat.

Vets have a simple trick for distinguishing a harmless *harumph* from a possibly serious infection like kennel cough.

"If you press gently on the front of the dog's throat, she will go into a coughing spasm if she has kennel cough," says Lee R. Harris, D.V.M., a veterinarian in private practice in Federal Way, Washington. "The virus particularly likes to irritate the lining of the trachea."

If your pet does not have kennel cough, however, pressing gently on her throat probably won't make her cough.

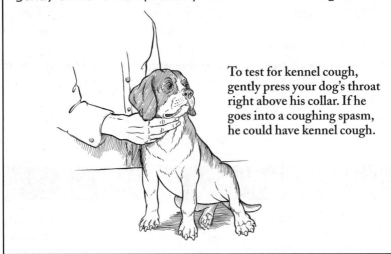

To test for kennel cough, gently press your dog's throat right above his collar. If he goes into a coughing spasm, he could have kennel cough.

future, never board your dog at a kennel that doesn't require proof of immunization. And always make sure she's had her shots before checking in.

PANEL OF ADVISERS

Jeffrey Feinman, V.M.D., is a house-call veterinarian in Weston, Connecticut.

Lee R. Harris, D.V.M., is a veterinarian in private practice in Federal Way, Washington.

Carol Macherey, D.V.M., is a veterinarian in private practice in Nashville.

Michael Richards, D.V.M., is a veterinarian in private practice in Cobbs Creek, Virginia, who also answers questions on dog and cat health in the Pet Care Forum on America Online.

Lameness

7 Ways to Get a Leg Up

You can't tell if he banged his knee, stepped on something sharp or pulled a muscle somewhere. But whatever happened, your pet is limping around the house like John Wayne in *True Grit*.

Lameness is often caused by nothing worse than a sore paw or strained muscle, which will often improve on its own within a few days. To get a leg up on lameness and keep your pet comfortable in the meantime, here's what vets recommend.

 **For Dogs and Cats**

Go feet first. "If your animal is lame, a paw may be injured," says Ronald Stone, D.V.M., clinical assistant professor of surgery at the University of Miami School of Veterinary Medicine and national executive secretary of the American Association of Pet Industry Veterinarians. "Look for a cut foot pad, broken toenails, a thorn or glass or other object stuck in the pad. There might even be bubble gum stuck between his toes."

Beware of thorny problems. If your pet comes limping home with a thorn, nail or piece of glass embedded in his paw, it's safe to gently remove it. But if the object has penetrated deeply, it may have punctured an artery deep inside. "If you pull it out, you've got a bleeder," warns Dr. Stone.

Stake a leg. If you suspect his leg is fractured, it's a good idea to get it immobilized before going to see the vet, says Dr. Stone. To make an emergency splint, roll a section of newspaper into a tube and cut it so it's the same length as your pet's leg. Then slip it over the injured leg, using tape to hold it snug.

You can also create a "Robert Jones" bandage with a roll of thick first-aid cotton, says Dr. Stone. "Take a big cotton roll, unroll it and wrap the leg in as much of the cotton as you can. Then take an Ace bandage or elastic bandage and wrap it around the cotton. You can't use tape because it won't stick to the cotton," he adds.

While a properly applied splint can help prevent further injury, don't waste time if you can't find the proper materials or you aren't sure exactly what to do. The most important thing, vets agree, is to get emergency help. Whether you're using a splint or not, pick your pet up carefully, keep the leg still and get him to a vet right away.

Give him some time off. If you can't determine what's bothering your pet, try letting him lounge around for a few days without going on your usual walks. Resting the leg for 48 to 72 hours is often all that's needed to help relieve pain and speed healing.

Put on a cold pack. If you suspect your pet is limping because he's recently strained a muscle, applying a cold pack to the area can help relieve pain and reduce swelling, says Wayne Wingfield, D.V.M., chief of emergency critical care medicine at the Colorado State University Veterinary Teaching Hospital in Fort Collins.

If you don't already have a cold pack in the freezer, you can make your own using ice (or even a bag of frozen vegetables) wrapped inside a small towel. "You should keep it on for five to ten minutes, four times a day at least," says Dr. Wingfield.

If he's still limping after two days and the area is sore to the touch,

When to See the Vet

Dogs and cats are naturally exuberant, and most leg injuries have more to do with enthusiasm—like pulling a muscle during a daring leap—than any sort of underlying problem.

Any leg problem that lasts more than 48 to 72 hours, however, or that obviously involves a serious injury—like a fracture or a gunshot wound—should be seen by a vet, says Steven Schrader, D.V.M., an orthopedics specialist and associate professor of small animal surgery at the Ohio State University College of Veterinary Medicine in Columbus.

In addition, while it's not uncommon for dogs to occasionally become lame, the problem is much less common in cats, and it's potentially more serious. So when your kitty is suddenly stepping gingerly, you should call the vet right away.

Make a "Robert Jones" bandage by wrapping the leg with cotton from a roll, then wrapping that with an elastic bandage.

To splint an injured leg, slip it inside a section of newspaper that's been rolled into a tube and cut to length. Seal the tube with tape to keep it snug.

you should take him to the vet for a checkup, Dr. Wingfield adds.

Switch to heat. Putting heat on a sore leg can also be very soothing. But don't use heating pads, because they can burn your pet, says Dr. Wingfield. Instead heat a gel pack, available at pharmacies, in the microwave until it's warm. Then wrap it in a towel and place it on your pet's sore leg. Just be sure to read the instructions carefully so it doesn't get too hot.

"You can also use warm water inside a rubber glove," Dr. Wingfield adds. "It conforms well to the injured area." To prevent burns, be sure the water's not too hot, and place a small towel between the glove and your pet's skin.

 For Cats Only

Look for war wounds. Cats tend to be more territorial than dogs, so it's not uncommon for them to come limping home after a squabble with a neighborhood rival, says Robert J. Murtaugh, D.V.M., associate professor in the Department of Medicine at the Tufts University School of Veterinary Medicine in North Grafton, Massachusetts. Bite wounds can be deep and often get infected, so check carefully for punctures. Thoroughly clean any wounds you find with soap and warm water.

PANEL OF ADVISERS

Robert J. Murtaugh, D.V.M., is associate professor in the Department of Medicine at the Tufts University School of Veterinary Medicine in North Grafton, Massachusetts.

Steven Schrader, D.V.M., is an orthopedics specialist and associate professor of small animal surgery at the Ohio State University College of Veterinary Medicine in Columbus.

Ronald Stone, D.V.M., is clinical assistant professor of surgery at the University of Miami School of Veterinary Medicine and national executive secretary of the American Association of Pet Industry Veterinarians.

Wayne Wingfield, D.V.M., is chief of emergency critical care medicine at the Colorado State University Veterinary Teaching Hospital in Fort Collins.

Lice

8 Soothing Solutions

Lately it seems as though your pet's favorite trick is trying to scratch herself in three places at once.

When you part her hair to take a look, what you see are nits—tiny white egg casings attached to the hair shafts. This means your pet has lice, six-legged insects that feed on blood and set off an intensely itchy reaction, explains Steven R. Hansen, D.V.M., a toxicologist at Sandoz Animal Health in Des Plaines, Illinois.

While pets in this country rarely get lice (it's actually more of a people problem), they aren't immune. When it's time to rid your pet of "lousy" guests, here's what vets recommend.

 ## For Dogs and Cats

Wash them away. Pet stores stock a variety of shampoos containing pyrethrins, chemicals that kill lice and fleas, says Paul Ruden, D.V.M., a veterinarian in private practice in Indianapolis. Look for a product containing a 0.05 percent solution, he advises. For more serious infestations, however, the 0.15 percent solution might be better. "Lice are real easy to get rid of," Dr. Ruden adds.

Wash your pet with the medicated shampoo once a week for three weeks. To make the treatment most effective, leave the shampoo on the coat for three to five minutes before rinsing.

Most cats, of course, would rather jump out of their skin than jump into the tub. For some tips, see "How to Give Your Cat a Bath" on page 186.

Protect their eyes. Any medicated shampoo can sting, so try not to get lather in your pet's eyes when giving her a bath, says Dr. Hansen.

Some vets recommend smearing petroleum jelly on the eyelids to keep shampoo out, but this probably isn't necessary and may actually cause harm, says Dawn Logas, D.V.M., assistant professor of dermatol-

When to See the Vet

One louse doesn't eat a whole lot, but when the *louse* is *lice*, your pet could literally be eaten alive.

"If a young dog or kitten has lice, she probably has fleas and ticks as well," says Steven R. Hansen, D.V.M., a toxicologist at Sandoz Animal Health in Des Plaines, Illinois. In severe cases, a pet could lose one-quarter of her blood volume within several weeks, causing severe anemia or even shock.

Symptoms of anemia include weakness and drowsiness. In addition, the inside of the pet's mouth will turn stark white. It's critical to get to a vet as soon as you notice symptoms. While the anemia will usually disappear once the parasite problem is resolved, some pets will need a blood transfusion to recover.

ogy at the University of Florida College of Veterinary Medicine in Gainesville. You're better off just being careful and flushing the eyes with running water if shampoo runs in.

See to his pals. Since lice can travel from pet to pet, it doesn't help to treat only one member of your household's four-footed crew. "If you have any other pets in the family, even if they don't have lice, be sure to treat them as well," says Pedro Rivera, D.V.M., a veterinarian in private practice in Sturtevant, Wisconsin.

If your cat has lice, however, you *don't* need to treat the dog—and vice versa. Lice are host-specific, meaning those that feed on cats won't move on to dogs. They don't move to humans, either, so if your head is itchy, relax—it's just your imagination!

Follow up with sprays. In addition to shampooing your pet, spray him twice a week with an over-the-counter lice or flea spray. Sprays will kill any new lice that happen to hatch between shampoos, Dr. Hansen explains.

Don't forget the powders. While lice powders usually aren't as effective as sprays, they can still assist in the eradication effort. Apply the powder generously from head to toe (and tail). When applying it to your pet's face, however, rub it in gently with your fingers to avoid getting it in her eyes or nose.

Go for the source. Even after your pet is lice-free, she can still be reinfested by lice lying in wait on floors, carpet or bedding. To prevent this, it's a good idea to wash all your pet's bedding, says Dr. Logas. In addition, grooming tools, kennels or pet carriers should also be scrubbed clean, either with a mild bleach solution or with soap and water, she says.

Stop the itch. The same stuff you take for hay fever—an antihistamine like diphenhydramine (Benadryl), for example—can provide itch control for your pet, says Dr. Rivera.

Vets recommend giving one to three milligrams for every pound of pet. Check with your vet for precise dosing instructions.

Soothe her with supplements. To heal your pet's lice-infested hide faster, many vets recommend giving supplements containing fatty acids, either alone or in combination with vitamin E and beta-carotene. "It increases certain beneficial fatty acids at the skin level and produces healthier skin," says Dr. Hansen.

You can buy a combination supplement (like Pet-Tabs Vitamin Supplement FA) in pet stores. Cats, puppies and dogs under ten pounds should be given half a tablet daily. Larger pets can take a whole tablet.

PANEL OF ADVISERS

Steven R. Hansen, D.V.M., is a toxicologist at Sandoz Animal Health in Des Plaines, Illinois.

Dawn Logas, D.V.M., is assistant professor of dermatology at the University of Florida College of Veterinary Medicine in Gainesville.

Pedro Rivera, D.V.M., is a veterinarian in private practice in Sturtevant, Wisconsin.

Paul Ruden, D.V.M., is a veterinarian in private practice in Indianapolis.

Licking

6 Steps to Dryness

Your cat grooms herself like it's a hobby. Your dog is constantly licking her paws, her tail and her haunches. If she gets any wetter, she could grow ferns.

While licking is part of a pet's normal grooming behavior, too much can lead to hair loss, infection or skin damage, says Karen Overall, V.M.D., Ph.D., a lecturer specializing in behavioral medicine in the Department of Clinical Studies at the University of Pennsylvania School of Veterinary Medicine in Philadelphia. "It can be a nightmare situation," she says.

Pets get into licking cycles for a variety of reasons. Some have allergies. Others are merely upset—because of a recent move, for example, or because there's another pet in the household, says Wayne Hunthausen, D.V.M., an animal behavior consultant in Westwood, Kansas, president of the American Veterinary Society of Animal Behavior and co-author of *Practitioner's Guide to Pet Behavior Problems*.

Here are some tips to help your pet dry out.

 For **Dogs** and **Cats**

Keep a "lick diary." It's difficult even for vets to diagnose specific allergies, says Richard Anderson, D.V.M., a veterinarian in private practice in Boston who specializes in dermatology. To help your vet get to the root of the problem, start keeping track of your pet's licking—when it began, what's happening at the time, how long it lasts and whether other pets in the family are affected. The more you can tell your vet about the problem, the more likely it is that he'll find a solution.

Lights, camera—lick! Since your pet probably won't lick on command in the veterinarian's office, it's good idea to make a videotape showing her in the act, says Dr. Overall. This will help the vet figure out what is wrong, she says.

When to See the Vet

Some licking is normal, but occasionally pets will lick themselves so vigorously and for such a long time that they damage the underlying tissue. The resulting sores are called lick granulomas, and they can lead to serious infections, says Richard Anderson, D.V.M., a veterinary dermatologist in private practice in Boston.

If your pet is licking a lot and her skin seems red and sore, call the vet right away, Dr. Anderson says.

Look for culinary culprits. Pets that are allergic to certain foods may get skin irritation and turn to licking, says Dr. Anderson. Try putting your pet on a different food—one that contains none of the ingredients in her usual chow—"then notice if the licking stops," he suggests.

Keep her honest. You'll never find out if your pet has food allergies if she's wandering the neighborhood and mooching from neighbors. "In some cases a neighbor may be feeding your pet, or the dog is eating the cat's food. You need strict control to determine food allergies," says Dr. Anderson.

Try an OTC. Pet stores sell topical anti-licking ointments that taste so bad that pets soon learn to keep their tongues where they belong. Dr. Anderson recommends an ointment that tastes like bitter apple, although other flavors may be equally effective.

Get her paws moving. Some pets get into licking because they don't have anything else to do. Taking your pet out for regular workouts will channel her energy in a healthier direction, says Dr. Hunthausen. He recommends taking a 20-minute walk twice a day.

PANEL OF ADVISERS

Richard Anderson, D.V.M., is a veterinary dermatologist in private practice in Boston.

Wayne Hunthausen, D.V.M., is an animal behavior consultant in Westwood, Kansas, president of the American Veterinary Society of Animal Behavior and co-author of *Practitioner's Guide to Pet Behavior Problems*.

Karen Overall, V.M.D., Ph.D., is a lecturer specializing in behavioral medicine in the Department of Clinical Studies at the University of Pennsylvania School of Veterinary Medicine in Philadelphia.

Lumps & Bumps

6 Ways to Beat Them

Your pet has always had a sleek physique, but lately his firm figure has started feeling more like a beanbag chair. What's going on in there?

It's not uncommon for middle-aged pets, particularly dogs, to develop all sorts of lumps and bumps, either on or just under the skin. In most cases the bumps are nothing more than harmless fatty tumors or cysts—fluid-filled sacs that resemble tiny balls filled with water. "Most lumps and bumps on dogs are benign," says Richard Anderson, D.V.M., a veterinary dermatologist in private practice in Boston.

In cats, however, as well as some dogs, lumps and bumps are a warning sign of more serious problems. Here's what vets recommend.

 For Dogs and Cats

Turn your back on cysts. Don't panic if your vet discovers cysts during a routine checkup. These fluid-filled sacs are almost always harmless, so the best thing is usually to ignore them, says Craig Griffin, D.V.M., a veterinary dermatologist in private practice in San Diego and a spokesman for the American Academy of Veterinary Dermatology.

Occasionally, however, cysts form in an area that gets a lot of friction—under the collar, for example, or around the anus—and they can get irritated and sore. If this happens, your vet may recommend having them surgically removed.

Keep them clean. Occasionally cysts will rupture on their own, which can cause the skin to become infected. "You can keep it clean with soap and water," says Dr. Anderson. Or you can apply rubbing alcohol several times a day. "That will keep it from getting infected and reduce the itching," he says.

Do a laying-on of hands. Frequently rubbing and stroking your pet is perhaps the best way to find potentially serious lumps early—and keep your pet happy at the same time! "Just as women check themselves for breast cancer monthly, go over your pet at least once a month," suggests Dr. Anderson. "Just by running your hands over him frequently, you can pick up lumps and bumps."

Put up the beach umbrella. It's not only two-legged sun-worshipers who are at risk for skin cancer. Pets that spend a lot of time outdoors—particularly light-colored breeds with thin coats that live in areas like California and the Southwest—are also at higher risk for developing dangerous lumps or bumps, says Dr. Anderson.

"There are some animals, like bull terriers, that love to sunbathe," says Dr. Anderson. "You need to keep them out of the sun."

Slather on protection. If you live in a sunny clime or your pets spend a lot of time outdoors, they need sun protection. Dr. Anderson recommends coating them with sunscreen—preferably the same strength you use on yourself, like SPF 15.

Apply sunscreen to his ears, nose and face, which are the areas most exposed to burning rays. Apply it every time your pet goes outdoors. Don't be concerned, however, if he licks it off. With the exception of products containing zinc, sunscreens aren't harmful to dogs or cats, says Dr. Anderson. Just apply some more.

Do a mouth check. It's not always fun to get up close and intimate, particularly when your best friend has been dining on liver and fish heads. But lumps that occur in the mouth are more likely to be dangerous than those found elsewhere on the body. It's important to periodically get your pet to open wide so you can do a careful inspection and perhaps catch them early, says Dr. Anderson.

When to See the Vet

While the vast majority of lumps and bumps are harmless, it takes expert eyes—and hands—to be sure. "Every big tumor started out as a little one, so you shouldn't overlook them," says Richard Anderson, D.V.M., a veterinary dermatologist in private practice in Boston.

Lumps are particularly worrisome in cats, since they're sometimes a sign of cancer, adds William Crane, V.M.D., a veterinarian in private practice in Colmar, Pennsylvania. So if you feel something unusual, call your vet right away.

What to Look For

Only your vet can say for sure if a lump or bump is harmless, but here are a few things you can look for.

- Uniformity. Benign lumps or bumps typically have a smooth shape, without irregular or jagged edges, says William Crane, V.M.D., a veterinarian in private practice in Colmar, Pennsylvania.
- Malleability. Lumps that are under the skin should move freely when you push against them. "Lipomas, for example, feel like a glob of fat under the skin," says Dr. Crane.
- Localization. The lump should feel like a solid object and be confined to one spot. If it's branched out and seems to be covering a larger area, you should see your vet.
- Growth. Lumps that are dangerous tend to grow rapidly and sometimes bleed. This type of lump should be seen by a vet right away.

Look at the tongue, around the lips and inside the mouth. You'll have to look carefully, because the lumps can be quite small—sometimes not much bigger than a pencil point, he says. If you find a lump you're not sure about, ask your vet to take a look.

PANEL OF ADVISERS

Richard Anderson, D.V.M., is a veterinary dermatologist in private practice in Boston.

William Crane, V.M.D., is a veterinarian in private practice in Colmar, Pennsylvania.

Craig E. Griffin, D.V.M., is a veterinary dermatologist in private practice in San Diego and a spokesman for the American Academy of Veterinary Dermatology.

Mange
11 Ways to Help Him Heal

It sounds like a disease associated with junkyard dogs, but even pampered pets can get mange, and it doesn't make for pretty dogs or cats.

"Mange can cause a small, red, hairless area, or there can be almost no hair, with big pimples and thickened skin oozing all over," says Dawn Logas, D.V.M., assistant professor of dermatology at the University of Florida College of Veterinary Medicine in Gainesville.

Mange occurs when mites burrow under the skin. One form of the disease, demodectic mange, occurs when mites that normally live on your pet suddenly multiply beyond their normal levels. Demodectic mange is much more common in dogs than in cats and typically results in hair loss and scaling around the eyelids, corners of the mouth and front legs.

A second form of the disease, commonly known as scabies, occurs when dogs or cats pick up a strange bunch of bugs from another animal. This type of mange is not only contagious but intensely itchy as well.

Only your vet can tell which type of mange your pet has, so it's important to get a checkup at the first signs of trouble. Once you know, here are some vet-recommended tips to make your pet beautiful again.

 For Dogs and Cats

Give it time. "If it's a young dog with a demodectic infection, it will probably cure on its own," says Sandra Merchant, D.V.M., associate professor of dermatology at the Louisiana State University School of Veterinary Medicine in Baton Rouge. As many as 90 percent of puppies with minor demodectic mange on the face or front half of the body recover with no treatment at all, adds Dr. Logas. However, if the problem isn't getting better within a month or is actually getting worse, call your vet for advice.

Douse it with dip. Pets with scabies often get intensely itchy. "It's like having mosquito bites on mosquito bites," says Paul Ruden, D.V.M., a veterinarian in private practice in Indianapolis. Soaking your

When to See the Vet

If your pet suddenly starts going bald because of mange, that receding hairline could mean he has a serious problem.

While the earliest stages of scabies (a common type of mange) can be treated at home, a more serious condition called demodectic mange always requires a veterinarian's care. It takes a vet to tell them apart.

"An older dog with demodectic mange probably has something else wrong that caused it," says Sandy Merchant, D.V.M., associate professor of dermatology at the Louisiana State University School of Veterinary Medicine in Baton Rouge. Rare in cats, this type of mange usually occurs when a dog's immune system isn't strong enough to "repel" the mites that cause it.

Conditions that can lead to demodectic mange include cancer and hypothyroidism—a hormone deficiency that can weaken the immune system, says Steven R. Hansen, D.V.M., a toxicologist at Sandoz Animal Health in Des Plaines, Illinois.

Don't take chances when you first notice hair loss or other problems, he advises. See your vet right away.

---

pet in a lime/sulfur medication, such as Lymdyp, diluted with water will kill the mites and help relieve the itching. The dip is available from Kennel Vet, P.O. Box 835, Belmore, NY 11710.

Put your pet in the tub and douse him with the dip for 10 to 15 minutes. Don't rinse when you're done and don't towel dry—the dip has to stay on the fur in order to work. In most cases, vets advise repeating the process once a week until the condition is better.

It's important to remember that products for dogs may be extremely dangerous if used on cats, so always check the label carefully. It's also a good idea to call your vet for advice. (For tips on bathing your cat, see "How to Give Your Cat a Bath" on page 186.

Don't neglect his housemates. If you have one pet with scabies, chances are good your other pets may get it, too. "You have to assume they've been exposed, and you should treat them," says Pedro Rivera, D.V.M., a veterinarian in private practice in Sturtevant, Wisconsin.

Screen your pet's friends. Certain mange mites can be picked up by direct contact with other animals or from contaminated areas. "If you see a dog that's baldish and scratching a lot, don't let your dog near it," says Dr. Rivera.

Do the laundry. While mites spend their entire lives on the host animal, some will occasionally slip off—and return to cause trouble another day. If your pet has recently been infested, it's a good idea to thoroughly wash his bedding and the area where he sleeps, says Dr. Merchant.

Fight it with fat. "Fatty acid supplements are fairly popular to use in skin disorders," says Steven R. Hansen, D.V.M., a toxicologist at Sandoz Animal Health in Des Plaines, Illinois. The supplements are available in pet stores. Ask your vet if one of these products might be right for your pet.

Pop some protection. To help control the itching caused by scabies, your vet may recommend giving your pet an antihistamine like diphenhydramine (Benadryl), says Dr. Rivera. The usual dose is one to three milligrams for each pound of pet. Ask your vet for precise dosing instructions.

Keep him clean. Regular grooming will help remove scaly skin and scabs caused by mange. Done regularly, it can also help keep your pet mange-free, particularly if he's been keeping company with a mangy crowd. "If you keep your pets clean with regular baths and brushing, they should be able to fight it," says Dr. Rivera.

Feed him well. Since mange often affects pets that are poorly nourished, giving your pet a quality food can help provide protection. "A better diet means a healthier, stronger animal," says Dr. Hansen.

Handle with care. The critters that live on your dog are perfectly capable of setting up shop on you. So if your pooch is infested, wait until after his first treatment before giving him loving hugs again, says Dr. Merchant. Even then, you should wash your hands afterward.

Forgo the oil treatments. "Pouring motor oil on your pet is a passed-down home remedy for mange, and it doesn't work," says Dr. Logas. In fact, since pets will lick the oil, it can be harmful. So leave the oil in the garage, she advises.

PANEL OF ADVISERS

Steven R. Hansen, D.V.M., is a toxicologist at Sandoz Animal Health in Des Plaines, Illinois.

Dawn Logas, D.V.M., is assistant professor of dermatology at the University of Florida College of Veterinary Medicine in Gainesville.

Sandra Merchant, D.V.M., is associate professor of dermatology at the Louisiana State University School of Veterinary Medicine in Baton Rouge.

Pedro Rivera, D.V.M., is a veterinarian in private practice in Sturtevant, Wisconsin.

Paul Ruden, D.V.M., is a veterinarian in private practice in Indianapolis.

Mating Problems
17 Ways to Spark Romance

You can't count on Cupid's arrow when planning the perfect pet romance. While experienced dogs and cats rarely balk in the boudoir, it's not always so easy for beginners.

"A lot of times inexperienced pets won't know what to do," says H. Ellen Whiteley, D.V.M., a veterinary consultant in private practice in Guadalupita, New Mexico, and author of *Understanding and Training Your Cat or Kitten.*

Performance anxiety can be a problem, particularly for males. Also a problem for males is balance—or the lack of it. And in some cases the chemistry simply isn't there. But with planning and patience, you can help your pet make a successful love connection. Here's what experts recommend.

 For Dogs and Cats

Start him young. "Breeding a five-year-old dog or cat for the first time often results in difficulties," says Dr. Whiteley. He may have a low libido or sperm count. Or he may not know what he's supposed to do.

"If you're going to use him as a stud, the first time should be before he's over 18 months old," says Dr. Whiteley.

It's also a good idea to have a vet examine your pet to make sure he (or she) doesn't have a sexually transmittable disease or unwanted genetic conditions—like hip dysplasia or certain eye diseases—that might be passed on to offspring. Your vet can also recommend the best time for breeding.

Find an experienced partner. Female dogs and cats generally have less trouble mating than males do, so matching a male with a more experienced partner will make his job that much easier.

Go to his place. Male dogs and cats occasionally get nervous when they travel to another dog's turf. "Take the female to the male, because males perform better and have more confidence when they're in their own environment," says cat breeder Elaine Wenner Gilbertson, of Vista, California, author of *A Feline Affair: Guide to Raising and Breeding Purebred Cats.*

Make her comfortable. "If it's the first time for the female, she is usually frightened being taken out of familiar surroundings," adds Gilbertson. "If she has a favorite toy or a cushion that she likes to sleep on, take it along. Give her something familiar from home."

Introduce them properly. While some dogs and cats are smitten at first sight, in many cases "blind dates don't work," says Marion Hunt, who breeds cocker spaniels in Howe, Texas. "She's not going to accept him if she doesn't know him."

Don't try to rush things, Hunt advises. Give them time—anywhere from a few hours to an entire day—to get comfortable with each other. When allowed to proceed at their pace (rather than yours), they'll eventually do what comes naturally, she says.

Send advance notice. When a prolonged face-to-face meeting isn't possible, Dr. Whiteley advises sending a personal "message"—a blanket, toy or some other object that has your pet's scent on it. Dogs and cats perceive the world largely through smell, and getting acquainted with their intended's scent ahead of time will make them more comfortable when they finally do meet.

When to See the Vet

When the course of four-legged love runs true, you can expect to have some new furry friends in about 63 to 65 days.

Sometimes, however, pregnancy doesn't occur. This is usually because the female wasn't at the right time in her cycle, says H. Ellen Whiteley, D.V.M., a veterinary consultant in private practice in Guadalupita, New Mexico. In some cases, however, it may mean that one of the pets is infertile,

There are a number of diseases that can cause infertility in pets, such as brucellosis in dogs and chlamydia in cats, she explains. When caught early, each of these bacterial infections can be treated with antibiotics. In some cases, however, the damage may be permanent.

If you've tried mating your pet several times without success, call your vet. "Today, veterinarians have some sophisticated techniques to help solve breeding problems," Dr. Whiteley says.

Prepare a comfortable boudoir. For first-timers particularly, it's important to give them a place without distractions. "Provide a quiet atmosphere," suggests Chris Walkowicz, who breeds bearded collies in Sherrard, Illinois, and is co-author of *The Atlas of Dog Breeds of the World* and *Successful Dog Breeding*.

"Some pets don't like anybody looking," Hunt adds. She suggests putting them in a place that provides a hidden view, like a garage with a window or a screen that you can peek around to make sure everything's going okay.

Give them encouragement. "Pets need a lot of coaxing and encouragement when they are unproven," says Walkowicz. If your pet seems unsure of how to proceed, speak to him in a calm, cheerful voice and reassure him that everything's going fine, she advises.

Give them support. A slippery floor is more than just distracting. It can also be dangerous if it causes the couple to slip and fall. "Always provide a rug or mat that provides good footing," Walkowicz suggests.

Find another partner. While most pets will breed with mates of your choosing, others can be extremely choosy. If one (or both) of the pair seems totally uninterested in the other or is getting mean and aggressive, it may be time to call it quits. "Try selecting another partner," suggests Dr. Whiteley.

 For **Dogs** Only

Move her to help him. Males that have never mated aren't always sure how to proceed. In fact, they commonly approach the wrong end or simply have trouble making contact.

Don't try to guide him, because this often causes males to lose interest, Walkowicz says. Instead try to maneuver the female into the appropriate position.

Give nature some help. When dogs have trouble with penetration, using an over-the-counter lubricant may help. Walkowicz recommends using a water-based lubricating product like K-Y Jelly.

Allow for bathroom breaks. "The mating act titillates more than just the libido," Walkowicz says. "It also sometimes makes them have to go to the bathroom."

Untie the knot. After mating, the female's muscles contract and the male's penis swells. The resulting "tie" will often keep the pair locked together for 30 minutes to an hour. "You need to watch that they don't hurt themselves," Hunt says. "An inexperienced male doesn't always know he has to get off and turn around backward."

If the two don't separate on their own within 60 minutes, make sure the male is in the original mounting position, then push down on his rump to help release the connection. "A little ice pack on the male's testicles may also help," Walkowicz says.

 **For Cats Only**

Practice makes perfect. Vets refer to cats as induced ovulators, meaning the female doesn't release an egg until after the mating act is completed. This isn't likely to occur the first time. "You must have more than one mating to produce a pregnancy," says Dr. Whiteley.

Breeders typically bring the pair together many times over the course of two or three days in order to make sure pregnancy occurs. Luckily, the process doesn't take too long. Cats can mate successfully in 30 seconds or less.

Provide an escape route. Experts aren't sure why, but it's natural for a female cat to strike out at the male immediately after mating. To prevent injury, "he needs a place of safety, a refuge to protect himself," Gilbertson says.

Professional breeders often put a high ledge nearby to make it easy for the male to escape in a hurry. His mate calms down fairly quickly, however, so he can usually descend within a few minutes.

Give her a trim. Another way to protect the male from his partner's wrath is to trim her claws beforehand. "Some females get kind of hostile," says Mary Jo Mersol-Barg, a cat breeder in Michigan. "Before putting them together, make sure all her nails are trimmed."

PANEL OF ADVISERS

Elaine Wenner Gilbertson is a cat breeder in Vista, California, and author of *A Feline Affair: Guide to Raising and Breeding Purebred Cats.*

Marion Hunt breeds cocker spaniels in Howe, Texas.

Mary Jo Mersol-Barg is a cat breeder in Michigan.

Chris Walkowicz breeds bearded collies in Sherrard, Illinois, and is co-author of *The Atlas of Dog Breeds of the World* and *Successful Dog Breeding.*

H. Ellen Whiteley, D.V.M., is a veterinary consultant in private practice in Guadalupita, New Mexico, and author of *Understanding and Training Your Cat or Kitten.*

Matted Coat

11 Ways to Ease the Tangles

Is your pet having a bad hair day? Is her coat so gnarly and matted that you'd unzip it and send it to the cleaners if you could?

It's not much fun getting tangled up with matted fur. "Hundreds and hundreds of hairs can be involved in just one mat," says Hazel Christiansen, owner of Blue Ribbon Pet Grooming in Lewiston, Idaho, and president of the American Grooming Shop Association. "It's not an easy task to break them up."

Unless your pet wears a buzz cut—courtesy of nature or the groomer—you'll probably have to deal with hair mats at some point. Here are a few tips from the experts to help smooth things out.

 For Dogs and Cats

Keep her dry. Once your pet's matted hair gets wet, "the mats will shrink up like a wool sweater when they dry and you'll never be able to get them out," says Kathe Barsotti, a certified master groomer and owner of Featherle Pet Care in Herndon and Sterling, Virginia. So keep her out of water—or even wet grass—until after she's been de-matted, Barsotti advises.

Let your fingers do the walking. Untangling a mat takes patience, but it can be done. Starting at the ends of the hairs and working inward—hair by hair, if necessary—divide the mat in half with your fingers. Then divide the halves into quarters, the quarters into eighths and so on until all the clumps are gone. Then run a comb through the hair to make the coat smooth, Christiansen says.

Give mats the brush-off. Your pet's brush can be a great mat-fighter, says Barsotti. Beginning near the tips of the hair and using short, rapid strokes, gently brush upward. As the hair gets smooth, gradually work your way down toward the skin. And don't dig the brush in too deep or you'll cause more tangling.

Once you've worked your way to the skin, brush the length of the hair, then finish the job with a comb. If the comb snags, go back with the brush and work out the tangle.

Coax them out with cornstarch. A light sprinkling of cornstarch makes stubborn mats easier to pull apart, says Barsotti. "It helps the hair glide right out of the mat," she says. As you work deeper into the mat, add more cornstarch as needed.

Or slide them out with spray. Pet stores sell sprays made specifically for detangling unruly snarls. The sprays, which typically contain lanolin, will help hairs slide out of the mat, Barsotti says. If you're working on your cat, however, read the label to make sure the product is safe for felines.

Take it in stages. If your pet has more than one mat or one big mat that's particularly tough, it's a good idea to do the job in stages. Linda A. Law, a certified master groomer and director of the Canine Clippers School of Pet Grooming in Dumfries, Virginia, recommends working on mats for only about ten minutes at a time. Then give your pet extra love and maybe a special treat. Come back to the mat a few hours later. "You want to make the dematting as pleasant an experience as possible," she says.

Try a clip job. If you come across a particularly stubborn mat, cutting it in half—by cutting straight down through the middle—will

When to See the Vet

Matted hair is never a pretty sight, but what's happening below the surface can be even worse, says David T. Roen, D.V.M., a veterinarian in private practice in Clarkston, Washington.

Unless mats are regularly combed out, they can provide an ideal hiding place for bacteria, yeast and other parasites. Over time, sores may develop under the mat, which in turn can cause a serious infection, says Dr. Roen.

So if you or the groomer finds an open, infected sore underneath a large mat—or if your pet experiences a fever or loss of appetite—see your vet right away. "These signs would indicate that a mat was much more than just a cosmetic problem," Dr. Roen says. "The animal could need medical attention quickly."

To brush out a hair mat, begin at the tips of the hair and gradually work down to the skin, brushing out small amounts of hair at time.

make it easier to work out with your fingers, Christiansen says.

In some cases it may be easiest just to cut the whole thing out, says David T. Roen, D.V.M., a veterinarian in private practice in Clarkston, Washington. "It's often the best thing to do for the animal's sake," he says.

Carefully push the tips of the scissors between the mat and the skin, then gently spread the tips to loosen the mat. Do this from several angles, advises Dr. Roen, then carefully use the scissors to cut the hairs between the mat and the skin, a few hairs at a time. "It's easy, with a thick mat surrounded by hair and a struggling pet, to cut the skin, so be very careful," he says.

Pet stores sell a variety of sharp grooming tools such as mat splitters, but in most cases it's best to leave such tools to the pros. Even sharp scissors can be dangerous, Barsotti warns. "We've seen too many pets come in for stitches after well-meaning owners used these tools."

Get thee to a groomer. Professional groomers have special tools to help untangle tough mats. It's important to remember, however, that even the best groomers sometimes give up and resort to a shortcut. "It's the most humane thing we can do sometimes," says Law.

Brush up on prevention. Once your pet is mat-free, giving her a daily brushing will help keep her coat smooth, says Barsotti. Be sure to brush out every layer of the coat down to the skin, she adds. "Too many owners just brush the surface layers and can't understand why their pet is all matted," she says. Since every animal's coat is different, ask a groomer what type of brush will be most effective.

Get her in condition. Regularly using a conditioner will help keep your pet's coat smooth and healthy, Law says. You should apply the conditioner about once a week. As always, read the label carefully to make sure the conditioner you choose is safe for your pet, be it a cat or a dog.

Take a short cut. One foolproof way to prevent matting is to keep your pet's coat cut short, Barsotti says. "It's much better in the long run to prevent mats than to have to get rid of them," she says. "A short coat is easy prevention."

PANEL OF ADVISERS

Kathe Barsotti is a certified master groomer and owner of Featherle Pet Care in Herndon and Sterling, Virginia.

Hazel Christiansen is owner of Blue Ribbon Pet Grooming in Lewiston, Idaho, and president of the American Grooming Shop Association.

Linda A. Law is a certified master groomer and director of the Canine Clippers School of Pet Grooming in Dumfries, Virginia.

David T. Roen, D.V.M., is a veterinarian in private practice in Clarkston, Washington.

Meowing

8 Tips for Quieting the Caterwauling

Most cats like to chat, but some loquacious kitties never seem to quit. They meow in the morning, cry in the afternoon and yowl at night.

"If you live with a cat, he believes you must live by his rules—and the rules are communicated through demanding meows," explains Jim Humphries, D.V.M., a veterinary consultant in private practice in Dallas and author of *Dr. Jim's Animal Clinic for Cats* and *Dr. Jim's Animal Clinic for Dogs*.

Some cats simply appear to like the sound of their own voices, adds Carin Smith, D.V.M., a veterinary consultant in private practice in Leavenworth, Washington, and author of *101 Training Tips for Your Cat*.

But if his catcalls are too much for you—or your neighbors—to handle, here's what experts recommend.

For Cats Only

Show 'em the door. Some cats, like people, can never make up their minds: When they're inside they ask to go out, and when they're outside they beg to come in. "Put in a kitty door," suggests Dr. Smith.

Pet stores stock dozens of pet doors, with prices beginning at about $25. In most cases they're easy to install yourself. "That's an easy solution," says Dr. Smith.

Feed him regularly. Rather than feeding your kitty only when he cries for food, try feeding him at the same times every day, suggests Deborah Edwards, D.V.M., a veterinarian in private practice in Largo, Florida. Once he understands the meal schedule, he'll be less inclined to give you reminders in between.

Extend the dinner hour. If you trust your cat not to overindulge, keeping his food bowl full will eliminate at least one cause for complaints, says Dr. Humphries. If he starts putting on the pounds, however, you may have to try another strategy.

Give him extra strokes. Frequent meowing is often a gambit for attention, says Dr. Smith. Spending a little more quality time with your pet—petting him, playing with him or even going for walks—will probably help keep him quieter.

Draw the line. While most cats will cool the chatter once they get what they're asking for, others rarely quit. Whatever you do, says Dr. Smith, don't encourage him.

"Even if you hold out as long as you can but then respond, what he's learned is that the longer he meows, the more likely it is he'll get your attention," she says. "Be strong. Simply ignore him."

Reward good behavior. Just as it's important to ignore him when he's talking, you'll also want to praise him when he's quiet, says H. Ellen Whiteley, D.V.M., a veterinary consultant in private practice in Guadalupita, New Mexico, and author of *Understanding and Training Your Cat or Kitten*.

"Wait until he's being quiet, then say, 'Oh, what a nice kitty!'" she suggests. "Then give him a tidbit of tuna or pet him and play with him."

Take tough action. The next time your chatty cat goes into his

When to See the Vet

While most meowing is a cry for attention, in some cases it means your pet is sick or in pain and needs a veterinarian's care.

Noting what your cat is doing when he cries can provide valuable clues as to what the problem is, says Jim Humphries, D.V.M., a veterinary consultant in private practice in Dallas. If he meows when eating, for example, he could have tender teeth or difficulty swallowing. Similarly, meowing in the litter box could mean he's constipated or is having trouble urinating.

"A change in the tone of your cat's meow typically means an upper respiratory or lung problem," adds Dr. Humphries. Excessive meowing can also be a symptom of a hormone imbalance called hyperthyroidism.

Don't take chances if your formerly quiet feline has suddenly joined the choir. Get him to a vet, Dr. Humphries advises.

meow cycle, try giving him a blast from a squirt bottle, suggests Dr. Smith. "They soon realize it's no fun to meow if every time they open their mouths, they get squirted."

Help him relax. Constant crying in cats could be a sign of boredom or stress, says Alan Parker, Ph.D., a veterinary neurologist and chief of staff of the Small Animal Clinic at the University of Illinois College of Veterinary Medicine at Urbana-Champaign.

He recommends introducing him to some new toys, preferably the kind that will keep him mentally challenged. A cat track with an enclosed ball is always a good choice. "You want to make his life more interesting," he says.

PANEL OF ADVISERS

Deborah Edwards, D.V.M., is a veterinarian in private practice in Largo, Florida.

Jim Humphries, D.V.M., is a veterinary consultant in private practice in Dallas and author of *Dr. Jim's Animal Clinic for Cats* and *Dr. Jim's Animal Clinic for Dogs.*

Alan Parker, Ph.D., is a veterinary neurologist and chief of staff of the Small Animal Clinic at the University of Illinois College of Veterinary Medicine at Urbana-Champaign.

Carin Smith, D.V.M., is a veterinary consultant in private practice in Leavenworth, Washington, and author of *101 Training Tips for Your Cat.*

H. Ellen Whiteley, D.V.M., is a veterinary consultant in private practice in Guadalupita, New Mexico, and author of *Understanding and Training Your Cat or Kitten.*

Moving Anxiety
12 Suggestions for Settling In

Your new house is beautiful. You and the family are going to be so happy here. But what's this? Do you detect a sourpuss in the crowd? Is that your cat scratching up the furniture, urinating on the rug, looking for a place to hide and perhaps plotting an escape from your lovely home?

"Moving can be very traumatic for a cat," says Sandy Sawchuk, D.V.M., clinical instructor of small animal medicine at the University of Wisconsin School of Veterinary Medicine in Madison. "Owners don't like to hear this, but cats are often more attached to their territory than they are to you."

Dogs, on the other hand, are usually much more attached to people than turf and so are less likely to have relocation trepidation, says Dr. Sawchuk.

To keep moving anxiety down, try these tips.

 For Dogs and Cats

Be a pack rat. If your pet is particularly fond of a certain piece of furniture, take it along. "Don't even think twice about whether it will fit into your new house," says Dr. Sawchuk. "Taking it along will help your pet become comfortable more quickly. Her scent is on it, she's used to it, and it's comforting for her."

Dr. Sawchuk says she once moved and left behind her cats' favorite old chair. "They wanted their chair, and they let me know in no uncertain terms," she says. She had to quickly get them a scratching post so they wouldn't engrave their marks on the new furniture.

Give her the shirt off your back. One way to help your pet get used to the new place is to make her sleeping area smell like you. "The olfactory world is extremely important to animals. They can be much more relaxed if they smell something or someone familiar around them," says Jeanne Saddler, owner of Myriad Dog Training in Manhattan, Kansas.

She recommends putting a T-shirt or sweatshirt you've worn but haven't washed for a while in your pet's sleeping area. "Use one you've sweated in during your move—that's perfect," she says.

Provide a quiet space. In the midst of moving, it's hard for your poor pet to get settled in her new abode. "Set aside a quiet place where your pet can go to escape from the noise, the boxes and the usual moving stuff," says Dr. Sawchuk.

To make the quiet place even more special, she recommends giving your pet lots of love and extra treats when you visit. That way there will be extra incentive for her to go to her retreat when she needs quiet time, says Dr. Sawchuk.

Be consistent. Keeping as close to your old routine as possible is very important after a move, says Patricia O'Handley, V.M.D., associate professor of small animal medicine at the Michigan State University College of Veterinary Medicine in East Lansing.

"Pets need patterns and predictability, especially after a move," she says. "Walk your dog at the same time, let your cat sleep with you if you did before and feed your pet the same food at the same time you did before," she says. "It can make a real difference."

Exercise away her angst. Keeping your pet well-exercised will help make her less anxious, says Dr. O'Handley. "Play games with your cat. Take your dog for fun walks. They'll enjoy their new lives a lot more and be healthier for it," she says.

Foil escape artists. It's critical to keep a close eye on your pet to ensure she doesn't sneak away while you're moving in, says Dr. Sawchuk.

"It can be easy to lose a pet during all the confusion," she says. Make sure your dog is under control—in a fenced yard, for example, or on a leash or in her own private kennel. If you plan on letting your cat go outdoors, let her get settled in for a month before you let her out. Even then, keep her on a leash the first few times, advises Dr. Sawchuk.

In addition, don't forget to get updated identification tags with the new address and phone number.

Be sure it's safe. A new home isn't necessarily a perfect home. Dr. Sawchuk advises going through the new house room by room and looking carefully for pet pitfalls, such as holes they could fall through, foamy packing material they might eat or dangerous exposed wires.

"This is important, take it from me," says Dr. Sawchuk. "Our new house had some floorboards that were lifted up, and my cat decided

Preparing for the Move

When it comes to keeping your pet safe and comfortable, what you do before the move can be just as important as what comes after, says Michael W. Fox, B.V.M., Ph.D., vice-president of bioethics and farm animal protection for the Humane Society of the United States in Washington, D.C., and author of *The New Animal Doctor's Answer Book.*

Be sure your pet has a collar with ID tags displaying both the old and the new addresses and phone numbers. "No matter how careful you are, your pet could escape. Proper identification could save his life," he says.

When moving to a new state, call the department of agriculture there and ask if there are special rules about moving with pets. "Hawaii, for instance, has a very long quarantine, and it's at your expense," says Dr. Fox. "Do your homework and don't let yourself be surprised."

---

this would be a great place to explore. He ended up falling a good ten feet down to the next floor and got wedged behind the brand new drywall we'd just painted. We had to saw a hole to get him out."

Plan ahead. "Try to schedule your move so someone in the family can spend several days at home with your pet before you go off to work and school again," advises Al Stinson, D.V.M., professor emeritus of animal behavior at the Michigan State University College of Veterinary Medicine in East Lansing. "The worst thing you can do for anxiety is move in and immediately leave the pet behind by himself all day."

 For Dogs Only

Check out the area. To help your dog feel at home, take him out on a leash for a 10- to 15-minute walk around the neighborhood, suggests Michael W. Fox, B.V.M., Ph.D., vice-president of bioethics and farm animal protection for the Humane Society of the United States in Washington, D.C., and author of *The New Animal Doctor's Answer Book.* "It's important for a dog to get his bearings, to get to know his neighborhood as soon as possible," says Dr. Fox.

Hire a sitter. If you're working long hours and your dog's alone all day, you may want to have someone visit and take him for a walk, suggests Dr. O'Handley. "Otherwise your dog can get very lonely for human companionship. He might not be able to wait that long to go to the bathroom, either."

 For Cats Only

Keep her nearby. It's not at all uncommon for cats to say adios to their new homes and head back to their old stomping grounds after a move. To prevent this, keep your cat inside or on a leash for at least a month following a move. When you do let her out, don't let her wander for long periods of time, vets advise.

Take it one room at a time. To help your cat feel secure in her new home, you may want to try introducing her to it gradually, says Dr. Sawchuk. For the first week, let her stay in one small section of the house, or even just a room (your bedroom would be ideal).

Put her bed there, along with her litter box, food and toys. Visit her frequently. Then, when she seems comfortable with that area, let her wander elsewhere. "The cat will explore slowly, cautiously, but eventually will come to terms with the new territory," Dr. Sawchuk says.

PANEL OF ADVISERS

Michael W. Fox, B.V.M., Ph.D., is vice-president of bioethics and farm animal protection for the Humane Society of the United States in Washington, D.C., and author of *The New Animal Doctor's Answer Book*.

Patricia O'Handley, V.M.D., is associate professor of small animal medicine at the Michigan State University College of Veterinary Medicine in East Lansing.

Jeanne Saddler is owner of Myriad Dog Training in Manhattan, Kansas.

Sandy Sawchuk, D.V.M., is clinical instructor of small animal medicine at the University of Wisconsin School of Veterinary Medicine in Madison.

Al Stinson, D.V.M., is professor emeritus of animal behavior at the Michigan State University College of Veterinary Medicine in East Lansing.

Nipping & Biting

11 Steps to Nip the Habit

Kittens love nothing more than to stalk and pounce, sometimes delivering a painful bite in the process. Puppies bite and chew—on furniture, shoes and sometimes you. Biting and nipping, in other words, is a normal part of a young pet's play behavior.

But what's cute in a puppy or kitten isn't so funny—or safe—in a full-grown pet. Delivered by a grown dog or cat, even a little "love bite" can cause injuries. Worse, behavior that starts out as play has a way of turning into genuine aggression later on. That's why it's so important to keep your pets under control from the beginning.

 For Dogs and Cats

Provide plenty of toys. Dogs and cats have a natural need to use their teeth. To help them put their mouths to good use, provide them with plenty of toys—and give them lots of praise when they use them, says Wayne Hunthausen, D.V.M., an animal behavior consultant in Westwood, Kansas, president of the American Veterinary Society of Animal Behavior and co-author of *Practitioner's Guide to Pet Behavior Problems*.

Dogs enjoy rubber or rawhide chews, while most cats appreciate cloth or rubber mice. "It's very important that the owner provide an alternate, acceptable outlet to biting," Dr. Hunthausen says.

Keep your skin safe. Pets will chew what you give them, and if their main "toy" happens to be your hand, they're learning a dangerous habit. Never let them chew directly on you, Dr. Hunthausen advises. Give them appropriate toys instead.

Act like an animal. The next time your pet puts the nip on you, let loose with a high-pitched yelp, just as another pet might do, says Andrea Fochios, D.V.M., a veterinarian in private practice in Ferndale, New York. This will make him realize he went too far. You'll know he's sorry when he licks the "wound," his way of apologizing for being too rough.

How to Spot a Problem Pet

It's normal for playful young dogs and cats to occasionally bite and scratch. As they get older and mellower, they gradually learn to control their toothsome exuberance and learn to play by your rules.

With some pets, however, the behavior doesn't stop—or it gets worse. "Some animals are more aggressive and have a real urge to establish control socially," says Steve Lindsay, a trainer and owner of Canine Behavioral Services in Philadelphia.

An aggressive cat, for example, may hiss or spit when people come too close, or begin attacking, with claws out, vulnerable human skin. An aggressive dog may growl when you approach his food or bite when you reach down to give him a pat.

Any show of defiance is potentially dangerous—not only to you and other family members but ultimately to the pet as well. This kind of behavior rarely gets better on its own and often gets worse, Lindsay warns. Don't take chances if you suspect your pet is becoming a biter or a scratcher. Call your vet or a professional trainer for advice.

As soon as he stops biting, reward him with strokes and praise, she says. This will help him understand that play can be fun without being rough.

Give him a chewing out. The next time he points his teeth in your direction, look him straight in the eye and firmly tell him "No!" says Dr. Hunthausen. Then ignore him for several minutes. Once he understands you're not happy with what he's doing, he'll try his best to please.

In most cases, it's best not to strike your pet when he bites, Dr. Hunthausen adds. Striking a pet could make him afraid of your hand, which in the future could cause him to bite even more.

Say it with spray. The next time your canine or feline friend tries a nip, blast him with a squirt from a water bottle, suggests Dr. Hunthausen. After a few impromptu washings, he'll get the hint and keep his teeth to himself. When he does, remember to praise him for his good behavior.

Try a hands-on approach. Young dogs and cats are sometimes uncomfortable with strangers, and they occasionally may nip when someone they don't know extends a friendly hand.

To help your pet get used to being touched, brush him several times a day, Dr. Hunthausen suggests. Encourage your friends to stroke and pet him as well. The more friendly touching he gets, the less likely he'll be to nip later on.

 For Dogs Only

Turn up the noise. An easy way to teach your dog not to bite is to rattle an empty can with some coins in the bottom. Dogs hate the sound, and eventually they'll learn that biting may have cacophonous consequences.

Shake him down. The next time your pooch gives a nip, grasp his collar with the fingers of both hands and cup his face between your palms. Make eye contact, give him a sharp shake and firmly say "Enough!" This will help him understand that you are the boss, explains Steve Lindsay, a trainer and owner of Canine Behavioral Services in Philadelphia.

After each "lesson," offer the back of your hand. If he nips at it again, give him another shake, Lindsay advises. If he continues to bite after that, however, don't take chances. Call your vet or a professional trainer for advice.

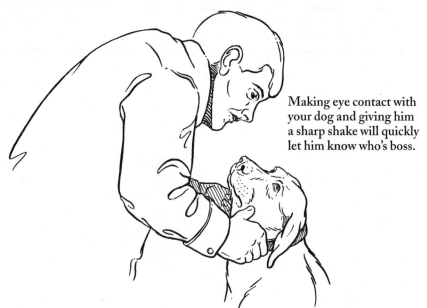

Making eye contact with your dog and giving him a sharp shake will quickly let him know who's boss.

Give him some quiet time. Dogs are social animals and don't like being banished to another room. So the next time he bites, put him in a room by himself for about five minutes, Lindsay suggests. Eventually he'll learn that nipping makes life lonely, and he'll learn to change his ways.

Make him sit. Dogs that are well-versed in the "sit" command are more likely to be calm in strange situations—and less likely to bite—than those that do whatever they please, Dr. Hunthausen says. By telling your pet to sit, you'll remind him that you're in charge—and he'll be less likely to misbehave.

 **For Cats Only**

Don't fight back. It's natural to pull away when your ferocious feline sinks her teeth—in fear, fun or anger—into you. Unfortunately, that makes *her* instincts tell her to bite harder, says Dr. Fochios. So the next time she nails you, try to let your hand go limp for just a second until she relaxes—then pull your hand free and give her a firm scolding.

PANEL OF ADVISERS

Andrea Fochios, D.V.M., is a veterinarian in private practice in Ferndale, New York.

Wayne Hunthausen, D.V.M., is an animal behavior consultant in Westwood, Kansas, president of the American Veterinary Society of Animal Behavior and co-author of *Practitioner's Guide to Pet Behavior Problems.*

Steve Lindsay is a trainer and owner of Canine Behavioral Services in Philadelphia.

Noise Anxiety

13 Ways to Silence It

During the Fourth of July fireworks, when everyone is oohing and aahing, is your dog under the bed, cowering and drooling? Does he tremble during thunderstorms or bark and pace when someone fires a gun?

A dog's hearing is extremely sensitive, and noise anxiety can be a resounding problem. "Dogs have crashed through plate glass windows and fallen a couple of stories after hearing a thunderbolt," says Elizabeth A. Shull, D.V.M., assistant professor of neurology, neurosurgery and animal behavior in the Department of Small Animal Clinical Sciences at the University of Tennessee College of Veterinary Medicine in Knoxville. "Fear of loud noises is not something to be taken lightly."

While cats may be startled by loud noises, they don't get panicky like dogs. So specialists focus their attention on the canine crew. Here's what they recommend.

 **For Dogs Only**

Give him his space. It's normal for a frightened dog to crawl into small spaces—under the bed or desk, for example, or even into the bathtub. "If the dog finds a place that seems to make him calmer, don't automatically try to pull him out," says John C. Wright, Ph.D., a certified animal behaviorist, professor of psychology at Mercer University in Macon, Georgia, and a member of the adjunct faculty at the University of Georgia School of Veterinary Medicine in Atlanta.

Create comfortable quarters. Dogs have been known to shove aside pots and pans and curl up inside a kitchen cupboard. You don't have to go this far, but you should make it easy for him to find a place to hide, says Dr. Wright. "If he likes it under the bed, clear out some room so he can get under it with ease," he suggests. Or add a small extension to your desk that will leave room for both your legs and him.

Calm him with a crate. Dogs tend to be less scared when they have a

Tranquillity at Your Fingertips

You may have the solution to your dog's noise phobia right in your own hands, says animal behaviorist Linda Tellington-Jones of Santa Fe, New Mexico, whose "Tellington Touch"—a system of therapeutic stroking—is widely practiced in homes, zoos and veterinarian's offices.

The technique is not quite massage therapy and not quite acupressure. Even Tellington-Jones, author of *The Tellington Touch*, isn't sure exactly why it works. "But it works wonders almost all the time," she says.

While there are several strokes for dogs with noise anxiety, an easy one to start with is the ear touch. Support your dog's head with one hand. With the other, gently hold his ear between your thumb and forefinger. "The main motion is a gentle stroke from the base of your dog's ear to the tip," says Tellington-Jones. "Repeat this motion several times, covering a different portion of the ear with each slide." You can also use your fingers to describe tiny circles, one at a time, all around the base of the ear.

The touches initially should be done when your dog isn't frightened. That way he won't come to associate the touches with whatever it is that's scaring him. Continue the touching for five to ten minutes. If your dog is just in heaven and you have nothing else to do, it's okay to go longer.

"This can calm even the most frightened animal," says Tellington-Jones.

place to call their own, says Robert K. Anderson, D.V.M., professor and director emeritus of the Animal Behavior Clinic at the University of Minnesota College of Veterinary Medicine in Minneapolis-St. Paul. "Crates and cages specially sold for dogs can act like dens in nature," says Dr. Anderson. "They can make a dog feel safer and more protected."

Covering the crate with a blanket or sheet will help your pet feel even more secure. Leave the door open, though, so he won't feel trapped. "It's important to make it comfortable and pleasant inside, with his favorite toy and a nice blanket," Dr. Anderson adds. But don't force him in if he doesn't want to go, because that will only make him more frightened.

Try a coverup. Putting a blanket or sheet over a petrified pooch will often have a calming effect, says Peter Borchelt, Ph.D., a certified applied animal behaviorist and owner of Animal Behavior Consultants in Brooklyn. Just make sure the blanket isn't covering his nose, he adds.

Lay on the love. Whether it's the bang of fireworks or the crash of thunder that has your pet trembling, giving him an extra dose of attention will help calm his nerves. "Give him plenty of comfort during a storm, just as you would a frightened child," says Dr. Borchelt.

Don't overdo it, however. Too much cuddling and pampering may encourage him to make a big deal out of being scared in the future. Soothing words and a few gentle pats are all he needs.

Dim the din. "Sometimes just masking the fear-causing sound with another sound can help your dog relax," says Dr. Shull. "Try a white noise machine. Or you can turn on your vacuum." Turning on the air conditioner can also help.

Ah, Bach. "Relaxing music that has a regular beat will help calm your dog," says Dr. Wright. "Play something like one of Bach's *Brandenburg Concertos*," he suggests.

If you know you're going to be gone during an upcoming thunderstorm or neighborhood skeet shoot, set a timer so the music turns on automatically. Just leave the tape or CD in continuous play mode and set the volume at a normal level.

Be calm yourself. It's difficult to soothe a frightened pet when you're jumping out of your own skin. "If you're looking tense and

When your pet is startled by loud noises, keep him calm by gently stroking his ear between your thumb and forefinger.

jumping when thunder cracks or firecrackers pop, you're not going to have a calming influence on your dog," says Dr. Wright.

Make noise time playtime. One of the best ways to prevent noise anxiety is to play with your dog—not only during thunderstorms or firecracker season but all the time, says Mary Lee Nitschke, Ph.D., an animal behavior therapist and assistant professor of psychology at Linfield College in Portland, Oregon. "If he's relaxed, he can't be tense. He'll learn he has nothing to fear," she says.

Consider pet therapy. To help animals overcome noise anxiety, experts use desensitization. While the process is complicated and requires a long-term commitment, the success rate is excellent, says Dr. Wright. "About three out of four dogs get much less anxious if the desensitization is done right," he says. Ask your vet or local Humane Society for the name of someone who specializes in this technique.

Ask about an Rx. When the Fourth of July rolls around, vets commonly prescribe medications—acepromazine or buspirone, for example—to help anxious pets get through the big booms.

Or go the natural route. Before resorting to prescription drugs, you might want to try an over-the-counter pet relaxant such as Pet Calm, suggests Dr. Nitschke. "They are very effective," she says.

Take a doggone vacation. If your dog is fearful of the Fourth, maybe this is a good time to retreat to a remote, quiet area until the noise blows over, suggests Dr. Shull. "The dog will surely appreciate it," he says.

PANEL OF ADVISERS

Robert K. Anderson, D.V.M., is professor and director emeritus of the Animal Behavior Clinic at the University of Minnesota College of Veterinary Medicine in Minneapolis-St. Paul.

Peter Borchelt, Ph.D., is a certified applied animal behaviorist and owner of Animal Behavior Consultants in Brooklyn.

Mary Lee Nitschke, Ph.D., is an animal behavior therapist and assistant professor of psychology at Linfield College in Portland, Oregon.

Elizabeth A. Shull, D.V.M., is assistant professor of neurology, neurosurgery and animal behavior in the Department of Small Animal Clinical Sciences at the University of Tennessee College of Veterinary Medicine at Knoxville.

Linda Tellington-Jones is an animal behaviorist in Santa Fe, New Mexico, and author of *The Tellington Touch*.

John C. Wright, Ph.D., is a certified animal behaviorist, professor of psychology at Mercer University in Macon, Georgia, and a member of the adjunct faculty at the University of Georgia School of Veterinary Medicine in Atlanta.

Overweight

12 Ways to Tip the Scales

Is your pooch a little pudgy? Is your cat a wee bit fat? They're not alone. Experts estimate that about one in three dogs and cats in America is overweight. That means there are some 39 million chubby pets waddling around.

Although weight gain occasionally indicates a medical problem, most overweight pets simply eat too much. "We're loving our pets to death with food," says Myrna Milani, D.V.M., a veterinarian in private practice in Charlestown, New Hampshire, and author of *The Body Language and Emotions of Dogs* and *The Body Language and Emotions of Cats.* "We give them all these treats and extra food, and then wonder why they're fat."

As with people, overweight pets can be plagued by problems such as high blood pressure, diabetes and even arthritis. To help keep your pet looking—and feeling—good, here's what experts recommend.

 **For Dogs and Cats**

Begin with the rib test. To tell if your pet is overweight or merely stocky, run your hand across his side. If you can't feel his ribs, you know it's time to trim his tummy, says nutrition expert Tony Buffington, D.V.M., Ph.D., associate professor in the Department of Veterinary Clinical Sciences at the Ohio State University College of Veterinary Medicine in Columbus.

Put on your walking shoes. Regular exercise is probably the best way to help your pet shed excess pounds, says Dave Dzanis, D.V.M., Ph.D., veterinary medical officer with the Food and Drug Administration in Bethesda, Maryland. "Taking your dog for a walk is great for your dog, great for you and a wonderful way to bond," he says. If your pet isn't used to regular exercise, you may want to start out with short walks—around the block, for instance—and gradually work up to longer, brisker adventures.

Many cats also enjoy walks, and some can even be leash-trained, says William D. Fortney, D.V.M., assistant professor of small animal medicine in the Department of Clinical Sciences at the Kansas State University College of Veterinary Medicine in Manhattan, Kansas. But if you and your feline friend are wary of walking on the wild side, playing vigorously at home can also be fine exercise, he adds.

Make it light. To help your pet slim down, some veterinarians recommend switching from his usual food to one that is high in dietary fiber and low in fat. (Or you can mix a higher-fiber food with his usual chow.) This can allow him to eat as much as before and still maintain a

If his abdomen protrudes beneath the ribcage and his head seems overly plump, your pet is probably overweight. A fit cat is lean, with ribs that are easily felt beneath the fur.

If you can't feel your dog's ribs and his belly is protruding underneath, it's probably time to start a diet. Dogs should have a clearly defined abdomen that's tucked up higher than the ribcage.

When to See the Vet

Your formerly svelte pet hasn't been eating more than usual, but lately he's begun to resemble a pot-bellied pig. While it's possible that all you're witnessing is the spread of middle age, his unexplained weight gain could also indicate something serious.

There are a number of dangerous conditions—among them diabetes and congestive heart failure—that make themselves known with weight gain, says Mark L. Morris, D.V.M., Ph.D., a nutrition consultant in Topeka, Kansas, and creator of Science Diet pet foods. That's why you should always check with your vet before starting your portly pet on a weight-loss plan. "Putting your pet on a diet in certain cases could lead to real trouble," warns Dr. Morris.

healthy weight, says Mark L. Morris, D.V.M., Ph.D., a nutrition consultant in Topeka, Kansas, creator of Science Diet pet foods and co-author of *Small Animal Clinical Nutrition*.

Cut back on the calories. When starting your pet on a diet, Dr. Buffington advises reducing the amount you feed him by about one-quarter. Then, after about two weeks, see if you can feel his ribs. If he still seems too plump, cut back on his food by another quarter. If two weeks go by and he still seems overweight, then it's probably time to see your vet, Dr. Buffington says.

Feed him often. To help your pet stave off hunger pangs while dieting, Dr. Milani recommends dividing his daily food allowance into four to six servings and giving him one serving every few hours. "It keeps him occupied and helps keep his stomach busy," she says. "He might not even realize he's not eating as much."

Spread the pleasure. Another way to help your pet feel satisfied while eating less is to make him eat more slowly, says Dr. Milani. For dogs, she recommends dividing the food into several bowls and spreading them around the kitchen. For cats, you can put the different bowls into open paper bags that have been laid on their sides. Between bites, your pet will have to walk from bag to bag, find the opening and crawl inside. "It's fun and time-consuming—just what the diet doctor ordered," she says.

Dividing your pet's food into several servings will prolong his eating pleasure, causing him to feel more satisfied even when he's eating less.

Nix the snacks. However tempting it may be to slip your pet a little something between meals, remind yourself that those are just additional calories he's better off avoiding, says Lisa Freeman, D.V.M., clinical instructor and a fellow in clinical nutrition at the Tufts University School of Veterinary Medicine in North Grafton, Massachusetts.

Or dole out low-cal treats. To please your pet's palate without packing on the pounds, you might want to give him high-fiber, low-fat snacks from your kitchen. "Lots of pets like foods such as cooked green beans, raw carrots or unbuttered air-popped popcorn," says Dr. Freeman.

Make a reservation. Another way to avoid fattening snacks is simply to set aside a small portion of your pet's usual food and dole it out during the day as an "added" treat, suggests Alan E. Schwichtenberg, D.V.M., a veterinarian in private practice in Indialantic, Florida. "You give him a piece of kibble here, a piece of kibble there, and everyone is happy," he says.

Go for the garlic. As bad as it can be for the breath, this pungent herb can be an effective weight-loss tool, says Ann-si Li, D.V.M., an expert in Oriental veterinary medicine in Oakland, California. "One of garlic's properties is that it helps regulate the liver and the gallbladder. That helps the digestive system get back on track," she says. For small

Weighing the Risks

Weighing your pet is a convenient way to measure the progress—or setbacks—of his weight-loss plan. For a small pet, it's easy: Just scoop him up and step on the scale. Then put him down and weigh yourself. Subtract your weight from what the two of you weigh together, and you'll quickly learn if your pet is still more hippo than gazelle.

It's not so easy, however, if your pet happens to be a big-time wiggler—or he's a 100-pound Labrador retriever. While bathroom scales work well for the upright among us, they're terribly inconvenient for our four-footed friends.

The solution to this weighty problem? Drop by your vet's office, suggests Alan E. Schwichtenberg, D.V.M., a veterinarian in private practice in Indialantic, Florida. Most vets have large platform scales that are easy for pets to stand on. In most cases they'll let you use the scale free of charge, particularly when you're working together to bring your pet back to fighting trim.

pets, she recommends crushing about one-quarter to half a clove and putting in their food. Larger pets can eat anywhere from one to two cloves a day.

Guard against theft. "Dogs and cats, especially cats, can be really sneaky when they're not getting as much food as they're accustomed to," says Dr. Fortney. His advice: "Keep the garbage out of their reach, keep an eye on your table, and by all means keep bread far away from your cat. Dieting cats really go crazy for bread."

 For Cats Only

Be prepared for the backlash. No one enjoys dieting, and few creatures enjoy it less than cats, says Dr. Fortney. "They whine, they meow, they bat at your ankles—they can be extremely difficult," he says. "Many of our clients decide at first that dieting or changing foods isn't worth it, but when they realize their cat's health is at stake, they give it another try."

Paw Problems

13 Steps to Comfort

You wouldn't walk barefoot over thorny fields, sun-baked rocks or jagged sheets of ice. But that's exactly what dogs and cats do every day. That's why their paws are so tough and thick, designed by nature to skip across terrain that would tear human soles to shreds.

Tough as their paws are, however, they can still get cuts, scrapes and painful burns. "Between the pads it is very sensitive," says M. Lynne Kesel, D.V.M., assistant professor of elective surgery in the Department of Clinical Sciences at the Colorado State University College of Veterinary Medicine and Biomedical Sciences in Fort Collins. "Cuts can be extremely painful," she says.

When your pet's paws are giving her pause, here's what you need to do.

 For Dogs and Cats

Do an inspection. If your pet is limping or favoring one foot, you need to take a close look to see what's wrong, says Scott Weldy, D.V.M., a veterinarian in private practice in El Toro, California.

Get down on the floor and gently raise the suspect paw. Look for redness, swelling, bleeding or other signs of irritation, he says. Press gently on the pads, around the claws and between the toes. If your pet winces or cries, move in for a closer look.

When doing a foot exam, always be prepared to back off, Dr. Weldy adds. Even the gentlest pet might nip when you hit a sore spot.

Beware of burrs. If your pet frequently romps outdoors, she may have picked up burrs—prickly seed cases that can stick painfully in the pads or between the toes.

To remove a burr, grab it firmly with a pair of tweezers and gently wriggle it free. If it's tangled in the hairs, however, you may need to clip it out with scissors, being careful not to snip adjoining skin, says

Breaking the Lick Cycle

Kids suck their thumbs, and more than one adult has been known to nibble a thumbnail. But who would have thought pets' lives are sufficiently nerve-racking to bring on a bout of paw-licking?

Pets that are bored, anxious or depressed will occasionally start licking one or more of their feet, not just for a minute or two but for hours at a time, says Bernadine Cruz, D.V.M., a veterinarian in private practice in Laguna Hills, California. The constant exposure to moisture can result in fungal infections or even tissue damage—sores that vets call lick granulomas, she explains.

To break the lick cycle and give paws a chance to dry, vets sometimes recommend using an Elizabethan collar—a cardboard or plastic device that slips over your pet's head and prevents her from licking. The collars are available from veterinarians and pet stores. Or you can try applying a repellent to the paw to make it less appetizing. One popular choice is bitter apple spray, says Dr. Cruz.

When home remedies don't seem to help, you should see your vet, Dr. Cruz advises. There is a variety of training techniques that can help keep your pet dry. "They're even using things like Prozac to control licking," she adds.

Mollyann Holland, D.V.M., a resident veterinarian in small animal medicine in the Department of Veterinary Medicine and Surgery at the University of Missouri College of Veterinary Medicine in Columbia.

Applying a little vegetable oil to the burr is another way to help loosen its grip. (For more tips, see Burrs on page 84.)

Take a little off the toes. It's not uncommon for long-haired pets to develop hair mats between the foot pads, which can chafe and cause irritation. "It's a good idea to keep hair trimmed back," says Dr. Kesel.

Get the mud out. Like hair mats, mud that accumulates between the toes can cause pain and irritation. After your pet has returned from a muddy romp, wash her feet thoroughly with soap and water to remove the grit, says Jan A. Hall, D.V.M., a veterinary dermatologist and referral specialist in Ville St. Laurent in Montreal.

Keep them dry. Like a baby's bottom, your pet's paws can become irritated from too much moisture. So after washing her feet—or when she comes indoors after a splashy run—dry her feet thoroughly with a soft towel, Dr. Kesel advises.

Douse the fire. Although your pet's paws are tough and hard, they're not immune to burns—from friction, for example, or from standing on a hot surface. Any burn should be thoroughly cleaned with soap and warm water to prevent infection, says Bernadine Cruz, D.V.M., a veterinarian in private practice in Laguna Hills, California. Then dry the paw well with a soft towel.

Put on a soothing ointment. After giving a burned paw a good wash, smooth on an over-the-counter antibiotic ointment, says Dr. Kesel. Then cover it loosely with a light gauze bandage to keep it clean. To keep the gauze in place, cover it with a light cotton sock.

Watch out for dryness. Like people, pets occasionally suffer from dry, cracked, callused skin on the bottoms of their feet. To keep the pads protected, Dr. Kesel says, try applying a moisturizer. The same stuff you use on your hands will work for your pet. Vitamin E oil, available in drugstores, also works well.

Once you've applied a moisturizer, "the big trick is to keep them from licking it off," says Nancy Scanlan, D.V.M., a veterinarian in private practice in Sherman Oaks, California. "Put the oil on at mealtime," she suggests. "They'll eat first, so the oil will have some time to soak in."

Occasionally, if your pet has a thick, uncomfortable buildup of dry, roughened callus, your vet may recommend bringing her in to have the callus trimmed, Dr. Scanlan adds.

Don't overdo it. While giving your pet the occasional lube job will help make her feet more comfortable, getting them too soft makes them vulnerable to injuries. So don't use lotion for more than a few days in a row, Dr. Cruz advises.

Get the salt licked. In winter, salt spread on sidewalks to melt snow can irritate your pet's paws and lead to cracking, Dr. Kesler says. She recommends removing the salt with soap and water immediately after winter walks. Dry the paw well, then apply a small amount of moisturizer with lanolin, she advises.

Clean up the oil slick. There are a number of common household chemicals, like motor oil, antifreeze and corrosive cleaners, that can be extremely hard on your pet's paws—and toxic should she lick them off. You don't need special stuff to remove the gunk, though: Washing your pet's feet with dishwashing detergent works well, says Dr. Cruz. Applying olive oil can also help.

Apply the detergent or oil to a damp washcloth and scrub the paw, repeating until it's clean. Don't rub so hard that you cause further damage. If whatever she's stepped in doesn't come off easily, give up and call your vet for advice.

Take a bite out of gum. If your pet has chewing gum stuck to her paw, you can use dishwashing detergent to help dissolve it. Or you can use gum removers, available at hardware and drugstores.

If the gum is really wedged into the hair, you may need to cut it out. Take a small pair of scissors and cut at the base of the hairs below the gum. Just be careful not to cut skin in the process, says Dr. Kesel.

 For **Dogs** Only

Forget the boots. While pet stores and specialty catalogs tout the virtues of rubber doggy boots—particularly for hunting dogs that spend their days traipsing over hill and dale—they're rarely needed, says Dr. Kesel. "Most of the time the dog walks out of them," she adds.

PANEL OF ADVISERS

Bernadine Cruz, D.V.M., is a veterinarian in private practice in Laguna Hills, California.

Jan A. Hall, D.V.M., is a veterinary dermatologist and referral specialist in Ville St. Laurent in Montreal.

Mollyann Holland, D.V.M., is a resident veterinarian in small animal medicine in the Department of Veterinary Medicine and Surgery at the University of Missouri College of Veterinary Medicine in Columbia.

M. Lynne Kesel, D.V.M., is assistant professor of elective surgery in the Department of Clinical Sciences at the Colorado State University College of Veterinary Medicine and Biomedical Sciences in Fort Collins.

Nancy Scanlan, D.V.M., is a veterinarian in private practice in Sherman Oaks, California.

Scott Weldy, D.V.M., is a veterinarian in private practice in El Toro, California.

Poisoning

14 Tips to Tackle Toxins

Pets are always poking their noses into interesting nooks and crannies, but sometimes what they find can be hazardous to their health.

Every year, thousands of dogs and cats are poisoned in the "safety" of their own homes. They don't read labels. Plus, things that would taste awful to us, like antifreeze, they find lip-smackingly good.

If you discover your pet eating—or rolling in—something dangerous, consider it an emergency and get him to the vet right away. With poisoning, every minute counts.

If you can't get professional help right away, here are some things you should do to make sure that curiosity doesn't kill the cat (or dog).

 **For Dogs and Cats**

Identify the problem. Even before you call the vet, you need to know *exactly* what your pet has gotten into. Don't just tell the vet that kitty polished off the pesticide. He'll need to know what the active ingredients are, in what concentrations they are used and any other information you can get from the package, says Larry Thompson, D.V.M., clinical veterinary toxicologist at the Diagnostic Laboratory at the Cornell University College of Veterinary Medicine in Ithaca, New York.

It's also a good idea to measure what's missing so you can tell your vet how much poison went from the package into your pet. If he's vomiting, save a small sample in a plastic bag. It may provide valuable clues, says E. Murl Bailey, Jr., D.V.M., Ph.D., professor of toxicology in the Department of Veterinary Physiology and Pharmacology at the Texas A&M University College of Veterinary Medicine in College Station.

Purge the poison. If your pet has gotten into pills, antifreeze or other toxic substances (but not caustic substances, such as lye), getting him to vomit will help eliminate some of the danger, says Dr. Bailey.

When to See the Vet

The sooner poisoning is treated, the better the odds of saving your pet. Since pets can't say where it hurts or what they ate, you need to know what to watch for—and then call your vet immediately. Warning signs include:

- Changes in behavior. Your pet may shiver or become anxious. He may lurch or stagger, have seizures or lose consciousness. In some cases he may drool excessively and paw at his mouth.
- Bleeding. Products used to control mice and other rodents often contain warfarin, a chemical that can cause bleeding from any body opening.
- Breathing problems, like panting or gasping. If your pet has been exposed to carbon monoxide, his lips and gums will turn bright red.

To make your pet vomit, give him household hydrogen peroxide (a 3 percent solution)—about one tablespoon for every ten pounds of pet. Draw the liquid into a syringe or turkey baster, tip your pet's head back and squirt it toward the back of his tongue, says Dr. Thompson.

In most cases your pet will vomit within five minutes (although it may not work with cats; even vets have trouble making them vomit). If he doesn't, wait ten minutes and try again. Don't give a third dose, however, because giving too much hydrogen peroxide can be dangerous, Dr. Thompson warns.

Don't use syrup of ipecac, he adds. While this over-the-counter product is safe for humans, it can be toxic to pets.

Neutralize the danger. If your pet has devoured something caustic—like drain cleaner or kerosene—don't induce vomiting, because the poison will do a double burn: going down *and* coming up. Instead give your pet something to neutralize the harsh chemicals.

If he got into something alkaline—like drain cleaner—give him about three teaspoons of vinegar or lemon juice diluted in an equal amount of water, suggests Dr. Bailey. Again, draw the liquid into a syringe or baster and squirt it toward the back of his mouth. This will help neutralize the harmful effects of the chemical in his belly, cooling the burn.

If he got into an acid—by chewing a battery, for example, or drinking bleach—"Milk of Magnesia will negate the acid," says Dr. Bailey. Give one teaspoon for every five pounds of pet, he advises.

Absorb it with charcoal. Giving your pet activated charcoal, either in tablet form or as a powder mixed with water, will quickly absorb toxins from the stomach before they have a chance to be absorbed into the system.

Even after giving charcoal, however, the original poison is still in the gut, so you'll want to see your vet right away.

Dilute it with milk. Giving your pet milk will help dilute poison while at the same time coating his stomach and mouth, helping soothe the irritation. "If the pet's alert," says Dr. Bailey, "you can't go wrong giving him milk."

If he seems woozy, however, don't give him anything to eat or drink, because it could cause suffocation.

Put medicines out of reach. The most ingenious childproof cap isn't a match for a curious cat or diligent dog. After commercial pesticides, human medications are the second most common cause of poisoning in pets, says Dr. Thompson.

"One extra-strength Tylenol can kill a cat," he warns. So keep all medications out of reach. That goes for drugs in your briefcase, purse or glove compartment as well.

Petproof the cabinets. Animals can be very creative when it comes to satisfying their curiosity. And a lot of products we store at their level—cleaners under the sink, for example—are potential poisons.

"If you don't have childproof locks on cabinets, pets can flip their paws and open them," says Tam Garland, D.V.M., Ph.D., veterinary toxicologist at the Texas A&M University College of Veterinary Medicine.

Guard the garage. One common cause of poisoning in pets is antifreeze. It has a sweet taste they like, and it's extremely toxic: One tablespoon could kill a cat, and less than a cup could kill a small dog. Don't leave open containers where pets can find them. And be sure to fix radiator or water-hose leaks before he discovers the puddles.

Cancel the candy. For pets, chocolate is a tasty toxin. It contains a compound called theobromine, which, like caffeine, is dangerous to dogs and cats when eaten in large quantities, says Mary Labato, D.V.M., clinical assistant professor at the Tufts University School of Veterinary Medicine in North Grafton, Massachusetts.

Baking chocolate, with nearly nine times more theobromine than milk chocolate, is particularly dangerous, but either kind can cause problems, she warns.

Don't panic, however, just because your pet sneaks a munch from your chocolate bar. A toxic dose of theobromine for a 20-pound dog is about 1,000 milligrams—the amount found in 28 ounces of baking chocolate. If you're not sure how much he ate, call your vet for advice.

Protect them from plants. There are a number of common house-plants, like philodendron, dieffenbachia, Jerusalem cherry and yew, that can cause an upset stomach in pets or even poison them. Usually the leaves must be swallowed to cause injury, but in some cases just chewing the leaves can cause problems, says Dr. Thompson.

Other plants dangerous to pets include caladium, spider plant, air-plane plant, cyclamen, foxglove, dragon tree, holly, mistletoe, azalea, poinsettia, rhododendron and mother-in-law's tongue.

Always put houseplants where adventurous dogs or cats can't get at them, Dr. Thompson says. If you have plants and aren't sure if they're safe, ask your vet for advice.

Don't use medicines creatively. In the belief that if some medicine is good, more must be better, owners occasionally give two or three times the normal amount—literally killing their pets with kindness. Or they forget to give one dose, then give twice as much later to make up for it.

Always read directions carefully and follow them exactly, Dr. Thompson says. If you have questions about your pet's medications, play it safe and call your vet for advice.

Clean the coat. Not all poisons must be swallowed to cause harm. Sometimes just coming into contact with them can cause damage or even death. Even products that are normally safe—like flea dips—can be harmful if the directions aren't followed exactly.

If your pet has gotten into something he shouldn't have, "immediately give him a bath to rinse off a topical toxin," says Dr. Thompson. "Rinsing even 12 hours later will help decrease the concentration."

First aid is the same as for humans, he adds. Rinse the affected area with water for at least ten minutes, even before you take him to the vet.

After the initial flushing, you can wash the coat with shampoo or dishwashing liquid to remove as much of the poison as possible, adds Dr. Garland. Even washing with plain water can help.

Beware of "helpful" poisons. While you may occasionally want to use household poisons to eradicate ants or other pests, always place them in places your pet can't go.

Even then, try to use them only in small amounts, adds Dr. Thompson—"enough to poison the mouse or roach but not enough to hurt your pet."

Give her air. If your pet has been exposed to high levels of carbon monoxide, natural gas or other types of gas, get him into fresh air as quickly as possible, says Dr. Bailey. Then call the vet right away.

PANEL OF ADVISERS

E. Murl Bailey, Jr., D.V.M., Ph.D., is professor of toxicology in the Department of Veterinary Physiology and Pharmacology at the Texas A&M University College of Veterinary Medicine in College Station.

Tam Garland, D.V.M., Ph.D., is a veterinary toxicologist at the Texas A&M University College of Veterinary Medicine in College Station.

Mary Labato, D.V.M., is clinical assistant professor at the Tufts University School of Veterinary Medicine in North Grafton, Massachusetts.

Larry Thompson, D.V.M., is a clinical veterinary toxicologist at the Diagnostic Laboratory at the Cornell University College of Veterinary Medicine in Ithaca, New York.

Porcupine Quills

6 Ways to Get the Point

A pugnacious porcupine (with 30,000 quills) didn't like your pet poking her proboscis into his personal business. And now your pet is stuck—quite literally—with a bit of a prickly problem.

Be forewarned: There's a good reason veterinarians often give an anesthetic before removing porcupine quills. "It can really hurt," says James B. Dalley, D.V.M., associate professor of small animal clinical sciences at the Michigan State University College of Veterinary Medicine in East Lansing.

If your pet escaped with just a few barbs, however, it's usually not too hard to remove them yourself. Here's what vets recommend.

 For **Dogs** and **Cats**

Go for your gloves. When removing quills, you want to make sure those nasty barbs don't end up in you. "Gloves with big leather palms do well to protect you," says Jan White, D.V.M., executive director of the International Wildlife Rehabilitation Council in Suisun, California, and an assistant wildlife health researcher at the Wildlife Health Center at the University of California, Davis, School of Veterinary Medicine.

Keep her calm. Your pet may not be herself when she has several barbed, three-inch projectiles jammed into her skin. Some pets go nearly mad with pain and will try anything—like bashing into walls or rolling on the carpet—to make the quills go away. "Speak to her, pet her softly, do whatever you have to reassure her and keep her from making matters worse," says William G. Brewer, D.V.M., assistant professor of small animal internal medicine in the Department of Small Animal Surgery and Medicine at the Auburn University College of Veterinary Medicine in Alabama.

Stay away from scissors. "The idea of cutting a quill to let the air out of it so it shrinks is an old wives' tale," says Susan Chadima, D.V.M., a veterinarian in private practice in Topsham, Maine. In fact, cutting a quill can cause small pieces to splinter off and jab into the skin. "You may actually create a more dangerous situation," Dr. Chadima says.

Get a grip. With either needlenose or blunt-nose pliers, grab a quill as close to the fur as possible. Using gentle pressure, pull steadily until

When to See the Vet

Pets tend to go after porcupines the same way they attack their food—with their mouths wide open. That's why quills often wind up inside the mouth and even toward the back of the throat. And when one quill is jabbed in a hard-to-see place, others may be lurking nearby.

If you find even one quill inside your pet's mouth or throat—or if she was on the receiving end of lots of quills—you'll want to take her to the vet right away. In fact, you should see the vet even if she got jabbed with a single quill that somehow broke off under the skin.

"Porcupine quills are excellent travelers. They're designed to travel in one direction—in," says Bernhard P. Pukay, D.V.M., a veterinarian in private practice in Ottawa, Canada, and host of the Discovery Channel's *Pet Connection.* "They can end up anywhere in the body, which can be very dangerous."

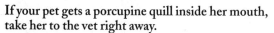

If your pet gets a porcupine quill inside her mouth, take her to the vet right away.

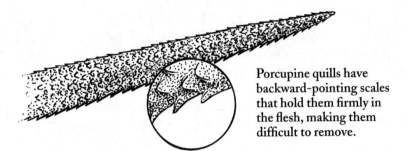

Porcupine quills have backward-pointing scales that hold them firmly in the flesh, making them difficult to remove.

the quill comes out. It's painful, so don't be surprised if your pet cries out. If she seems overly distressed, however, you may want to leave the remaining quills and get professional help.

Dab it with disinfectant. Since even porcupines sometimes get jabbed, nature provided protection by coating quills with a fatty acid to help reduce the risk of infection. But it's still a good idea to apply a topical antiseptic like Betadine Solution after removing a quill, say porcupine pros. "It makes it easier to prevent a possible problem this way," says Lynda Bond, D.V.M., a veterinarian in private practice in Cape Elizabeth, Maine, who hosts a weekly pet segment for a Portland television station.

Feel for hideaways. While the largest porcupine quills can be as long as four inches, others may be only ½ inch—small enough to get lost under your pet's fur. "Now that you've pulled out all the quills you were able to see, let your fingers do the walking," says Dr. Dalley. "Feeling carefully for quills will help you get any you may have missed. You'll know a quill when you feel it," he adds.

PANEL OF ADVISERS

Lynda Bond, D.V.M., is a veterinarian in private practice in Cape Elizabeth, Maine, who hosts a weekly pet segment for a Portland television station.

William G. Brewer, D.V.M., is assistant professor of small animal internal medicine in the Department of Small Animal Surgery and Medicine at the Auburn University College of Veterinary Medicine in Alabama.

Susan Chadima, D.V.M., is a veterinarian in private practice in Topsham, Maine.

James B. Dalley, D.V.M., is associate professor of small animal clinical sciences at the Michigan State University College of Veterinary Medicine in East Lansing.

Bernhard P. Pukay, D.V.M., is a veterinarian in private practice in Ottawa, Canada, and host of the Discovery Channel's *Pet Connection*.

Jan White, D.V.M., is executive director of the International Wildlife Rehabilitation Council in Suisun, California, and an assistant wildlife health researcher at the Wildlife Health Center at the University of California, Davis, School of Veterinary Medicine.

Prostate Problems
6 Helpful Hints

Tough-guy dogs and he-man cats don't shave twice a day or hang out in the club showing off their pecs, but they still have ample amounts of testosterone.

What's good for macho swagger, however, isn't necessarily good for the prostate gland. The purpose of the prostate gland is to supply the fluid needed to transport sperm. As male pets age, this gland—which encircles the urethra below the bladder—gradually swells. Eventually it may begin pressing on the urethra, making urination difficult. Bowel movements may also become difficult.

In addition, dogs and cats occasionally develop a painful inflammation or infection of the gland called prostatitis, says Frank L. Moore, D.V.M., a veterinarian in private practice in Westminster, California, who specializes in small animal medicine.

If your pet's prostate problems are causing pain, difficulty walking or urinary problems, your vet may recommend drugs or surgery. In addition, there are things you can do at home to relieve the ache and help keep your pet comfortable.

 For **Dogs** and **Cats**

Get him outside. It's often difficult for a pet with an enlarged prostate gland to urinate all at once, so he may need to go out more often, says David Polzin, D.V.M., Ph.D., professor of veterinary medicine at the University of Minnesota College of Veterinary Medicine in St. Paul. Not only will he feel more comfortable, but frequent urination can also help prevent urinary tract infections.

Give him recovery time. Although frequent outings can be helpful for pets with prostate problems, you have to be careful not to overdo it. In some cases, the prostate gland gets tender and inflamed, and even mild exercise can be painful, Dr. Polzin adds. So if your pet is having

When to See the Vet

An enlarged prostate gland isn't always painful, but for some pets it's a lifelong problem, causing back pain as well as difficulty walking or urinating. That's when you need to see a vet for treatment.

In most cases, however, the cure is a snip away. Testosterone is what causes the prostate gland to enlarge. "Remove the source of the testosterone, which is the testicles, and the process reverses," says W. Jeffery Alfriend, D.V.M., a veterinarian in private practice in Los Alamitos, California, who specializes in small animal medicine. The prostate gland may decrease in size by 70 percent after a pet is neutered.

In fact, dogs and cats that are neutered when they're young may never have the problem, Dr. Alfriend adds.

trouble walking or the back end of his body seems tender, limit your outings to a stroll around the yard, he advises.

Reduce the pressure. Occasionally an enlarged prostate gland will begin pressing on the large intestine, making defecation difficult. To help your pet stay regular, your vet may recommend giving a prescription stool softener such as lactulose, says Lauren Prause, D.V.M., a veterinary resident in small animal internal medicine in the Department of Clinical Sciences at the Colorado State University College of Veterinary Medicine and Biomedical Sciences in Fort Collins.

Experts recommend giving about one teaspoon of stool softener for every 20 pounds of pet two to four times a day. Ask your vet to recommend a dose that's right for your pet.

Provide pain relief. For dogs with prostate pain, aspirin is a safe, effective remedy, says Dr. Polzin. Give about one-quarter of a 325-milligram tablet of buffered aspirin per ten pounds of pooch once or twice a day, he advises.

Aspirin can be dangerous for cats, however, so give it only under a vet's supervision. Other painkillers like ibuprofen and acetaminophen can also be dangerous for pets. Don't use them, vets say.

Fill his water tank. Since a pet with prostate problems may have trouble emptying his bladder, urine tends to stagnate, increasing the risk of urinary tract infections, Dr. Polzin says.

Encouraging your pet to drink more water contributes to more frequent urination. This in turn makes it harder for bacteria to build up to infection-causing levels, he explains.

Give medicines at the right time. If your vet has prescribed antibiotics for a prostate infection, be sure to give them immediately after your pet has urinated. This will allow the drugs to reach higher levels in the body rather than quickly being eliminated in the urine, Dr. Prause says.

PANEL OF ADVISERS

W. Jeffery Alfriend, D.V.M., is a veterinarian in private practice in Los Alamitos, California, who specializes in small animal medicine

Frank L. Moore, D.V.M., is a veterinarian in private practice in Westminster, California, who specializes in small animal medicine.

David Polzin, D.V.M., Ph.D., is professor of veterinary medicine at the University of Minnesota College of Veterinary Medicine in St. Paul.

Lauren Prause, D.V.M., is a veterinary resident in small animal internal medicine in the Department of Clinical Sciences at the Colorado State University College of Veterinary Medicine and Biomedical Sciences in Fort Collins.

Ringworm

10 Healing Solutions

Just because your pet's getting balder doesn't mean he's suddenly getting older. In fact, if his coat is starting to resemble the putting green on the 18th hole, it could be due to the fungal infection called ringworm.

Dogs and cats of all ages may occasionally get ringworm, a type of fungus that causes ringlike, flaky, bald patches on the head, ears, paws and back, says Frank L. Moore, D.V.M., a veterinarian in private practice in Westminster, California, who specializes in small animal medicine. It can also infect the nails, he adds.

While ringworm often goes away on its own within one to three months, in the meantime it can make your pet uncomfortably itchy as well as ugly. Worse, it's contagious—both to pets and people, says Dr. Moore. To clear up the infection fast, here's what vets recommend.

 **For Dogs and Cats**

Take a little off the top. Trimming hair around the bald spots will help prevent the fungus from spreading and also make the area easier to treat, says Lauren Prause, D.V.M., a veterinary resident in small animal internal medicine in the Department of Clinical Sciences at the Colorado State University College of Veterinary Medicine and Biomedical Sciences in Fort Collins.

Depending on how fast your pet's hair grows, you'll probably have to repeat the trim every week to two weeks until the infection has cleared up. Using scissors is okay, but it's better to use an electric trimmer, says Dr. Prause. "I can't tell you how many animals I see with cuts inflicted by well-meaning owners," she says.

Haul away the hair. Since ringworm thrives on hair both on and off the pet, be sure to clean up well after giving your pet a haircut, says Dr. Prause.

Wash it well. To keep the "rings" clean and infection-free, wash them daily with an over-the-counter antiseptic soap containing povidone iodine (such as Betadine Skin Cleanser) or chlorhexidine (such as Nolvasan), advises Patrick McKeever, D.V.M., professor of veterinary medicine at the University of Minnesota College of Veterinary Medicine in St. Paul. This will help prevent minor fungal problems from turning into a more serious bacterial infection, he says.

Spread on protection. There are a number of over-the-counter antifungal creams, liquids and ointments that are very good for controlling ringworm, Dr. McKeever says. For the treatment to be effective, rub a small amount of the medication into the skin twice a day, he advises. Ask your vet which medication will work best for your pet.

Practice prevention. To eliminate ringworm and prevent it from spreading, wash your pets with an antifungal shampoo. This will not only kill any fungus that's already present, it will also help prevent further infection. So even if only one pet in the family is infected, it's a good idea to shampoo *all* your pets, says Dr. McKeever.

Soak your pet thoroughly—either in the tub or outside using a hose. Then work up a good lather with the shampoo. Wait about 15 minutes to give it time to work, then rinse well, Dr. McKeever says.

Keep him brushed. To prevent ringworm from spreading, regular grooming is very important, says Dr. McKeever. Brushing or combing

When to See the Vet

While many pets with ringworm experience nothing worse than a bald spot or two, sometimes the infection can spread over the entire body, causing large, red, weepy sores.

If this happens, see your vet right away, advises Patrick McKeever, D.V.M., professor of veterinary medicine at the University of Minnesota College of Veterinary Medicine in St. Paul. Your pet may need griseofulvin (Fulvicin P/G tablets)—a powerful prescription drug, taken orally, that attacks fungal infections from the inside out.

Griseofulvin does more than stop infections in progress. Because it's actually absorbed into the growing hair, it also helps prevent infection (or reinfection) from occurring, adds Dr. McKeever.

your pet at least once a day will help remove fungal spores before they can cause further infection, he says.

To prevent reinfecting your pet, however, it's important to clean the brush or comb thoroughly after grooming by dunking it into a solution made with 1 part bleach to 32 parts water. Dip combs, scissors and clipper blades into the solution several times, then set them aside to air-dry, says Dr. Prause. Brushes take longer to disinfect, so allow them to soak for several minutes, she advises.

Take precautions. While pet problems usually aren't passed to people, ringworm is a contagious exception, warns Dr. Prause. So until your pet is infection-free, keep the cuddling to a minimum. And always wash your hands well after petting or treating him.

Soap and water alone won't kill the fungus, she adds, so it's a good idea to first douse your hands with a mild bleach solution, then wash that off with regular soap and water.

Protect his pals. Since ringworm is readily spread from pet to pet, it's a good idea to keep your infected friend away from your other pets until the "rings" clear up—or better yet, until you get a clean bill of health from your vet, says W. Jeffery Alfriend, D.V.M, a veterinarian in private practice in Los Alamitos, California, who specializes in small animal medicine.

Vacuum often. Since ringworm survives even on hair that's not on your pet, vacuuming the house often will help reduce the risk of reinfection, Dr. McKeever says. "Make sure you vacuum well and get all the hair that's been shed," he says.

Cover his bases. Draping an old sheet or blanket over your pet's bedding—or on carpets, furniture or anyplace else that he calls home—makes it easier to prevent "contagious" hair from spreading.

Every day or two, scoop up the covers and wash them in hot water, Dr. McKeever suggests. For extra protection, add a mild bleach solution to the wash, he adds.

PANEL OF ADVISERS

W. Jeffery Alfriend, D.V.M., is a veterinarian in private practice in Los Alamitos, California, who specializes in small animal medicine.

Patrick McKeever, D.V.M., is professor of veterinary medicine at the University of Minnesota College of Veterinary Medicine in St. Paul.

Frank L. Moore, D.V.M., is a veterinarian in private practice in Westminster, California, who specializes in small animal medicine.

Lauren Prause, D.V.M., is a veterinary resident in small animal internal medicine in the Department of Clinical Sciences at the Colorado State University College of Veterinary Medicine and Biomedical Sciences in Fort Collins.

Separation Anxiety

12 Ways to Ease the Angst

While virtually all pets are sorry to see their owners leave the house, "others truly go off the deep end," says Karen Overall, V.M.D., Ph.D., a lecturer specializing in behavioral medicine in the Department of Clinical Studies at the University of Pennsylvania School of Veterinary Medicine in Philadelphia.

Vets tell tales of anxious dogs chewing through drywall, bending metal bars on crates or jumping through closed windows. And while some cats also suffer from separation anxiety, it's more of a canine problem. "Dogs are pack animals. Some are utterly lost when left alone," says Myrna Milani, D.V.M., a veterinarian in private practice in Charlestown, New Hampshire, and author of *The Body Language and Emotions of Cats* and *The Body Language and Emotions of Dogs*.

To help calm your canine, here's what experts recommend.

 **For Dogs Only**

Separate slowly. To help your pet get used to your absences, you'll have to begin gradually. "Give your dog a treat and leave the room for a minute, shutting the door behind you," suggests Micky Niego, an animal behavior consultant in Airmont, New York.

"When you come back, your dog will act like you're just back from a long European vacation, but at least she'll know she can survive one minute without you," Niego says. Gradually work your way up to the point where your dog can spend an hour or two in a separate part of the house without being concerned.

Step out for a moment. After your dog gets used to being in another part of the house without you, try leaving the house for very short periods, suggests Bob Gutierrez, animal behavior coordinator at the San Francisco Society for the Prevention of Cruelty to Animals.

"One Saturday I practiced leaving 20 times for just a few minutes at a time. For 15 homecomings, my dog acted like God had returned.

As part of a training program, leaving the house for a minute or two at a time can help your pet adjust to longer absences.

Then something clicked and he barely even noticed when I was coming and going," Gutierrez says. "He was pretty much fine after that."

Don't coddle her. When you leave the house, don't make a big fuss. "Say, 'See you later,' and leave," says Gutierrez. Be equally nonchalant when you come home. "This way you're telling your dog it's no big deal when you come or go—that it's okay to be alone," he says.

But leave her a special treat. When you leave the house, give your dog something special to chew—something she never gets when you're together. "That way the dog may come to look forward to the treat more than she worries about you saying good-bye," says Dr. Overall.

She recommends stuffing a hollow shank bone or rubber chew toy with goodies like peanut butter or cream cheese. "Dogs can spend hours at a time working on these and forget about everything else," she says.

Work out her worries. Before leaving your dog alone, take her out for a romp, Dr. Overall suggests. If you get her thoroughly tired, there's a decent chance she'll sleep the entire time you're gone.

Practice her lessons. To make the most of outdoor jaunts, Dr. Milani recommends using them for extra training time. "When a dog knows what you want and what's expected, she's likely to be more confident. And a confident dog is less anxious," she says.

Find her a friend. Since dogs are pack animals by nature, the company of another pet might make her feel completely different about your departures, says Carol Lea Benjamin, a New York City dog trainer and author of *Mother Knows Best: The Natural Way to Train Your Dog* and *Surviving Your Dog's Adolescence.* "Getting another dog might be great, but even having a cat around can decrease your dog's anxiety and make her feel comfortable," she says.

Make suitcases fun places. "Some dogs get really upset when they see the suitcases come out," says Dr. Overall. To allay the anxiety, she recommends occasionally taking luggage out of the closet even when you're not taking a trip.

"Play fetch by the suitcase, or put toys in it and let your dog find them," she suggests. "That way when you get ready for a trip, your dog won't have that 'Oh, my God' reaction."

As a special reward, Dr. Overall says, she always brings her dog a gift when she returns from trips. "I don't fuss over her when I get back, but I let her shuffle through the suitcase and unpack her toy."

Light up her life. If you leave on a light or two when you're gone in the evening, your dog may feel more at ease, says Benjamin. "Anything you can do to make the situation more like it is when you're home can help."

Tune in to tune out. Turn on the radio so your dog can't hear little noises nearby, says Niego. Just set it to a station you normally listen to, at the usual volume. Or try putting on "white noise" from a fan or special noise machine. "If your pet isn't always listening for the sound of

---

Prescription Relief

When nothing you do seems to calm your panicky pooch, your vet may recommend medications that can help take the fear away, says Karen Overall, V.M.D., Ph.D., a lecturer specializing in behavioral medicine in the Department of Clinical Studies at the University of Pennsylvania School of Veterinary Medicine in Philadelphia.

There are a number of prescription drugs that boost levels of a brain chemical called serotonin, which has been linked to relaxation, says Dr. Overall. Unlike tranquilizers, which merely make panicked dogs sleepy, drugs such as amitriptyline (Elavil) and buspirone (BuSpar) can actually help them feel normal. "To some people, these are miracle drugs," says Dr. Overall. "They give them back the pet they thought they'd lost forever."

Encouraging your pets to play in suitcases will help
them feel less anxious when it's really time to take a trip.

your car or your footsteps, she can do something other than spend
every bit of energy waiting for you to come home," she says.

Beware of Blue Mondays. You think *you* hate Mondays. Try
being a dog that has spent all weekend being a beloved part of the
family and then wakes up to an empty house Monday morning. "The
animal doesn't know what to do with herself. Her world is turned
upside down," says Niego, who recommends being extra-attentive on
Monday mornings. "Be sure your dog gets a good exercise session in
the morning, leave some music on and give her a favorite chew toy,"
she says.

Comfort her with a crate. For some dogs, the security of a dog
crate or cage is the only way to keep panic away, says Stanley Coren,
Ph.D., professor of psychology at the University of British Columbia
in Vancouver who also teaches at the Vancouver Dog Obedience
Training Club and is author of *The Intelligence of Dogs*. "It's like a den.
They get in there and realize everything is okay," he says. If your dog
isn't already crate-trained, talk to your vet about choosing a crate and
helping your dog get used it, he suggests.

Some dogs, however, don't do well in crates, adds Gary Landsberg,
D.V.M., a veterinarian in private practice in Thornhill, Ontario, who
specializes in animal behavior. "Put her in a crate and leave for short
periods to see how she does," he says. "If she panics, she could really
hurt herself. You don't want to be crating a panicked dog."

The Psychic Connection

Did you ever wish your frightened dog could speak up and tell you what's wrong? "Your dog *can* talk, and you can talk with her," insists Jeri Ryan, a therapist in Oakland, California, who believes people can communicate telepathically with their pets. "You can actually converse with your dog without saying a word," she says.

According to Ryan—whose clients include both humans and pets—separation anxiety is a common complaint. "This one dog was extremely frightened of being left alone," she recalls. "I talked with him and found out he had been abandoned by his last owners. I was able to assure him that his current owners had a lifetime commitment to him, and his sadness and fear lifted like a curtain."

To try conversing with your own canine, Ryan recommends going into a quiet place and relaxing completely. "Think about your pet, reach out and touch her in your mind," she says. Be ready for everything—and remember, it takes practice."

Of course, if your "sixth sense" tells you your pet's fears are out of hand, don't try to treat her yourself. Call your vet right away.

PANEL OF ADVISERS

Carol Lea Benjamin is a dog trainer in New York City and author of *Mother Knows Best: The Natural Way to Train Your Dog* and *Surviving Your Dog's Adolescence*.

Stanley Coren, Ph.D., is professor of psychology at the University of British Columbia in Vancouver, teaches at the Vancouver Dog Obedience Training Club and is author of *The Intelligence of Dogs*.

Bob Gutierrez is animal behavior coordinator at the San Francisco Society for the Prevention of Cruelty to Animals.

Gary Landsberg, D.V.M., is a veterinarian in private practice in Thornhill, Ontario, who specializes in animal behavior.

Myrna Milani, D.V.M., is a veterinarian in private practice in Charlestown, New Hampshire, and author of *The Body Language and Emotions of Cats* and *The Body Language and Emotions of Dogs*.

Micky Niego is an animal behavior consultant in Airmont, New York.

Karen Overall, V.M.D., Ph.D., is a lecturer specializing in behavioral medicine in the Department of Clinical Studies at the University of Pennsylvania School of Veterinary Medicine in Philadelphia.

Jeri Ryan, Ph.D., is a therapist in Oakland, California, whose clients include humans and pets.

Shedding

15 Ways to Keep Fur from Flying

Whether you have a short-haired calico or a long-haired collie, the coming of summer means there's more than just pollen in the air.

"Your pet can drop thousands of hairs a day when she's losing her winter coat," says Renee Harris, manager of Mission Pet Hospital grooming services in San Francisco. Your pet's loss, unfortunately, is your gain, as the drifting hairs coat floors, carpets and furniture.

While indoor pets can shed all year long, most shedding occurs in spring as dogs and cats change into their summer coats. Long-haired pets may appear to shed more than their short-haired friends, but that's only because the hair is longer and more likely to form visible clumps, says Harris.

To keep your pet comfortable and the house clean, try these tips.

 ## For Dogs and Cats

Give hair the brush-off. "If you're going to do only one thing when your pet is shedding, you should brush, brush, brush," says Harris.

Not all brushes are the same, however. You need a brush that's tailor-made for your pet's coat, and cats need a softer brush than dogs do. "What works with a greyhound won't work with a malamute," Harris adds. Ask a salesperson at the pet store which brush is right for your pet.

Depending on how much hair your pet is shedding, plan on brushing her as often as once a day or as little as once a week.

Go deep. For brushing to be effective, you need to use firm, deep strokes. Short strokes are better than long ones because they penetrate the coat more thoroughly. "Too many people just quickly run over the top of the coat and never brush into it," says Harris. "That doesn't help much for shedding."

Rub her the wrong way. After brushing your pet from head to tail, reverse direction and go against the grain, suggests Harris. This will help loosen hair you might have missed the first time. Then finish off the job by brushing in the normal direction.

Don't give her any static. Brushing against the grain will occasionally be a shocking experience for you and your pet. "Her coat can build up a static charge, and you can spark her," says Harris. To prevent this, try using a static-free brush, she suggests.

Switch to a comb. After giving your pet a thorough brushing, you can pick up loads of additional hair by switching to a comb, says Loretta Marchese, owner of Hal Wheeler's Grooming Academy in Cedar Grove, New Jersey. "It's a great way to really say good-bye to that shedding hair," she says.

Take a rake to it. Pet stores sell grooming rakes, which are actually big combs with a handle attached. The advantage of using a rake is that it's easier to grip than a comb and less fatiguing to use. "A rake is a terrific tool in the shedding battle," says Harris.

Curry her favor. Rubber curry combs, which are used on horses, are also great for grooming short-haired dogs and cats. When using a curry comb, go in the direction the hair grows, Harris advises.

Try another horse trick. Another great trick from the stable for rooting out loose hair is to use a shedding blade. This consists of a strip of metal with a serrated edge that's attached to a handle. "The results will blow you away," Harris says.

When to See the Vet

Your furry friend has always shed some hair during the warm months, but this year it looks like he's going bald—you can actually see skin beneath that gorgeous coat. What's going on?

"Shedding is one thing, getting bald is quite another," warns William D. Fortney, D.V.M., assistant professor of small animal medicine in the Department of Clinical Sciences at the Kansas State University College of Veterinary Medicine in Manhattan, Kansas.

There are a number of conditions that can cause bald patches, including ringworm, skin irritations and hormonal disorders. So when shedding seems to be going skin-deep, play it safe and call your vet right away, Dr. Fortney advises.

"If your pet has a long coat, you could have a real snowstorm, so you may want to try this outside," she adds.

Put on a glove. Pets that won't stand still for the usual grooming equipment may welcome a little hands-on care. "That's when you reach for a grooming glove," says Shirlee Kalstone, a New York City groomer and author of *The Complete Poodle Clipping and Grooming Book.*

Grooming gloves are coated with tiny plastic or rubber teeth, which are ideal for removing loose hair from a skittish pet. "Your pet will think you're just stroking her with your hand," Kalstone says. "It feels good to her, and you can go to town on the hair."

Comb after bathing. Bathing your pet in warm water will help loosen hair in her coat, so that's a perfect time for grooming, says Kalstone. You may want to brush or comb her while she's still in the tub. Or you can groom her later while you're drying—or blow-drying—her fur.

If your pet's coat is unusually matted, however, it's best to get the mats out before getting her wet. Otherwise they'll be even harder to remove later on.

Condition her coat. Occasionally applying a little hair conditioner will make her coat smoother and easier to brush, Kalstone says.

You can apply a conditioner after shampooing, or you can use a spray-on conditioner between baths. "Conditioners make it easier on you and your pet during grooming time," says Kalstone. "When the coat is smoother and less tangled, your grooming session will be smoother."

Grooming gloves slip easily over your hand and are ideal for removing loose hair from skittish pets.

Turn down the heat. If you routinely keep the thermostat set at tropical heat, your pets may shed more than usual, even during the cold months.

"They go through sheds that can be heavy if they're really warm," says Harris. She recommends turning down the thermostat slightly until you find a level that seems comfortable for you and your pet. And if your pet sleeps next to a heater, moving her bed farther away may help, she adds.

 **For Dogs Only**

Give her a new 'do. When summer is coming and your long-haired pooch is shedding enough to stuff a pillow or two, giving her a haircut will help keep the problem under control.

"The dog will still shed, but at least she will shed short hairs instead of long ones," making the problem less noticeable, says Marchese.

 **For Cats Only**

Put on protection. While some cats love nothing more than being brushed, others would rather exercise their claws than submit to a good grooming. Donning a pair of leather gloves, or gauntlets, will help protect your hands and wrists from your feisty feline, Harris says.

Get a grip. Holding your cat firmly by the scruff of the neck will help control her wilder instincts during grooming. "You have to be firm," Harris says.

PANEL OF ADVISERS

William D. Fortney, D.V.M., is assistant professor of small animal medicine in the Department of Clinical Sciences at the Kansas State University College of Veterinary Medicine in Manhattan, Kansas.

Renee Harris is manager of Mission Pet Hospital grooming services in San Francisco.

Shirlee Kalstone is a New York City groomer and author of *The Complete Poodle Clipping and Grooming Book.*

Loretta Marchese is owner of Hal Wheeler's Grooming Academy in Cedar Grove, New Jersey.

Sinus Problems

7 Ways to Assuage the Sniffles

When it comes to using their noses, dogs and cats are the champs. They use them to greet friends, explore new territory and sniff everything that doesn't run away.

In their enthusiasm, however, sometimes they snort up something they shouldn't—a schnozz-tickling virus, for example, or a small grass seed that causes inflammation or congestion inside the nose. This in turn can lead to an infection of the membrane-lined cavities inside the skull, known as sinusitis.

While full-blown sinusitis requires a veterinarian's care, there are ways to relieve some of the nose-related problems—like sneezing and runny nose, says Susan M. Cotter, D.V.M., professor of medicine and head of the Section of Small Animal Medicine at the Tufts University School of Veterinary Medicine in North Grafton, Massachusetts.

To help make your pet more comfortable, here's what vets recommend.

 For **Dogs** and **Cats**

Serve it hot. Giving your pet a hot, steaming meal will do more than tickle his taste buds. The heat will also help unclog blocked sinuses, helping him to breathe easier, Dr. Cotter says.

To fix him a hot meal, just add warm water to his kibble to make a soothing, steaming broth. Or pop his usual food in the microwave for a minute or two. Just don't get it so hot it burns his mouth, she warns.

Upgrade the menu. While a pet with sinusitis may not feel like eating, it's important to provide good nutrition to keep his immune system strong and help him recover. Dr. Cotter recommends tempting him with some of his favorite food. For cats, tuna is always a good choice, while dogs will enjoy a snack of cooked liver.

Keep his nose clean. Sinusitis may cause large amounts of mucus to accumulate around the nostrils, which will make your pet uncomfortable and possibly interfere with breathing. Sponge his face with a warm, damp cloth to remove secretions before they cause problems, says Carin Smith, D.V.M., a veterinary consultant in private practice in Leavenworth, Washington, and author of *101 Training Tips for Your Cat.*

Rub his face gently. "If the nose is already very irritated or sore, you've got to be gentle," adds Jim Humphries, D.V.M., a veterinary consultant in private practice in Dallas and author of *Dr. Jim's Animal Clinic for Cats* and *Dr. Jim's Animal Clinic for Dogs.*

He recommends wiping the nose with baby wipes, moistened towelettes that contain soothing ingredients such as aloe vera.

Turn up the steam. Putting moisture into the air is an easy way to soothe irritated mucous membranes and unclog blocked sinuses, says James Richards, D.V.M., assistant director of the Feline Health Center at the Cornell University College of Veterinary Medicine in Ithaca, New York.

He recommends taking your pet into the bathroom with you when you bathe or shower. "A steamy bathroom can be helpful," he says.

Plug in the vaporizer. Another way to put soothing moisture into the air is with a hot water vaporizer, says Dr. Humphries. Adding a little menthol ointment or liquid to the mix can be particularly helpful. "The menthol has a soothing action on delicate tissues and helps open the sinuses," he says.

When to See the Vet

While sinus problems may be caused by nothing more serious than a grass seed sniffed into the schnozz, in some cases it's a warning sign that a bacterial infection has taken hold, says James Richards, D.V.M., director of the Feline Health Center at the Cornell University College of Veterinary Medicine in Ithaca, New York. In fact, nasal discharge from one nostril can also be a sign of cancer.

If your pet has a fever and thick, discolored mucus and seems to be unusually tired or lethargic, call your vet. He may prescribe antibiotics or other medications to keep the infection under control.

Using a cold water humidifier will also help keep the mucous membranes moist and comfortable, he adds.

Drop in relief. Putting several drops of sterile saline nose drops, which are available in drugstores, into your pet's nostrils will help relieve irritation and temporarily thin secretions, helping unclog the sinuses. Just tip your pet's head back and put one or two drops into each nostril, says H. Ellen Whiteley, D.V.M., a veterinary consultant in private practice in Guadalupita, New Mexico, and author of *Understanding and Training Your Cat or Kitten.*

PANEL OF ADVISERS

Susan M. Cotter, D.V.M., is professor of medicine and head of the Section of Small Animal Medicine at the Tufts University School of Veterinary Medicine in North Grafton, Massachusetts.

Jim Humphries, D.V.M., is a veterinary consultant in private practice in Dallas and author of *Dr. Jim's Animal Clinic for Cats* and *Dr. Jim's Animal Clinic for Dogs.*

James Richards, D.V.M., is assistant director of the Feline Health Center at the Cornell University College of Veterinary Medicine in Ithaca, New York.

Carin Smith, D.V.M., is a veterinary consultant in private practice in Leavenworth, Washington, and author of *101 Training Tips for Your Cat.*

H. Ellen Whiteley, D.V.M., is a veterinary consultant in private practice in Guadalupita, New Mexico, and author of *Understanding and Training Your Cat or Kitten.*

Skunk Spray

7 Tips to Stifle the Stench

Your pet has always had a certain presence—but it never preceded him quite like this before. In fact, you can smell him coming a mile away. He's oily. He's odoriferous. He's been skunked.

There are few smells as unpleasant—and penetrating—as skunk spray. "But if you think it smells bad to you, imagine how your poor dog or cat feels being covered with the odor," says Jan White, D.V.M., executive director of the International Wildlife Rehabilitation Council in Suisun, California, and an assistant wildlife health researcher at the Wildlife Health Center at the University of California, Davis, School of Veterinary Medicine. Try these tips from the experts to help clear the air.

 **For Dogs and Cats**

Check his eyes. Skunk spray is irritating, and your pet's eyes may be watery or red after getting blasted. "It won't make him blind, but it's very painful," says Veronika Kiklevich, D.V.M., instructor and head of the community practice division at the Washington State University College of Veterinary Medicine in Pullman.

She advises rinsing his eyes with the same type of eyewash solution people use. "Just follow the directions and your pet should get quick relief," she says.

Wash him well. "This is best done outside, if weather permits. Otherwise your entire house could smell for weeks," says Lynda Bond, D.V.M., a veterinarian in private practice in Cape Elizabeth, Maine, who hosts a weekly pet segment for a Portland television station. Wear rubber or latex gloves to protect your hands and scrub your pet well with pet shampoo. Then rinse him off and scrub again, she advises.

Pour on the juice. Experts aren't sure what it is about tomato juice that helps quell skunk smell, but this traditional remedy may be worth a try. After washing and drying your pet, "just pour it on," says Hazel

When Skunks Go to the City

As if smog isn't enough, an increasingly common scent in city settings is *eau de skunk*.

"Skunks are everywhere these days," says Jan White, D.V.M., executive director of the International Wildlife Rehabilitation Council in Suisun, California, and an assistant wildlife health researcher at the Wildlife Health Center at the University of California, Davis, School of Veterinary Medicine. "When they get displaced from a rural or suburban habitat, they pack their bags and go to another location. They can do pretty well in cities," she says.

If you've noticed a skunk moving in next door, you can discourage it from signing a long-term lease by following a few simple rules, says Dr. White.

Since skunks like cool, dark areas, clear away such attractions as brush and piles of bricks or wood.

It's also important to be sure there are no holes beneath your house that a skunk can enter. If skunks are already in residence, wait until they wander out at night, then seal up the hole behind them, says Dr. White. Make sure, however, that there aren't babies left behind. If there are, you may want to wait until fall or winter when they're old enough to follow their mother out of the house.

Skunks go where there's food, so if you feed your dog or cat outside, don't leave the food out overnight. "Skunks love cat food and dog food," says Dr. White.

It's also important to use garbage cans that close securely. "An open garbage can is an open invitation to a skunk," says Dr. White.

Christiansen, president of the American Grooming Shop Association and owner of Blue Ribbon Pet Grooming in Lewiston, Idaho.

Depending on your pet's size, you may have to use several large cans. Make sure the juice saturates his coat and let it soak in for 10 to 20 minutes—whatever he'll tolerate, she says. Then rinse it off and wash him again with his regular shampoo.

If he still reeks, repeat the whole procedure until he smells a little sweeter.

One caution: If your pet's fur is normally white and you douse him with tomato juice, be prepared for some temporary color changes. "He could end up pink or orange for a while," says Christiansen.

Massage him with Massengill. This over-the-counter medicated douche has long been a favorite of pet groomers, whose four-legged clientele is often redolent of skunk. "Massengill works miracles," says Tracey McLaurin, a dog breeder and groomer in Winchester, Virginia. "It's all we ever use for skunked pets."

For small to medium pets, she recommends mixing two ounces of Massengill with one gallon of water. For large dogs, you'll want to double the amount of water and Massengill.

"Pour the mixture over your pet until it really soaks in and wait 15 minutes to rinse it out," says McLaurin. Then wash him with his regular shampoo and rinse thoroughly.

Use your bean. A shower of vanilla can help sweeten your stinky pet, says Christiansen. She recommends dousing him with $1^1/_4$ cup of vanilla extract mixed in a gallon of water. Let it soak in for about ten minutes, then wash him with his regular shampoo and rinse thoroughly.

Try some chemistry. According to chemist Paul Krebaum of Lisle, Illinois, you can make an excellent deskunking formula by mixing $^1/_4$ cup of baking soda and one teaspoon of liquid soap in a quart of hydrogen peroxide. Work the solution into your pet's fur, then rinse well.

A similar formula, minus the soap, has been used in laboratories to quell the stench of hydrogen sulfide, and it may help deodorize your pet as well.

Shop for the solution. Pet stores stock a variety of deodorant rinses and sprays, including products with names like Skunk Kleen. "They work pretty well, and they're easy to use because they're sprays and prepared rinses," says Dr. Bond.

PANEL OF ADVISERS

Lynda Bond, D.V.M., is a veterinarian in private practice in Cape Elizabeth, Maine, who hosts a weekly pet segment for a Portland television station.

Hazel Christiansen is president of the American Grooming Shop Association and owner of Blue Ribbon Pet Grooming in Lewiston, Idaho.

Veronika Kiklevich, D.V.M., is instructor and head of the community practice division at the Washington State University College of Veterinary Medicine in Pullman.

Tracey McLaurin is a dog breeder and groomer in Winchester, Virginia.

Jan White, D.V.M., is executive director of the International Wildlife Rehabilitation Council in Suisun, California, and an assistant wildlife health researcher at the Wildlife Health Center at the University of California, Davis, School of Veterinary Medicine.

Sleep Problems
10 Ways to Ease the Zzzs

Click, click, click goes your dog. *Lick, lick, lick* goes your cat. *Tick, tick, tick* goes the clock.

If everyone in this house doesn't hurry up and get to sleep, in the morning you're going to feel sick, sick, sick.

Not getting enough sleep is rarely a problem for our furry friends. Dogs are asleep or drowsy more than half the day, while cats typically spend more than 18 hours a day nodding off. "Sleeping is a real strength with these pets," says Edgar A. Lucas, Ph.D., director of All Saints Episcopal Hospital and Sleep Disorders Center in Fort Worth, Texas.

Sometimes, however, dogs and cats don't get enough Zzzs to please. When your pet's restless nights are keeping you awake, here are some tips that can help.

 For **Dogs** and **Cats**

Make a nice bed. How would *you* like to sleep on the floor every night? A hard floor makes for restless sleep. "If you've ever gone camping and slept on the cold, hard ground, you know how hard it is to sleep when you're uncomfortable," says William D. Fortney, D.V.M., assistant professor of small animal medicine in the Department of Clinical Sciences at the Kansas State University College of Veterinary Medicine in Manhattan, Kansas.

He recommends providing your pet with a soft, comfortable bed of her own. Pet stores stock a variety of pet beds, or you can improvise by giving her a soft blanket or large pillow to sleep on.

Plan for bathroom breaks. "Very young pets and older pets are more likely to have trouble getting through the night without needing to go out, so be especially aware of their needs," says Barbara Simpson, D.V.M., Ph.D., a certified applied animal behaviorist and adjunct assistant professor at the North Carolina State University College of Veterinary Medicine in Raleigh.

Always let your pooch out before you bed down for the night, she advises. For cats, make sure the litter box is where they can get to it.

Tucker her out. Pets that are restless at night may need more exercise during the day, says Karen Overall, V.M.D., a lecturer specializing in behavioral medicine in the Department of Clinical Studies at the University of Pennsylvania School of Veterinary Medicine in Philadelphia.

"If you really exercise your kitty or dog during the day, she should settle right down at night," she says.

Rub away aches. Older pets occasionally have pain from arthritis that keeps them up at night, says Raymond Deiter, V.M.D., a veterinarian in private practice in Sausalito, California, who specializes in acupuncture. "Do anything you can to relieve the pain, and the animal might sleep better," he says.

Massaging the sore area will help your pet relax, he says. In addi-

When to See the Vet

While a little insomnia isn't anything to worry about, some pets develop serious sleep problems that require a veterinarian's care.

Dogs that are overweight, for example, may develop a condition called sleep apnea, in which breathing frequently stops during sleep, says Adrian Morrison, D.V.M., Ph.D., professor of behavioral neuroscience in the Laboratory for Study of the Brain in Sleep at the University of Pennsylvania School of Veterinary Medicine in Philadelphia.

Dogs with this condition sometimes need medications to help their breathing. "Getting the dog down to a more normal size will also help," adds Dr. Morrison.

Pets can also suffer from a sleep disorder called narcolepsy. This is a neurological condition that can cause them to suddenly collapse and fall asleep at the most inappropriate times—like in the middle of eating.

There is no cure for narcolepsy, but the symptoms can be partially controlled with medication, Dr. Morrison says.

tion, massage improves circulation to the area, which can help speed healing and relieve the pain.

Try an OTC. Giving your pet a mild painkiller can help ease sore joints and make it easier for her to sleep. Vets sometimes recommend giving dogs with arthritis aspirin twice a day. The usual dose is one-quarter of a 325-milligram tablet of buffered aspirin per ten pounds of dog.

Don't give cats medication without first checking with your vet, because drugs (and doses) that are safe for dogs can be dangerous for cats.

Give her a room of her own. Some pets are simply night owls, and no matter what you do they'll always stay up burning the midnight oil. To keep your pet occupied, give her plenty of toys and a place to play—preferably one that's far enough away from the bedroom that she won't keep you up as well.

"It's a simple solution, but it makes everyone happy," says Dr. Simpson.

Blow her away. Some pets are early risers. They figure if they're ready to get up and play, so are you—and they're all too happy to give you a reminder.

Dangerous Dreams

It's normal for dogs and cats to move their paws while they sleep. It probably means they're dreaming of exciting things, like chasing a rabbit or taking a swim, says Dennis O'Brien, D.V.M., Ph.D., associate professor of neurology at the University of Missouri College of Veterinary Medicine in Columbia.

In some cases, however, pets may thrash so violently during sleep that they hurl themselves several feet across the floor. "My cat would occasionally propel herself five feet from where she was sleeping," says Dr. O'Brien. "It was a little disconcerting."

Vets refer to this unusual disorder as REM without dystonia, which means the animal has an unusual degree of muscle tension during deep sleep. While it's rare for dogs or cats to hurt themselves during sleep, your vet may recommend giving your pet tranquilizers to help her snooze more peacefully, says Dr. O'Brien. It's also a good idea not to let her sleep in high places like your bed, he adds.

To discourage your early bird from getting you up before you're ready, try arming yourself with a blow dryer the night before, suggests Dr. Simpson. "The moment she pounces on you, give her a quick little blast," she says. "It will startle her away but won't hurt her. She probably won't feel like coming back for more."

Share the care. Some pets get resentful—and wakeful—when their owners' new friends come over and spend the night. "The animal could be uncomfortable with the new person to the point where she just can't sleep," says Dr. Deiter.

He recommends that you and your friend take turns feeding and playing with your pet. Once everyone's happy and secure again, the sleeping will probably improve.

Make her night a little brighter. Some pets have trouble sleeping because of nighttime anxiety. "She may be losing her sight or may just have developed a fear of the dark for some reason," says Dr. Fortney.

Leaving on a nightlight can be a reassuring touch. "The nightlight can make her more relaxed with her surroundings," Dr. Fortney says.

Soothe with soft music. "Playing a relaxing radio station or tape with the volume low could be of some comfort," Dr. Fortney says.

PANEL OF ADVISERS

Raymond Deiter, V.M.D., is a veterinarian in private practice in Sausalito, California, who specializes in acupuncture.

William D. Fortney, D.V.M., is assistant professor of small animal medicine in the Department of Clinical Sciences at the Kansas State University College of Veterinary Medicine in Manhattan, Kansas.

Edgar A. Lucas, Ph.D., is director of All Saints Episcopal Hospital and Sleep Disorders Center in Fort Worth, Texas.

Adrian Morrison, D.V.M., Ph.D., is professor of behavioral neuroscience in the Laboratory for Study of the Brain in Sleep at the University of Pennsylvania School of Veterinary Medicine in Philadelphia.

Dennis O'Brien, D.V.M., Ph.D., is associate professor of neurology at the University of Missouri College of Veterinary Medicine in Columbia.

Karen Overall, V.M.D., is a lecturer specializing in behaviorial medicine in the Department of Clinical Studies at the University of Pennsylvania School of Veterinary Medicine in Philadelphia.

Barbara Simpson, D.V.M., Ph.D., is a certified applied animal behaviorist and adjunct assistant professor at the North Carolina State University College of Veterinary Medicine.

Spraying

12 Drying Tips

Has your formerly fastidious feline suddenly taken to spraying the house, despite having a perfectly good litter box down the hall? Don't rush to let him out. Odors to the contrary, spraying has nothing to do with going to the bathroom.

"It's a way of identifying property and covering other cats' scents," explains Gary Landsberg, D.V.M., a veterinarian in private practice in Thornhill, Ontario, who specializes in animal behavior. "It's a cat's way of reassuring himself that he owns what he's sprayed."

Spraying wouldn't be such a big issue if a cat's sense of ownership were limited to a tree at the back of the yard. In most cases, however, he makes his claims closer to home—on the drapes, for example, or against the living room sofa.

Female cats will occasionally spray, but in most cases it's a guy thing, Dr. Landsberg says. And once your pet gets the habit, it can be very hard to make him stop. Here's what experts recommend to keep spraying under control.

 **For Cats Only**

Spare the rod. Even if you happen to catch your cat in the act, punishing him for spraying absolutely doesn't work, stresses Dr. Landsberg. "It's a natural, innate behavior in cats and can't be punished out of them," he says.

Start with detective work. The only way to control spraying is to find out what's causing it, says Peter Borchelt, Ph.D., a certified applied animal behaviorist and owner of Animal Behavior Consultants in Brooklyn.

If your cat was looking out the window just before he sprayed, for example, he might have spied another cat. Was there more than one pet in the kitchen? Maybe he felt crowded. Did you have company? Perhaps he smelled another cat on the visitor's clothes. "Try to think like a cat," Dr. Borchelt advises.

Restrict the view. Many cats will spray indoors when they spot other cats outside, says Dr. Landsberg. "If you cannot keep the other cat off your property, keep your cat away from the windows and doors so he can't see or smell the interloper."

One way to restrict his view is to remove desks, couches or other furniture from in front of windows, Dr. Borchelt says. Heavy drapes will help keep him from looking out. You may even want to cover the bottom portion of windows with frosted "privacy" paper, he suggests.

Provide separate quarters. It's not uncommon for cats to spray when they feel competitive with other pets in the household. Keeping them separated—on different floors, for example, or in different rooms of the house—will often relieve the problem, Dr. Landsberg says.

Promote team building. Cats that get along are far less likely to spray than those in competition with each other, so it's worth your time to encourage their friendship. Dr. Borchelt recommends setting aside playtimes every day when you can all get together and have a good time—chasing pull toys, for example, or batting balls across the floor.

"Any activity that promotes a friendly, playful, interactive mood in your cats will help reduce competition," he says.

Lick the problem. It's natural for cats to groom each other, and once they get started they can literally wash away bad feelings. Once or twice a week, wipe down all your cats with a wet towel, vets advise. After grooming themselves, they may begin grooming each other. This will help keep their aggressions—and spraying—under control.

Give them equal time. Paying more attention to one cat than another will often foster feelings of jealousy and competition. Dr. Borchelt recommends not paying too much attention to your cats indi-

When to See the Vet

Most cats use spraying as a way of marking their territory or because something in their life (or yours) is making them upset. Sometimes, however, spraying is a warning sign that something is wrong physically, like diabetes, a blocked urethra or a urinary tract infection.

If your cat has just started spraying or is suddenly straining to urinate or urinating more often, don't take chances, advises Robert J. Watson, D.V.M., a veterinarian in private practice in Toronto. Call your vet right away.

vidually but really laying on the strokes when they're all together. "This will increase their social interaction and reduce the competition, and that may stop the spraying," he says.

Make a common bed. Cats that sleep in the same area will gradually get used to each other, which may help keep aggression in check. Dr. Borchelt recommends putting a bed for each cat in a comfortable, favored spot, like near a sunny window. "The more they hang out together, the better they will get along," he says.

Create a "no spray" zone. If your cat is repeatedly spraying in the same place, applying a pet repellent may help turn him away. Many vets recommend repellents containing bitter apple.

While pet repellents can help protect certain areas, they are unlikely to stop the spraying, Dr. Borchelt adds. Eventually your cat will probably just move on to a new area, and you'll have to start the process all over again.

Do a deep cleaning. If you've recently moved and your cat has just started spraying, it may be that he smells traces of other cats. Dr. Borchelt recommends scrubbing the rugs with a combination enzyme and bacteria cleaner, like Outright Pet Odor Eliminator or Nature's Miracle, which are available in pet stores. The enzyme in the cleaner will dissolve old urine crystals, while the bacteria devour the residue, he explains.

Keep him calm. Cats sometimes spray in response to change. Keeping his schedule consistent will help prevent problems before they occur. "Keep his bed and litter box in the same place, feed him in the same place and try to keep the same routine," advises Dr. Borchelt.

Practice prevention. "Ninety percent of male cats that spray will stop entirely when you get them neutered," says Dr. Landsberg. In spayed females the success rate is even higher, about 95 percent. Vets recommend having kittens neutered at about six months.

PANEL OF ADVISERS

Peter Borchelt, Ph.D., is a certified applied animal behaviorist and owner of Animal Behavior Consultants in Brooklyn.

Gary Landsberg, D.V.M., is a veterinarian in private practice in Thornhill, Ontario, who specializes in animal behavior.

Robert J. Watson, D.V.M., is a veterinarian in private practice in Toronto.

Sunburn

13 Tips to Cool the Fire

Oh, those dog (and cat) days of summer! Pets delight in sunny romps, and invariably they play, dig, scratch and snooze in the brightest patch of sunlight they can find.

Sometimes, however, they get too much of a good thing. The result can be sunburn—on the tips of their ears, the bridge of their noses and even on their tender tummies, where fur is thinnest.

At the very least, sunburned skin is sore, painful skin. "One of the dangers with sunburn and long-term sun exposure in dogs and cats is that it can develop into cancer," adds Lowell Ackerman, D.V.M., Ph.D., a veterinary dermatologist in private practice in Scottsdale, Arizona, and author of *Skin and Haircoat Problems in Dogs*.

White pets are most susceptible to sunburn, as are those with fair skin and sparse fur, says Carin Smith, D.V.M., a veterinary consultant in private practice in Leavenworth, Washington, and author of *101 Training Tips for Your Cat*. In addition, pets that live at high altitudes—near the Rocky Mountains, for example—are more likely to burn than those that live at lower elevations.

To quench the pain of sunburn and help protect your pet from burning rays in the future, here's what vets advise.

 ## For Dogs and Cats

Mist away the pain. To quickly soothe sunburn pain, Dr. Ackerman recommends spraying the area with cool water from a squirt bottle every half-hour or so.

Most dogs enjoy the coolness and will welcome the "treatments." Cats, however, hate getting their faces wet and may not stick around for the whole thing. To keep your cat calm, try cupping one hand in front of her face while you spray, vets advise.

Ease it with a compress. Putting a cold compress on a burn is a

When to See the Vet

Sunburn rarely results in anything worse than a little discomfort. In severe cases, however, it can result in raw, blistered and infected skin. "Whenever an animal has been exposed for a number of hours and she's in pain or there is a break in the skin, she should see the vet," says Lowell Ackerman, D.V.M., Ph.D., a veterinary dermatologist in private practice in Scottsdale, Arizona, and author of *Skin and Haircoat Problems in Dogs*.

The danger of sunburn can be more than just temporary. Repeated exposure to the sun can result in skin cancer as well. This is particularly true of white pets, particularly cats, which are especially prone to squamous cell carcinoma on the tips of their ears. So don't take chances if your pet *isn't* tickled to be pink. Take her to the vet right away.

great way to soothe the pain, says Dr. Smith. She recommends wetting a washcloth or towel with cold water, wringing it out and then draping it over your pet's sunburned areas. Hold it gently in place for a few minutes, making sure it's not so tight that she has trouble breathing. Once it warms up, rewet it and apply it again, she advises.

Give her a soak. Bathing your pet in cool water in which you've mixed colloidal oatmeal (like Aveeno) can be very soothing, says Steven A. Melman, V.M.D., a veterinarian with practices in Palm Springs, California, and Potomac, Maryland, and author of *Skin Diseases of Dogs and Cats*.

Switch to witch. Applying witch hazel to burned skin causes almost instant cooling due to the liquid's sudden evaporation, says Dr. Ackerman. He recommends soaking a cotton ball with the witch hazel and applying it to the burned area three or four times a day.

Numb the pain. There are a variety of over-the-counter sprays, like Solarcaine and Lanacane, that contain local anesthetics. "They make the pet feel better fast," says Ken Lawrence, D.V.M., a veterinarian in private practice in Sherman, Texas.

While these products are fine for dogs, they should be used judiciously for cats: They could cause the cat's tongue to become numb during her usual grooming. Before treating your feline friend, call your vet for advice.

Replace the moisture. Sunburned skin is dry skin. "You want to re-hydrate the skin as much as possible," says Dr. Ackerman. "Things like jojoba, coconut oil–based creams or even petroleum jelly help seal in the moisture." He recommends coating the sore spot with a thin layer of cream two or three times a day.

Reach for aloe vera. While virtually any moisturizer can help soothe burned skin, you may not have to look any farther than your windowsill. "Aloe vera works great," says Dr. Smith.

To extract the healing gel from the plant, simply break off a bit of leaf and squeeze. Or you can buy aloe vera–based creams and lotions at your pharmacy.

Put on protection. If your dog or cat frequently spends long periods of time in the sun, you may want to apply a sunscreen to her vulnerable areas. "Use a sunscreen with a minimum SPF (sun protection factor) of 15, and preferably higher," says Dr. Ackerman. "The higher the SPF, the better protection she'll get."

To make sure the sunscreen stays put, Dr. Smith recommends feeding your pet immediately after applying it. "She'll forget it's there and won't try to lick it off right away," she explains.

Pet stores stock a variety of sunscreens. Human products will also work, but because dogs and cats will eventually lick off the lotion, avoid those containing PABA or zinc oxide, which can be dangerous if swallowed.

Cover her head. "There are caps that animals can wear to keep the areas that are prone to burn shielded from direct sunlight," says Dr. Ackerman. The caps should shade the ears and the tender bridge of the nose. Pet stores also sell muzzles that will provide sun protection, he adds.

Dress to a T. For dogs that love to spend their days lying flat on their backs or for thin-coated pets without a lot of natural protection, your best bet is to cover them up. "Putting them in a T-shirt when they're outside will protect their skin," says Dr. Ackerman.

For cats and small dogs, you may need to use an infant-size shirt, while larger pets will probably fit into a small or medium. Just pull the opening and neck of the shirt over their heads and fit their front legs into the armholes.

Draw the blinds. If your pets won't stay away from bright sun even when they're inside, it may be time to pull the drapes or blinds. This is particularly true for cats, which like nothing better than perching in sunny windows. "If they always sit by a window, you'll want to keep your shades partly drawn," says Dr. Smith.

Beware the hot times. "The best way to prevent sunburn is to keep pets out of the sun between 9:00 A.M. and 3:00 P.M.," says Dr. Melman.

Put up protection. "Make sure your pets have shade available at all times," says Dr. Smith. In fact, you may need to put up a fence or confine them in some other way to a shaded area inside the yard.

PANEL OF ADVISERS

Lowell Ackerman, D.V.M., Ph.D., is a veterinary dermatologist in private practice in Scottsdale, Arizona, and author of *Skin and Haircoat Problems in Dogs.*

Ken Lawrence, D.V.M., is a veterinarian in private practice in Sherman, Texas.

Steven A. Melman, V.M.D., is a veterinarian with practices in Palm Springs, California, and Potomac, Maryland, and author of *Skin Diseases of Dogs and Cats.*

Carin Smith, D.V.M., is a veterinary consultant in private practice in Leavenworth, Washington, and author of *101 Training Tips for Your Cat.*

Tail Problems

8 Happy Endings

Whether they're wagging in doggy delight or lashing out in feline fury, pets' tails tell tales.

Sometimes, however, this expressive part of their anatomy goes where it shouldn't—into their mouths, for example, or on a collision course with an expensive vase. Tails can also get red, sore and infected.

To help your pet put tail problems behind him, here's what vets recommend.

 For Dogs and Cats

Ferret out fleas. Flea bites are the number one reason cats and dogs chow down on their nether regions, says H. Ellen Whiteley, D.V.M., a veterinary consultant in private practice in Guadalupita, New Mexico, and author of *Understanding and Training Your Cat or Kitten*.

Getting rid of fleas will often stop the nibbling. She recommends spraying or powdering your pet with products containing pyrethrins— fast-acting medications that kill fleas and help prevent them from coming back. The medications are available in pet stores and from your vet. (For more tips, see Fleas on page 185.)

Keep it dry. Dogs and cats have small, football-shaped glands at the base of their tails that sometimes release large amounts of fluid, causing the surrounding skin to get oily, sore and inflamed. Since the problem is more common in males than females, vets refer to this condition as stud tail.

To absorb secretions and give the tail a chance to heal, vets recommend applying a light dusting of cornstarch or fine cornmeal, says Carin Smith, D.V.M., a veterinary consultant in private practice in Leavenworth, Washington, and author of *101 Training Tips for Your Cat*.

When to See the Vet

Just as some people become obsessed with certain behaviors—like washing their hands 50 times a day—some pets won't leave their tails alone, says veterinarian Nicholas H. Dodman, B.V.M.S., professor in the Department of Surgery and director of the Behavior Clinic at the Tufts University School of Veterinary Medicine in North Grafton, Massachusetts.

"The attacks may last a few minutes several times a day or may be continuous the whole day," adds Alan Parker, Ph.D., veterinary neurologist and chief of staff of the Small Animal Clinic at the University of Illinois College of Veterinary Medicine at Urbana-Champaign. In rare cases, pets may attack their tails so vigorously that they cause serious injury.

If your pet is constantly chasing—and catching—his own tail, it's a good idea to call your vet. He may recommend giving your pet tranquilizers or other medications to help keep his tail-chasing under control.

After powdering the tail, wait five minutes, then comb it out, she advises. Then repeat once or twice a week until the condition heals.

Keep it clean. If your pet's tail looks like, well, something the cat dragged in, it's a good idea to wash it thoroughly, says Dr. Smith. Wet it well, then lather thoroughly with a pet shampoo. Rinse, then repeat two more times, she advises.

For convenience, you can set a cat or small dog on the edge of a sink and let his tail drape into the water. For larger dogs, however, it's usually easier to use the tub. (For tips on bathing cats, see "How to Give Your Cat a Bath" on page 186.)

Wash away infection. If the tail is sore and tender and has one or more bald areas, it's probably infected. Wash the area well with an antibacterial cleanser like Betadine Solution, says Jim Humphries, D.V.M., a veterinary consultant in private practice in Dallas and author of *Dr. Jim's Animal Clinic for Cats* and *Dr. Jim's Animal Clinic for Dogs.* Washing the area several times a week will help soothe the irritation and speed healing.

Try an OTC. Pets occasionally get clogged glands that cause blackheads and other forms of acne to appear on the tail. "An over-the-counter ointment with benzoyl peroxide, like Oxy 2.5, may be helpful," says James Richards, D.V.M., assistant director of the Feline Health Center at the Cornell University College of Veterinary Medicine in Ithaca, New York.

"Don't use anything stronger than a 5 percent ointment," he adds. "They can be pretty irritating."

An anti-inflammatory ointment containing hydrocortisone can also help ease tail travails, says Dr. Humphries. "Most people have Cortaid or something like that at home, which will help soothe the area so the pet doesn't chew himself as much," he says. Applying the ointment once or twice a day for several days will usually help clear things up.

Find a diversion. It's not uncommon for dogs and cats to suddenly become fascinated by their own tails. They spin like dervishes to catch the prize, and once they start nibbling, they may not know when to stop.

To prevent your pet from chewing his tail into rawness, try making a loud noise to distract him, suggests Alan Parker, Ph.D., veterinary neurologist and chief of staff at the Small Animal Clinic at the University of Illinois College of Veterinary Medicine at Urbana-Champaign.

"You can whack a newspaper against the chair or floor to shock the pet out of the behavior," he says. Or shake an empty can with a few

To help your cat put his tail problems behind him, it's good idea to wash his tail thoroughly.

Tail Travails

Pets' tails have a language all their own. They droop low when life is sad and swing high when things are grand. Tails can be jaunty or depressed, alert or downright sleepy. They can even be filled with nervous energy, just like tapping feet.

Sometimes, however, these energetic appendages find their way into trouble—like under the wheels of a car or into the works of a reclining chair.

The tail is an extension of the spine, and "broken tails can have serious consequences," says Jim Humphries, D.V.M., a veterinary consultant in private practice in Dallas.

You can recognize a broken tail because the damaged portion generally hangs limp, Dr. Humphries explains. In addition, there may be scrapes, swelling or other signs of a recent injury.

If you suspect your pet has a fractured tail, call your vet right away. While some tail fractures, particularly those near the tip, will heal on their own, in most cases the damage is permanent. Your vet may recommend having the tail docked to prevent further injury. It's a simple procedure, Dr. Humphries says, and most pets soon forget what they're missing.

coins in the bottom. You can also try giving him a blast from a squirt bottle, he adds.

Make every day play day. "Tail-chasing and chewing often are caused by stress and anxiety," says Dr. Whiteley. It may be that your pet simply needs to have more fun.

She recommends giving him a variety of new toys, particularly those that involve a certain amount of exercise. For cats, fishing pole–type toys are a good choice, while most dogs love chasing balls or flying disks.

 For Dogs Only

Clear away clutter. A large, enthusiastic dog can sweep a coffee table clean with just one wag—and perhaps cause injury if his tail happens to wag the wrong way, such as into a moving fan. You can't control his tail, but you can make it a point to keep potentially dangerous (or delicate) items out of range, says Dr. Humphries.

PANEL OF ADVISERS

Nicholas H. Dodman, B.V.M.S., is professor in the Department of Surgery and director of the Behavior Clinic at the Tufts University School of Veterinary Medicine in North Grafton, Massachusetts.

Jim Humphries, D.V.M., is a veterinary consultant in private practice in Dallas and author of *Dr. Jim's Animal Clinic for Cats* and *Dr. Jim's Animal Clinic for Dogs.*

Alan Parker, Ph.D., is a veterinary neurologist and chief of staff of the Small Animal Clinic at the University of Illinois College of Veterinary Medicine at Urbana-Champaign.

James Richards, D.V.M., is assistant director of the Feline Health Center at the Cornell University College of Veterinary Medicine in Ithaca, New York.

Carin Smith, D.V.M., is a veterinary consultant in private practice in Leavenworth, Washington, and author of *101 Training Tips for Your Cat.*

H. Ellen Whiteley, D.V.M., is a veterinary consultant in private practice in Guadalupita, New Mexico, and author of *Understanding and Training Your Cat or Kitten.*

Teething

9 Tips to Chew Over

You've had your puppy for only a month and already he's left an imprint on your heart. Unfortunately, he's also left an imprint or two on a paperback book, your best leather shoes and the leg of the kitchen table.

Teething is a natural behavior that usually occurs between three and six months of age, when your pet's deciduous (or baby) teeth are replaced by adult teeth. All puppies do it, and even kittens will occasionally give their teeth a workout.

"Teething helps relieve discomfort and may help the new tooth penetrate the gum," says Steven Holmstrom, D.V.M., a veterinarian in private practice in Belmont, California, president of the American Veterinary Dental College and author of *Veterinary Dental Techniques*. "It's not something you want to prevent."

Of course, you don't want to sacrifice your favorite belongings, either. Here are a few ways to accommodate your pet *and* take a little bite out of teething.

For Dogs and Cats

Keep temptation beyond her teeth. Leaving toothsome dainties—like that soft new pair of leather gloves—where she can get to them is just asking for trouble. "Give your puppy or kitten a break—don't leave tempting articles for her to get into," says Debra L. Forthman, Ph.D., a certified applied animal behaviorist at Zoo Atlanta in Georgia.

It's also a good idea to tape down electrical wiring so your pet can't get her jaws around it. And be sure to keep household chemicals out of her way. "A determined, teething puppy can be very clever at getting into things," warns Dr. Forthman.

Do give her chewing satisfaction. Just as birds have to fly and fish have to swim, young pets have to chew. So give your puppy or kitten a few special toys to work over. That way she won't have to turn her teeth to forbidden objects, says Linda Tellington-Jones, an animal behaviorist in Santa Fe, New Mexico, and author of *The Tellington Touch*.

Although pet stores have literally hundreds of chew toys to choose from, don't go overboard, adds Tellington-Jones. "It's better that your pet knows what is definitely okay to teethe on, so keep her choices simple," she says.

Make it mouth-watering. To ensure that your pet teethes on her toys (while leaving yours alone), you need to make them tempting. Bob Gutierrez, animal behavior coordinator at the San Francisco Society for the Prevention of Cruelty to Animals, suggests soaking chew toys in broth or coating them with peanut butter. Or rub them all over with your hands. "She loves your scent and is more apt to chew something that smells like you," he says.

Help her learn right from wrong. When you catch your puppy or kitten teething on something she shouldn't, "just give her a big 'No!'" says Dr. Forthman. "Then hand her a toy and praise her with a 'Good girl!' when she starts chewing on it instead."

But don't hold a grudge. All pets make mistakes, and if one day you come home and find that your kid leather gloves have been shredded to bits, don't scold your pet unless you actually catch her in the act. Otherwise, "she won't know why you're yelling at her," explains Dr. Forthman.

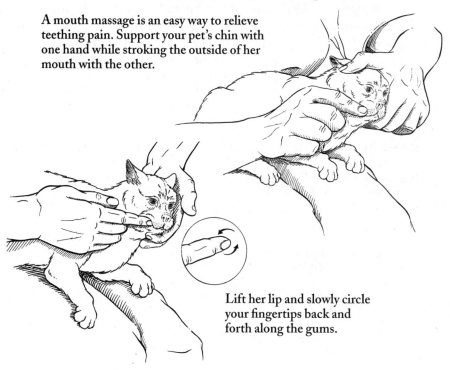

A mouth massage is an easy way to relieve teething pain. Support your pet's chin with one hand while stroking the outside of her mouth with the other.

Lift her lip and slowly circle your fingertips back and forth along the gums.

Have some playtime. Pets that are given an abundance of attention are less likely to do extra chewing, says Tellington-Jones. "Exercise will tire them out and make them content so they won't be as apt to chew as much." Kittens adore batting at ribbons swung from a long stick, while most puppies enjoy chasing balls. "Play whatever games your pet likes," she says.

Put the pain on ice. Giving your pet ice cubes or chipped ice to chew on will often help ease teething pain and reduce the urge to chew, says Liz Palika, a dog obedience instructor in Oceanside, California, columnist for *Dog Fancy* magazine and author of *Fido, Come: Training Your Dog with Love and Understanding* and *Love on a Leash*.

"They really seem to feel better when they can mouth a little ice," she says. You can put the ice in your pet's bowl or feed it to her by hand.

Or chill it with a cold rag. Another cool solution for teething pain is give your pet a towel to chew on. Palika recommends tying a knot in a dish towel, wetting it, wringing it out and putting it in the freezer to chill. "They love these frozen rags because they're fun to gnaw on," says Palika. "Their gums get a little numb so they get relief."

Rub her the right way. Massaging your pet's mouth and gums will help ease the ouches of teething, says Tellington-Jones.

Sitting slightly behind your pet, support her chin with one hand while gently stroking the outside of her mouth until she's relaxed. Lift her lip a little and slowly circle your fingertips back and forth along her upper and lower gums, using light to medium pressure. Doing this for even a few minutes will help ease the pain, she says.

PANEL OF ADVISERS

Debra L. Forthman, Ph.D., is a certified applied animal behaviorist at Zoo Atlanta in Georgia.

Bob Gutierrez is animal behavior coordinator at the San Francisco Society for the Prevention of Cruelty to Animals.

Steven Holmstrom, D.V.M., is a veterinarian in private practice in Belmont, California, president of the American Veterinary Dental College and author of *Veterinary Dental Techniques*.

Liz Palika is a dog obedience instructor, columnist for *Dog Fancy* magazine and author of *Fido, Come: Training Your Dog with Love and Understanding* and *Love on a Leash*.

Linda Tellington-Jones is an animal behaviorist in Santa Fe, New Mexico, and author of *The Tellington Touch*.

Ticks

11 Ways to Keep 'Em Off

They get under everyone's skin, suck up to anyone they can and spend much of their lives with their mouths buried in mammalian flesh. They're also responsible for spreading such things as Rocky Mountain spotted fever and Lyme disease, and they can blow up to more than 50 times their normal size after a good blood meal.

It's no wonder that ticks give even veterinarians the creeps. "I don't like ticks one bit," says Philip Kass, D.V.M., Ph.D., associate professor of epidemiology at the University of California, Davis, School of Veterinary Medicine. "There's just not much good about them at all."

Fortunately, there are ways to keep the creepy crawlies at bay. Here's what vets recommend.

 For Dogs and Cats

Mow 'em over. Ticks like to congregate several feet off the ground on vegetation along paths and roadsides. They patiently bide their time until dinner—your pet—comes padding by.

Keeping grass and weeds trimmed to below ankle height will put ticks at a disadvantage, says Tanya Drlik, pest management specialist for the Bio-Integral Resource Center, a nonprofit group that investigates pesticide alternatives, in Berkeley, California. "The ticks won't have a good vantage point, and they will have fewer opportunities to attach themselves," she says.

Abolish the nursery. Although mature ticks "stalk" large prey, younger ticks typically feed on mice and other rodents before graduating to pets. Making your yard inhospitable to rodents will help eliminate the ticks as well, Drlik says.

"Remove brushy cover and rock piles and secure trash cans with spring-top lids," she suggests. It's also a good idea to stack firewood

When to See the Vet

All weekend your dog romped through fields and forests with sheer joy, and your cat prowled through tall grass in pursuit of mice, real or imagined.

But after having all this fun, your poor pets haven't been themselves. They don't feel like eating and their joints seem to hurt. Or maybe they have sores, fever and diarrhea. They may even be partially paralyzed.

Call your vet right away. Ticks can transmit a number of diseases that cause these and other unpleasant symptoms, says Steven R. Hansen, D.V.M., a toxicologist with Sandoz Animal Health in Des Plaines, Illinois.

A toxin found in the salivary glands of a tick, for example, can cause a rare but dangerous condition called tick paralysis. This causes the pet's hindquarters—and possibly his whole body—to become progressively weaker. Once the tick is removed, however, your pet should recover nicely, says Dr. Hansen.

Other conditions your vet may look for include Lyme disease, Rocky Mountain spotted fever and ehrlichiosis. While dangerous, each of these diseases can be cured with antibiotics, particularly when they're caught early, says Dr. Hansen.

Even if you haven't seen any ticks, you should call the vet as soon as you notice worrisome symptoms, Dr. Hansen adds. Ticks can be extremely small, so not spotting one is hardly proof it was never there. "It's best to err on the side of caution," Dr. Hansen advises.

---

away from the house. Move bird feeders away, too, since rodents may be attracted to the seed.

Keep mice tick-free. Another way to end the tick/mouse relationship is with a product called Damminix. Consisting of cotton balls soaked with insecticide, Damminix is placed in strategic sites outside to attract mice, which use the cotton to build nests. The insecticide-soaked cotton kills fleas and ticks but doesn't appear to harm the mice, Drlik says. Damminix is available through farm supply catalogs.

Take the road most traveled. When hiking in areas that harbor

Although ticks can be extremely small, once they start feeding, they expand to many times their normal size.

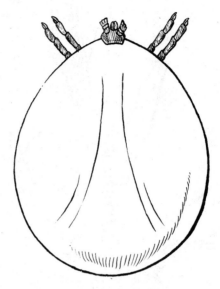

ticks, don't be a trailblazer, says Robert Hilsenroth, D.V.M., executive director of the Morris Animal Foundation in Englewood, Colorado. "Just stick to the trails and make sure your pet sticks with you," he says. "That way you avoid the longer grasses or wooded areas where ticks are waiting."

Give him a new coat. Before heading into tick country, protect your pet with a spray, dip or powder containing pyrethrins, insecticides made from chrysanthemums, suggests Walter Doolittle, D.V.M., a veterinarian in private practice in Groton, Connecticut. Other products that may work include D-limonene, linalool or permethrin.

Before using insecticides on your feline friends, be sure to check the label. Products and doses that are safe for your dog may be dangerous when used for cats.

Watch out for hitchhikers. After you and your pet return home, give him a careful going-over. While some species of ticks are easy to see, others aren't much bigger than the period at the end of this sentence. It takes sharp eyes to spot them all, says Steven R. Hansen, D.V.M., a toxicologist with Sandoz Animal Health in Des Plaines, Illinois.

Ticks like being warm and protected, so pay special attention to the areas under your pet's legs and in or around his ears.

Comb them out. If you do spot ticks, first spray your pet lightly with a tick insecticide and then comb his fur with a fine-toothed

To remove a tick, grasp it with tweezers right at the skin line.

Then drop it in a small jar of alcohol. This kills the tick and also keeps it preserved in case your vet needs to test for diseases.

comb. Pet stores sell flea combs (which are also used for ticks) that will remove critters that aren't already embedded.

Take fast action. If you should spot a feeding tick, it's important to remove it quickly. The longer it feeds, the more likely it is to transmit Lyme disease, says Dr. Doolittle.

Don't play with matches. "Forget all those old wives' tales about how you're supposed to remove embedded ticks," Dr. Doolittle says. "Making them back out with matches or cigarettes doesn't work and could badly burn your pet."

Give a gentle pull. With his veterinary practice only five miles from Lyme—the small town in Connecticut where Lyme disease was identified—Dr. Doolittle has had plenty of experience removing ticks. "The best way is to take a pair of tweezers or forceps, grab as close to the tick's head as possible and gently pull it out," he says. "This way it comes out nicely—head and heels and all."

For extra protection after removing the tick, dab the area with a topical antiseptic like Betadine Solution or an antibiotic ointment, he adds.

Dispose of them carefully. Once you've removed a tick, don't just throw it in the trash or toilet, Dr. Doolittle advises. "They don't die just because they're detached. You could end up with ticks crawling out of your toilet at an inopportune moment."

He recommends putting detached ticks in a jar partly filled with rubbing alcohol or insecticide. Then cover the jar and either dispose of it or keep it to show your vet just in case your pet develops symptoms of Lyme disease.

PANEL OF ADVISERS

Walter Doolittle, D.V.M., is a veterinarian in private practice in Groton, Connecticut.

Tanya Drlik is a pest management specialist at the Bio-Integral Resource Center, a nonprofit group that researches pesticide alternatives, in Berkeley, California.

Steven R. Hansen, D.V.M., is a toxicologist with Sandoz Animal Health in Des Plaines, Illinois.

Robert Hilsenroth, D.V.M., is executive director of the Morris Animal Foundation in Englewood, Colorado.

Philip Kass, D.V.M., Ph.D., is associate professor of epidemiology at the University of California, Davis, School of Veterinary Medicine.

Travel Problems

15 Tips for Cruising in Comfort

If pets planned vacations, you'd never have to worry about renting a car or making hotel reservations. You wouldn't even need a map. Just dashing across the park or splashing in a nearby creek would be excitement enough.

Unfortunately for pets, it's their people who make the plans—and human travel, for dogs and cats, can be uncomfortable travel, says Grace Long, D.V.M., a veterinarian with the Ralston-Purina Company in St. Louis. Dogs get carsick. Cats get lost. Everyone gets hot and thirsty. "For a lot of pets, car rides end in some experience that's just not very desirable," says Dr. Long.

Don't nix your trip down Route 66. Here are some tips to keep your pets comfortable.

 ## For Dogs and Cats

Take a practice cruise. If the only time your pet gets in the car is when she's going to the vet, she's bound to get a little balky, says Dr. Long. Before taking a long trip, get her used to the idea by taking shorter rides, she suggests. Drive around the block. Better yet, take her to the park a few times. That way she'll associate the car with pleasant experiences and will be more likely to relax during longer trips.

Be a tag team. No matter how careful you are, dogs and cats have a genuine talent for getting loose—and lost. So before setting out, make sure your pets are wearing the appropriate tags, says Michael Kaufmann, education coordinator for the American Humane Association in Englewood, Colorado.

At the very least they should have identification tags with your name, address and telephone number. Since you won't be home (you're on vacation, after all), it's also a good idea to fit them with temporary tags listing the motel or campground where you're staying. Temporary tags are available at pet stores, Kaufman says.

Pack the paperwork. Many campgrounds—and virtually all national parks and foreign countries—won't admit pets without proof that they've had their rabies shots. "Always carry a rabies certificate with you," advises David Barnett, D.V.M., a veterinarian in private practice in Colma, California, and past president of the American Veterinary Medical Association.

It doesn't hurt to get a general health certificate from your vet before setting out, he adds. That way, if border or other officials have questions, you won't be stuck hundreds of miles from home without the answers.

Provide a cozy crate. Few things are more uncomfortable—and potentially dangerous—than having pets loose in the car. What's more, most dogs and cats naturally feel more secure when they have their own space.

"Even pets that hate to travel will often hunker down and wait it out once they're in a crate," says Sherbyn Ostrich, V.M.D., a veterinarian in private practice in Wernersville, Pennsylvania.

To help your pet feel at home, he recommends padding the crate with her favorite rug or pillow and putting in some of her favorite toys. In addition, it's critical that the crate get plenty of fresh air, so leave space around it when packing the car.

Buckle up. Whether your pet is snug in a crate or curled up on the seat, it's important to keep her buckled in. "Loose animals in a car are not a good idea," says Dr. Ostrich. "Just braking can cause a pet that's loose in the car to fly through the air."

Pet stores sell harnesses that work in conjunction with lap and shoulder belts to keep your pet secure. These are most effective with larger pets weighing 25 pounds or more, experts say. Smaller pets are best kept in a crate that's buckled to the seat or firmly attached to the floor.

Moisten her muzzle. It's extremely easy for dogs and cats to overheat in the car, so providing plenty of water is essential. Pet stores sell traveling water dishes that have a deep hole in the middle with a lid on top. The design makes it difficult for the bowl to tip or spill.

A neater alternative is to freeze a small dish of water ahead of time and let her lick the ice whenever she gets thirsty, suggests Dennis Wilcox, D.V.M., a veterinarian in private practice in Port Angeles, Washington. Or you can simply stop every hour or two and pour a little water in a dish, he adds.

Flying the Friendly Skies

Just as some travelers have gone to New York while their luggage went to Los Angeles, it's not unheard of for dogs and cats to temporarily get lost in cargo holds or airports or even to be sent to the wrong city.

Major mishaps are rare, of course, and most pets traveling by plane experience a minimum of discomfort. To make sure your pet's flight goes smoothly, here's what experts recommend.

Take her on board. Most airlines will allow cats and small dogs to travel with their owners on the plane—but only if they fit into a kennel small enough to fit beneath the seat. Some vets recommend Sherpa Carriers, padded carry-on pet bags that may be more comfortable than the hard plastic kind.

Make reservations early. Airlines may allow only one on-board pet per flight, so it's important to make your travel plans in advance.

Give her space. If your pet is traveling in the luggage hold, taping a bag of food to the top of her crate will help ensure that nothing gets stacked on top.

Provide water. Most crates include a small water bowl that fits on the door. Filling the bowl with water and freezing it ahead of time will prevent it from spilling.

Book a nonstop flight. This way your pet won't experience the turmoil of being moved from plane to plane. It also means there's no chance she'll make the wrong connection. If the flight is delayed before takeoff, you're justified in asking that your pet be unloaded so you can see to her safety.

Ask about medications. Most pets can travel comfortably without the use of tranquilizers, but if your pet barks or meows excessively or seems especially stressed during travel, ask your vet if medications might help.

Don't forget the chow. It's common for dogs and cats to get uncomfortable when they suddenly change from one food to another—and that's the last thing you want when you're traveling. To keep them fed and their tummies calm, take along their usual food, vets say.

Remember rest stops. Even dogs and cats with great control may need frequent "rest" breaks when traveling. Plan on stopping every hour or two so they can stretch their legs and have a romp, says M. Ward Crowe, D.V.M., professor emeritus in the Department of Veterinary Science at the University of Kentucky in Lexington and chair of the Animal Welfare Committee of the American Veterinary Medical Association.

Keep her under control. Nothing's more frightening than losing a pet in a strange place—or having her dart into traffic at the rest stop. To be absolutely safe, always attach the leash *before* you open the door, Dr. Crow says.

Settle her stomach. Like kids, young dogs and cats are particularly prone to car sickness, although older pets can get it, too. Not feeding pets for about six to eight hours before traveling will help keep their stomachs calm, says Clayton MacKay, D.V.M., director of the veterinary teaching hospital at Ontario Veterinary College at the University of Guelph in Canada and president of the American Animal Hospital Association. But giving them water is okay.

Give a seat with a view. Pets are less likely to get carsick when they can see the passing scenery, so try to give her a window seat. Opening the window and letting in fresh air will also help, Dr. MacKay adds.

Take precautions. The same over-the-counter drug people use for preventing car sickness also works for pets. Dimenhydrinate (Dramamine) is safe for most healthy dogs and cats, although pets with glaucoma or bladder problems shouldn't take it without a veterinarian's approval.

Medium to large dogs should be given 25 to 50 milligrams of Dramamine at least an hour before traveling, vets say. (Dramamine should always be taken before traveling because it's more effective at preventing car sickness than at stopping it once it occurs.) Cats and small dogs should get about 12.5 milligrams. Dramamine is available in 50-milligram tablets that can be split into quarters to provide the right dose for your pet.

Park with care. Even on cool days the inside of a parked car can get uncomfortably hot. Don't take chances, Dr. Wilcox warns. When it's time to eat, consider using drive-throughs rather than leaving your pet behind. Or eat in shifts, with one family member staying behind with your pet—preferably *outside* the car.

If you have to leave your pet in the car—while you run into a store, for example—always park in a shady spot, preferably where a breeze blows through the windows. But even then, don't stay away for more than a few minutes, vets warn.

 **For Cats Only**

Take the litter. Unlike dogs, which will treat roadside rest stops like their own backyards, cats are often reluctant to relieve themselves at the end of a leash. So always take a litter box when you travel, Dr. Long advises.

"The best thing is to have a crate big enough that you can put the litter box at one end," she says.

Don't clean it too well. To help your cat feel at home, vets recommend not starting a trip with fresh litter. Taking litter she's already used is like putting out a little sign that says "mine."

PANEL OF ADVISERS

David Barnett, D.V.M., is a veterinarian in private practice in Colma, California, and past president of the American Veterinary Medical Association.

M. Ward Crowe, D.V.M., is professor emeritus in the Department of Veterinary Science at the University of Kentucky in Lexington and chair of the Animal Welfare Committee of the American Veterinary Medical Association.

Michael Kaufmann is education coordinator for the American Humane Association in Englewood, Colorado.

Grace Long, D.V.M., is a veterinarian with the Ralston-Purina Company in St. Louis.

Clayton MacKay, D.V.M., is director of the veterinary teaching hospital at Ontario Veterinary College at the University of Guelph in Canada and president of the American Animal Hospital Association.

Sherbyn Ostrich, V.M.D., is a veterinarian in private practice in Wernersville, Pennsylvania.

Dennis Wilcox, D.V.M., is a veterinarian in private practice in Port Angeles, Washington.

Treed Cat

12 Down-to-Earth Solutions

Whether he's chasing birds, escaping from dogs or simply catching a high-altitude snooze, one of a cat's favorite activities is climbing trees.

But while cats are naturally great climbers, they aren't always so good at getting down, says Gary Landsberg, D.V.M., a veterinarian in private practice in Thornhill, Ontario, who specializes in animal behavior. Sometimes they refuse to budge because they're afraid of falling. Or they may be nervous about all the commotion down below—like you and 20 of your friends calling, "Here, kitty!"

A cat that refuses to come down from his perch for a long time could get dehydrated, says Dr. Landsberg. In addition, cats sometimes slip and fall, which can cause serious injuries.

To help get your cat down to earth or prevent him from going too high in the first place, here's what experts recommend.

For Cats Only

Don't rally 'round the tree. Just because your cat is out on a limb doesn't mean he needs your help. In fact, he'd probably prefer it if you'd go away and leave him alone rather than begging him to come down. "Give your cat some space," Dr. Landsberg advises.

Give him time. While it's not impossible for a cat to be truly stuck in a tree, chances are he just hasn't gotten around to coming down, says Steve Bell, an intake officer and animal ambulance technician in Scarborough, Ontario. "Most cats are fully capable of coming down by themselves," he says.

Bell recommends giving your cat an entire day to come down on his own. If he's injured, however, or is wearing a leash that could cause him to choke, you may have to go after him sooner. The same is true if it's getting dark. Cats that stay in trees overnight could be attacked by wild animals like raccoons, Bell says.

Tempt his taste buds. Even cats in trees get hungry, and putting some of his favorite food where he can see (and smell) it may get him down in a hurry, Dr. Landsberg says.

Mount a rescue mission. If your cat is simply too scared (or injured) to get down on his own, "the easiest thing is to climb the tree and get him," says Todd Spencer, president of Wildlife Removal and Prevention Services in Toronto.

If the tree doesn't have the right kind of branches for easy climbing, you'll need a ladder. An extension ladder generally works better than a stepladder, Bell adds.

Don protection. A treed cat is a scared cat, and many people have been bitten or scratched while trying to rescue a frightened feline. "Always wear heavy work gloves and a thick jacket to protect yourself," Bell advises.

Go for the neck. When grabbing a scared cat, it's best to catch the skin on the back of his neck. This is the same place mother cats use when carrying kittens, and most cats will go limp once you've taken hold and lifted them up.

Make the first effort count. When grabbing for a treed cat, make sure you don't miss. "You may only have one chance to get hold of your cat before he jumps higher," Bell warns, "so make your first grab count."

Call in the cavalry. If your cat has been in the tree for more than a day and you can't get him down yourself, it's probably time to call in the pros. Your local humane society may be able to help, or you can call an animal rescue service. "They know what they're doing and can rescue any cat from anywhere in just a few minutes," Spencer says.

Animal rescue services are usually listed in the Yellow Pages, or you can call your vet for advice.

Make a staircase. If your cat frequently gets "stuck" in the same tree, you can make life easier for both of you by nailing up a few boards, Bell suggests. This will give your high-climbing pet something to grab onto when making his descents.

Keep him away. "If your cat only seems to have trouble getting down from one particular tree, you can stop him from climbing that tree by putting up some kind of barricade," suggests Dr. Landsberg.

He recommends enclosing the tree with wire fencing or the type of metal cone that's used to keep squirrels away. Just make sure it's high enough so your cat can't get over it with a flying leap.

Try a big bang. Another way to keep your cat away from a troublesome tree is to use a "pull" firecracker. Commonly used as party favors, these firecrackers have two strings. First tie one string to the tree and then sit a few feet away, holding the other string. As soon as your cat puts his first paw on the tree, pull the string, advises Peter Borchelt, Ph.D., a certified applied animal behaviorist and owner of Animal Behavior Consultants in Brooklyn. The resulting noise may be enough to keep him out of the tree for good, he says.

Teach him new tricks. "Believe it or not, you can actually teach your cat how to come down from a tree," says Dr. Borchelt.

1. First place your cat in the tree about four feet off the ground. He should have no trouble jumping off. Then place him higher—say, six feet off the ground. He may hesitate but probably won't have too much trouble coming down.
2. Using a ladder, place your cat higher and higher in the tree—up to eight or ten feet, for example—until you reach a height that really makes him nervous.
3. When he refuses to come down, pick him up and place him lower on the tree, preferably at the last height from which he felt comfortable getting down. Return him to that same place several times to build up his confidence. Then put him higher again. In time he should become as comfortable climbing down from higher points as from lower ones.

"You might have to do this exercise a few times over a couple of weeks, but eventually he will be able to come down any tree from any distance," Dr. Borchelt explains.

PANEL OF ADVISERS

Steve Bell is an intake officer and animal ambulance technician in Scarborough, Ontario.

Peter Borchelt, Ph.D., is a certified applied animal behaviorist and owner of Animal Behavior Consultants in Brooklyn.

Gary Landsberg, D.V.M., is a veterinarian in private practice in Thornhill, Ontario, who specializes in animal behavior.

Todd Spencer is president of Wildlife Removal and Prevention Services in Toronto.

Ulcers

7 Stomach-Soothing Tips

Your cat isn't a hot dog in a New York law firm. Your dog doesn't furrow his brow over the evening news. But even without a full calendar and worries about world peace, pets still can suffer from ulcers—small, painful sores in the lining of the stomach or small intestine.

Most pets that develop ulcers get them because they're taking aspirin for long-term conditions such as arthritis, says Lisardo Martinez, D.V.M., a veterinarian in private practice in Miami. Kidney or liver problems can also cause ulcers, as can noshing on irritating snacks, like pennies. "Those things are very toxic," says Eugene Snyder, D.V.M., a veterinarian in private practice in Kettering, Ohio.

While curing an ulcer frequently requires help from a veterinarian, there are things you can do to keep his insides safe.

 **For Dogs and Cats**

Don't trust his appetite. Some cats and almost all dogs will chew—and perhaps swallow—just about anything that catches their interest. Be sure not to leave batteries, pennies or other potentially harmful articles where they can get them, advises Dr. Snyder. If you see your pet swallow something he shouldn't and you even suspect it might be dangerous, call your vet right away.

Provide plenty of toys. "Many of the ulcers we see tend to be started by the ingestion of rough material, such as wood and bone," says Lee R. Harris, D.V.M., a veterinarian in private practice in Federal Way, Washington. Giving your pet safe, chewable toys, like rubber bones, will help keep his adventurous appetite under control.

Keep up with brushing. For cats particularly, regular brushing will help reduce the amount of hair they swallow during their grooming sessions. Although this may not prevent ulcers from occurring, it may help reduce irritation of the stomach and small intestine that will make existing problems worse, Dr. Harris says.

Be cautious with painkillers. Just as over-the-counter analgesics like aspirin, ibuprofen and naproxen can cause ulcers in people, they are a major cause of ulcers in dogs and cats as well. "These drugs are very potent," says Dr. Snyder. A dose that's right for a human could be dangerous for your pet, particularly when it is given for long periods of time. So check with your veterinarian before starting any treatment plan.

Whatever you do, don't give acetaminophen to cats, adds Dr. Harris. "They lack the enzyme that gets rid of it, and their livers can't handle it," he says.

Mealtime's the best time. If your vet has recommended that you give your pet aspirin, always give it with food so it won't directly irritate the stomach lining, advises Dr. Snyder.

Pick a buffered variety. Aspirin is very acidic, so look for a buffered brand, which is easier on the stomach, says Dr. Harris.

Aim for a stress-free life. While emotional stress doesn't appear to be a major cause of ulcers in pets, it may play a role, says Janet R. Childs, D.V.M., a house-call veterinarian in Fairview, Tennessee. To help keep your pet healthy and relaxed, make sure to include plenty of fun time in his life.

When to See the Vet

While some ulcers will heal on their own, others can result in dangerous internal bleeding. Symptoms to watch for include blood in the stool or vomit that looks like it has coffee grounds mixed with it, says Janet R. Childs, D.V.M., a house-call veterinarian in Fairview, Tennessee. "You may also see blood in vomit," she says.

Get to your vet as soon as you notice symptoms. In most cases, ulcers can be treated with prescription drugs like cimetidine (Tagamet) and sucralfate (Carafate), which help reduce the amount of irritating acid in the stomach.

In addition, don't take chances if you see your pet contentedly swallowing a battery, coin or other nonfood delectable. Call your vet right away, says Dr. Childs.

Having another pet at home, be it a dog or a cat, will give your friend someone to play with, Dr. Childs says. In addition to another pet, taking regular walks will help keep him exercised and happy—and less prone to getting an upset stomach.

PANEL OF ADVISERS

Janet R. Childs, D.V.M., is a house-call veterinarian in Fairview, Tennessee.

Lee R. Harris, D.V.M., is a veterinarian in private practice in Federal Way, Washington.

Lisardo J. Martinez, D.V.M., is a veterinarian in private practice in Miami.

Eugene Snyder, D.V.M., is a veterinarian in private practice in Kettering, Ohio.

Urinary Tract Infections

4 Helpful Hints

She used to go all day without a break, but lately your pent-up pet can hardly wait to get outside. And no sooner does she come back in than she has to go out again. If this goes on much longer, you're going to need a revolving door.

Urinary tract infections (UTIs) aren't just the bane of bathroom-hopping humans. Dogs and occasionally cats also get infections of the urethra or bladder. UTIs make it difficult to urinate—which is why your pet has to go so often. What's more, the inside of the urinary tract can get painfully inflamed.

To keep UTIs under control and help prevent them in the future, here's what vets recommend.

 For **Dogs** and **Cats**

Pour some juice. It's a home remedy for people that works for pets, too. Cranberry juice and orange and other citrus juices boost the acidity of urine, reducing the number of bacteria and helping relieve discomfort from UTIs, says W. Jeffery Alfriend, D.V.M., a veterinarian in private practice in Los Alamitos, California, who specializes in small animal medicine.

The problem with juice is getting pets to drink it. "I don't know any pet that likes cranberry juice," he says. You can try putting out a bowlful and see what happens. Or just mix an ounce or two of juice with her breakfast, he advises.

Provide frequent potty breaks. When urine remains in the bladder for a long time, any bacteria that happen to be floating around have more time to multiply, possibly to infection-causing levels. "A pet that urinates only two times a day is more likely to develop an infection than one that goes ten times a day," says Lauren Prause, D.V.M., a veterinary resident in small animal internal medicine in the Department

When to See the Vet

While some urinary tract infections will clear up on their own even without treatment, occasionally the bacteria will swim upstream, causing a dangerous kidney infection vets call pyelonephritis.

Symptoms of kidney infection include frequent or difficult urination and possibly blood in the urine, says Lauren Prause, D.V.M., a veterinary resident in small animal internal medicine in the Department of Clinical Sciences at the Colorado State University College of Veterinary Medicine and Biomedical Sciences in Fort Collins. Some pets get feverish and lethargic as well.

Don't take chances if you notice any changes in your pet's normal urinary habits, says Dr. Prause. She may need oral antibiotics to prevent a small infection from turning into a major problem.

If your vet does send you home with antibiotics, the best time to give them is right after your pet urinates, adds Dr. Prause. "That way you get the highest concentration of drugs in the animal's system," she explains.

of Clinical Sciences at the Colorado State University College of Veterinary Medicine and Biomedical Sciences in Fort Collins.

It's a good idea to let your pet outside every few hours to flush away bacteria before they cause problems, she says. If you have an indoor cat, make sure the litter box is always accessible.

Ask for assistance. Your pet may have great control, but if the only times she goes outside are before you go to work and after you get home, bacteria have plenty of time to do their dirty work.

If you can't get home during the day, perhaps you can ask a neighbor to let her out for you. In return, you can offer to let *her* pet out when she needs help.

Get those paws moving. Most dogs and cats can't go around the block without making a deposit. Taking at least two 20-minute walks a day will increase urination and reduce the risk of infection, says Frank L. Moore, D.V.M., a veterinarian in private practice in Westminster, California, who specializes in small animal medicine.

PANEL OF ADVISERS

W. Jeffery Alfriend, D.V.M., is a veterinarian in private practice in Los Alamitos, California, who specializes in small animal medicine.

Frank L. Moore, D.V.M., is a veterinarian in private practice in Westminster, California, who specializes in small animal medicine.

Lauren Prause, D.V.M., is a veterinary resident in small animal internal medicine in the Department of Clinical Sciences at the Colorado State University College of Veterinary Medicine and Biomedical Sciences in Fort Collins.

Vision Problems

7 Coping Strategies

Your pet has always been a sure-footed beast, but lately (ever since you rearranged the house) she's been bumping into things and looking lost. And when you go on walks, she has trouble finding you.

For some reason your pet's sharp vision has faded. Some dogs and cats suffer from progressive retinal atrophy, which makes it hard for them to see in dim light. Others can get cataracts, glaucoma or other eye diseases that cause their sight to dim. Fortunately, there are a number of treatments as well.

"Some of the treatments available for pets are as sophisticated as people's," says Mary B. Glaze, D.V.M., professor of ophthalmology at the Louisiana State University School of Veterinary Medicine in Baton Rouge and co-author of *The Atlas of Feline Ophthalmology*.

Even if your pet never regains her 20/20, there are many things you can do to make her life easier. Try these tips from the eye experts.

 For **Dogs** and **Cats**

Don't play musical chairs. Moving furniture can confuse dim-sighted pets and even cause injuries—if your pooch barrels into a table leg, for example, says Art J. Quinn, D.V.M., professor of ophthalmology at the Oklahoma State University College of Veterinary Medicine in Stillwater. "If you don't have to, don't move your furniture," he says.

Show her around. If you do shuffle the furniture or your pet's vision has suddenly faded, lead her around on a leash for a day or two to help her find her way, says Dr. Glaze.

It's also a good idea to confine her to one or two rooms until she knows them well. Once she's familiar with the layout, you can introduce her to new territory. Most pets want to be around people, so you can keep her in rooms you frequent so she won't be all alone.

Be predictable. Stability is important for poorly sighted pets, says

Dr. Glaze. "Leaving their food and water in the same place will help give them a sense of order and security," she says. The same goes for litter boxes and beds: The less you move them around, the better, she says.

Give her a leash on life. If your pet has even the slightest trouble seeing, don't let her wander outside unless she's on a leash or in a fenced area where she can't escape, warns Dr. Quinn.

Guard the pool. Swimming pools can be deadly for pets that can't

When to See the Vet

It's tough for humans to lose their sight, but animals are more adaptable. Because of their fine-tuned senses, "visually impaired cats and dogs have an uncanny ability to get around," says Mary B. Glaze, D.V.M., professor of ophthalmology at the Louisiana State University School of Veterinary Medicine in Baton Rouge.

Some pets can actually *hear* whether a door is open or closed and then walk through (or stop) without hesitation. "It's as if they can see," says Dr. Glaze.

Take your pet into new territory, however, and her vision problems may become more evident—and more dangerous. Blind pets can bump into furniture or bash into walls. If they get outside unattended, they could walk into traffic.

Any pet with vision problems needs to be seen by a vet. How can you tell if your pet is going blind? She may have trouble finding you when you call. Blind dogs are often reluctant to go up or down stairs. Blind cats may not jump up on furniture as much as they used to.

"If your cat has been sleeping on your bed for years and she gradually stops, blindness could be a reason," says Art J. Quinn, D.V.M., professor of ophthalmology at the Oklahoma State University College of Veterinary Medicine in Stillwater.

Another way to tell is with the cotton ball test, advises David C. Smith, D.V.M., a veterinarian in private practice in Tulsa, Oklahoma. Stand several feet in front of your pet and drop a cotton ball. If you do it a couple of times and your pet doesn't even glance at it, she may be having trouble seeing. Call your vet right away, he advises.

Some poorly sighted dogs have so much hair in their eyes that their vision is impaired even further.

see where they're going. "I've had blind pet patients that have fallen into pools and drowned," says Dr. Quinn.

Bring in a friend. Sometimes a pet with vision will help one without it. In many cases, "they're willing to be very giving to the pet that can't see," helping to guide her around, says Dr. Glaze.

Even if they aren't good friends, having two pets in the family still can help. For example, attaching a bell to the collar of the sharp-sighted pet will make it easier for her companion to follow her around and stay out of danger, says David C. Smith, D.V.M., a veterinarian in private practice in Tulsa, Oklahoma.

Try a new hairdo. If your pet has vision problems and her bangs are hanging in front of her eyes, trim them away, says Dr. Smith. "I've seen dogs, like Old English sheepdogs, that have so much hair in their eyes that it can further impair vision that's already questionable," he says.

PANEL OF ADVISERS

Mary B. Glaze, D.V.M., is professor of ophthalmology at the Louisiana State University School of Veterinary Medicine in Baton Rouge and co-author of *The Atlas of Feline Ophthalmology*.

Art J. Quinn, D.V.M., is professor of ophthalmology at the Oklahoma State University College of Veterinary Medicine in Stillwater.

David C. Smith, D.V.M., is a veterinarian in private practice in Tulsa, Oklahoma.

Vomiting

8 Soothing Solutions

Sure, it's a dog-eat-dog world out there. But it's also a dog-eat-rancid-garbage world. And a cat-eat-dead-mouse world.

Not surprisingly, your pet came into this lip-smacking world with a vomiting reflex to match his adventurous appetite. "Dogs do it at the drop of a hat, and cats are pretty good at it, too," says James B. Dalley, D.V.M., associate professor of small animal clinical sciences at the Michigan State University College of Veterinary Medicine in East Lansing.

While dogs and cats usually vomit because of Dumpster-diving, eating too much or eating too fast can also upset their tummies. To help your pet hold down his lunch, try these tips.

 **For Dogs and Cats**

Give him fast relief. "When your pet is vomiting, his stomach needs a time-out," says Martin J. Fettman, D.V.M., Ph.D., professor of pathology and clinical nutrition at the Colorado State University College of Veterinary Medicine and Biomedical Sciences in Fort Collins. Don't let him have any food for 24 hours, he advises. A short fast may be all it takes to get his stomach back to normal. If he's still vomiting after 24 hours, call your veterinarian.

Fill the water bowl. Once the worst of his vomiting is over, encourage your pet to wet his whistle during his fast, says Dr. Fettman. "The last thing you want is dehydration," he says.

Let him lick ice. If water makes him queasy, give him ice cubes instead. "He'll lick the water off more slowly, and it usually stays down better than when he drinks," says David Hammond, D.V.M., a veterinarian in private practice in Pleasant Hill, Oregon, and veterinary affairs manager for Hill's Pet Nutrition. "Besides that, pets like playing with the ice cubes. It's a real source of entertainment."

He recommends putting an ice cube in your pet's bowl or on a part

When to See the Vet

Your pet's all-consuming appetite has made him sick more than once, but never like this. He's lethargic, disoriented and stumbling around like he's drunk. And he's throwing up with alarming frequency.

Call your veterinarian—immediately. There's a chance your pet may have been munching poisonous plants, like dieffenbachia or philodendron, or lapping up toxic chemicals, like antifreeze. "Every minute counts if you suspect your pet ate something poisonous," says Fred Oehme, D.V.M., Ph.D., professor of toxicology, medicine and physiology in the Department of Clinical Sciences at the Kansas State University College of Veterinary Medicine in Manhattan, Kansas.

Serious vomiting can also be a sign of other serious troubles, including brain tumors, ulcers and kidney and liver disorders.

Unappealing as a close-up inspection may be, by noting what the vomit looks like, you can help your vet make an accurate diagnosis. Things to look for include blood, yellowish-green fluid, material that looks like coffee grounds or clumps of stool-like material. "Vomiting can mean so many different problems, it helps us immensely to have good observations from owners," says James B. Dalley, D.V.M., associate professor of small animal clinical sciences at the Michigan State University College of Veterinary Medicine in East Lansing.

---

of the floor you don't mind getting wet. To make sure the water stays down, don't give him more than one cube every 15 minutes.

Keep a lid on it. To prevent your pet from drinking too much, keep the toilet lid down, says David Simmons, D.V.M., a veterinarian in private practice in Castro Valley, California. "Otherwise your animal could have a double treat—an unlimited supply of water he shouldn't have and water that's chock-full of bacteria that aren't going to help his situation," he says.

Make the menu bland. After fasting for 24 hours, your pet may be ravenous for food. "Start with a bland diet to gently work his system back into digesting, or else you could end up back at square one," says Dr. Hammond.

Vets recommend mixing two parts cooked white rice with one part cottage cheese or boiled skinless white chicken. At first, feed him small amounts about every four hours. After a day, if he's still holding the bland food down, you can begin feeding him his usual amount.

Bring back his favorite food—slowly. After two days on the bland diet, you can start reintroducing his usual fare. Vets recommend replacing about one-fourth of the bland food with his regular food every day for four days until he's back to normal.

Calm it with Kaopectate. Even after the vomiting stops, your pet may not be feeling up to par. Kaopectate will help soothe his stomach. "It's chalky and not exactly delicious, but it works," says Dr. Hammond.

Give one teaspoon of Kaopectate for each ten pounds of weight. Since dosages vary widely from pet to pet, however, be sure to ask your vet for advice.

 For **Dogs** Only

Get in the pink. Giving your pet Pepto-Bismol will help soothe his tummy just as it does yours, says Dr. Hammond. He recommends giv-

---

When Your Pet Is Crazy about Grazing

No one's sure why, but virtually all dogs and cats occasionally eat grass and then vomit as a result. Some vets say they do it to purge unpleasant things from their systems. Others suspect grass-eating may be more of a culinary thing.

"Humans might not think grass is tasty, but humans also don't think garbage-can contents are delicious," says James B. Dalley, D.V.M., associate professor of small animal clinical sciences at the Michigan State University College of Veterinary Medicine in East Lansing.

"As long as the grass isn't treated with chemicals and it isn't eaten in excessive quantities, grass-eating probably isn't anything you need to prevent your pet from doing," says Lisa Freeman, D.V.M., clinical instructor and a fellow in clinical nutrition at the Tufts University School of Veterinary Medicine in North Grafton, Massachusetts.

ing about one teaspoon for every 20 pounds of dog every four to six hours for up to two days. "Dogs don't like it much, though, so don't be surprised if more ends up on you than in your dog," he adds. A neater solution is to use an oral syringe, which is available at pharmacies.

Never give Pepto-Bismol to cats without a veterinarian's supervision, he warns. It contains ingredients cats don't metabolize well, so it can make them sicker.

PANEL OF ADVISERS

James B. Dalley, D.V.M., is associate professor of small animal clinical sciences at the Michigan State University College of Veterinary Medicine in East Lansing.

Martin J. Fettman, D.V.M., Ph.D., is professor of pathology and clinical nutrition at the Colorado State University College of Veterinary Medicine and Biomedical Sciences in Fort Collins.

Lisa Freeman, D.V.M., is clinical instructor and a fellow in clinical nutrition at the Tufts University School of Veterinary Medicine in North Grafton, Massachusetts.

David Hammond, D.V.M., is a veterinarian in private practice in Pleasant Hill, Oregon, and veterinary affairs manager for Hill's Pet Nutrition.

Fred Oehme, D.V.M., Ph.D., is professor of toxicology, medicine and physiology in the Department of Clinical Sciences at the Kansas State University College of Veterinary Medicine in Manhattan, Kansas.

David Simmons, D.V.M., is a veterinarian in private practice in Castro Valley, California.

Whisker Problems

4 Ways to Keep Them in Trim

Bloodhounds can sniff a scent for miles. Afghan hounds can spy a mouse a block away. Pretty impressive—but even the most gifted dog can't top the sensory abilities of a cat.

A cat's whiskers—located above his eyes and under his chin as well as on the sides of his face—are embedded in bundles of nerves. The slightest change in air currents causes his whiskers to move, providing kitty with sophisticated information about his surroundings, says veterinarian Nicholas Dodman, B.V.M.S., professor in the Department of Surgery and director of the Animal Behavior Clinic at the Tufts University School of Veterinary Medicine in North Grafton, Massachusetts. "They are exquisitely sensitive," he says.

While whisker damage—from a candle flame, for example, or from being scissored off by a neighbor's preschooler—is hardly a life-threatening event, it can be discombobulating and sometimes very painful. Without whiskers, your cat may have trouble maneuvering through tight spaces or judging distances when hunting at night.

Dogs also have whiskers, of course, but they depend on them far less than cats do, Dr. Dodman says.

If your pet's whiskers have been inadvertently trimmed, here's what vets recommend.

 For **Cats** Only

Keep him indoors. Since cats depend on their whiskers for navigation, any damage could cause them to misjudge distances or crash into obstacles, says Bernadine Cruz, D.V.M., a veterinarian in private practice in Laguna Hills, California.

A cat without whiskers, for example, could suffer eye damage from walking through prickly underbrush and not getting the signal in time to shut his eyes. "Without whiskers they can get wedged into a tight space," adds Nancy Scanlan, D.V.M., a veterinarian in private practice in Sherman Oaks, California. This can be particularly dangerous in life-or-death moments—like when he's running from a dog.

To keep your cat safe, it's best to keep him indoors for several months until his new whiskers grow, says Dr. Cruz.

Don't make big changes. If your cat has just had his whiskers shorn, it's probably not the best time to be moving furniture or remodeling the house, says Mollyann Holland, D.V.M., a resident veterinarian in small animal medicine in the Department of Veterinary Medicine and Surgery at the University of Missouri College of Veterinary Medicine in Columbia. "He could have some difficulty with depth perception," she says.

Groom with care. While some whisker injuries occur in the wild, they can also be a result of careless grooming. "Sometimes when owners groom their pets themselves they'll trim the whiskers," says Jan A. Hall, D.V.M., a veterinary dermatologist and referral specialist in Ville St. Laurent in Montreal.

The next time you're giving kitty a trim, take a little off the top—but be sure to leave his whiskers alone.

Douse the flames. While it's unlikely that curiosity actually killed a cat, it can cause them to get a little singed—particularly when they approach a candle flame or stove burner whiskers first. While whiskers that have been cut will usually grow back, those burned off at the base probably won't, says Dr. Cruz. So if your pet persists in showing more curiosity than common sense, you may want to put him in another room until the flames are out.

PANEL OF ADVISERS

Bernadine Cruz, D.V.M., is a veterinarian in private practice in Laguna Hills, California.

Nicholas Dodman, B.V.M.S., is professor in the Department of Surgery and director of the Animal Behavior Clinic at the Tufts University School of Veterinary Medicine in North Grafton, Massachusetts.

Jan A. Hall, D.V.M., is a veterinary dermatologist and referral specialist in Ville St. Laurent in Montreal.

Mollyann Holland, D.V.M., is a resident veterinarian in small animal medicine in the Department of Veterinary Medicine and Surgery at the University of Missouri College of Veterinary Medicine in Columbia.

Nancy Scanlan, D.V.M., is a veterinarian in private practice in Sherman Oaks, California.

Wool Sucking
8 Ways to Guard Your Garments

Cats do the darnedest things. They fall asleep in utensil drawers. They unfurl rolls of toilet paper and shred them to bits. They indulge in catnip and stare at their reflection in the mirror.

Just when you thought you'd seen everything, you discover that your favorite feline has become a material girl: She sucks on sweaters, gnaws on carpets and chews on socks, gloves, towels and blankets. Your vet calls it wool sucking. You call it sheer destruction.

"Almost any kind of soft texture will do, although wool is a favorite," says John C. Wright, Ph.D., a certified animal behaviorist, professor of psychology at Mercer University in Macon, Georgia, and a member of the adjunct faculty at the University of Georgia School of Veterinary Medicine in Atlanta.

Vets aren't sure what causes cats to become wool suckers, although it seems to be more common in those that were weaned too early. Siamese have a particular penchant for wool-sucking, vets say, but it occurs in other breeds as well.

To find a solution before you lose your shirt—or sweater, or blankets or anything else—try these tips.

 **For Cats Only**

Raise temptation. "The easiest way to keep your cat from munching your sweaters is to keep them out of her reach," says Dr. Wright. Keep sweaters and other wool clothing in closed drawers and closets, he advises.

If your cat likes to suck on items that can't be put away—the carpet or bedspread, for example—your only solution may be to keep her out of rooms where she does the most damage.

Toy around. Cats with plenty of chew toys may be less likely to set their sights—and teeth—on favorite clothing, says Dr. Wright. Pet stores sell a variety of wool toys that will appeal to wool-sucking cats. "Experiment and see which work best," he says.

Fix it with fiber. Switching your pet to a cat food that's high in dietary fiber can help quell the urge, says Peter Borchelt, Ph.D., a certified applied animal behaviorist and owner of Animal Behavior Consultants in Brooklyn. "I've had cases where just switching the cat to a dry food seemed to make the cat's desire for chewing wool diminish."

Produce results. It's not clear why, but giving your cat a little lettuce may take his mind off wool, says Dr. Wright. "Cats seem to prefer Romaine lettuce. Some really take to it and forget about their other habits."

He recommends giving your cat a leaf or two of lettuce—whole or shredded, whichever she prefers—each day.

Go for the crunch. Cats that aren't distracted by lettuce may respond to crunchier items like green beans, cooked potato skins or even a little bacon, says Dr. Borchelt. "Sometimes these things do the trick very well."

Create a stink. To keep your cat out of trouble, try spraying at-risk clothing with pet repellent, suggests Suzanne Hetts, Ph.D., a certified animal behavior consultant in Littleton, Colorado. She recommends products such as bitter apple.

When you spray you should also place a tempting wool toy nearby, she adds. "Your cat might come to realize that toys are good, but the object of her desire is too unpleasant," she says. "It could change her behavior."

Mix them with mothballs. The strong odor of mothballs in your laundry bin or closet can help keep destructive felines away, says Dr. Hetts. Be sure to put the mothballs inside a small sealed basket, since some pets actually have a taste for them, she adds.

Sound the alarm. Putting a motion-detecting alarm inside your closet can help keep sweaters and other clothing safe. "When your cat hears the alarm, she will get startled and back off or run away from the closet," says Dr. Wright. "Eventually, the cat will think, 'Forget it.'"

PANEL OF ADVISERS

Peter Borchelt, Ph.D., is a certified applied animal behaviorist and owner of Animal Behavior Consultants in Brooklyn.

Suzanne Hetts, Ph.D., is a certified animal behavior consultant in Littleton, Colorado.

John C. Wright, Ph.D., is a certified animal behaviorist, professor of psychology at Mercer University in Macon, Georgia, and a member of the adjunct faculty at the University of Georgia School of Veterinary Medicine in Atlanta.

Worms

7 Gutsy Solutions

It's unsettling to see something alive in your pet's bathroom deposits, but intestinal worms are anything but rare.

Virtually all puppies and kittens are born with worms or get them soon after birth. And in areas where worms thrive—some of the Southern states, for example—many adult dogs and cats are also affected.

While the worms you see may be unpleasant, they rarely cause anything worse than a little diarrhea or vomiting. Worms you *can't* see, however, like hookworms or whipworms, can cause anemia, dehydration or nutritional deficiencies, says Michael Willard, D.V.M., professor in the Department of Small Animal Medicine and Surgery at the Texas A&M University College of Veterinary Medicine in College Station.

Since specific medicines are necessary to treat each type of worm, you'll want to see your vet, says Dr. Willard. In addition, here's what you can do to ease the symptoms and also to prevent the problem in the future.

 ## For Dogs and Cats

Worm them young. "Almost every puppy and kitten will be born with worms or will pick them up from nursing their mother," says Dr. Willard.

Vets advise worming puppies and kittens as young as six weeks. The medication is available from veterinarians and in pet stores.

Finish the fleas. Most pets that have tapeworms got them originally from infected fleas, which they swallowed during their normal grooming. While there are medications that will eliminate tapeworms, it's also important to eliminate the fleas that cause them, says Michael Dryden, D.V.M., Ph.D., associate professor of veterinary parasitology

When to See the Vet

While worms are rarely a serious problem, without treatment they can multiply to dangerous levels in the body, says Michael Willard, D.V.M., professor in the Department of Small Animal Medicine and Surgery at the Texas A&M University College of Veterinary Medicine in College Station. That's why it's important to see your vet at the first sign of trouble.

Symptoms of worms include vomiting, bloody diarrhea or stool that looks like black tar. In addition, worms in the body may shed small segments of their bodies, which appear in the pet's stool.

at the Kansas State University College of Veterinary Medicine in Manhattan, Kansas.

Pet stores stock a variety of flea sprays and powders. Vets often recommend those containing D-limonene or pyrethrins, which are effective and less toxic than some other insecticides. Or you may want to try products containing methoprene, a synthetic hormone that prevents flea eggs from maturing.

Products that are safe for dogs, however, may be dangerous for cats, so read labels carefully, advises Tam Garland, D.V.M., Ph.D., a veterinary toxicologist at the Texas A&M University College of Veterinary Medicine.

Calm tummies with Kaopectate. This over-the-counter medication is a safe, effective way to reduce diarrhea and calm your pet's insides, says Dr. Willard.

"Kaopectate is pretty safe for cats and dogs," he says. "It adds some solidity to the stool."

To give the medication, draw some up in a syringe or turkey baster. Tip your pet's head back and squirt the medicine in his mouth toward the back of his tongue. Hold his mouth closed and stroke his throat until you see him swallow.

A rule of thumb is to give one teaspoon of Kaopectate for each ten pounds of weight two or three times a day. Doses vary widely from pet to pet, however, so be sure to ask your vet for advice.

Stop the stalking. Another way pets get worms is from eating mice, rabbits or other rodents, says Dwight Bowman, D.V.M., associate professor of parasitology at the Cornell University College of Veterinary Medicine in Ithaca, New York. To reduce the risk, keep your pets inside the yard or on a leash when you go roaming, he advises.

Keep the yard clean. A variety of intestinal parasites thrive in soil that's contaminated with wastes from dogs and cats. "Dogs can get worms by digging in contaminated soil," says Thomas Craig, D.V.M., Ph.D., professor in the Department of Veterinary Pathobiology at the Texas A&M University College of Veterinary Medicine. In addition, pets can get an intestinal infection called giardiasis from drinking dirty water.

"Hygiene will handle 90 percent of your problem," says Dr. Bowman. He recommends keeping the yard clean by removing stools before they have a chance to contaminate the soil underneath.

Take precautions. Some of the same medicines that vets recommend for preventing heartworms will help reduce certain intestinal worms, says Dr. Willard.

Watch for culprits. While it's extremely common for pets to get worms, catching them early makes the problem much easier to treat.

Dr. Craig recommends regularly checking your pet's bottom and droppings. Look for rice-shaped tapeworm segments or the longer, spaghetti-like roundworms. In addition, you should have your vet check your pet's stool once a year.

PANEL OF ADVISERS

Dwight Bowman, D.V.M., is associate professor of parasitology at the Cornell University College of Veterinary Medicine in Ithaca, New York.

Thomas Craig, D.V.M., Ph.D., is professor in the Department of Veterinary Pathobiology at the Texas A&M University College of Veterinary Medicine in College Station.

Michael Dryden, D.V.M., Ph.D., is associate professor of veterinary parasitology at the Kansas State University College of Veterinary Medicine in Manhattan, Kansas.

Tam Garland, D.V.M., Ph.D., is a veterinary toxicologist at the Texas A&M University College of Veterinary Medicine in College Station.

Michael Willard, D.V.M., is professor in the Department of Small Animal Medicine and Surgery at the Texas A&M University College of Veterinary Medicine in College Station.

Wounds

11 Ways to Give Aid

In your view, she may be man's best friend, and he may be the purr-fect pet. Unfortunately, the other critters in your neighborhood may not hold your four-legged companions in the same high regard. That's why, sometimes, dog literally tries to eat dog—or at least attempts to take out a hearty chunk. And those nightly cat fights can occasionally take on the proportions of an Ali-Frazier duel.

Add to that the reality of accidents, abrasions and other mishaps and you've got the makings of some nasty wounds, abscesses and bleeding. So here's what you can do.

 **For Dogs and Cats**

Take precautions. Most experts recommend muzzling a dog or cat before trying to treat injuries. "If you touch the area that gives them the most discomfort, they're going to bite you," warns Alan Lipowitz, D.V.M., professor of small animal surgery at the University of Minnesota College of Veterinary Medicine in St. Paul.

If you don't have a muzzle handy, you can improvise one from a roll of gauze or a length of rope, Dr. Lipowitz says. Just wrap it firmly several times around the animal's muzzle, then pull the ends back and tie them behind her ears. But keep a pair of scissors handy, he adds. If your pet starts to vomit, you'll want to remove the muzzle promptly to prevent her from choking.

Try wrapping her up. If your pet is too small to wear a muzzle, you can wrap her head in a pillowcase, towel or blanket before beginning treatment, advises C. B. Chastain, D.V.M., associate dean for academic affairs and professor of veterinary medicine and surgery at the University of Missouri College of Veterinary Medicine in Columbia. To avoid making it difficult for her to breathe, however, don't wrap her too tightly or for too long.

First aid comes first. "Stopping the bleeding is number one," says William D. Fortney, D.V.M., assistant professor of small animal medicine in the Department of Clinical Sciences at the Kansas State University College of Veterinary Medicine in Manhattan, Kansas. As soon as possible, apply firm pressure to the wound with your hand or a clean piece of gauze or cloth. Maintain the pressure until the bleeding stops, usually within a few minutes. If the bleeding doesn't stop, get your pet to a vet right away, he advises. (For more information, see Bleeding on page 72.)

Make the fur fly. Once bleeding is under control, the next step is to clean the wound thoroughly. Start by trimming away the fur surrounding the area. Scissors are fine, but vets usually recommend using electric clippers. "You need to keep that hair away from the wound, because if it mats down it keeps the infection in there," says Wayne Wingfield,

When to See the Vet

While most wounds can be managed at home, deep cuts or scrapes are going to need an expert's care. This is particularly true when the wound is deep or bleeding heavily or seems to be unusually painful, says Wayne Wingfield, D.V.M., chief of emergency critical care medicine at the Colorado State University Veterinary Teaching Hospital in Fort Collins.

"If the laceration is deep enough to involve tendons or muscle, you should seek some kind of professional care," he says. Deep cuts often require anesthesia and stitches. Even scrapes can be dangerous if there's been a lot of blood loss or if infection sets in.

In fact, infection is the main risk from most wounds, experts say. Danger signs include pus, redness, swelling or tenderness that doesn't go away. Infections are particularly common in bite wounds, especially those caused by cats, because a cat's mouth is teeming with bacteria, and his sharp, pointed canines can cause deep puncture wounds.

"If it's a severe bite wound or puncture wound, you probably ought to see somebody and get antibiotics," advises Alan Lipowitz, D.V.M., professor of small animal surgery at the University of Minnesota College of Veterinary Medicine in St. Paul.

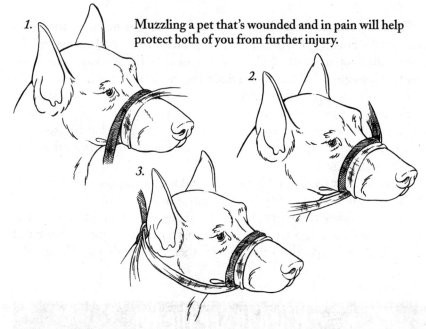

1.

Muzzling a pet that's wounded and in pain will help protect both of you from further injury.

2.

3.

D.V.M., chief of emergency critical care medicine at the Colorado State University Veterinary Teaching Hospital in Fort Collins.

But first, paste on protection. To prevent freshly clipped hairs from falling into the wound, Dr. Lipowitz recommends coating it with a thin layer of water-soluble K-Y Jelly. The hairs will adhere to the jelly, which then can be easily washed away.

Do some deep cleaning. It's especially important to flush deep cuts or punctures with water to expel germ-covered hair or debris that might contaminate the wound. "Soap and water are the very best antiseptics to use," says Dr. Wingfield. You may also want to apply an antibacterial ointment.

Bubbles mean trouble. Although doing a thorough cleaning is critical, veterinarians generally don't recommend applying antiseptics like hydrogen peroxide or rubbing alcohol because they can further irritate injured tissue.

Let 'em lick. When dogs or cats get injured, their tongues automatically go to work. Don't interfere with Nature's plan. Licking does no harm, and it may actually help the healing process because it mechanically cleans the wound of debris, says Dr. Wingfield.

Heads up. Although some licking may be good for a wound, dogs or cats that have gotten stitches will often try to lick or chew them loose. To prevent this, your vet may recommend fitting your pet with an Elizabethan collar, a conical plastic shell that fits around your pet's head and prevents her from licking her wounds.

Elizabethan collars are sold in pet stores, or you can make your own by cutting a hole just big enough to go over her head in a plastic bucket or food container, Dr. Wingfield says. Be sure, however, that the collar fits comfortably and doesn't prevent your pet from reaching her food or water.

"Sometimes collars are put on automatically when maybe they're not necessary," adds Dr. Wingfield. He generally counsels a wait-and-see approach. If your dog or cat isn't worrying about the wound excessively, she'll probably do fine without the collar.

Let the sunshine in. Although a firmly tied bandage can help slow bleeding soon after an injury occurs, in most cases it isn't necessary and can actually be harmful, says Dr. Wingfield. "We do know the more material you put on a wound, the slower the healing."

Watch out for abscesses. While most minor wounds will heal on their own, occasionally an abscess will form. An abscess is a pocket of pus beneath the skin that indicates an infection is gathering strength.

To make your own Elizabethan collar, cut a hole in a plastic bucket that's just large enough to fit over your pet's head. It should fit securely but comfortably around the neck. Just be sure it doesn't prevent her from eating or drinking.

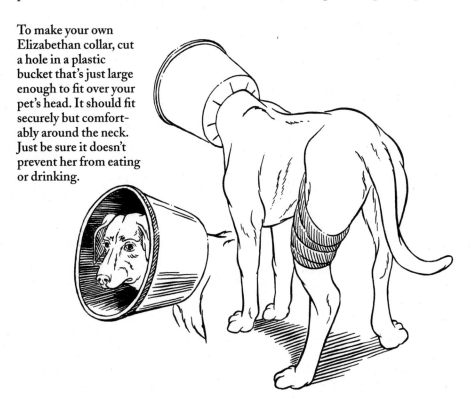

"Because it does not drain, the infection is much more likely to spread internally," Dr. Fortney says.

Once your pet has an abscess, she'll probably need to have it drained. In addition, your vet may recommend that she take oral antibiotics. Don't try to treat an abscess yourself, says Dr. Fortney. If you do, he says, "you've probably lost valuable time."

PANEL OF ADVISERS

C. B. Chastain, D.V.M., is associate dean for academic affairs and professor of veterinary medicine and surgery at the University of Missouri College of Veterinary Medicine in Columbia.

William D. Fortney, D.V.M., is assistant professor of small animal medicine in the Department of Clinical Sciences at the Kansas State University College of Veterinary Medicine in Manhattan, Kansas.

Alan Lipowitz, D.V.M., is professor of small animal surgery at the University of Minnesota College of Veterinary Medicine in St. Paul.

Wayne Wingfield, D.V.M., is chief of emergency critical care medicine at the Colorado State University Veterinary Teaching Hospital in Fort Collins.

Index

Note: <u>Underscored</u> page references indicate illustrations.
Boldface references indicate primary discussion of topic.

Attention, to prevent
   chewing problems, 342
   dung eating, 161
   meowing, excessive, 271
   noise anxiety, 283
   spraying, 329–30
Aveeno, 25, 122, 230, 231
Avon Skin-So-Soft, 230, 233

Baby oil, to treat ear mites, 164
Back and disk problems, **45–47**
Bad breath, 6, **48–51**, 78, 147
Baking soda
   to clean litter box, 155, 224
   to treat
      insect bites and stings, 228
      skunk spray, 323
Balding, 315
Balloons, water-filled, in training, 87–88
Bandages
   Ace, 247–48
   "Robert Jones," 247–48, <u>249</u>
   to treat
      bites, 67
      claw problems, 107
      wounds, 67, 74, 75
Bandannas, for drooling, 157–58, <u>158</u>
Barking, excessive, **52–55**
Bark-speak, understanding, 54
Bathing. *See also* Hygiene
   cats, 185, 186–87, <u>187</u>
   excessive, 77
   eye care and, 251–52
   grooming and, 316
   to treat
      allergies and hay fever, 25, 28
      anal sac problems, 30
      body odor, 76
      dandruff, 121
      fever, 174
      fleas, 185, 186–87, <u>187</u>, 233
      insect bites and stings, 230
      itching, 231–32
      lice, 251
      mange, 259–60
      poisonings, topical, 298
      ringworm, 307
      shedding problems, 316

   skunk spray, 321
   sunburn, 332
Bathroom breaks, ample
   to prevent
      bladder control problems, 69–70
      constipation, 115–16
      sleep problems, 324–25
      travel-related problems, 350–51
      urinary tract infections, 359–60
   prostate problems and, 303
Bedding
   arthritis and, 36
   hip dysplasia and, 208
   ringworm and, 308
   washing to treat
      allergies, 27
      fleas, 190
      lice, 252–53
      mange, 261
Begging for food, **56–58**
Behavioral problems. *See specific types*
Bells, deafness and, 125–26
Benadryl, 25–26, 120, 210, 233, 253, 261
Benzoyl peroxide, to treat acne, 337
Beta-carotene
   to prevent heart problems, 203
   to treat lice, 253
Betadine Skin Cleanser, 307
Betadine Solution, 75, 212, 302, 336
Bird feeders
   heartworm-carrying insects and, 205,
      206
   to prevent
      boredom, 81, 140
      depression, 140
Birthing, **59–64**, <u>62–63</u>
Biscuits
   to prevent
      bad breath, 50
      dental problems, 132
Bites, **65–68**
   animal, 65–68, 250, 377
      protection from, 65–66, 73
      rabies from, 68, 157
      treating, 66–67, 250
   insect, 210, 228–30
   veterinarian care for, 66
Biting, 65–66, **277–80**
Bitter apple, to prevent
   chewing problems, 101
   licking, excessive, 255, 292
Blackheads, 336–37. *See also* Acne
Bladder control problems, **69–71**

H